< >

FISCAL CRISES, LIBERTY, AND REPRESENTATIVE GOVERNMENT, 1450-1789

THE MAKING OF MODERN FREEDOM

General Editor: R. W. Davis

FISCAL CRISES, LIBERTY, AND REPRESENTATIVE GOVERNMENT, 1450-1789

< >

*Edited by Philip T. Hoffman
and Kathryn Norberg*

STANFORD UNIVERSITY PRESS
STANFORD, CALIFORNIA
1994

Stanford University Press
Stanford, California
© 1994 by the Board of Trustees of the
Leland Stanford Junior University

Printed and bound by CPI Group (UK) Ltd,
Croydon, CR0 4YY

CIP data appear at the end of the book

Stanford University Press publications
are distributed exclusively by Stanford
University Press within the United
States, Canada, and Mexico; they are
distributed exclusively by Cambridge
University Press throughout the rest of
the world.

‹ ›

Series Foreword

THE STARTLING AND MOVING events that swept from China to East-ern Europe to Latin America and South Africa at the end of the 1980s, followed closely by similar events and the subsequent disso-lution of what used to be the Soviet Union, formed one of those great historic occasions when calls for freedom, rights, and democracy echoed through political upheaval. A clear-eyed look at any of those conjunctions—in 1776 and 1789, in 1848 and 1918, as well as in 1989 —reminds us that freedom, liberty, rights, and democracy are words into which many different and conflicting hopes have been read. The language of freedom—or liberty, which is interchangeable with free-dom most of the time—is inherently difficult. It carried vastly dif-ferent meanings in the classical world and in medieval Europe from those of modern understanding, though thinkers in later ages some-times eagerly assimilated the older meanings to their own circum-stances and purposes.

A new kind of freedom, which we have here called modern, gradu-ally disentangles itself from old contexts in Europe, beginning first in England in the early seventeenth century and then, with many con-fusions, denials, reversals, and cross-purposes, elsewhere in Europe and the world. A large-scale history of this modern, conceptually dis-tinct, idea of freedom is now beyond the ambition of any one scholar, however learned. This collaborative enterprise, tentative though it must be, is an effort to fill the gap.

We could not take into account all the varied meanings that free-dom and liberty have carried in the modern world. We have, for ex-ample, ruled out extended attention to what some political philoso-phers have called "positive freedom," in the sense of self-realization of the individual; nor could we, even in a series as large as this, cope with the enormous implications of the four freedoms invoked by Franklin D. Roosevelt in 1941. Freedom of speech and freedom of the press will have their place in the narrative that follows, certainly, but not the boundless calls for freedom from want and freedom from fear.

We use freedom in the traditional and restricted sense of civil and political liberty—freedom of religion, freedom of speech and assembly, freedom of the individual from arbitrary and capricious authority over persons or property, freedom to produce and to exchange goods and services, and the freedom to take part in the political process that shapes people's destiny. In no major part of the world over the past few years have aspirations for those freedoms not been at least powerfully expressed; and in most places where they did not exist, strong measures have been taken—not always successfully—to attain them.

The history we trace was not a steady march toward the present or the fulfillment of some cosmic necessity. Modern freedom had its roots in specific circumstances in early modern Europe, despite the unpromising and even hostile characteristics of the larger society and culture. From these narrow and often selfishly motivated beginnings, modern freedom came to be realized in later times, constrained by old traditions and institutions hard to move, and driven by ambition as well as idealism: everywhere the growth of freedom has been *sui generis*. But to understand these unique developments fully, we must first try to see them against the making of modern freedom as a whole.

The Making of Modern Freedom grows out of a continuing series of conferences and institutes held at the Center for the History of Freedom at Washington University in St. Louis. Professor J. H. Hexter was the founder and, for three years, the resident gadfly of the Center. His contribution is gratefully recalled by all his colleagues.

R.W.D.

Contents

Contents

⬟

Acknowledgments

Several foundations have generously supported The Making of Modern Freedom series, and this volume in particular. The National Endowment for the Humanities provided funding for planning meetings. Liberty Fund Inc. sponsored the autumn 1988 conference where the volume was first discussed. The John M. Olin Foundation contributed towards meeting administrative expenses and salaries at the Center for the History of Freedom. Last, but far from least, of our outside supporters is the Lynde and Harry Bradley Foundation. This volume largely took shape in the second of our annual Institutes in the spring semester of 1989. The Institutes, which bring the authors together as Fellows of the Institute for the History of Freedom, have been fully funded by the Bradley Foundation. We are grateful for all the support we have received, including the strong backing we have always enjoyed from Washington University.

R.W.D.

The idea for this volume came from the fertile minds of J. H. Hexter and Douglass C. North. Along with Richard Davis, Hexter also selected the volume's contributors and invited them to pass a delightful semester at Washington University's Center for the History of Freedom, where work on the book began. Our task was to edit the volume, but fortunately we had considerable assistance from Richard Davis, Elisabeth Davis, and especially Elisabeth Case. Without their help and their patience—patience that we sorely tried at times—this volume would never have reached completion.

P.T.H. and K.N.

CONTRIBUTORS

Philip T. Hoffman
California Institute of Technology

J. R. Jones
University of East Anglia (Emeritus)

Kathryn Norberg
University of California, Los Angeles

David Harris Sacks
Reed College

I. A. A. Thompson
University of Keele (Emeritus)

Augustus J. Veenendaal Jr.
Instituut voor Nederlandse Geschiedenis

< >

FISCAL CRISES, LIBERTY, AND REPRESENTATIVE GOVERNMENT, 1450-1789

Introduction

PHILIP T. HOFFMAN AND KATHRYN NORBERG

BETWEEN THE END of the Middle Ages and the outbreak of the French Revolution, western states were sucked into a vortex of near permanent war, war that grew more costly with every battle call. For rulers traditionally obliged to "live on their own," the cost of fighting soon exceeded their income from Crown lands and customary dues. Their pockets nearly empty, they were often forced to strike deals with their subjects, deals that meant sharing political power in return for higher taxes. In some instances, the eventual result was "representative" government. In others the ruler reasserted his supremacy and absolutism prevailed. But whatever the outcome, the fiscal crises marked turning points along the path of both fiscal and political development.

It is the reciprocal relationship between political development and the growth of state finance that forms the subject of this book. Political development here cuts a rather broad swath, encompassing both the growth and demise of political institutions—particularly representative ones—and the shaping of political thought—particularly about fundamental liberties. Our concern is thus twofold: first, to trace how fiscal crises and the evolution of state finance affected political thought and political institutions; and second, to show how politics in turn affected the fisc. Throughout, we shall cast our nets wide, not limiting ourselves to moments of fiscal panic. We shall explain, for instance, how countries such as the Netherlands managed the seemingly miraculous and escaped fiscal crises almost altogether. It will be fair game as well to explore a tax system's economic consequences or to analyze its glaring peculiarities—for example, France's extraordinary reliance on the sale of government offices.

The fisc, of course, has long attracted historians, and the literature on fiscal crises alone is voluminous.[1] There is even more to read about political development—or as it is often called, state making. Much of the existing literature, however, fails to link the seemingly arcane details of state finance with the development of political ideas and political institutions. The historical works on state making (even classic ones, such as those by Otto Hintze, Roland Mousnier, and Hans Rosenberg) sketch the evolution of political institutions and relate them to social groupings, but they usually ignore the connection to the mechanics of state finance.[2] As for the writings on fiscal history, they fail to connect taxes and government borrowing to political development. Worse yet, they overlook the reasons behind the seemingly quaint fiscal practices of early modern monarchies, preferring to dismiss this or that institution as merely another example of chaotic early modern governance. Fortunately, in the past decade a number of works have appeared that break with this older literature. They go beyond it to provide a new vantage point from which both the state finance and the state making of early modern Europe can be understood.[3] Our volume is a part of this new fiscal history.

Here one might object that early modern politics involved much more than raising taxes and disbursing funds. One might invoke the Reformation and the Counter Reformation, which fortified states with sermons on obedience but also buffeted them with calls for godly rebellion. And one could point out that early modern states drew considerable sustenance from public ceremony, artful legend, and court ritual. But the fisc is so important that it deserves undivided attention.

Given our concern with fiscal crises, we ought to define what they are. For us a crisis is a jump in expenses beyond both revenues and the ability to borrow. Suppose, for example, that a prince goes off to war and spends more than he collects in taxes. If he borrows to make up the difference, there is no fiscal crisis. But if he cannot borrow enough, or if he is forced to default on old loans, then a crisis has erupted. The same is true if he resorts to measures of desperation, such as seizing his subjects' property or withholding payment from his troops. If he wished to avoid the fiscal crisis altogether, he could try to raise taxes or cut expenses. He might, for example, eschew the costly quest for dynastic hegemony or military glory, but that would not be an easy choice for an early modern ruler.

Obviously fiscal crises, like the tax man himself, haunted all of early modern Europe. The subject thus speaks to the history of the entire continent, but covering it all would require an encyclopedia, one that would sacrifice analysis for irrelevant detail. Our attention, it seems, must be restricted, and in our case we have limited ourselves to England, the Netherlands, Spain, and France. To be sure, one might lament the lack of a chapter on Italy or Germany, for the Italian city states were the first to rely upon long term public debt, and in various German states parliamentary bodies were deeply involved in state finance.[4] Yet there are sound reasons to exclude them and to concentrate on the four states we have chosen. Unlike Italy and Germany, largely geographical expressions until the nineteenth century, they became nation states very early, and their political life was not complicated by the lingering powers of the Papacy and the Holy Roman Empire.

More important, the four countries present a number of sharp contrasts. In the Netherlands, representative institutions, an unusual constitution, and a vibrant economy permitted the government to borrow at low rates of interest and to wage war without great difficulty, while in Spain, her arch-enemy, the costs of war bankrupted the government and shackled the economy. Eighteenth-century England also enjoyed fiscal advantages; eighteenth-century France did not. Similar contrasts exist in the realm of political ideas. In France the debate over tax reform was particularly sensitive to the issue of equality; elsewhere equality was of lesser importance. And each country fashioned its own beliefs about what political liberties were fundamental and how they were to be safeguarded.

Although our book stretches over four countries and nearly four centuries, it is not intended to be either a textbook or a complete account of the political and fiscal history of England, the Netherlands, Spain, and France from 1450 to 1789. Rather, it is a work of synthesis, synthesis based not on detailed narrative but on fresh analysis and generalization. We have concentrated on what we deemed important and left out what would add little to our story. We omit the British Empire, gloss over the eighteenth century in both the Netherlands and Spain, and fix our gaze on Castile to the exclusion of the rest of the Iberian Peninsula. Nor have we wasted time belaboring the obvious: for example, that the representative institutions of interest—Parliament, Cortes, Estates—concerned only an elite of wealthy males.[5] In early modern Europe, political voice and fundamental liberties were never democratic.

We begin with two chapters on England. The first, by David Harris Sacks, traces the politics of government finance from the fifteenth century to the eve of the Civil War. Sacks examines the role of king and Parliament and analyzes fundamental beliefs about what was owed the state and what was rightfully free from the state's claims. The second chapter, by J. R. Jones, carries the relationship between politics and state finance from the reign of the later Stuarts into the early eighteenth century, when England began to raise enormous sums from borrowing and taxation. Jones not only surveys the threats posed to English liberties by the actions of the later Stuarts; he also probes the more subtle dangers created in the aftermath of the Glorious Revolution, as representative government was jeopardized by new and powerful financial interests.

The third chapter, by Augustus Veenendaal, is devoted to the Netherlands. Here the task is to account for the Netherlands' exceptional ability to raise money via taxes and loans in the sixteenth and seventeenth centuries. The reasons Veenendaal gives involve not only the thriving economy, but more important, the Estates and the unusual constitution of the Netherlands. Chapters four and five, by I. A. A. Thompson, concern Spain, with a spotlight on Castile and its Cortes. Thompson follows the changing fortunes of the Cortes, relates its role to the ever more desperate operations of the Spanish treasury, and all the while emphasizes the liberties that Castilians believed would preserve them against deception. These liberties were far more robust than Whiggish historians would suppose.

The sixth chapter, by Philip Hoffman, looks at France from the end of the Middle Ages up to the early eighteenth century; the seventh, by Kathryn Norberg, continues the story from the Law affair to the French Revolution. Both authors reflect on the nature of absolutism. Hoffman notes the fiscal effects of privileges and particularism and explores the political consequences of the country's repeated fiscal crises. Norberg then explains why the fiscal crisis of 1788 brought down the monarchy, even though numerous preceding ones had never done so.

The conclusion compares our four countries and draws general lessons about the relationship between state finance and political development. It attempts to answer a number of general questions. How, for example, did state finance influence political outcomes? Did it determine the shape of the state and the success of representative institutions? What was the relationship between state finance and political thought—in particular, the various conceptions of liberty and liberties we encounter throughout early modern Europe? And how did politics affect the fisc? Could absolute states raise more money and thus fight war more effectively? Or was the fisc ultimately more powerful when backed by representative institutions?

The Paradox of Taxation: Fiscal Crises, Parliament, and Liberty in England, 1450-1640

DAVID HARRIS SACKS

IT IS A PRINCIPLE of modern life that "taxes are what we pay for civilized society."[1] It is equally a maxim of the modern state that "the power to tax is the power to destroy."[2] By extracting excessive wealth from individuals or institutions, taxes can squeeze their life from them or crush their capacity for independent action, thereby depriving them of their liberty. But without the protection offered by the tax-supported forces of the organized state, neither life nor liberty would be secure.[3] Taxes, then, can uphold rights and freedoms as well as threaten them.

This paradox lies at the heart of the political economy and political sociology of the modern state during its period of formation in late medieval and early modern Europe; its resolution had a lasting affect on the character of the regimes that emerged in this period. As Jean Bodin said, paraphrasing an ancient orator and anticipating many modern ones, "the sinews of the state are in its finances."[4] The methods used to gather the money, to employ it for the benefit of the commonweal, and to provide reserves for emergencies gave the state its characteristic features, affected its capacity to act, and shaped the personality of the society it served and dominated. In Joseph Schumpeter's words, "the fiscal history of a people is above all an essential part of its general history." In consequence, "the spirit of a people, its cultural level, its social structure, the deeds its policy may prepare—all this and more is written in its fiscal history, stripped of all phrases."[5]

Just how particular countries faced the paradox of taxation varied a good deal in the late medieval and early modern period. The scheme followed in the absolutist state, which Bodin called "*la Monarchie*

Seigneuriale" or "Lordly Monarchy,"[6] permitted the ruler to collect
taxes for public necessity on his sole judgment. It was up to him, with
the aid of his principal servants, to determine when his demand for
revenue and his predatory instincts risked long-term harm to the productive, revenue-producing capacities of his subjects or threatened to
incite them to rebellion.[7] In this kind of monarchy the king governs
"his subjects as the father of a family does his slaves" and is "lord
of their persons and goods."[8] Nevertheless freedom could still reside
where the royal will was not effectively enforced by the existing instruments of government. To adapt the modern sociological idiom of
Michael Mann, freedom in such places exists where the "despotically
strong" state, empowered to act "without routine, institutionalized
negotiation with civil society groups," is "infrastructurally weak,"
lacking the "capacity . . . to actually penetrate civil society, and to
implement logistically political decisions throughout the realm." In
other words, liberty under a lordly monarchy existed in the inter-
stices of command, where the muscles and sinews of power were
weak how ever willing its spirit of despotic rule.[9]

In late medieval and early modern England the situation was different. Its solution to the paradox of taxation lay in the establishment of a form of mixed monarchy that the fifteenth-century lawyer
and theorist Sir John Fortescue labelled *dominium politicum et regale*. By this phrase, Fortescue designated a realm where the "king
may not rule his people by other laws than such as they assent unto,
[a]nd therefore . . . may not set upon them . . . impositions without
their own assent." He distinguished this kind of realm from "*dominium regale*," a form of rule roughly equivalent to Bodin's "lordly
monarchy" in which the king made laws and levied taxes by himself
without his people's consent.[10]

For Bodin the idea of a mixed monarchy was an oxymoron. Still
he recognized the existence of states where the monarch left "every
man his natural liberty and the propriety of his goods." In such places,
the king "yielded himself in obedience to the laws of nature as he desired his subjects to be towards him."[11] Here a man's freedom, his capacity to live as he pleases[12]—it should be apparent that we are dealing with a discourse primarily concerned with men—was not lost in
his obedience to rule as it was under lordly monarchy, but retained
through his willing commitment of person and property to the needs

of the commonweal. To a considerable degree, of course, the vitality of this participatory form of rule depended on the work of political institutions—the Parliament and the courts—which themselves had the capacity to encroach on the personal freedoms and the property of individuals.[13] Nevertheless mixed government of this type made it possible for liberty to prevail even when the "infrastructural power" of the state, to adapt Mann's sociological terminology once again, overcame the technical and logistical limitations with which it struggled. For Fortescue, this kind of liberty—liberty understood as a concrete set of social and cultural traditions and practices—was uniquely manifested in the English polity.

≺ I ≻

Fortescue's Polity

Fortescue is one of the earliest English thinkers to frame his understanding of his nation's institutions around a sense of its special— its specially blessed—character. His work provided the foundation myth on which many in early modern England grounded their rights as Englishmen and many in Britain and America today base their devotion to ideals of popular sovereignty. Ideas—even ones rooted in historical misperception or jingoistic self-congratulation, as were many of Fortescue's—sometimes have extraordinary political force. They can shape a people's understanding of just rule and establish their individual and collective goals.

But along with performing these ideological functions for the Anglo-American world, Fortescue also had a remarkably astute understanding of the way in which a "style-of-rule," to borrow a term from twentieth-century political scientists,[14] grows out of the interrelationships among governmental institutions, social structure, and economic order. His work offers us a model which we can use to explore the broad development of mixed government in England, especially in its fiscal aspect.[15]

We can profitably begin with Fortescue's remarks on the English jury system. He held that its effectiveness as a means of finding the facts in law cases was the result of England's socio-economic structure, which assured that in every community there would always be sufficient numbers of men "well-off in possessions" to sit on juries. England, he made clear, was a country possessed not just of the wealthy and the poor, but also of a wide middle rank, made up of men sufficiently free from the power of others to act independently for the good of their communities. "[I]t is unthinkable," he said, "that such men could be suborned or be willing to perjure themselves, not only because of their fear of God, but also because of their honour, and the scandal which would ensue, and because of the harm they would do to their heirs through their infamy." What Fortescue meant is that such men of property necessarily engaged with their neighbors in regular transactions of all sorts—political, legal, and economic— and hence depended upon their reputations for honesty for their continued success. In other, less prosperous countries—he meant France in particular—"men of great power, great wealth and possessions" normally do not live in close proximity to one another. "How, then, can a jury be made up in such regions from among twelve honest men of the neighbourhood where the fact is brought to trial, when those who are divided by such great distances cannot be deemed neighbours . . ."[16] In those places it would be necessary to make up juries either of persons remote from the disputed facts or of paupers "who have neither shame of being infamous nor fear of loss of their goods . . . and are also blinded by rustic ignorance so they cannot clearly perceive the truth." Hence these other countries must follow the civil law, where facts are established only "through the deposition of witnesses," with the attendant risk that those "lacking in conscience" will "for fear, love, or advantage . . . contradict every truth."[17]

This same point carried through to other aspects of governance as well. England, Fortescue argued, had a distinctive social geography which manifested a much more even distribution of wealth than was common elsewhere. It "is so well stocked and replete with possessors of land and fields," he said, "that in it no hamlet, however small, can be found in which there is no knight, esquire, or householder of the sort commonly called franklin . . . nor numerous other free tenants, and many yeoman," sufficiently wealthy to bear local offices.[18] Unlike its continental neighbors, then, England was able to draw on the unpaid services of its own inhabitants to provide justice and adminster law to the country. It did not require a swarm of greedy royal officials, eager to bleed it of its fiscal resources for their own advancement.

Fortescue attributed this English exceptionalism in part to England's natural endowment and in part to the productive spirit of its people, which enabled them to live in prosperity without contracting the "rusticity of mind" that necessarily followed from overfamiliarity "with the soil." Not only did England's fruitful pastures and fields provide subsistence without the undue strain, but its exchange economy, which is implicitly assumed, permitted its population to convert the wool of their flocks into the other products necessary for their survival. This co-existence of market-oriented agriculture with the subsistence economy made it possible for England to enjoy the benefits of enclosure, which, as Fortescue explains, allowed its sheep and cattle to graze freely behind the protection of ditches and hedges, and to fertilize the land as they "lie by night in the fields without guard in their cotes and folds."[19]

This prosperous commonwealth, created by God's beneficence and nurtured by its people's enterprise, was upheld by its mixed constitution. Where kings rule "merely regally," as they do in France, Fortescue argued, evils of all sorts arise. For example, soldiers commonly are quartered in villages without paying anything, and if any villagers decline to accept the charges they are "quickly compelled by cudgeling." Similarly,

all villages and towns pay to the king annually huge sums assessed on them for men-at-arms, so that the king's troops, which are always very numerous, are kept in wages every year by the poor of the villages, towns, and cities of the realm . . . Notwithstanding all these, other very heavy tallages are levied to the use of the king every year, on every village of their realm, from which they are relieved not in a single year.[20]

In England, by contrast, "no one billets himself on another's house against its master's will," nor requisitions his goods with impunity. Although the king may take necessaries for his household by purveyance, "he is obliged to pay" for them "at reasonable price . . . because by those laws he cannot despoil any of his subjects of their goods without due satisfaction. Nor does the king . . . impose tallages, subsidies, or any other burdens whatever on his subjects, nor change their law, nor make new ones, without the concession of his whole realm expressed in parliament."[21] Fortescue here mentions Parliament, but his interest is primarily on the role of consent in the English polity, not on the institutional means by which it was expressed; he has very little to say about the latter issue.[22]

The consequences of this regime of consent bring benefit to both people and king. In France, Fortescue believed, "the people live in no little misery" and "are so impoverished and destroyed" by taxation that of necessity they must "labor and grub in the ground for their sustenance so strenuously that their nature is wasted." In consequence, they are "not able to fight, nor to defend the realm," nor even to buy weapons, so that their king "hath not men of his own realm able to defend it, except his nobles, which bear no such impositions," and is therefore "compelled to make [up] his armies and retinues for the defense of his land" from foreign mercenaries.[23] But England, as an island, was unable readily to obtain assistance from other lands. Hence if it "were ruled under such a law and under such a prince, it would be . . . a prey to all other nations that would conquer, rob, or devour it."[24] Fortunately, every Englishman "uses at his own pleasure the fruits which his land yields, the increase of his flocks, and all the emoluments which he gains, whether by his own industry or that of others, from land and sea . . . Hence the inhabitants . . . are rich, abounding in gold and silver and all the necessaries of life."[25] As a result, the people are not in penury, "nor thereby hurt in their persons," but are "wealthy and have all things necessary to the sustenance of nature. Wherefore they be mighty, and able to resist the adversaries of this realm, and to beat other realms that do or would wrong them." They are ready therefore to do their king more good and to be more profitable to him than are the subjects of the French king.[26] According to Fortescue, "these are the fruits which the political and regal government yields."[27]

Nevertheless Fortescue is quite adamant that the power of kings ruling merely regally is neither greater nor less than the power of those ruling according to the principles of *dominium politicum et regale*. In each case, this power grants to the king the same authority to defend the realm against invasions and to protect the inhabitants from crimes by natives. Both equally represent the image of godly rule on earth, both being "monarchs in their kingdoms, as God is sole monarch in the world." Hence each must be reckoned as operating under "equal laws, without disparity of power and dignity."[28] Fortescue's point, of course, is that neither kind of ruler has legitimate power to do wrong, to rule against the law of nature. For a ruler who exercises his power "only to his own profit and not the good of his subjects," is not a true king, but "a tyrant."[29]

Yet Fortescue is equally clear that because "their authority over their subjects is different," the king ruling merely regally is much more susceptible to the temptations of tyranny than his counterpart. For unchecked by the need to seek the consent of his subjects for changes in the law and the grant of taxation, and therefore more vulnerable to be "overcome by his own passions or poverty," he impoverishes his people, "and does not allow them to live and be supported by their goods."[30] Although Fortescue believed with Aristotle that "it is better for a city to be ruled by the best man than the best law," he also understood that "it does not always happen that the man presiding over the people is of this sort." Hence it is better "that a kingdom be constituted such that the king may not be free to govern his people tyrannically, which only comes to pass when the regal power is restrained by political law."[31]

Fortescue's virtues as a reporter of actual political and fiscal conditions in mid-fifteenth-century England and France hardly commend him. It would be foolish to think that his rosy depiction of well-dressed, well-fed, and industrious villagers in merrie England is any more accurate than his lugubrious account of the downtrodden and oppressed peasants in absolutist France. But we can excise the canker of jingoism from his account without abandoning all the other features of the theory. In particular, his account links together three features of English life that will require further attention: its reliance on consent—granted in Parliament—to make laws, grant taxes, and check the potential for tyranny inherent in monarchical government;[32] its dependence on a sufficient population of prosperous and responsible men in the localities to serve the needs of justice and self-rule; and its grounding in a market-oriented economic order. For all his myth-making, Fortescue suggests that these elements not only appear together as distinguishing characteristics of English political culture, but are inextricably intertwined, each providing support for the other two.

≺ II ≻

The Medieval Foundations of the English Tax State

The theme of exceptionalism recurs frequently in English historiography. But there are exceptionalisms of different kinds. For many twentieth-century scholars, exceptionalism provides the basis for viewing the country's history as a "great arch" of political and social change from which the modern liberal state and contemporary bourgeois society have emerged. In this interpretation, already apparent in the work of whiggish writers like G. M. Trevelyan,[33] and more recently cast in Marxist terms by Edward Thompson, the English are considered to have entered the modern age—as Thompson puts it—at the genteel pace of a cricket match, with breaks for lunch and tea, instead of in one massive upheaval such as many believe transformed French society at the end of the eighteenth century.[34] Here the exceptionalism has a teleological and progressive quality. It resides in the belief that England, and later Britain, experience history differently from the rest of Europe.

For Alan MacFarlane, in contrast, the exceptional characteristics of the English are retrospective. They depend on the early disappearance in England of the defining features of a peasant society. In place of collective restraints on property use posed by joint family ownership, MacFarlane argues that the English enjoyed individualized ownership of their lands and possessions by the early thirteenth century and lived in a highly mobile and open society based on a market-oriented individualism. From this early date, he says, life in England was systematically different "not merely in degree but in kind from the peasantries" found elsewhere in Europe and in consequence almost every aspect of English culture was "diametrically opposed to that of the surrounding nations."[35]

Fortescue's ideas should cast some doubt on both these visions. Although like MacFarlane he sees England's distinctive characteristics as already long in place by the fifteenth century, his account suggests that these differences were not rooted in the kingdom's socio-economic order but primarily concerned the polity and its governance. Fortescue, of course, was no historian. He considered the institutions and habits of his England, even those of relatively recent origin, to be beyond memory. His exceptionalism is mythologi-

cal—almost religious. Nevertheless, he points us to an unusual feature of English rule—namely the existence in the Middle Ages of an
effective centralized regime based on feudal customs and other traditional practices. Following him, we can see England entering into
the early modern period with an endowment of governing institutions and political habits and an inheritance of laws and liberties
that significantly distinguished it from its continental cousins. Even
though medieval England frequently suffered from political disorder,
it had already become a politically integrated realm long before Fortescue's day, while the French monachy was still struggling to assert its authority over semi-independent provinces, Spain had not yet
been united under a single Crown, and the Netherlands were no more
than a collection of distinct provinces in the possession of the dukes
of Burgundy.

From at least the end of the twelfth century, and possibly from
before the Norman Conquest, England was possessed of strong, central governing institutions that normally commanded the obedience
of the entire realm. Where else in Europe could so massive an administrative achievement as Domesday Book, systematically surveying
the rights on the land in every shire in England, have been accomplished? If these governmental authorities did not yet command a
complete monopoly of rule-making or of the means of violence—the
church and the barons saw to that—they at least ruled uniformly over
the kingdom and brought its subjects together in what was increasingly called the "community of the realm." It is striking, for example,
that the very barons who resisted King John in 1215 did so not as a
collection of feudal warriors pursuing individual ends but on behalf
of this very same community and that the agreement they exacted
from the king in *Magna Carta* protected a wide range of rights and
liberties in church and society and not just their own.[36] By the time
of the baronial revolt in 1258, the idea had developed into something
having the character of a constitutional theory.[37]

In this early period, the most significant features of centralized
governance lay in the king's capacity to offer effective justice to his
subjects. From the end of the twelfth century, his courts, set up in
competition with the feudal jurisdictions, were able to provide definitive resolution to most disputes between private parties and already
depended upon a coherent body of common law focused on the defi-

nition and preservation of property rights.[38] What this system did to
bring a modicum of peace and security to the realm is well known.
Not even in the bad days of bastard feudalism in the fifteenth century, did England descend to the daily terrors of private violence
that so often marked the lives of landholders elsewhere in medieval
Europe.[39]

This centralization of the law transformed the king's authority
into genuine power to serve the realm and control it. It established
him and his institutions in practice as the final source of remedy
for wrong. At the same time it brought him the profits of justice, a
not insignificant item of revenue especially in those early days when
his fiscal resources were largely limited to his own lands.[40] From the
time of Bracton in the mid-thirteenth century, civil law concepts regarding royal authority as well as property rights played some role in
shaping the thinking of English judges. But these ideas were incorporated into the common lawyers' learning rather than substituting for
it. The result was to give the English judges an extraordinary responsibility for settling cases of broad political and constitutional significance as part of their regular judicial business. It is instructive, for
example, to follow certain fifteenth-century common law cases concerning the king's taxing power, in which the judges authoritatively
discussed whether acts of Parliament or Convocation could abrogate
a tax exemption made by royal patent. They explored not only the
"validity" of these royal grants themselves, but as Charles Gray has
shown, also "the general criteria of validity" in such matters, thereby
demonstrating the existence of a legal system perfectly capable of
dealing with large issues of constitutional weight. The English law
courts, Gray says, "had to and *could* modulate the interaction of royal
and parliamentary authority."[41] It is hard to think of another place
in medieval Europe where such issues would be settled—and indeed
settled independently—by judges talking the common language of
their profession rather than by the political maneuvering or coercion
of the parties. The fact the judges could do so tells us much about the
degree of integration achieved by the English state under the impetus of the law.

The same fifteenth-century tax cases call Parliament into focus
for us. Although this body was hardly unique in medieval Europe,
the course of its development in the later Middle Ages already gave

it a special place in the history of representative institutions. In the first instance, Parliament was a court, bound up with the very same legal system we have just been discussing and very much a symbol of its centralization. In the thirteenth century, before there was any thought of including representatives of the commons, it brought together the judges and great men of the realm to assist the king in the dispensing of justice through the considering of petitions and hearing of pleas. But even at this early date it was not only that. It was also there to consider any business on which the king might wish to consult its members, and for the monarch and his counsellors it was often these other matters—great affairs, *"grosses busoignes"* the chancery clerks called them in 1280—that were the most important. As J. G. Edwards has argued, this body was the "high" court of Parliament "not merely because it was judicially above other courts, but also because it was in itself more than a judicial court; it was an omnicompetent organ of government at the summit of lay affairs in England."[42]

Out of this combination of judicial and consultative functions arose Parliament's important legislative role, since it was here that petitions for the remedy of individual wrongs and common grievances were brought together with the knowledge and concerns of royal judges and advisors, whose duty it was to devise, enact, and administer new general policies for dealing with them. By the fourteenth century, the burden of parliamentary work had so shifted that the body virtually ceased being a court for private suits and became what G. R. Elton has called "a predominantly political institution" focusing primarily on larger matters of common concern.[43] Thereafter Parliament became the primary and then the sole place for legislation. Although technically only the king made law by statute, since without his assent a parliamentary bill had no legal status, it was already clear by 1500, and a matter of strict legal formula by the 1530s, that a statute became law not only by the king's will but "by the authority" of Parliament as well.[44]

A second line of development concerns Parliament's role in taxation, already evident in the fifteenth-century cases to which we have just referred. From very early in its medieval history England had a tradition of national taxation. The Anglo-Saxon and Anglo-Norman kings, for example, were able to impose the Danegeld to cope with the Danish invasion and its aftermath. Although this was strictly an emergency levy, limited in scope and size and subject to widespread avoidance and exemptions, it recognized in practice—though perhaps not in theory—that public necessity might, in G. L. Harriss's words, "override private rights and royal concessions."[45] By 1207, this principle was enshrined in a theory of taxation in England that viewed the power to tax as growing from the king's responsibility for the safety of the realm and his subject's duty to support its defense.[46] Equally striking, this levy was explicitly authorized by the advice and consent of the king's great council, which removed from it the taint of arbitrary action. Strictly speaking, the consent was not to the tax itself but to the king's plea of necessity, which once given bound the subject to come to his aid in defense of the realm. Hence it was, as Harriss argues, "in part at least ritualistic," since agreement signified "that the state served the common profit of ruler and ruled"; it affirmed "a common unity and obligation" of Crown and subject. But taxation framed on this basis also obliged the king to negotiate with the political nation for these revenues, which imposed important political, if not legal, restraints on his actions. Since the taxes were for the common profit of the realm, the way was opened for making a connection between taxation and the redress of grievances, especially those associated with the revenue needs of the Crown. In this way, the negotiation of taxes extended to wide discussions of good government.[47]

The rise of national taxation on this basis brought with it the need for the granting of formal consent to provide legitimacy for the exactions. At first, consent was given in the king's great council, made up of the magnates representing the community of the realm and voicing its common counsel.[48] But by the end of the thirteenth century, it became the practice to summon representatives to consent on behalf of their communities to what the magnates had agreed upon, thereby recognizing that the great men by themselves lacked the authority to commit the whole realm to the granting of a tax.[49] But until the mid-fourteenth century it was not settled just what form the body or bodies granting this consent would take. In the early fourteenth century, for example, the *maltolt*, a tax levied on wool exports, was assented to not by the Commons at large but by the merchants who held the wool and were involved in shipping it abroad. Later, in 1346, the great council, independent of Parliament, authorized the renewal of the grant on its own judgment of the common necessity. In other words, this tax opened the possibility that the king might bypass Parliament in national taxation in favor of direct negotiation with sectional interests or of reliance on his council, as became the common practice in France. And it was to this danger that Parliament objected when it insisted that it be the sole body to grant consent for all taxes falling on free men in England. The relationship the merchants formed with the king in the course of their mutual dealings, it was feared, would lead, in effect, to the trading of special privileges for funds. Parliament claimed for itself the sole right to grant taxes to prevent them from becoming sources of singular profit to particular groups of subjects with whom the king might negotiate separately.[50]

The significance of this development is all the more enhanced by the Crown's poor fiscal situation during most of the medieval period. It was generally understood that the king would come to the nation for taxes only in emergencies and that taxes therefore would be of short duration and for specific purposes beyond the resources possessed by the king himself. Broadly speaking these came from three broad areas: his rights as a landlord and feudal lord; his profits from the administration of justice and performance of other governmental activities; and finally his revenues as head of state, which consisted of customs duties and taxes granted in Parliament and by Convocation. But it was only relatively late in the medieval period that the monarch acquired and held an endowment in lands sufficient to meet a significant amount of the Crown's ongoing expenses. Before then most of his properties were granted away to support family members or political allies.[51]

Of course, the king had non-parliamentary sources of income that could be exploited by his agents in times of financial strain. For example, his feudal rights had important fiscal implications that he could call on from time to time and that in the hands of clever Crown lawyers led to a considerably expanded income from the fifteenth century.[52] His household officers could also take foodstuffs and other goods by purveyance, paying only customary charges. Sometimes, in some districts, those subject to purveyance were allowed to compound for these commodities, in effect turning the royal right into a money tax. Impositions, called prises, were levied on wines coming into certain privileged ports and operated in the same way. The prerogative of purveyance and related charges were often a nuisance to those whose livelihoods depended on the food markets, but they became a special problem in wartime when officials were not simply supplying the king's household but victualling his armed forces.[53]

Yet it was not possible for the king to live of his own for much of this period. Even in peacetime, the Crown was habitually short of funds, especially if it had accumulated debts in a recent war. In wartime it was pressed even further. In the 1340s, for example, its regular revenues brought in only about £28,000 per year. Clerical and lay taxation, which could be counted on for almost twice that sum, was necessary to cover the extra expenses. The king also took sums known as benevolences and forced loans. The former were granted outright by individuals at the king's request. Technically those asked had the right to refuse, but they normally did so at their peril. Forced loans were anticipations of taxes not yet granted or collected; they were intended to be paid back, but without interest. These grants grew out of the same doctrines of necessity and consent that govern parliamentary taxation. They constituted an exception to the control Parliament enjoyed over the main means of raising revenue—customs and exactions from personal and real estate—and they were so understood and treated in political practice. But since only the very richest members of the community ever were asked for a benevolence or forced loan, none of these grants could do more than modestly reduce the king's need for funds. They did not allow him to escape the need for parliamentary taxes, particularly when his affairs on the Continent drew him into extended military operations. Since war was never very far from the king's business in the Middle Ages, its occurrence provided the opening for the rapid development of Parliament as an essential part of royal government, called on regularly by the king to grant the taxes necessary for the maintenance of the realm against his enemies, which for all its efforts to obtain redress of grievances it dependably did. Medieval English kings necessarily lived by the frequent grant of extraordinary taxes and in consequence always depended for a substantial part of their revenues upon the consent of those with property and power.[54]

So long as the wars brought victory, it was possible to sustain the burdens in this fashion. When the Hundred Years' War began to sour for the English, however, this need for taxation resulted not only in petitions for the remedy of specific grievances but also in more general demands for a restructuring of royal finances in order that the king might indeed live of his own. The king was urged by Parliament to recover or resume direct control of all Crown lands and to avoid relying on extra-parliamentary exactions, such as purveyance, in the conduct of his affairs. The implementation of this program was the foundation of late medieval household government, which originated as a Yorkist demand for reform in the profligate households of Lancastrian monarchs and became the policy of Edward IV and Henry VII. By the end of the fifteenth century, then, we find a relatively new fiscal situation in which the king—almost for the first time—was able to pay for the bulk of his recurring expenses through careful management of his own regular income.[55]

From our perspective, however, the most important medieval developments concern the evolving conception of Parliament as a fundamental element in the governance of the realm. Because from very early its place in English affairs required calling all the interests of the nation to it, the English were justified in thinking of it as standing for the whole body politic. Already in the mid-fourteenth century Chief Justice Thorpe could claim in response to a plea of ignorance to a statute that "Parliament represents the body of all the realm."[56] By the sixteenth century, this was little more than a commonplace.[57] Although the earliest parliaments usually consisted of the magnates and the king's judges and principal servants, who collectively might be considered to speak for the "community of the realm," representatives of the commons, as we know, were also regularly summoned to consider taxation from Edward I's reign. Until the beginning of the fifteenth century, the Commons was not formally part of Parliament in a technical or legal sense, but nevertheless served, in Elton's words, as "the voice of the nation, bringing grievances before the king and his Great Council in Parliament and granting money for extraordinary purposes." In the course of the fifteenth century, however, this already essential element of parliamentary politics became the constitutional equal of the Lords in that each was required to assent to the making of laws and the granting of taxes; the modern system of two Houses emerged.[58] By this time, too, the majority of those representatives had already come to be members of the gentry. In the early and mid-fifteenth century half or more of the borough representatives were gentlemen rather than mere burgesses and by the end of the sixteenth century at least eighty percent were.[59]

These changes in the social make-up of the membership were crucial, because they gave substance to the representatives' *plena potestas* which granted them full powers to settle matters in Parliament without explicit instruction on each occasion from their communities. Because the Commons already contained within it the leading men of the land, or their representatives, it was unlikely that its actions would be effectively challenged in the shires by those who objected to the result. These figures often served at home to administer the very taxes they had voted, turning the formal consent of Parliament into actual consent in the counties and boroughs. When the king negotiated with Parliament, then, he could be confident that the agreements would be final, since Parliament was both legally and politically competent to make the necessary decisions. Only once during the medieval and early modern period, in 1339, did the MPs, faced with local opposition to taxation, refuse to make a grant on their own judgments, asking instead to refer back to their communities for further authority.[60]

An even more important development affected the role of the king. For Fortescue and the men of his era, he was the head of the body politic represented in Parliament and not himself a member; the Parliament was his court, serving him. Although it was composed of the three estates of the realm—the lords spiritual and temporal and the commons—it was not yet an exemplification of both the head and the members of the whole body politic. Laws were made by the king and Parliament acting together, not by the king-in-Parliament forming a unified, single, though mixed body.[61] But by 1543, Henry VIII could comfortably tell the members of Parliament that they belonged to an institution "wherein we as head and you as members are conjoined and knit together into one body politic."[62] This conjoining gave the body a sovereign status in the sense that it, as Elton has put it, enjoyed "absolute discretion in the making and unmaking of law."[63]

Hence, Sir Thomas Smith was fully justified in saying in his *De Republica Anglorum* that Parliament "representeth and hath the power of the whole realm both the head and the body. For everie Englishman is entended to be there present . . . of what preheminence, state, dignitie or qualitie soever he be, from the Prince (be he King or Queen) to the lowest person of England. And the consent of Parliament is taken to be everie man's consent." By thus making the whole realm present in microcosm, Parliament allowed the English commonwealth to act in pursuit of the common good. "The most high and absolute power of the realme of Englande," Smith says, "is in the Parliament." For there the nobility, bishops, and commons "bee present to advertise, consult and shew what is good and necessarie for the common wealth," which "the Prince himselfe in presence of both the parties doeth consent unto and alloweth." "That is the Prince's and the whole realmes deede," Smith declares, "whereupon justlie no man can complaine, but must accommodate himself to find it just and good and obey it." Their duty to obey is an obligation, something to which they have become bound by their own promises—that is, by consent.[64]

Nor was this consent purely formal in character. Parliamentary taxation was assessed and collected by the same people (or people of the same kind) as granted it; parliamentary statutes were enforced in the same fashion. By the fifteenth century, then, the governance of England depended in a very direct fashion on the willingness of these figures—the prominent gentry in the counties and the members of the local corporations in the towns—to participate with the king and his principal servants in the governance of the realm. This relationship simultaneously strengthened and limited those who joined in it—the members of the political nation as well as the king. Together they could do what could not be done separately but not without accepting restraints on their framing of policy and exercise of power. It was this combination—or should we say integration—of centralized rule and local participation that gave late medieval and early modern England its distinctive legacy of rights and institutions.

< III >

The Course of Economic Change

We must now turn to examine England's tax base—its economy. While market exchange remained deeply "embedded" in social and political relations, as Karl Polanyi has put it, markets and marketing were important aspects of the medieval scene, as Fortescue himself well knew. In consequence, society was not entirely free from the pressures the market could bring upon social relations and the distribution of power. However, market pressures were not necessarily felt continuously or uniformly. A host of moral and ethical considerations—ideas of justice and expectations of fairness serving wide social and religious ends beyond the needs of production and profit— also played a governing role. In consequence the allocation of resources still depended on cooperation and command and not simply on competition between producers and the operations of the price mechanism.[65] In certain respects, late medieval and early modern England had a rather backward economy, especially when compared to Italy and the Low Countries. Its trade had many of the characteristics of colonial dependency. Agricultural produce, raw materials, and the products of labor-intensive industry were exported in return for high-priced manufactures and luxury wares. England, moreover, was still overwhelmingly an agrarian country, with only a handful of significant-sized cities. In the fifteenth century, even London was not yet the dominating metropolis it would become—in 1500 its population was about 50,000, only three to four times larger than those of its nearest rivals. At the same time, England's financial and commercial institutions were primitive compared to those of Venice or Florence or of the key cities of the Netherlands.

Nevertheless, a national market existed to a surprising degree. Late medieval England relied on a single currency for the whole realm and did not suffer the hindrances and inconveniences of internal tolls on wholesale trade. While regional differences remained in weights and measures, only a few systems were in use and they were easily reconciled. Moreover, in the aftermath of the Black Death in the mid-fourteenth century and with the loss of France in the mid-fifteenth, some important changes had occurred. First, an increasing portion of the agrarian population was freed from villein status and thereby came to enjoy the benefits of the common law, especially as regards property rights. As a result those with clear claims to their property received greater security in their possessions and status, though perhaps those without such clear claims became more vulnerable to exploitation and displacement. Under these conditions, there was positive encouragement to farmers to undertake genuine improvements on their lands.[66]

Simultaneously the agrarian population became increasingly dependent upon participation in the money economy for a significant share of its livelihood. Some were drawn to sell their agricultural produce in the national and international market, and some came to depend in part on manufacturing as well as agriculture. But more important was the conversion of their obligations to their landlords into money rents. The need to pay in money, or in money equivalents, meant that even customary tenants were incorporated into the market economy, at least to the degree that tenants felt pressure from their landlords for higher rents. It also meant that landlords increasingly peopled their estates with large leaseholders, willing and able through their introduction of improvements like enclosure to pay market rents for their holdings. Moreover, when a tax fell upon these figures it competed—even though every effort was made not to include what was owed in rent in official tax assessment—with the rents owed to their landlords.[67]

At the same time, an increasing share of the English economy came to depend on trade and manufacture, especially the latter. In the high Middle Ages, England traded wool for what it needed from the Continent. In the later Middle Ages it was woolens. This change encouraged more and more English villagers, especially in upland locations, to devote themselves to clothmaking as well as their customary agrarian pursuits.[68] It also helped shift the burden of the king's customs—a main source of his revenue from the thirteenth century —from agriculture narrowly construed to manufacture. Furthermore England's loss of all but a foothold in France led it to the development of a much more diversified trading economy, focused even more than earlier on the Low Countries and to an increasing extent on the Iberian Peninsula and Mediterranean. This trade was very much concentrated on luxury imports. But it also was the harbinger of a consumer revolution.[69]

These considerations lead us to one further point. Although England was far from having the most sophisticated economy in Europe, its commercial sector was admirably well-structured for the purposes of fiscal exploitation. Throughout the Middle Ages its overseas trade was heavily focused on one bulky commodity—first wool and then

cloth—exported by a relatively small community of merchants concentrated in London and only a few other places. Therefore it was possible not only to construct out of medieval administrative traditions
and practices an effective revenue-gathering regime—the customs—
to tap into this wealth but to establish effective political means
which could be exploited to the interests of both the merchants and
the Crown. We have already seen the results with the *maltolt*. The
establishment of commercial monopolies to exploit trade, such as the
Merchant Adventurers of England, only furthered this kind of sym-
biotic relationship.

There is also no doubt that from the second half of the sixteenth
century England was experiencing economic change and its discon-
tents in various ways. According to the best available estimate, the
combined population of England and Wales stood in 1541 at about
2.8 million; by the death of Elizabeth I it was about 4.1 million, a
more than two-thirds increase. Although the rate of growth was not
uniform in the next century, by 1688 the population stood at nearly
4.9 million.[70] Nor was this growth confined to the countryside or
merely cumulative. In a very real sense it is reflected in important
economic developments as is shown by the population history of
the towns. London reached 150,000 to 200,000 inhabitants by 1600
and was on the order of ten to twelve times larger than the next
biggest urban centers. Although growth in the provincial towns did
not keep pace even with the rise in national population, more urban
places of significant size—5,000 or more—became established and
we can begin to see a widely elaborated urban network in England,
dominated by London, integrating the entire nation into a single system of interdependent regions. During the course of the seventeenth
century, when London grew to about 575,000 inhabitants, the number of towns with populations over 5,000 increased by more than 50
percent, further elaborating the hierarchy of urban places that had
already been established in the earlier period. During this same era,
the proportion of the population living in cities also rose. It went
from perhaps 5.25 percent in 1520, to 8.25 percent in 1600, to 13.5
percent in 1700.[71]

But for all this evidence of economic development, the economic
picture was not uniformly rosy in this era. During the sixteenth century, population growth exceeded the capacity of the economy to

supply it. Real wages may have fallen by as much as 40 percent from 1520 to 1600. This deterioration persisted into the early seventeenth century, when it bottomed out; real wages then began to rise significantly, especially after 1660.[72] The effect was to create a genuine problem of poverty and an underclass of the poor in both country and town, particularly in the later sixteenth and early seventeenth centuries. Moreover, the great inflation of the sixteenth century that affected real wages also hit those living on fixed incomes, such as rents or governmental salaries, which were slow to adjust to changes in prices and the market. Price levels may have increased by as much as 450 percent between the first decade of the sixteenth century and the last and a further 34 percent between then and the 1650s. Only in the last half of the seventeenth century did prices truly stabilize.[73]

To understand the way economic pressures affected the state and were affected by it, it is perhaps helpful to think that England in this period possessed a "two-tiered economy." One segment of it depended upon buying and selling in large-scale regional, national, and international markets. The other operated outside these markets, relying upon exploitation of resources in the forests, commons, and wastes; cooperation among neighbors or gift exchange; customary services owed to superiors; and engagement only in a very localized trade in a limited number of items. The resulting complexity of relations between market-oriented and non-market-oriented economic activities is illustrated by the case of rural manufactures, such as clothmaking. In the late medieval and early modern period, weaving—to name only one of the various stages of production—was not carried out by specialist craftsmen who devoted their lives exclusively to production for the market. Rather it was performed by residents of upland villages who spent part of their time at their looms but also raised animals and tilled the soil for their own use. In many rural places, manufacturing was a by-employment carried out in conjunction with stock raising or other agrarian pursuits by practitioners who lived simultaneously in the market and non-market sectors of the English economy. Scholars have learned to speak of these inhabitants of the pastoral-industrial areas of England as depending on a "dual economy."[74] That is, their very communities and their very lives represent the existence of a two-tiered economy in a single place.

The implications of this view are large. It suggests that one side of

this duality might expand at the expense of the other and that competing principles might be at work in particular communities at the
same time. A similar point can be made about the nucleated arable
villages in the regions where traditional forms of open-field agriculture still prevailed. These places too were not entirely free of the
pressures of the market, as the evidence of agrarian improvements
and enclosure makes abundantly clear. The production of agricultural
staples could as readily be subject to the forces of economic expansion as could the production of manufactures. If the inhabitants of
these open field villages were less frequently caught up in the Janus-
faced dilemmas of daily life in the "dual economy," whole villages
could very well find themselves being pulled from one economic tier
into the other.[75]

In the towns, of course, the story was bound to be somewhat different. Although urban life depended in some measure upon the gift
economy and cooperation, and perhaps even on other non-market
modes as well, it centered on the exchange of goods and services
in the marketplace. Nevertheless, the history of towns is consistent
with the picture of economic change we have been outlining. In the
medieval period urban markets were highly regulated, and access
to them was severely limited. As a result, the economy as a whole
was less dependent upon them than it became in the course of the
early modern period and the proportion of the overall population participating in their market life was relatively small. In the sixteenth
and seventeenth centuries, however, the picture changed as effective
regulation broke down and as the percentage of the total population
living in substantial towns increased. Hence, the towns not only led
but responded to the growing importance of market exchange in the
early modern era.[76]

These increases in economic complexity owed much to changes
in England's trade and manufacture. In the later medieval period,
England's market economy was dominated by the production of cloth
and its export. The cloth industry remained important right through
the early modern period. But during the sixteenth and seventeenth
centuries, England's commercial and industrial activities came to
depend on more and more varied products and commodities. Metal
wares and other manufactures appeared alongside woolens among
exports and in domestic trade, and a wide variety of imported items,

joined later by colonial goods, played a significant role as well. That is, the increasing importance of the market-oriented tier of the English economy was a matter not merely of its share but also of its scope. With the explosion of trade that began in the later sixteenth century, the market came to supply a wider and wider variety of needs for a larger and larger portion of the population. These developments are closely related to fiscal matters. For example, more and more of the customs revenue came potentially from this developing sector of England's overseas trade. But it had to be tapped by adjustments to the rates at which various goods were assessed for *ad valorem* duties, a process that as we shall see led to difficulties over impositions. At the same time, the luxury trade encouraged the development of domestic sources for many of these goods, which in turn encouraged the creation of methods to exploit the wealth created by this sector of the economy. Out of them came the corruption we associate with the royal monopolies and the origins of the London money market.[77]

In other words, the dichotomized economy of which we have been speaking was continually being subverted by the processes of economic change that brought it into being in the first place. This fact has considerable relevance to the story we must tell. For it suggests that as more and more Englishman found more and more of their lives dependent upon market-oriented economic activity, their own needs for money competed directly with the fiscal needs of the state. These circumstances did not in themselves account for the existence of and reaction to fiscal crisis. Such a view artificially reduces the problem to a single cause. But here is a necessary—though not sufficient—condition for the emergence of and increasing importance of the resistance many Englishmen mounted against the intrusions of the state into their economic lives.

≺ IV ≻

The History of the English State

In the language of modern political sociology, a state is "a territorially and jurisdictionally defined political entity in which public authority is distinguished from (though not unconnected to) private power, and which is manned by officials whose primary (though not sole) allegiance is to a set of political institutions under a single, i.e. sovereign and final, authority"[78] which enjoys "a monopoly of *authoritative binding rule-making*, backed up by a monopoly of the means of violence."[79] This kind of state was only just coming into being in the early modern period. In almost every dimension its characteristics were contested or not yet sharply delineated. It was well understood, of course, that monarchy was an office that survived intact as one king died and the next succeeded him. But even in the days of the last Tudors and early Stuarts, when this doctrine of the king's two bodies had achieved its refined articulation, the loyalty of the subject was as much to the person as the office, which in ordinary circumstances were united as the body is to the soul. In practice there was no neat division between what belonged to the king as an individual, as the head of a family or dynasty, and as the ruler of the realm. Moreover, if loyalty to the Crown was personal, so was service. Although in many instances the leading offices of state imposed well-defined duties on the officeholders and required them to follow precisely encoded procedures, they were not constitutional officers in our sense of the term, exercising their principal functions according to a legally binding table of organization. They were primarily royal servants doing their master's bidding, capable of being employed no matter what their titles in tasks far removed from their official responsibilities.

Nor were these figures so selflessly loyal to their master as to lack personal ambition, independent interests, and social roles outside their official positions. Some officeholders, among them a few of the most important, were the recipients of gifts and gratuities (and bribes) from subjects who wanted favor or assistance. Lawrence Stone and Joel Hurstfield have told us about the successes of the Cecils, especially Robert, in turning their offices to financial effect for themselves and their family.[80] To add to this picture, it can only be said that at a lower level lesser officials were no less reluctant to turn their duties to their own good. The customs officers, for example, regularly converted what would otherwise have been customs revenue into wages for their offices.[81] In other words, only part of an official's income derived from what we might call official sources. It has been estimated, for example, that in the 1630s between £250,000 and £400,000 a year, equal to perhaps 40 percent of the royal revenues, came into officeholders' hands through gifts, gratuities, and other irregular means.[82]

Indeed, the salaries and fee schedules established for their posts assumed that this would be so, especially in the age of inflation in the sixteenth century. In effect, an informal system of taxation existed to pay for the services—or at any rate to enhance the income of suppliers of those services—where the formal system of salaries and fees did not.

This already complex picture is further complicated when we consider the role played by unpaid officials in many important services. Already in the fourteenth century there was a rich assortment of these figures—many of them centrally appointed—in both the counties and boroughs: sheriffs, escheators, coroners, constables, keepers of the peace, mayors, bailiffs, and the like. They offered vital assistance in the local administration of justice, the maintenance of law and order, and the remission of revenue to the Crown. In the succeeding age, this practice of relying on the services of local notables to perform these duties only became more important with the rise of the justice of the peace and of Quarter Sessions in the counties and the emergence of select boards of aldermen in the boroughs. The church too served political and administrative functions, even before the Reformation turned it into a second arm of monarchical rule. It not only provided high officials, like Cardinal Wolsey, to handle the king's principal business, but served as an instrument of propaganda, social discipline, and public welfare in the dioceses and parishes and performed legal functions such as the probate of wills and enforcement of marriage contracts.

All of this is to say that we are speaking of a state that was not yet established on a modern bureaucratic footing. Nevertheless, it would be wrong to conclude that there was no conception of the state in Tudor and Stuart England. Elizabeth I, for example, distinguished what she called "matters of state" from "matters concerninge the commen wealth" when granting freedom of speech in the House of Commons. As regards the former, she said, the Commons were not "to meddle" except with "such as should be propounded unto them."[83] This idea of the "state" owes a debt to medieval terminology. It refers to something static—the queen's estate; her accumulated powers, rights, and possession; her being or condition. But by thus distinguishing this state from the queen's person, by indicating that like the commonwealth it too might have the need of legislative action consented to by the whole realm, and by emphasizing that royal officials would propound those needs in Parliament on its behalf, this formulation already had come half way towards a modern conception of the state as positive legal and constitutional order, capable of collective action in its own interests, that the ruler and his or her officials have a duty to uphold.[84] It was not long before this concept had evolved further. In the 1590s, for example, when the dangers of international war and the prospect of the inevitable end of the Tudor dynasty loomed large in the political imagination, it was not unusual to find discussions of policy framed in terms of the state's long-term interests as involving the general welfare of England, not just the interests of the present monarch.[85] This state, as Elizabeth herself recognized in distinguishing its business from that of the commonwealth, was in the monarch's care and in that of her duly appointed servants.

This idea is given further specification and elaboration in "The Maxims of State," a work attributed to Sir Walter Ralegh. There the state is defined as "the frame or set order of a commonwealth, or of the governors that rule the same, especially of the chief and sovereign governor that commandeth the rest." This "state of sovereignty" consisted in five points, namely "making or annulling of laws," "creating and disposing of magistrates," "power over life and death," "making of war or peace," and "highest or last appeal." "Where these five points are, either in one or in more, there is the state." In this definition, the state is understood to be a feature of a commonwealth, in the sense that without a commonwealth there would be no state. But was the state just the government or was it the entity over which and in whose interest the government rules? In the end, the "Maxims" take the former view: the state is the collectivity of institutions and officials charged with caring for the common good.[86]

Nevertheless, monarchical government had only partly disentangled itself from the web of relations in what modern commentators like Michael Mann often call "civil society."[87] It is no surprise, therefore, to find it equally common for some thinker to treat the state as a synonynm for the whole body politic. Already in the 1530s, Thomas Starkey was using the word in this fashion, not only as something to be ruled by whoever had "authority upon the whole state," but as an organism whose health depended on the joint efforts of its various members—the ruler who was its heart wherein reason resided; the officials who were its eyes, ears, and other senses; the craftsmen and warriors who were its hands to protect it and work to make things necessary for collective well being; and the plowmen and tillers of the soil who were its feet in that they sustained and supported the rest of the body.[88] By the 1590s, this usage was also well established.[89] On this interpretation, all subjects in the realm shared responsibility for the welfare of the state.

A similar tension was reflected in the sociology of the political nation. Was it a narrow elite or a widely ramified social organism? According to one widely-held modern view, the political as well as the economic horizons of most English men and women before the modern day were extremely circumscribed. They lived, it is said, in "self conscious and coherent" communities, each a "little self-centred kingdom on its own" where the everyday needs of family life and survival predominated over politics.[90] Accordingly, when conflict arose between the community and the state, local issues and local loyalties usually prevailed over national ones. Only a small elite, operating at court or in council, concerned themselves primarily with great matters of state and engaged in the national political arena.

In the judgment of Peter Laslett, the political nation in early modern England consisted of just one class—"one body of persons"—the gentry—"capable of concerted action over the whole area of society"; only its "opinions" mattered. This class he estimated to consist of "a twenty-fifth, at most a twentieth, of all the people alive in the England of the Tudors and Stuarts." Its members alone enjoyed the "instituted, recognized power over other individuals" that made one "free of the society of England."[91] Edward Thompson, however, has stressed that the pre-capitalist age knew not one but two significant social groupings: "the rulers and the ruled, the high and the low people, persons of substance and of independent estate and the loose and disorderly sort. In between, where the professional and middle classes, and the substantial yeomanry should have been, relations of clientage and dependency were so strong that . . . these groups appear to offer little deflection of the essential polarities."[92]

The emphasis placed by Laslett and Thompson on the distinction between the limited number who rule and the vast majority who do not reflects earlier usage. Sir Thomas Elyot, for example, explicitly adopted the phrase "public weal" to describe the English body politic for fear that "common weal" would associate the "plebs," the commons, with a role in governance.[93] Sir Thomas Smith also distinguished the rulers from the ruled. But he saw a far wider participation in the political nation. He included citizens and burgesses among the rulers because they "serve the common wealth, in their cities and burrowes, or in corporate townes where they dwell." Yeomen—the famous forty shilling freeholders—fell into a similar category. They bore all the burdens of local governance and law enforcement in the countryside not undertaken by the gentry. Even "the fourth sort or classe"—such as poor husbandmen and artificers—who had "no free lande" and who traditionally had "no voice nor authoritie in our common wealth," often served in the towns as jurors and in the villages as churchwardens and constables.[94]

On Smith's view, therefore, early modern England was a realm in which all were considered "subjects and citizens" except "bondmen who can beare no rule nor jurisdiction over freemen," and women, children, and infants who fall into a similar condition. Hence the middling sort exercised considerable public responsibility, extending to "administration in judgementes, corrections of defaultes, in election of offices, in appointing tributes and subsidies, and in making lawes."[95] Clearly, the nobility and gentry bore the greater authority and power, but we would fail to grasp the nature of the early modern English polity if we dismissed this picture of wide participation by "the little people" in its public affairs. They are the very folk on whom Fortescue saw the basic institutions of law and governance depending in England's *dominium politicum et regale*.

Equally important, as Fortescue had stressed, is the fact that the gentry, yeomanry, and others capable of participating in local governance were plentiful in number in the early modern period. The gentry, of course, had emerged as a distinct element in rural society in the course of the fourteenth and fifteenth centuries, and by the sixteenth century every county had a significant population of such figures involved in local political affairs and willing and able to bear the burdens of local governance when called upon. According to Thomas Wilson, there may have been 16,000 gentry families in England in 1600, which if correct would mean that they represented perhaps 2 percent of the entire population. Of these, only about a sixth were men with serious ambitions for advancement at court or in national office; the rest would have been leaders only within their counties or more likely still within their home parishes. Wilson's estimate of the number of freeholders in 1600 suggests that the yeomanry may have amounted to 8 or possibly even 10 percent of the English population.[96]

The yeomanry, however, were steadily on the increase throughout the period. Gregory King indicates that by 1688 there were more than 180,000 such families, representing something in excess of 18 percent of the total population. By the end of the seventeenth century, their share of the land in England had increased by perhaps a third from the levels of the late fifteenth and early sixteenth centuries.[97] In the towns, too, the numbers of the middling sort were on the rise as urban populations grew and more and more diverse occupational structures became established during the course of the sixteenth and seventeenth centuries, though here we are not able to establish the numbers with any exactitude. If, as King estimated, the population living in English cities and towns stood at about 1,400,000 at the end of the seventeenth century, there were perhaps 75,000 to 100,000 families in them capable of supporting the system of popular participation in local governance.[98] Whether the political expectations and aspirations of all of them could be accommodated, however, is more open to doubt.

Since service in some offices was completely unpaid, and most other officers were underpaid, the Crown was, in a very genuine sense, the beneficiary of a kind of *corvée* levied on the nobility and gentry, and, to a certain degree, the better off elements in town and village society. Without these resources English monarchs would have had even greater difficulties in making ends meet than they otherwise did, even in peacetime. Nevertheless, this singularly unsystematic aspect of the fiscal system might be thought of as the most telling feature of the political order. It gives us a clear example of "self-government at the king's command," in which local communities existed in a co-ordinated relationship with the central authorities to form a single organic whole. This Fortescueian form of governance placed heavy reliance on unpaid officials ranging from the great magnates who held the highest offices of the state and served as royal lieutenants in the counties, through the justices of the peace and city magistrates who maintained law and order in the localities, to the constables and other petty officials whom Smith praises and Laslett and Thompson disparage.

Nevertheless, it would be wrong to think that late medieval or early modern England entirely lacked a class of professional office-holders. Grants of life tenure, the awarding of posts in reversion, the widespread use of deputies, and even the sale of offices undermined the control the monarch could exercise over his own officials, but there was an increased stress on selecting officials from an educated elite, learned in the classics and the law, committed not only to service to their king but to traditions of public duty to the commonweal.[99] A number of governmental departments—such as the Exchequer and the Chancery—served the Crown (and not the king's person), were separate from the royal household, and operated within established codes of routine and legally binding systems of control. That these departments suffered from considerable inefficiency and corruption does not completely defeat their significance as centralized hierarchies of officials engaged in the organized pursuit of the interests of the state.[100] These characteristics were already present in the medieval period and were enhanced in the course of the sixteenth century as effective political control of the regime came under the Privy Council and as more and more governmental posts went to laymen who relied on them as the primary source of their status, income, and power.[101]

However, this civil service, if we can call it that, was never very large. It has been estimated that in Elizabeth I's reign about 600 officials administered the Crown lands and a further 600 the other central departments of state, meaning that there was one royal official for every 4000 inhabitants or thereabouts. In Charles I's reign the size of this civil service was not much larger, even though the demands of the royal household were considerably increased by the need to attend to his wife and children.[102] Moreover, there was not a large professional military to complement and support the work of the officials. Throughout the Tudor and early Stuart periods, the military strength of the nation still depended primarily on mercenaries, the followings of the great landlords, and the national militia; although there were permanent posts in the armory, ordnance and forts and castles and the reform of the militia under the lords lieutenant reduced the independent military power of the nobility and improved the strength and efficiency of the county musters. As for the Navy, it was still pri-

marily a defensive force, intended for guarding the coasts, and was
made up of only a small number of royal ships. Elizabeth I left only
29 vessels of 100 tons or more on her death and these were captained
either by members of the nobility or by privateers. When war came,
the size of the naval force was built up by employing privateers or
requisitioning private vessels and crews into national service.[103]

The English state, then, lacked the scale of modern bureaucratic
regimes as well as many organizational features on which they typically depend. Nevertheless, by the close of the sixteenth century the
English had long understood themselves to be living in a polity on
whose welfare their own interests critically depended and to which
they owed service as well as allegiance. In this sense early modern
England in principle was a state, even though it lacked the state apparatus of its counterparts and rivals on the continent.

≺ V ≻

The Royal Endowment

If the distinction between state and society was just being formed
in England in the early modern period, so too were the differences
of function among the institutions and agencies of its governmental regime. Although by the mid-sixteenth century, if not before,
many royal offices and central departments—particularly those concerned with revenue—had well-defined administrative responsibilities,[104] most performed a multiplicity of other political duties, participating in the processes of patronage and social exchange that
characterized public life, especially among the kingdom's elite.[105] In
consequence, even so well-established an administrative arm as the
Exchequer could not completely disentangle itself from the web of
society.[106] The government did not—because it could not—form a
full-fledged fiscal system in which each element meshed with the
others to make a smoothly running bureaucratic machine. Hence not
much is to be gained from an overly precise catalogue of the various
institutional elements involved in revenue gathering and expenditure in early modern England. We need rather to understand how the
attendant processes of state-building helped shape the social and economic practices, outlooks, and ideologies of the English.

First we must consider the sources of revenue that adhered to the king's person by virtue of his title. The main component here is the Crown lands, the income-producing properties of the Crown. Some of these belonged to the ancient demesne, the original endowment of the kingship, which could not be completely alienated. But throughout the Middle Ages the royal practice had been to encumber them with charges. Hence it is said that in Edward IV's reign he received only five-eighths of their rental.[107] Of course, new lands came to the Crown through forfeitures, which were especially important in the fifteenth century, and to a lesser degree through escheats. Even these properties, however, rarely remained in the king's hands for very long—typically they were given away as rewards to followers.

Nevertheless, from the mid-fifteenth century there was a general improvement in this aspect of royal revenue, much of it under the stimulus of reforms, promoted by Edward IV and Henry VII as well as by the aristocracy, intended to assure that the king would indeed live of his own.[108] In 1433, the combined income from Crown lands and the Duchy of Lancaster amounted to about £9,300. But under these two monarchs an aggressive policy of resumptions, improved management of the estates themselves, the attainder of enemies, and a certain amount of dynastic luck—combined with the contributions of the Yorkist and Tudor patrimonies—brought this figure up to £42,000 in 1509.[109] Although income from this source declined somewhat during the early stages of Henry VIII's reign as the king granted certain of his estates away, the fiscal side of the Reformation more than restored its importance to the Crown. For example, as the recipient of first fruits and tenths after 1534, Henry received some £40,000 annually from Church lands. This income was reduced to half after the dissolution of the monasteries, but the dissolution more than made up for the loss. Between 1536 and 1539, land worth £135,000 to £140,000 annually was added to the Crown estate. While a good deal of this land was sold off right away, between 1536 and 1544 the net yearly receipts of the Court of Augmentations, created to deal with this influx of properties, averaged more than £112,000. Henry VII's entire annual income at his death had been just about the same.[110]

In the short run, then, the dissolution put the royal revenue on a new and secure footing for the first time in generations. Had the Crown been able to hold on to these properties, there can be little doubt that the subsequent constitutional and political history of

England would have been far different from what it became, since Parliament's role as a tax-granting body almost certainly would have atrophied. But within a very brief interval, largely under the pressure of war and the indebtedness it produced, the practice of alienating properties began eroding this position. Between 1539, when rumors of war were first heard, and the end of Henry VIII's reign some £800,000 worth of monastic lands were sold. Taken together with what had been given away, the Crown's holdings of former monastic properties had been reduced by two-thirds. The process continued under Edward VI, even though the confiscation of chantry lands had added to the royal holdings.[111] Given an inflation rate of about 250 percent between 1509 and 1558, by the beginning of Elizabeth I's reign revenues from Crown lands had actually fallen by about 25 percent from the level Henry VII had achieved. A further 75 percent inflation between 1558 and 1603 wiped away the nominal gain achieved in this period. Indeed, any chance for an increase in land revenues in real terms was defeated by extensive land sales at the beginning and end of her reign to pay debts and meet current expenses and by the Crown's failure to raise rents on its properties during these years.[112] Nor did the situation improve in the next century. It has been estimated that during his first decade on the throne, James I each year sold lands worth £27,000; and that Charles I, during his first decade on the throne, did about the same.[113]

This history of decline meant that income from land came to play a smaller and smaller role in the royal revenues for our period. At the beginning of Elizabeth I's reign, it accounts for about 40 percent of ordinary receipts; at the end only a bit more than 30 percent. By the 1630s it was about 14 percent.[114] There were, however, several sources of royal revenue that could be made to yield greater returns. One arose from the king's position as a feudal overlord. These so-called feudal incidents gave the monarch the wardship of underage heirs to the estates of his tenants-in-chief and the right to arrange the marriages of their heiresses should no sons have survived. Starting in Henry VII's reign, if not earlier, Crown lawyers operating according to the principles of *prerogativa regis* in feudal relations found new ways to exploit this source of income.[115] At the end of Henry VIII's reign the net profits to the king of this "fiscal feudalism," as Joel Hurstfield called it, stood at about £7,000 annually. During Elizabeth I's reign the yearly income from this source fluctuated between £15,000 and £20,000. But again inflation took its toll, so that it was only in the last decade of the sixteenth century, under the eye of Sir Robert Cecil, that income from this source began to catch up with levels reached in the mid-sixteenth century.[116] Cecil's exploitation of this source of revenue taught a lasting lesson. By 1640, income from fiscal feudalism had risen to about £84,000 annually, which in real terms represents roughly a doubling of income from the levels of the 1540s.[117] Over the same period, it went from providing about 7.5 percent of ordinary royal revenue to 12 percent, and more if we add to it the £175,000 or so raised from another feudal right—distraint of knighthood—in the 1630s.[118] In effect, then, by Charles I's reign the Crown was able to use these ancient feudal rights to tap into the rise in landed incomes that had occurred during the Tudor and early Stuart era, though of course only those families holding their estates as tenants-in-chief of the king and unlucky enough to have left under-age or female heirs were required to bear this burden.

Purveyance and the creation of monopolies provided other sources of additional income for the Crown, which by tapping directly into the market economy could keep up with inflation. Whether purveyance was made in kind or by one or another form of composition, the effective tax involved the difference between the king's price and the actual market price of the goods in question. Hence, if the purveyance officers could successfully keep the agreed upon king's price from rising with market prices, they could effectively impose a tax that transferred the benefits of inflation from the taxpayers to the Crown. However, the activities of the clerk of the Market, an official of the royal household who had the power to fix prices in markets throughout England and Wales, created a complication. It was his duty to prevent market prices from rising too steeply, lest pressures for altering the composition agreements in the counties became overwhelming or the king himself be forced to bear the burden for goods bought directly for his household. Nevertheless, the value of purveyance appears to have been growing from Elizabeth's reign until it was finally abolished in 1660. According to Fabian Philipps, writing in the 1660s, it was worth about £25,000 to the Crown in 1592–93, £37,544 annually under James I, and perhaps £50,000 a year under Charles I. If this is correct, there was about a 40 percent increase in the value of purveyance in real terms between the 1590s and the 1630s. Although these sums were relatively small in comparison with the total wealth of the England, the burden fell very unevenly over the realm, with the counties nearest the king's main residences in and about London bearing the heaviest load. It should be no surprise, then, that with the intrusions of the clerk of the Market, the corruption that followed from dealings with the officials of the household, and the uneven incidence of the tax, purveyance became a significant grievance in this period.[119]

The grant and sale of patents of monopoly represented another source of the royal revenue with the potential to cause grievance. Grants of the exclusive right to trade or to perform some public function were hardly new to the early modern period. The medieval records of the Chancery abound with them. But in the mid-sixteenth century they took on a new character when the monarch began issuing them ostensibly to promote new manufactures. Many of them were, in effect, forms of excise tax, since they added to the cost of certain consumer items in such a way as to benefit the state as well as the monopolist. It is not clear just how much accrued to the royal accounts from this source in the early years. But most patents in Elizabeth I's reign contained clauses reserving a part of the profit to the Crown specifically to offset any losses to the customs revenue that might come from the grant. Moreover, many of these patents went in the first instance to courtiers, in effect supplementing their official incomes. A number of these grants were made to Crown creditors—courtiers and non-courtiers—as ways of paying back loans. In addition, we should recall that any grant involved fees, gratuities, and outright bribes to various officials, whose incomes also benefited thereby. But unfortunately we cannot estimate the total benefit to the Crown or cost to the consumer. For the 1630s, we can be a bit more definite. The monopolies of starch, coal, salt, and soap in those years were raising perhaps £80,000 annually for the Crown, at an estimated cost to the consumer of £200,000 to £300,000 a year. Although the grievance of monopoly touched on many other issues, this burden alone would have been enough to excite complaint.[120]

The above-mentioned groups of revenue sources required no special grant of authority each time the monarch wished to collect. They could therefore be counted upon to support royal government whenever the monarch chose to draw from them, even though they might not be exploited at all or might vary from year to year in the amounts actually received. To them we should also add the first fruits and tenths, already mentioned, which from 1534 were levied annually, producing at first, as we have seen, about £40,000 annually and after the dissolution of the monasteries, an average of about £20,000. But the most important of the revenues that the monarch could count upon throughout his or her reign came from the customs.

England has had a national system of customs since at least 1275 when Edward I first began collecting a tax on the export of wool, woolfells, and hides. Once established in the later thirteenth and fourteenth centuries, rates on various goods—usually referred to as the "great and petty custom"—remained in place until the early modern period. The customs on wool, woolfells, and hides, for example, continued to be collected until James I's reign while the cloth custom of 1347 persisted until Queen Mary's. Strictly speaking, these older customs payments were not parliamentary taxes since they were habitual charges on export and import, imposed by royal will and permanent in duration. Even though the so-called ancient custom of 1275 was made by the community of merchants with the assent of the great men of the realm, it was recognized to belong to the Crown as of right and not contested. The more important part of the customs revenues, however, came from the subsidies, taxes which at their inception were granted by consent for specific purposes and limited periods. We have already mentioned the *maltolt* on wool collected in the mid-fourteenth century to support Edward III's wars. Of much longer history were the subsidies of tonnage and poundage. At their inception, these subsidies were granted to defray royal expenses during specific wartime emergencies and lasted only a limited number of years before they had to be renewed. But in the fifteenth century Henry VI and Edward IV each received life grants, though not during their first regnal year. With Richard III began the practice of making life grants at the start of the reign, and until Charles I every subsequent monarch received such a grant in this fashion. With this change, the tax became officially devoted to assuring the safety of all Englishmen upon the seas.[121]

These revenues represented a significant share of the king's resources throughout the sixteenth and early seventeenth centuries. At the end of Henry VII's reign about 35 percent of the ordinary income of the Crown came from them.[122] By the end of Henry VIII's, however, customs revenue, which fell continuously through his reign because of decreased wool exports and the disruptions to trade caused by war, had declined to only half the level it had been at its outset.[123] But reforms in the customs under Queen Mary, especially the establishment of a new book of rates in 1558, helped restore the income somewhat. It brought in about £86,000 annually at the beginning of Elizabeth I's reign, and after a decline in the 1570s, stood at approximately £100,000 a year at the end. Given that the queen's annual ordinary revenue was only around £200,000 during her first decade on the throne and £300,000 at the end, the contribution of the customs was substantial indeed. Customs revenues account for almost 45 percent of the total at the beginning and about 33 percent at the end.[124]

The customs revenues posed two great difficulties to the Crown, both the consequence of their dependence on the market. First, the revenues were subject to significant fluctuations as market conditions varied, sometimes very sharply, from year to year. In addition, the return from them depended on a wide network of customs officials in the ports, who given the limited administrative resources available to the Crown could not be closely supervised in their dealings with the merchants. Much income was certainly lost each year to collusion and peculation. Here the Crown could guarantee the contribution the customs would make to its revenue through tax-farming, by which individual entrepreneurs or groups of entrepreneurs paid the Crown a fixed rent in return for collecting a particular tax or group of taxes. The effect was to accept the certainty of a fixed income each year during the term of the farm in place of bearing the burdens, risks, and delays in annual tax collection. Since the leases were renegotiated when their terms ended, however, it was also possible for the Crown to take advantage to some degree of the gains in the base revenues derived from customs over the preceding period. Tax-farming, therefore, yielded a degree of predictability to the customs income and placed the burden and cost of supervising the customs officials out of the hands of the Crown.

Customs farming also created an important relationship between the monarchy and particular groups of financiers and merchants, who stood ready to advance loans to the king in emergencies and who in return not only pocketed the benefits of improved trade but received special privileges in the economy—especially in their control of colonial enterprises and foreign trading monopolies. This relationship became especially important under the early Stuarts, who in effect turned the customs over to a tight-knit group of Crown clients and concessionaires, based primarily in London. Hence there was a heavy price paid for the advantages derived from the farming of the customs. In an era when royal income had difficulty keeping pace with costs, the Crown not only passed up taking the full benefit of the trade expansion which its own policies brought about but contributed further to the grievances that were associated throughout this period with its patents and grants.[125]

The second great problem posed to the Crown by the customs was inflation. Since there had been at least a fourfold increase in prices during the sixteenth century, customs revenues at the end of Elizabeth's reign were actually worth only about half of what they had been at the end of Henry VII's. Here increases could be achieved through the exercise of extraordinary royal powers. For example, in anticipation of the farming of the customs some improvement was gained in 1604—following the example of 1558—through a unilateral increase in the rates used to assess *ad valorem* duties. This increase raised the assessed values on many goods by 25 to 50 percent. The *Book of Rates* was revised again in 1635.[126] More important was the levy of impositions, that is of special charges over and above the ordinary customs due on certain commodities. In 1573, Elizabeth I had settled such an extra charge on the importation of sweet wines, and in the 1590s additional impositions were placed on the export of such items as lamb and sheep skins, beer, and coal. Early in James I's reign a further levy fell on currants imported from the Levant, which in 1606 gave rise to the famous decision in *Bate's Case* on behalf of the royal prerogative to use such charges to regulate the realm's relations with foreign powers. On the basis of this decision, a full list of items subject to impositions was created in 1608 and although the rates were modified after heated parliamentary protest in 1610, these so-called "new impositions" became a regular part of the royal revenue thereafter. They were expanded and extended further during the reign of James I and Charles I. According to one estimate, by 1640 the annual return from these sources came to almost £250,000. In addition, leases on the customs farms were renegotiated to produce almost £270,000 annually.[127] In this way, the early Stuarts managed finally to advance the customs revenues beyond inflation. Evaluated in real terms, the customs revenues in 1640 amounted to more than a doubling of the revenues enjoyed by Henry VII at the end of his reign and about a fourfold increase over Elizabeth I's customs revenues at the end of her reign. By 1640, the customs accounted for more than 50 percent of the total Crown revenue.[128]

≺ VI ≻

Extraordinary Income

We need now to consider the extraordinary income of the Crown, those sources of revenue that were collected only under special conditions, largely having to do with the need to finance warfare or more broadly to conduct foreign affairs and protect the national security. Some depended on well-established and widely accepted procedures for their grant and collection, while others came to the Crown only by virtue of the exercise of special (or emergency) powers for the preservation of the realm. Among the sources of revenue we have already considered, the income from the Crown lands, the royal rights of wardship and marriage, the customs revenues, and even purveyance can be said to come to the Crown in the first way. The income from the patents and the impositions, however, falls into the second category—which we can now designate "prerogative taxation." Among the "extraordinary" revenues, this same pattern obtains. Parliamentary subsidies, and the related clerical subsidies, normally voted by Convocation each time a lay subsidy was levied in Parliament, also came to the Crown through settled and accepted avenues. Aids, benevolences, forced loans, and ship money, however, fall into our second category; they depended upon the prerogative of the king or queen. The difference turns on the concept of consent. With parliamentary and clerical subsidies, taxation was granted by the collective act of the realm taken by the representative assemblies in which each man was said to be present either in person or by his agent. With the benevolences and other examples of "prerogative taxation" the money was collected in response to direct requests from the monarch for assistance in a time of emergency.

By the fifteenth century, the main form of parliamentary subsidies was the so-called "fifteenth and tenth," first levied in 1332 as an assessed tax. As originally conceived it was to fall on a fifteenth of the value of all movables in the shires and on a tenth in all boroughs; the clear object was to tap the actual wealth of each taxpayer as it grew in market value. After two troubled years of avoidance and protest, however, the government abandoned any pretense of actually assessing the tax and agreed to accept a fixed sum, amounting conventionally to £37,430 per grant, divided among the counties. In the early Tudor period, after reductions to reflect losses of taxable property and deductions for the costs of collection, the net yield was £29,800 per grant.[129] With roughly this yield, the fifteenth and tenth continued to be collected down to 1623, sometimes in the form of multiple grants.

But the most important development in taxation before the mid-seventeenth century Tudors was the reintroduction under the early Tudors of the directly assessed lay subsidy, a tax whose incidence and yield varied according to the terms laid out by statute at the time of the grant. Although there were seven such grants in the fifteenth century before 1485,[130] it was only under Henry VII and Henry VIII, and especially after 1523, that this form of direct taxation become fully established. The central feature of the tax was its direct assessment of incomes from land or personal property by local officers under the supervision of centrally appointed commissioners. Since no attempt was made to limit the yield of the tax in advance or to fix a minimum, the success of the grant depended entirely on the accuracy of the assessment. In its early manifestations, the scope of the tax was also very broad. It was intended to fall on wages, starting at £1 a year, as well as on property, and therefore to draw contributions from the laboring poor as well as the wealthy, though in some grants there was a graduated scale so that richer subjects paid at a higher rate than poorer ones. After the middle of the sixteenth century, the attempt to tax the poor was abandoned. In the early Tudor period, also, assessments seem to have been reasonably accurate, especially in their treatment of the landed elite who typically had escaped full payment of their tax obligations during the Middle Ages. But by the end of the sixteenth century the assessments again tended to markedly under-estimate the taxable wealth of those most able to pay. At about the same time, the assessments became for the most part merely nominal—fixed by custom and tradition—and the subsidy acquired some of the features of the fifteenth and tenth as a tax with a fixed yield. The voting of each subsidy, then, had become instead something like a unit of account, intended to produce so much income, though in this case the yield tended to diminish with each successive grant.[131]

There can be no doubt, however, that direct taxation by parliamentary grant could produce significant sums in times of necessity, provided the members of the Commons and the local assessors were persuaded of the need. To cover the expenses of war between 1540 and 1545, for example, parliamentary grants contributed £489,000 in subsidies and fifteenths and tenths; another £112,000 was granted by forgiving the repayment of a loan raised among the propertied classes in 1542. In 1559 and 1560, at the outset of Elizabeth I's reign when the queen was burdened by the heavy war debts that her sister had accumulated, some £195,400 was raised; and in 1572 and 1573, when dangers at home and abroad again seemed exceptionally severe, parliamentary grants brought in another £175,000.[132] In periods of crisis, it was possible to sustain taxation at these levels for years at a stretch, even though the sums raised met only a fraction of the total need. According to Sir Robert Cecil, parliamentary subsidies produced £1,562,224 in the war-torn years from 1594 to 1603.[133]

But as the yield of the subsidy declined in the later sixteenth and early seventeenth centuries it became harder and harder to achieve these levels. For the first four subsidies of Elizabeth I's reign, granted from 1559 to 1571, the average yield was almost £128,000. It had fallen precipitously by the 1620s. The yield in 1621 was approximately £72,500, in 1624 about £67,000, in 1625 around £63,000, and in 1628 only £55,000. To make up for the decline the Crown requested and was granted multiple subsidies to reach a particular return. This procedure, however, probably contributed to the MPs' reluctance to grant as much as was desired, since it was politically difficult to vote additional subsidies even to keep up with the declining yields. Moreover, inflation took a heavy toll on the actual value of these grants. The £275,000 collected in 1628, for example, purchased about 17 percent less that the £175,400 collected in the early 1570s.[134]

In the fourteenth and fifteenth centuries, as we know, the theoretical justification for taxation had been the doctrine of necessity. When the realm faced emergency, when it was in danger, it was the duty of all its members to come to its aid. Sometimes, to be sure, peacetime projects were also funded by direct parliamentary taxes, but to include them the Crown's lawyers had to find clever ways to treat them as preparations for the national defense in the face of impending crisis. In the mid-sixteenth century, however, this legal and rhetorical foundation for the grant of taxes underwent important modifications as the Crown itself began asking for funds not only to support its military needs but to assist it with the general costs of providing good government. In 1534, when in fact there was no pressing military need, the preamble of the subsidy bill explicitly grounded the grant on

the entier love & zeale which the Kinges saide Highnes alwayes hath borne and nowe intendeth to the conservacyon mayntenaunce & increase of the welthe estate of this Realme & the weal profitte commoditie & quietnes of his people & subjectes of the same.[135]

For the next twenty years, similar terms were regularly used in the subsidy statutes to justify taxes. Even after this language had been largely purged from the legislation under Elizabeth I, royal propagandists continued to make reference to the theme of good government in giving the reasons for calling Parliament and the subsidy statutes themselves persisted in referring in shorthand to the great benefits accruing to the commonwealth from the royal government.[136] These innovations in rhetoric introduced new ideological and political considerations to the granting of taxation, even where they failed to alter the legalities. They enlisted the members of Parliament in assuring the provision of good government and established standards against which the Crown's actions could be criticized, redress of grievances could be sought, and a legislative program of reform could be mounted. In this way, then, the new terminology brought the language of commonwealth from the realms of legal theory and royalist propaganda into political debate.[137]

< VII >

The Anti-Tax Motif

Compared to most continental countries, England was relatively little taxed in the period before 1640.[138] In the 1630s the annual cost of its central government came to perhaps £1 million to £1.2 million, counting not only the revenues coming into the Exchequer but hidden expenditures on gratuities and bribes that went directly to royal officials. It has been estimated, however, that its economy produced an annual income of perhaps £25 to £30 million in this same period, which suggests that the economic burden of the central government on society amounted to less than 5 percent. The figure would be higher, of course, if we included local taxes—such as the poor rates and the costs of maintaining the militia—and tallied up in money terms the contributions made by unpaid officials. But even so, it is hard to imagine that the English state in this period extracted anything approaching the percentages of the national wealth that the French and the Spanish states were able to manage.[139] Nevertheless, the MPs' reluctance to grant adequate taxation was not entirely the result of selfishness or tight-fistedness, or confusion about how much each such grant would bring in. It was also the consequence of some very practical economic considerations, having to do especially with the limitations of the existing system of credit.

By its very nature, the payment of taxes in this period depended upon the transfer of coin from one set of pockets to another. It was not enough to promise to pay, in effect drawing on one's future income to pay present expenses. In simple terms, the obligation to pay a tax was like a debt that could be acquitted only through the actual exchange of hard currency. The reasons for this are simple. Since there was no established banking system that could support the deferred payment of taxes (or supply the king's creditors with long-term backing for their future transactions), taxpayers had to pay their obligations in coin, thus depleting their own abilities to quit their other debts or conduct their personal business in cash. The problems this caused would have been minimized, of course, had the Crown distributed the received funds evenly through the realm. The system of assigning exchequer tallies, in use from the Middle Ages, was designed in part to make this possible. It allowed those to whom the king owed money to draw payment from funds collected in the shires rather than from the Exchequer itself. But in the period we have been discussing only a relatively small portion of the royal income—normally less than ten percent of the total—was handled in this fashion.[140] In fact, widespread use of this procedure was never in the cards, since the flow

of coin necessarily tended to concentrate around the central governing bodies, most of them in and near London, and the monarch, also
based primarily in the metropolis. In wartime, the effects were exaggerated not only by the way the funds moved into certain regions
and certain hands—those of the victuallers of ships for example—
but also by the way that they were used up at sea or abroad.

The effect of a tax grant, therefore, was to funnel coin to the Exchequer without redistributing it on an equal basis to the regions.
Taxes, then, produced on a regional basis just that scarcity of coin
that merchants and others habitually complained of in this period.
They sapped the monetary resources necessary for ordinary subjects—rich and not so rich—to conduct their ordinary business. This
effect was openly complained about in 1523, when Wolsey proposed
a heavy tax of 4s in the pound. The tax, it was said, could not be
paid since "there was not so much money, out of the kynges handes,
in all the realme." Gentlemen's possessions were in lands, husbandmen's in cattle and corn, merchants' and artisans' in goods, not in
money. "If all the coyne was in the kynges handes," the MPs asked,
"how should men live?"[141] Nor was this mere parliamentary hyperbole. In 1525, when Wolsey attempted to raise a benevolence—an un-
parliamentary grant—of one-sixth on the laity and one-third on the
clergy over and above the heavy burdens of the subsidy granted for
four years in 1523, there was significant evidence of scarcity of coin
throughout the realm, and the mayor and aldermen of Norwich even
offered to pay their share in the city plate.[142] Similar complaints were
made in 1593 and Francis Bacon explicitly said that what with "poore
mans rents . . . they are not able to yeald" anything towards the subsidy, while "gentlemen . . . must sell their plate and the farmers their
Brasse pottes before" the subsidy "wilbe payed."[143]

The strains such a scarcity created in personal relations between
debtor and creditor could be large, whether we are looking at tenants and landlords or merchants and clothiers or even gentlemen
and their mercantile suppliers. The resistance to taxation in England
during the early modern period has much to do with this feature of
the economy. So long as taxes had to be paid in coin, and coin was
scarce, the payment of small sums could be a problem even for the
relatively well-to-do and could affect the economy of a district or region far out of proportion to the amounts demanded. Only in the

1540s, when the government systematically devalued the currency and thereby increased the size of the circulating medium in England, was the pressure somewhat relieved. With the revaluation at the beginning of Elizabeth I's reign, however, this era had ended.

A number of modern scholars have traced the unwillingness of MPs to face the requirements of financing the early modern state to their habitual tendency to place the interests of themselves and their particular communities above the larger interests of the realm.[144] But as Bacon said in 1593, "the danger" of over taxation "is this: wee breed discontentment in the people and in a cause of Jopardie her Majesties saftie must consist more in the love of her people then in their welthe."[145] Short of an actual invasion of the realm by a foreign power, many MPs undoubtedly thought that no crisis could be severe enough to warrant undermining of the very fabric of social relations in the localities by draining away more of their fiscal resources and coin than they could afford. Every other threat required the careful assessment of the risks entailed by the proposed course of action.

From the Crown's viewpoint, however, this logic was by no means self-evident. As Elizabeth I made clear in her famous "Golden Speech" of 1601, the monarch had a godly duty to protect the realm from every "Peril, Dishonour, Shame, Tryanny and Oppression," which could come to it as easily from outside as inside the realm.[146] To provide this protection not only demanded vigilance but the exercise of power, which in turn required money, the sinews of war, as Bacon also said in 1593.[147] But warfare was becoming ever more costly in the early modern period as Europe underwent what has been quite correctly described as a "military revolution." There were a number of factors producing this technological upheaval. Changes in tactics promoted the use of larger and better disciplined armies, while military affairs came increasingly to depend on the use of heavy equipment— especially artillery—and on massive fortifications or big ships. Hence war became ever more costly—especially so if an army and navy had to be assembled and organized almost from scratch, as was very nearly the case in England any time war broke out. From the viewpoint of strategy and tactics, it was far more costly as well as harder to make up the shortcomings of the forces on short notice than it was to anticipate them in advance. The increased emphasis on military technology also meant that the conduct of war had come to depend more on the centralized control and coordination of the various components. The problems this need for coordination could cause were only too apparent when the Duke of Buckingham organized his expedition to La Rochelle, when ships, supplies, and men all had to be brought together at the same time and place for concerted action. The costs of war, therefore, rapidly outstripped inflation, making the need for taxation in wartime all the greater. Under these conditions, however, the demand for money in wartime often far exceeded the traditions of support stored in the collective memory of the taxpayers.[148]

In the face of these limitations, peace was the only sensible policy for an English ruler and his or her servants to follow. On the whole English monarchs understood this truth, especially Elizabeth I and James I. As a result, England experienced the military revolution negatively, as it were. Lacking the fiscal resources to support huge increases in its armed forces, it counted on the protection of the seas to keep it from invasion and focused its desire for dominion on the British Isles, particularly after the loss of Calais in 1558. Instead of mounting a standing army and building a massive fleet, therefore, it relied on trained militia for home defense and reinforced its naval forces with requisitioned vessels and privateers when necessary. Hence the share of ordinary expenditures devoted to the army and navy did not rise in England anywhere as far or as fast as it did on the Continent.[149]

But peace was not always possible. It could not be upheld in the face of a threat to the national well-being, such as was mounted by the Spanish at the end of the sixteenth century. And it could not be upheld in the face of a humiliation to the honor of the realm and its prince as occurred in the 1620s. And when war could not be avoided, the government was hard pressed to find the resources to fight it. Costs of the war mounted by Henry VIII and by Edward VI's councillors between 1542 and 1550 came to the staggering sum of £3.5 million, while the great Spanish War at the end of Elizabeth I's reign cost about £4 million between 1586 and 1603. In the wars with Spain and France in the late 1620s the known disbursements for the navy alone came to almost £800,000 between 1625 and 1630, but these figures are incomplete and say nothing about the other costs of military operations on land during this period. Almost certainly the total costs of these wars was more than twice this figure.[150] Secretary Coke told the Commons in 1625 it was costing £50,000 per month to support soldiers and allies in the war, which suggests, as Conrad Russell has pointed out, that the maintenance of the land forces required almost the whole of the king's annual income.[151] It would be wrong, however, to attribute every problem experienced by the state in this period to war. War only exposed the structural weaknesses inherent in the various regimes of the day. Or to change the metaphor—it had the capacity to bring chronic ailment to acute crisis.

≺ VIII ≻

Fiscal Devices

If Parliament, the one national institution authorized to grant taxes on the principle of consent, was unwilling or unable to provide the fiscal resources government officials believed they needed to conduct the vital business of the realm, what was to be done? A number of devices could make up the difference. According to well-established medieval practices, it was possible for a king facing a state of emergency to demand money—or if need be military equipment, victuals and ships—from his subjects to meet the necessity. In Henry VIII's reign, for example, there were so-called "forced loans" in 1522 and 1542, a failed attempt at an "amicable grant" in 1525, and somewhat more successful ones in 1545 and 1546. His daughters Mary and Elizabeth also resorted to forced loans and free gifts to help settle their accounts; and in the 1590s Elizabeth demanded ships, and money in lieu of ships, to fight her war with Spain.[152] As is well known, Charles I used these same devices in the 1620s and 30s. His notorious forced loan of 1626–27 raised some £260,000, the equivalent of about five subsidies, while from 1634 his demands for ship money brought in an average of £107,000 a year, more than any previous peacetime direct tax.[153] Given the monarchy's positive duty to preserve the kingdom, it is no wonder that its servants felt themselves justified in using every possible device to enhance the income of the state, even against bitter complaint and outright resistance.

Demands for such non-parliamentary taxation came in two forms: loans, which it was intended would later be paid from parliamentary grants; and outright gifts or benevolences, which would not. Both had a long history. In principle, the granting of loans was obligatory, in the sense that once the necessity had been properly attested by the king in council the subject could not legitimately refuse the request to contribute. But it was not compulsory; it depended upon the subject's consent, which he was bound to give because of the service he owed the commonwealth in emergencies and because he would later be repaid from lawfully granted taxes, although in many instances the loans in fact were never repaid. Since the raising of loans rested on the subject's obligation, refusals to contribute to them could not be couched in the language of resistance; the only way to argue against such loans in principle would be to deny the duly agreed upon necessity to which the law would give no credence. Refusals, then, usually took the form of what G. L. Harriss calls "excuse," which were largely arguments about inability to pay. A benevolence, however, was a free gift, which subjects could legitimately refuse to make, as was done in 1525.[154]

In other words, the underlying theory of taxation in regard to "prerogative taxation"—loans, benevolences, and ship money—was the same as for parliamentary taxation. Every Englishman was expected to come to the aid of the realm in time of general need, whether the request was made collectively to the whole body politic, or separately to individuals or communities. And in terms of the general response to these requests, the reactions of taxpayers were consistent with this view, at least superficially. Few challenged the royal right to claim and exact financial support for national purposes, but they tended to resist the size of the requested grant. In Parliament, where the key consideration was how many notional subsidies to grant on a given occasion, the MPs habitually cut back the number they were willing to vote, sometimes acting from the mistaken belief that a smaller number would produce more revenue than in fact they did and sometimes acting from the belief that their constituents would not accept more. With "prerogative taxation" the argument was usually cast in terms of ability to pay: ship money, for example, was most commonly resisted by communities and individuals claiming that they could not pay the sums demanded.

By the time of the early Stuarts the various forms of "prerogative taxation" were open to a kind of resistance that parliamentary subsidies were not, since it was indeed possible to doubt the validity of the exaction and not merely the size. What made this new kind of argument possible? Two points deserve notice. First, by the early seventeenth century the doctrine of "absolute property" had emerged in English law in a form insisting that "the propriety of any man's goods and chattels neither can nor ought to be changed, neither ought the same goods and chattels to be any way charged, by any absolute authority of the King's Majesty without assent of Parliament." At the same time, the notion of property had been extended to cover such matters as one's occupation—the source of one's livelihood—as well as lands and goods. Property had become an abstract right that inhered to the individual as part of his life and could not lawfully be taken from him without his consent.[155] Initial resistance to Charles I's forced loan of 1626, for example, concerned whether a man "should have the libertie of a subject to dispose of his money and estate at his pleasure," as Sir Thomas Darnell himself put it.[156]

Since the doctrine of consent was also implicit in the rationale for "prerogative taxation," this new conception of property would not by itself have been enough to promote resistance. What also had changed were ideas regarding the provision of consent. With the transformation of the broadly constructed king's council of the Middle Ages into the Privy Council of the early modern era, composed exclusively of close advisors and servants of the monarch, only Parliament remained a sufficiently representative body to certify emergencies for the realm as a whole. This new thinking lay at the foundation of John Hampden's defense in the *Ship Money Case*. His lawyers accepted the need to aid the commonweal in time of emergency, but insisted that the only acceptable mode for doing so was through Parliament—the "*commune concilium regni*, in respect that the whole kingdom is representatively there." Parliament, Oliver St. John said on Hampden's behalf, "is best qualified and fitted to make this supply for some of each rank," since "through all the parts of the kingdom being there met, his Majesty having declared the danger, they best knowing the estates of all men within the realm, are fittest, by comparing the danger and men's estates together, to proportion the aid accordingly."[157]

These new forms of resistance to "prerogative taxation" together suggest the emergence of a new kind of politics in the 1620s and after—constitutional politics.[158] Drawing on the capacities of the

English law and law courts to address the most fundamental questions touching the polity, the language used for debating fiscal issues moved from considerations of what might be called equity, which asked whether the amounts requested were reasonable, to considerations of authority and right, which asked whether correct forms had been followed. Hence, in place of a rhetoric in which high claims of royal prerogative were met by self-interested excuses, taxes came to be debated in terms of their rectitude as well as their fairness.

< IX >

The Liberties of the Subject

Complex societies normally are held together through one or both of two broad processes: social interchange in the form of market transactions and the giving and receiving of favor, friendship, and benefit; and the exercise of state power to impose rules and enforce them within a specific territory. But before the emergence of modern market capitalism, with its capacity to create national and transnational forms of social organization, it was not possible to maintain stable social relations over large geographical areas solely through the gift or the market economy. Social interchange in the gift economy could produce effective solidarity only within circumscribed social groupings or small communities and over fairly narrow fields; while in the absence of fully established capitalistic markets, economic interactions were too intermittent to bind individuals and groups firmly together beyond their home bases. In the early modern period, state power was required to provide the means to bring the inhabitants of broad regions together in effective, stable relations.

Law-making and revenue-raising are among the principal means for accomplishing this task of social development. It is here that Parliament played a vital role in turning the coercive powers of a feudal monarchy into the much more diverse functions of a working territorial state—functions that include the maintenance of internal order and protection of person and property; promotion of international interests and defense against foreign enemies; creation and development of internal communications and markets; and provision for the social and moral welfare of the people.[159] As Tudor and early Stuart commentators themselves recognized, Parliament was a permanent feature of the English polity, representative of the whole realm, which alone could perform vital functions for its welfare.[160]

From this perspective, it matters little that, as some scholars have argued, Parliament was rarely an oppositional force in politics or that it failed to use its right of consent to taxation to gain effective redress of grievances from the king.[161] For in a very genuine sense its role as a tax-granting assembly marked the existence of the commonweal served by the state. The requesting and granting of consent to statutes or taxes, then, was less the striking of a bargain between competing parties or interests than the ritual recognition that a social and political bond held the governed and the governors together for common profit. Completion of the negotiation signified the renewal of the ties that made the realm a healthy body politic, while failure of king and subject to reach concord, as they frequently failed to in the early seventeenth century, indicated nothing less than the presence of disease in that same social body.[162]

For early modern English monarchs, however, the strategies employed to cope with fiscal problems largely involved the exercise of power to improve their command over the market. In particular, many of the devices available to add to Crown income in the face of inflation—especially monopolies, purveyance, and impositions—focused particularly on the royal prerogative, that is on the special rights, powers, and privileges that belonged to the monarch as the result of his or her exalted position in the state. Hence the raising of taxes—which necessarily involved encroachments on the subjects' property rights for the public good—was no less a political act whether it was achieved with ready agreement or by prerogative action.

What then of liberty or freedom? For the monarchs and royal officials busy exploiting one fiscal device or another to make ends meet—especially in war—the freedom of Englishmen depended critically on the capacity of the state to protect itself against attack and uphold its interests in the international arena. A conquered state was a slave state. This was not only because its own leaders no longer would control its policies, but because the fact of conquest carried with it the wiping away of all laws. Protections coming to the subjects from their customs and traditions would be no more, and they themselves would be subject to the will and whim of their conqueror. In effect, they would be slaves. Hence it was important that the ruler have the necessary authority and power to serve the state, which meant of course having the necessary financial resources to do so.[163]

There was also a second view, one that turned like the first on the distinction between freedom and slavery. It connected liberty with the right each freeborn Englishman had to dispose as he would of his own labor and property. Behind this notion of freedom was the idea that every member of the commonwealth—every free citizen and subject—owed a duty to preserve and advance it according to his skills and capacities. A shoemaker did so by making shoes; a landlord by upholding production on his property and maintaining good relations with his tenants. Depriving either unlawfully of his rights was tantamount to turning him from a freeman into a slave, since it destroyed his ability to perform his obligations to his community. If sums of money were exacted from an individual without his consent, it undermined his capacity to use his property for the common good. In effect, it turned him into a villein, whose person and property were subject to the authority of his lord. A man could become a villein by his own action—explicitly by acknowledging himself as one or implicitly by accepting without protest treatment "in a court of record," such as Parliament, that was fit in legal terms only for the unfree. On this theory it was imperative that every freeborn Englishman resist any attempt to tax him without his consent, lest he be reduced to servile status.[164]

Therefore, to those aggrieved by the Crown's fiscal actions in the markets—a growing number in the early modern period as industry and trade became more important—the preferred line of defense involved adopting strategies of freedom, strategies that carved out areas of daily life in which the state should not interfere. This move resolved the paradox of taxation for those who took it. It allowed them to willingly engage in service to the commonwealth through their contributions to the fiscal needs of the realm, granted by their consent, or through the commitment of their skills and property to the general welfare, granted by their actions in their own communities.

This line of thinking had a long period of gestation. In the Middle Ages, the "liberties" Englishmen possessed were exclusive privileges and immunities.[165] They belonged to individuals according to their membership in recognized legal ranks or established communities.

Being free was understood to be a status—an attribute or quality or property of a certain type of person. Those who possessed it were contrasted to bondmen. To put this point in another way, when applied to individuals freedom referred to their place in the social order, not to universal characteristics of their human nature or to their uniqueness as human beings. These medieval ideas recognized no sharp distinction between individual and collective liberties and were in this way very similar to the conceptions of freedom that prevailed into the early modern period in Spain, France, and the Netherlands, where rights, several and discrete, were enjoyed primarily according to the rank, community, or province to which one belonged.[166]

By the end of the sixteenth century, however, some new ideas of political liberty had found their way into English political discourse. It became commonplace to talk of the "liberties"—and increasingly of the "*liberty* of the subject." This usage has an obvious link to the language of the Middle Ages, because liberty still belonged to one by virtue of his status, in this case as a subject. In a sense, then, the kingdom was viewed as a corporate entity in its own right, and its subjects were freemen, in the same way as citizens were freemen in the privileged towns. Within the bounds of the realm, this liberty was inclusive. It belonged to free-born Englishmen as their birthright. As the last vestiges of villeinage disappeared, this birthright became the inheritance in theory of virtually every adult male in the realm. Once the term was opened in this way interesting things happened to its use. For the "liberties of the subject" were not narrow privileges, but primarily guarantees of equal justice and hindrances to excessive meddling by officials into an individual's affairs. They were not, therefore, just a collection of separate and distinct franchises and immunities, but rather the specific rights and freedoms that followed from being a freeman under the English common law.

These issues arose in a particularly relevant way during the Parliament of 1610, in which the lawyer Thomas Hedley made a memorable speech attacking the impositions recently levied by the Crown on a variety of imported commodities. As a matter of "policy and government" as well as law, he found these taxes to be illegal because they threatened every Englishman's right to his lands and goods. What worried Hedley was not that impositions would deprive the English of their wealth, "but [of] the power of holding it."

For that is nothing else but bondage, or the condition of a villein, whose lands and goods are only in the power of his lord, which doth so abase his mind, even the lack of liberty in this point, that he is neither fit to do service to his country in war nor peace . . . So if . . . their lands and goods be any way in the king's absolute power . . . , then they are . . . little better than the king's bondmen.[167]

Hedley believed that because Englishmen freely enjoyed their possessions, they were as fit to be soldiers "as the chivalry or gentry of . . . other states . . . for their courage is equal, because their freedom and liberty is equal to theirs." The prowess of the English proved that the "ancient liberty of the subject in England" is what had always maintained and upheld "the sovereignty of the king" and made him able "to stand of himself without the aid of any neighbor princes or states and so to be an absolute king which dependeth immediately upon God."[168]

But once take away this ancient liberty from the commons, so they perceive their lands and goods not absolutely their own but in the absolute power and command of another, they will neither have the care for that wealth and courage that they now have, but a drooping dismayness will possess and direct them . . . for seeing their liberty and condition no better than the bondmen or the peasants in other places, their courage will be no better than theirs; for it is not the nature of the people or climate . . . that makes this difference; but it is the laws, liberties, and government of this realm.[169]

"Therefore," he said, "let no man think liberty and sovereignty incompatible, that how much is given to the one is taken from the other; but rather like twins, that they have such concordance and coalescence, that the one can hardly subsist without the other."[170] Like Fortescue, on whom he based his argument, he attributed England's capacity to preserve the property of its inhabitants against plunder by neighbors and to defend itself against foreign enemies to its political—that is its consent-based—form of rule.

Hedley was in no way denying the king's right to raise taxes in support of the necessities of the kingdom. It is implicit in his speech that no member of the realm could legitimately deny his king assistance in time of common need, provided he was duly asked. But Hedley was answering a question concerning *meum*—what is mine—not what a subject owed his community once his property had been secured. On this second important issue, the common position concerned the giving and receiving of benefits. If the king informed his subjects that the realm was in danger, the latter were morally obligated to help as far as their wealth would allow. To do otherwise would signify their withdrawal in moral terms from membership in the body politic from which they received protection for their lives and liberties and to which they, like the king himself, therefore owed their willing service. A king who took the property of his subjects without their consent, however, undermined the moral sinews that held this political community together, since the realm no longer could depend on the voluntary exchange of service and good will between ruler and ruled. It became, instead, no better than the manorial estate of the monarch, in which only the king enjoyed the freedom to perform ethical acts.[171]

Hedley's arguments were explicitly answering the judges in Bate's Case of 1606, especially Thomas Fleming, chief baron, whose opinion had strongly upheld the Crown's right to levy a duty on currants without a parliamentary grant. Fleming's judgment was rooted in a civil law view of royal prerogative. "To the king is committed the government of the realm and his people," he said. "[A]nd . . . for his discharge of his office, God had given him power, the act of government, and the power to govern." This "power is double." Ordinary power concerns only "the profit of particular subjects" and here the "laws cannot be changed without parliament." But "the absolute power of the king" concerns "the general benefit of the people" and is not guided by the common law, but by "policy and government"— it was these words that Hedley was referring to in his speech. "As the constitution of [the body politic] varieth at the time," Fleming said, "so varieth this absolute law according to the wisdom of the king for the common good; and these being general rules and true as they are, all things done within these rules are lawful." On this foundation, Fleming went on to show how the levying of customs rates arose out of the king's absolute right to conduct foreign policy, which in turn required him to protect and therefore to regulate commerce with foreign states according to his own discretion and political wisdom to the benefit of the commomweal as a whole.[172]

Fleming first developed this theory of law and politics in Darcy v. Allen of 1602, the famous case of the playing card monopoly in which Fleming, at that time solicitor general, appeared for Sir Edward Darcy, the playing card patentee. The central legal argument against the monopoly patents, as articulated by Nicholas Fuller who later also strongly opposed impositions, was that by granting exclusive manufacturing and trading rights to a few private individuals they deprived free men of their livelihoods, and therefore of the liberties assured them by chapter 29 of *Magna Carta*. Hence such patents were against common right and common good, and void on their face. In this, England was conforming itself to the law of God, which required men to labor for their livelihoods and which therefore prevented anyone from interfering with this duty. The key is the idea that every free man had a godly obligation (not just a right) to earn his bread—a duty to himself, his family, and the commonwealth—that could not be abridged without his consent. A monopolist was understood—actually said—to be a *vir sanguinis*, a man of blood who in preventing competitors from exercising their crafts threatened their very existence as free men. He put them into "bondage"—this word was repeatedly used in the discussions—not only because a monopoly deprived established craftmen of the profits of their own skills, which were their rightful possessions as land was to a gentleman, but also because it interfered with the free exercise of their wills in their callings—that is, in their spiritual as well as worldly commitments. Or to state this conclusion another way, under the theory articulated in *Darcy*, legal rights were not mere protections for a person's opportunities. They were considered, rather, to guarantee freeborn Englishmen what was duly theirs, starting with their own persons, and to secure them in the performance of their duties, that is, in meeting their responsibilities to themselves, their families, and the commonwealth as their consciences dictated.[173]

In responding to this position, Fleming argued in *Darcy* that "the ancient and fundamentall lawes" of England were those of "an absolute Monarchie," in which "plenarie fullnes of power" belonged to the Queen "in her princely wisdome and care to Commande things good and forbidd thinges evell" for the "health of the Comon wealth." "Absolute is the [monarch's] power and infinite are his Prerogatives," Fleming said, and in consequence "the Kinge . . . hath attributed vnto him plenarie fullnes of power domynacon and rule over all. All things and all persons are committed and submitted vnder his charge and subiection" and "there is neither Lawes Justice magistrate or goverment of anie power whatsoever vnlesse the same be deryved from his Imperiall Matie and power." Furthermore,

> vnder his absolute power are comprehended all those markes and rights of Soveraintie . . . to take order and provyde for the benefitt and safety of the Realme from Enemies abroad, from evell manners at home and to doe all thinges for the health of the Comon wealth as the occurrents and affaires of the state requires. To all wch because we must presumme that their generall end doth tend to sett order and policie amongst vs we must submit and not dispute of their reason and causes.

Hence English monarchs enjoy absolute power to use "their owne princely prudence and wisedome publickly . . . according to the occurrents and necessarie affairs of state and as the nature of the Causes happening required."[174]

In *Bate's Case* and *Darcy*, we see Thomas Fleming undoing the linkage between consent and national welfare so deeply embedded in the Fortescueian view of the English polity. The security of the realm, Fleming was saying, could not depend on the voluntary participation or collective will of the people, which was inherently uncertain. Instead it required the absolute power of the monarch who alone could mobilize the necessary forces and maintain effective command. It can be no surprise, therefore, that Hedley and the other common lawyers who entered the fray in the imposition debates in 1610 did so in starkly Fortescueian terms. Fleming was making a profound challenge to their Fortescueian *mentalité*, to their habits of thought about the moral foundations of the realm and the effects of time on institutions which underpinned it. It was necessary therefore to move against it with a full panoply of arguments in defense.

According to the theory of liberty articulated in the debates over monopoly and impositions, it was no contingent matter that these two evils should be intimately linked. For the fundamental connection between property and liberty established by this theory saw any assault on the first leading inevitably and inextricably to assaults on the second. The Petition of Right of 1628, offering its protection against non-parliamentary taxes, imprisonment without cause, the quartering of soldiers without consent and due compensation, and the exercise of martial law on ordinary subjects, far from simply enumerating the liberties of freeborn Englishmen, made explicit the underlying links between control over one's property and the exercise of personal freedom. If the English lived in a *dominium politicum et regale*, liberty necessarily went hand in hand with consent. Loss of control over one's material possessions would lead inevitably to loss of control over one's person, including one's freedom to act as God demanded. The two were inextricably interconnected as property is to propriety, as what is possessed is tied to the right to possess it.[175]

This view of freedom emphasized two important principles. The first was the role of participation in upholding the commonweal. To maintain a free state, it was not sufficient for the monarch to exercise authority and project power; it was also necessary for each subject— low as well as high—to perform his due function for the general welfare. Anything that might hinder his actions not only turned a freeman into a slave, but perforce weakened the commonweal against its enemies at home and abroad. According to the theory, a free commonweal upheld its strength and prosperity precisely because its subjects necessarily acted in their own interests when they supported the state. This was true for paying taxes as well as for service in public office or exercise of a calling.

In placing this stress on participation, however, this idea of freedom recognized that each member of the commonwealth had a secure place within it. Accordingly, the duty of the state was to assure that each individual received what was his due. It was to avoid doing anything that would bring harm to anyone's legitimately held social position and thereby disrupt the existing organization of society. But arbitrary taxation—like arbitrary imprisonment—threatened to do just this. By undermining the ability of those with a duty to serve, such actions disrupted the intricately formed hierarchies on which social relations were thought to depend. In other words, one's liberty under this conception was not the freedom to be just what you wanted to be, but the freedom to be unhindered in performing what were your personal and social obligations. Hence, this idea of freedom called forth another principle, namely that being free depended upon living in a particular kind of community with a particular structure of social and political institutions—one in which authority was exercised only by recognized leaders with an established place in the networks of deference and command and decisions touching the property and welfare of free subjects were taken with their consent.[176]

≺ X ≻

Conclusion

"Liberty and the law are high sounding words," as Sir Ronald Syme has said of the late Roman republic. "They will often be rendered, on a cool estimate, as privilege and vested interest."[177] There can be little doubt that in early modern England the "liberties of the subject," and the protection of private property to which they principally referred, were far more valuable to substantial landholders and prominent commercial or industrial entrepreneurs than to the day laborers, customary tenants, petty artisans, and small tradesmen who made up the vast majority of the English commons. But words have their own force. By shaping political understanding, they become sources for political action in their own right and can be deployed by persons and for purposes undreamed of by those who first uttered them. The high sounding words we have been discussing in this chapter enjoyed just such a subsequent history. In the 1640s they became the foundation for the Levellers' defense of the lawful rights of all freeborn Englishmen to consent to their own governance[178] as well as for King Charles I's eloquent speeches against the tribunal that conducted his trial.[179] In the 1650s they led small shopkeepers and craftsmen to argue, as did some in Bristol, that the "Rights, Liberties [and] Fundamental Laws" of the English demanded the "administration of impartial and equal Justice" by which "the Magistrates without respect of persons, judge according to the Law, not their own wills or lusts."[180] Later still similar ideas gave support to the ideology of freedom which grew up to justify the Glorious Revolution.

≺ APPENDIX ≻

A Note on the Tax Burden

Accurately estimating the overall tax burden on the English in the sixteenth and early seventeenth centuries is not possible. Not only did the kingdom lack a system of national economic accounting, but its fiscal records were designed less to report revenues than to hold particular administrative officers legally accountable for moneys that had passed through their hands. In addition, many of the costs of government were paid for in kind or in the form of services donated by unpaid officials, while the most important taxes were collected only in periods of national emergency. Nevertheless, a very crude gauge of the scale of taxation can be calculated. According to Sir Robert Cecil, emergency conditions during the war years at the end of Elizabeth's reign produced a total revenue of £1,562,224 in parliamentary subsidies from summer 1594 to 24 March, 1603, or approximately £174,000 per year.[181] During this same period the net revenue from the other principal source of national tax income, the customs, amounted to approximately another £100,000 per year.[182] This £274,000 per year is equivalent in wages to 5,480,000 man days for craftsmen in the building trades.[183] With the population of England and Wales standing at about 4.1 million,[184] this meant an annual tax rate of about 16 pence per person in this war period, roughly equivalent to one and a third days wages of a skilled building craftsman. Put another way, this £274,000 a year would have purchased about 1,300,000 bushels, or about 473,000 hectoliters, of wheat at average prices for the same period—approximately 0.1 hectoliters per person.[185]

Beyond what the subsidy and the customs brought in, annual royal revenues in this same period might have amounted to a further £200,000–£250,000. If for the sake of argument we consider this income as part of the overall tax burden, it would have paid for a further 4,000,000 to 5,000,000 man days of labor from skilled building craftsmen. Put in terms of the price of wheat, these sums amount to another 950,000 to 1,182,000 bushels, or 346,000 to 430,000 hectoliters. If these sums can be accepted, the total tax burden in the years from 1594 to 1603 came to approximately £474,000 to £524,000 per year, equal approximately to the wages of 9,480,000 to 10,480,000 man days of labor from skilled workers in the building trades or the purchase price of 2,250,000 to 2,482,000 bushels, or 818,000 to 903,000 hectoliters, of wheat at current prices. The annual tax rate in this wartime era, then, was about 28 to 31 pence per person, roughly the equal of 0.2 hectoliters of wheat, or of 2.3 to 2.5 days wages for a skilled building craftsman.

Fiscal Policies, Liberties, and Representative Government during the Reigns of the Last Stuarts

J. R. JONES

THE REVOLUTION OF 1688–89, like earlier attempts during the century to secure the constitutional liberties of the English nation, had entirely unintended and major consequences. Few Englishmen saw in advance that it would result in a long and extremely expensive war against France, and that this involvement in a continental European war would require fiscal and administrative developments which threatened to disturb the balance between the executive and legislative branches of government. This war necessitated a greatly expanded army. Its maintenance and that of a large navy as well—and no other state including France could for long support the expense of both—brought into being what has been termed "the fiscal-military state." Taxation rose to levels never attained before. Long-term government borrowing required systematization, leading to the establishment of a new institution, the Bank of England. An enlarged fiscal bureaucracy levied excises.[1]

These developments created alarm, particularly among the Whig and Tory Country elements, that is the conservative-minded noble and gentry landowners in both parties. They failed to understand the economic principles on which post-1688 fiscal and economic policies were based and contested the need for them. They were accustomed to simpler and more confrontational problems. Before 1688 recurrent threats to liberties—by the Cabal ministers in 1672–73, the earl of Danby in 1678, and James II in 1686–88—were blatantly provocative and direct, but after 1688 the dangers appeared in more subtle and oblique forms. The army was not used to extort money or overawe London; but the expanded patronage it gave to ministers increased their ability to control Parliament. The Crown still needed parliamentary consent for all votes of taxation; but a new form of dependence on the London credit market, and the certainty that a Jacobite restoration would result in a general repudiation of public debts, locked the administration into a permanent relationship of mutual dependence with the new financial or monied interest of bankers, financiers, and rentiers. Theoretically the Commons continued to have exclusive control over the supply of finance: in practice, because of commitments made by the Crown and ministers to foreign allies and London bankers, its freedom of action became restricted. Ministers, MPs, and peers had to work out the answers to entirely new questions about the nature of the relationship with the financial interest which would preserve the integrity of English liberties and yet give successive administrations the ability to wage a successful war against France. And—even more important—politicians, publicists, and financiers during the decades after 1688 were having to address themselves to what is still today, and particularly because of the collapse of Marxism-Leninism, the central issue in democratic countries: how to ensure the co-existence of effective representative government and economically efficient capitalism.

< I >

Armies, Money, and Law

Once the former Cromwellian army had been paid off and disbanded, the financial settlement that followed the restoration of the monarchy in 1660 displayed uniformly conservative characteristics. The Commons preferred the traditional subsidy to the more efficient and productive monthly assessment. Parliament even resorted to the obsolescent Tudor device of a benevolence or "voluntary" present. When Charles II asked for a revision of the demonstrably defective revenue voted him for life and which from the start resulted in an annual deficit, even the ultra-loyal MPs of the early years of the Cavalier Parliament failed to vote him sufficient extra revenue, assuming that if the king became financially self-sufficient he would not have to call frequent sessions, as he did until 1681.[2]

Charles II did not follow his father's fatal example of attempting to levy money that had not been voted by Parliament. But significantly and damagingly, most of the cases reported of attempts by his servants to do so were connected with the armies raised in 1666–67, 1672–73, and 1678 for the two wars against the Dutch and during a crisis which could have ended in war against France. None of these cases concerned large amounts of money; but they clearly breached the law and cumulatively they provoked the fear that a royal army would try to live off the country by free quarter, as the Commonwealth troops had done in the winter of 1659–60. MPs complained of requisitioning, the diversion of money due under statute for the militia for the maintenance of the army. Householders not legally liable to billet troops were being made to compound with payments in return for observance of their right. It was alleged that attempts to hold soldiers responsible for criminal actions were being systematically obstructed, with justices who attempted to enforce the law being summoned to appear before councillors and often the king in person; instead military discipline was being enforced by courts martial composed of army officers.[3]

The outcome of these complaints was that the Commons voted the army of 1672–73 a "grievance," meaning something contrary to law and a source of illegalities.[4] They also made it possible for Country MPs to generalize the issue, contending that they demonstrated that it was difficult "for armies and properties to stand together," that is to co-exist.[5] This may seem a ridiculously exaggerated conclusion when the cases of soldiers illegally extorting money were small in scale and intermittent, but such practices were very generally employed in continental absolutist monarchies, particularly France where many of the English army's officers had been in service, and they represented a direct infringement of the 1629 Petition of Right. Consequently the Commons reacted strongly with a bill in 1674, which lapsed with a prorogation but was reintroduced in 1675 and 1677, "to prevent the levying of any Tax, Tillage or Subsidy, but by Parliament." Its formal title, "A Bill to prevent the Illegal Exaction of Money from the Subject," sounds defensive, but the proposed provisions represented a substantial encroachment on the royal prerogative. The bill would remove from the Council the power to summon before it any person refusing to pay charges that had not been voted

by Parliament, including duties on goods imported or exported; this
would have prevented James II continuing to impose customs duties
in 1685 before Parliament had the opportunity to vote them.[6]

The most innovative provision, which carried far-reaching implications, declared that all attempts to levy, or compel subjects to
pay, illegal taxes would in the future constitute acts of high treason. The supreme crime in law, both then and still in the twentieth
century, treason is a crime against the person or the right of the sovereign. The bill would give the crime a much wider meaning: under
it actions judged certain to undermine the law of the constitution
would be placed in the same category as the most dangerous and
subversive action against the sovereign. In practical terms it would
have closed the door on the operationally easiest method of imposing non-parliamentary taxation, by making it illegal to extend taxes
arbitrarily beyond the time limits set by Parliament.[7]

The fear that the king and his ministers might resort to levying
taxes which had not received explicit parliamentary approval was invariably linked with suspicions that the main purpose was to raise
and maintain a "standing" or professional army that would enable
them to impose absolutist methods of government.[8] No Parliament
would ever vote money for this purpose, but MPs identified the tactics which the administration could use to manipulate them into providing the money for a standing army. These centered on the use made
of taxes voted for the two Dutch wars which Charles II launched in
1665 and 1672. Declarations of war and the making of peace, and all
decisions on how war was to be waged, formed part of the royal prerogative: parliamentary consent was not required although the king
could ask for advice, as Charles did before the war of 1665–67 but not
before that of 1672–74. Once money was voted—in 1665 in unprece-
dentedly large amounts—Parliament had no further control over the
methods employed by the king, and experience led the majority of
MPs to fear that under the cover of these wars the king and his ministers were pursuing a "design" to make the Crown more powerful or
even absolute.

The disturbing development during the war of 1665–67 was the
emergence of the London bankers as potential royal auxiliaries who
threatened to reduce the leverage that the Commons could exert on
the administration through its control over the voting of taxes. This

applied particularly to the device which the Commons began to use systematically and which Charles resented as an improper (and effective) restriction. Suspecting that money voted for the war in general had been diverted for other purposes, the Commons tied its votes of extraordinary supply to particular uses and enforced this appropriation of money by appointing a public accounts committee composed of MPs, rejecting the king's preemptive attempt to establish a committee of his own nominees, all non-members. Loans from bankers, secured on taxes already voted or on the permanent revenue, could enable the Crown to evade the restrictions imposed by appropriation, and they would also significantly reduce the bargaining power exerted by the Commons when, in return for desperately needed money, it could extort the royal assent for legislation initiated by independent MPs.[9]

The activities of the bankers created an additional and more basic cause for concern. By the last winter of the war, in 1666–67, the Crown had run out of money and the economy was so weakened that new taxes could produce little in time for a third campaign at sea. Consequently the Crown had to turn to the London bankers and goldsmiths for large advances of money, invariably at high rates of interest, that is 10 percent or more. This provoked alarm that the future was being mortgaged, a vista of indefinitely high taxation to pay off debt and meet interest charges at extortionately high levels. Equally significant in setting the agenda for public discussion and polemics for the next seventy years, was the emergence of the so-called Financial Interest as a new and intrusive rival to the currently predominant landed interest that provided the Lords and Commons with most of its personnel. This provoked furious and revealing social indignation.[10]

The best that official spokesmen could offer in defense of the bankers was that they had been "necessary evils" and that money could not have been obtained without their services. The bitter attacks directed against bankers were fuelled by social contempt: MPs who were landed gentlemen depicted them as upstarts who had been born in relative poverty but now flaunted their wealth, for example by indulging in the most publicly ostentatious show of conspicuous expenditure, parading through Hyde Park in London in "glass coaches." Samuel Pepys as a rising official invested in one, a coach with expensive and fragile windows of glass but no springs, and then wondered if he was wise to exhibit his wealth and raise questions as to how he had acquired it. Bankers as men of serious new money had no such doubts. But others recalled their plebeian origins as usurers exploiting the landed nobility and gentry before they found greater opportunities in taking advantage of the king's necessities.[11]

In extended criticisms MPs laid responsibility for the depression that followed the end of the war in 1667 on the activities of the bankers. By offering high rates of interest on deposits they were alleged to be draining money away from the provinces to London, creating a shortage of coin that was crippling local economies. In debates MPs were taught that a direct relationship existed between prevailing interest rates and the price and rental levels of agricultural land. By raising interest rates bankers were said to be plunging proprietors of land into permanent depression. The axiom, that "as Interest goes up, Land goes down, like a pair of scales," formulated by John Birch, a former parliamentarian colonel and a fiscal expert, was to justify the hostility of Country MPs to the Financial Interest for the next seventy years. Polemicists who appealed to the less affluent gentry used it to construct the story of a conspiracy to ruin landowners, manipulate Parliament, and bring to power a new and artificial ruling class of financiers and their political accomplices.[12]

Some of the more venomous attacks on the Financial Interest in 1668 and 1670 went so far as to advocate suspending or repudiating part or most of the debts encumbering the treasury as a result of the Dutch War. But these unthinking proposals, mostly distillations of personal animosity towards nouveaux riches and moneylenders, simplistically ignored wider considerations.[13] The hatred directed against bankers encouraged the Cabal ministers to act against them in an entirely arbitrary fashion just before Charles launched a new war against the Dutch in April 1672. Whereas in 1664–65 the administration had taken care to involve Parliament in resolutions against the Dutch as obstructors of English trade, and then to vote massive sums of money for a war, in 1672 the king did not call Parliament or receive any grants of money. The Treasury used a short-term tactic to make money immediately available, by a partial and selective suspension of interest payable on debts and advances. This was the so-called Stop of the Exchequer, on 2 January 1672, which ordered a suspension for one year, although in the outcome some money was not to be repaid until the end of the century.[14]

The postponement of a session of Parliament for over a year ensured a limited reaction to the Stop, but eventually it was seen to constitute a critical threat to the property, and so to the liberties, of the nation. At various times the Stop was described as the "greatest invasion of Property," and as being particularly dangerous because money was the most vulnerable form of property. As one MP said, "no part of our Liberty is dearer to us than that of our Money: with it we lose our Liberty."[15] If the king could arbitrarily deprive the hated bankers of the interest due to them, he could act similarly against all forms of property belonging to any other subject: his agents "might have sent to your house, or my house, as well as the bankers" commented the Master of the Rolls. He held his office for life, having paid for it, but if the Stop was valid there was nothing to prevent the king arbitrarily dismissing him, changing his tenure to deprive him of his property in his office.[16] It was in 1672–73 that Charles reverted from granting judges their commissions during their good behavior to ones "during pleasure," which allowed him to dismiss them at will. This converted them into instruments of royal policies and meant that the bankers could not expect to receive justice in the law courts. It was not until 1691–92, when judges again held commissions during good behavior—although this was not put on a statutory basis until 1701 with the enactment of the Act of Settlement—that the bankers' case received fair legal consideration. However even then judgments in their favor were reversed on appeal by the Lord Keeper, a politician, who went against the opinions of his legal advisers.[17]

In 1672 the Stop of the Exchequer formed only one part of a package of measures accompanying the war against the Dutch which convinced most peers and MPs, and indeed opinion generally, that the liberties of the nation and the Protestant religion, as well as the very existence of Parliament, were all directly threatened. All the crucial royal policies were based on the assumption that the king was not subject to limitations prescribed by, and enforceable at, the common law. The Stop overrode property rights. The Declaration of Indulgence embodied a claim to a prerogative power to suspend statutes, specifically all those enforcing religious uniformity including several which had been passed recently by the existing Parliament. A

large army was raised and stationed in England. It was disciplined
by courts martial composed of officers. More generally the war was
being fought in alliance with the France of Louis XIV, seen as the
model of absolutism. And much of the money expended on the war
against the Dutch had been voted by Parliament in 1670 and 1671
for almost the opposite purpose, to implement the Triple Alliance of
1668 with the Dutch and Sweden to keep the French out of the Spanish Netherlands. Aware that the king and his ministers were deceiv-
ing them, most informed opinion concluded that a covert "design"
was being attempted, although they were unaware of the terms of the
French alliance concluded in the secret treaty of Dover.[18]

The most acute threat to liberties appeared to come from the expanded army. When Parliament had to be reconvened because the
king needed more money some MPs declared that the war was simply
a pretext: "the war was made rather for the army, than the army for
the war."[19] It followed that the constitution remained in danger so
long as the war continued: a king of France was quoted as saying that
"he was hors de Pairs, free from his Estates" once he had obtained a
standing army.[20] Consequently the Commons forced Charles to make
peace early in 1674 by refusing him further money. To justify this
effective sabotage of royal policies, which included the withdrawal of
the Declaration of Indulgence, the Commons proclaimed themselves
to be acting as the "people's trustees," a concept which was becoming
familiar by the increasing use by lawyers of devices of trusteeship
in elaborate and sophisticated forms for the purpose of ensuring the
transmission of estates to future generations of heirs.[21]

The parallel between guaranteeing liberties for the enjoyment
of future generations and preserving estates intact to safeguard the
rights of heirs was real and appropriate. Like land, liberties were being
seen as a form of property, the one the possession of freeholders, the
other of freemen.[22] The prefix "free" applied equally to rights of which
the legal possessor could not be arbitrarily deprived. An MP defined
the duty vested in the Commons to secure both forms of right: "the
people have trusted us with their money, and Magna Carta is not to
be given up, with their money and liberty into a bottomless pit."[23]
This theme received repeated emphasis. A barbed rhetorical question, "What is the difference betwixt breach of property and slavery?"
had a particular resonance because "slavery" was the term given by

contemporary Englishmen to the status of the subjects of absolute monarchs and especially of those under Louis XIV.[24] They meant all ranks of French subjects, including even the nobility whose privilege of exemption from direct taxes could be suspended (as in 1695) on the plea of necessity, of which Louis (like Charles I in the Ship Money levies of the 1630s) was the sole and nonaccountable judge. By contrast the Commons could frustrate policies which it judged to pose a danger to the constitution by refusing supply. An MP could claim "we carry on all things for the interest of the nation, and assist him (the king) upon the public interest of the nation, and no further."[25] This was the theory. But the Commons experienced the greatest difficulties in restraining royal policies in 1678, and James II was able in 1686–88 to initiate and develop policies that could have made him absolute but for the Revolution of 1688.

In 1678 an army was raised to enable Charles to enter the war against France that the Dutch had been waging since 1672. The Commons voted money, although insufficient. When the French and the Dutch concluded peace it provided further supply expressly for the disbandment of the new units, but Charles and his minister, the earl of Danby, used it for exactly the opposite purpose, to keep the new units under arms. Suspicions that the army had been raised to establish "military government," not to fight a foreign war, received apparent confirmation when it was revealed that the king had been simultaneously negotiating for subsidies from France, against whom he was proposing to go to war.[26] Sir Richard Temple was drawing on this experience when, in 1685, he warned the Commons that liberties might be lost by inadvertance. Stating that no country had ever enacted "a Law to set up an Army," curiously overlooking the example of Scotland, he meant that no representative entity had consciously voted permanent revenues and legal immunities to establish a standing army. Rather rulers had used foreign wars and domestic insurrections as a cover. Temple predicted that if Parliament ever established an army by giving the king sufficient money to maintain a professional army "you can disband them no more."[27] It would be an irrevocable move. Ironically this was what Parliament had already done earlier in 1685 by giving James additional taxes for the suppression of the rebellion instigated by the duke of Monmouth, which was actually achieved quickly and inexpensively. These extraordinary grants of supply made it possible for James to dispense with Parliament, to expand his army considerably, and to initiate policies intended to transform the entire set of relationships between the sovereign and his subjects.[28]

< II >

Political Arithmetic and Royal Policies, 1686–88

In 1679–81 a determined political campaign had been mounted by the first Whigs to exclude James from the succession on account of his conversion to Catholicism and his absolutist tendencies. As king he therefore believed in the necessity to strengthen royal authority, and the methods which he employed in 1686–88 were eventually to convince most of his subjects that he designed to deprive them of their liberties: the outcome was the defection of the nation in the Revolution of 1688. However while James was politically authoritarian he initiated religious and economic policies which were innovative: one can almost use the term experimental.[29]

James set out in 1686–88 to appeal to the interests of his subjects and to secure their obedience to the sovereign by establishing a community of interests between the Crown and the nation, and in particular its economically most industrious and useful members. He established religious toleration for all so as to unite his subjects to himself "by inclination as well as duty."[30] In terms of religion James intended to create favorable conditions for the Catholic Church to make progress in reconverting England. But this constituted a long-term aim: in the shorter perspective religious toleration was expected to stimulate economic activity, to create popular contentment as people became wealthier. Toleration would particularly benefit useful and industrious people—merchants, shipowners, and seamen engaged in overseas trade; entrepreneurs and artisans engaged in manufacturing—a disproportionate number of whom were dissenters in religion and had been attracted to the Whig cause in 1679–82. Such people would no longer suffer harassment from magistrates and clergy to disrupt their working lives by fines, distraints, and imprisonment. Absorbed in the peaceful and profitable pursuit of their own vocations they would increase the wealth of the nation without the need for the kind of subsidies, protective tariffs, and officially-sponsored organizations that J.-B. Colbert, Louis XIV's finance minister, had to provide in France.[31]

In return for religious toleration and economic prosperity, useful and industrious people—located in London and its suburbs, provincial towns, and industrialized villages—would cease to constitute a constituency of support for demagogic leaders of political opposition. Instead they would be bound by ties of mutual interest to the king, and as auxiliaries or even instruments (rather than as allies able to impose terms), they would free the Crown from its dependence on those whose loyalty James disparaged as conditional—the landed nobility and gentry, and the Anglican clergy. Such reliance on merchants, tradesmen, and artisans, when it has been noticed at all, has usually been dismissed as foolish and of course it did end in failure in 1688—but only because of intervention from outside. But it was based on systematic processes of fact-finding, and on scientific and experimental method, such as had never previously been applied to politics. Statistical inquiry and analysis replaced conjectures based on historical examples and axioms derived from classical antiquity by such mediating theorists as James Harrington.[32]

The overwhelming electoral successes of the Whigs in 1679–81 had revealed the political power that could be derived from "useful people" in the urban areas. James was reminded of this in a memorandum on government which Sir William Petty presented to him shortly after his accession. Petty was the most prominent of the first generation of political economists or, to use the more accurate term they used themselves, political arithmeticians, whose imprint can be found on all James's innovative policies. The practice of political arithmetic followed Baconian methods: first the accumulation of "examples" and then their categorization. Its relevance is explicable by the visible changes that were affecting England: the growth of London, despite much-studied, devastating outbreaks of plague; the expansion of oceanic trade with the Americas, Africa, India, and East Asia; the settlements in North America; and, not least, continuing political instability. Petty and his colleagues set out to quantify these changes as the preliminary to explaining them.[33]

Political arithmeticians were primarily concerned with making measurements. Petty's fame derived from two forms at opposite ends

of scales of size; his medical dissections and his Down survey of Ireland, so called because he put down on paper all that anyone needed
to know about its physical characteristics. His aim in accumulating
statistical material was practical: to improve material conditions, for
example how to prevent plague spreading, how to design fast yet safe
ships (his model sank), and above all how to ensure that the means of
subsistence kept pace with population increases. His work was free
from all moral values, being concerned with quantities, not qualities, of life. The chilling impersonal objectivity of his method is seen
in his proposals for large-scale compulsory transfers of populations,
which the Down survey was to facilitate. Like the rulers of twentieth-
century Marxist states he simplistically estimated the worth of individuals and classes exclusively by their economic value, and significantly he was one of the first to grope conceptually towards the labor
theory of value. Consequently he rated tenant farmers as useful, landlords as useless, and he saw no need for so many lawyers, clergy, and
university teachers.[34]

    In Petty's advisory memoranda, as in James's policies, there was
no place for civic humanism, for active participation in public affairs
by the subject. Affairs of state should be the concern of the sovereign:
had he had enough time James would have professionalized local as
well as central administration.[35] In 1686–88 he deliberately allowed
most county militias to lapse into inactivity; they had proved useless
during Monmouth's rebellion but citizen-soldiers could not be relied on if they thought their liberties were endangered. As he showed
in the relentless prosecution of a deserter, in order to establish a
test case, James demanded absolute obedience from all serving in his
standing army.[36]

    But for William's intervention James would have called a Parlia-
ment in November 1688, one that he had been working since the
spring of 1687 to ensure that it would follow royal directives. His
parliamentary strategy involved managing the general election to
return a majority preengaged to collaborate with the Court. This
strategy and the managerial techniques used were heavily influenced
by Petty's method and analysis of parliamentary representation. He
demonstrated the existence of a fatal weakness in the political as-
cendancy exercised by the landed classes. He showed that freeholders, some of whom were very minor landowners but most of whom

were men of some substance, returned a mere 91 MPs, the county members. The number of freeholders he estimated at 160,000, but in the corporate towns and boroughs the number of persons eligible to vote was far smaller, only 40,000, and most of them were far from well-off. Petty's purpose in submitting this memorandum may have been to urge reform, but James's response was to seek to exploit the anomalies Petty uncovered. The latter concluded that fewer than 2000 "active men" governed, that is decided, the election of a majority of MPs.[37] To James and his electoral agents this made it practical to think of depriving such a relatively small number of men of their influence and of replacing them with an approximately similar number of royal nominees. Systematic fact-finding and the correlation of information in a central office in London preceded royal intervention in the constituencies. In counties lords lieutenant canvassed the gentry, an operation involving thousands of individuals, which had indifferent success. Itinerant agents reported on the composition of the governing bodies in the towns, canvassed individuals, and then recommended dismissals and names of those suitable as replacements. The fact that they found it necessary to undertake several purges was not necessarily an admission of failure: rather it can be seen as literally experimental, the operation of a succession of tests to achieve a secure local majority.

William's invasion in 1688 prevented James from testing his policies in general elections, and we cannot now say whether he would have been successful in packing and manipulating Parliament. The economic and social assumptions that underlaid his attempts to reconcile the manufacturing and mercantile interests to a greatly strengthened royal authority can be criticized as grossly simplistic. In expecting that personal enrichment would make large numbers of economically enterprising people passively obedient to royal domination James and his advisors ignored evidence that the pursuit of private interest produced not passivity but new sets of tensions and antagonisms. Men whose lives were dominated by commercial competition were unlikely to accept the role of political neuters, and they were already forming pressure groups to further their economic interests.

The frequency with which Parliament met between 1660 and 1681 led to a sharp increase in the number of petitions directed to the Commons (rather than the Crown) which called for legislation, mostly on economic issues. There was an increase in the number of private bills initiated and passed. Organized lobbying quickly developed. MPs received entertainment and occasionally evidence surfaced of bribery. Consequently corrupt practices threatened to taint the reputation of the Commons as they had done previously in the case of the royal Court. It was said that bills introduced on behalf of corporate bodies were "never good for the Nation," that is that they put private interests before the public good.[38] Because interest groups were by their nature inherently competitive and acquisitive, James was living in an illusion to think that the pursuit of interest by his most energetic subjects would produce domestic harmony, or immunity for himself and his ministers from pressures and from recriminations by the disappointed.

More generally, the basis for royal or ministerial decisions and judgments on commercial and industrial questions would have been challenged. The variant forms of mercantilist-inspired policies on which James gave signs of intending to embark—particularly in controlling and channelling colonial trade—can be regarded as unrealistically reactionary. They represent an update of the system (and concepts) articulated during the reign of James I by Gerald de Malynes. Malynes regarded all commercial activity (including manufacturing for export) as being contained within an ordered system which was related to a patrimonial order in which every aspect of life must be subject to the authority of the sovereign. But even in James I's time critics such as Edward Misselden and Thomas Mun presented an alternative set of concepts which became widely accepted by the 1680s. They claimed to demonstrate that all commercial, industrial, and financial activities were governed by objective economic laws which lay beyond the power of any prince to control or nullify.[39] Some intellectuals, and especially clergy, remained skeptical, but the majority of those actively engaged in commerce, industry, and finance—and in England though not in France this included many of the nobility and gentry—accepted these conclusions and also the corollary added by Petty, that all economic relationships "were amenable to scientific investigation."[40]

In terms of practical politics acceptance of the proposition that objective laws governed all economic activities did not prevent Parliament intervening crudely on behalf of favored interests, notably with the Irish Cattle (prohibition of imports) Acts in the 1660s, further discriminatory measures against Irish trade in the 1690s, the Navigation Act directed against the Dutch, and the institution of the bounties on corn exports. But a *general* direction of all trade and export-orientated industry would have been difficult to justify or enforce. The strength of the reaction which James would have provoked had his policies not been aborted by the Revolution of 1688 can be grasped by an analysis of the controversies provoked by broadly similar policies introduced in France by Colbert. He organized and subsidized new trading companies and industries in order to produce a favorable balance of payments by eliminating the need for most imports and boosting exports. This would augment France's resources of precious metals and encourage a brisker circulation of money throughout the provinces, facilitating a prompter and fuller payment of taxes to the central government.[41]

Nothing so intensive was ever attempted in England, and the reaction against Colbert was greatest (ironically, considering James's religious mission to reconvert England) from the *dévôt* party within the Catholic Church, whose most prominent spokesman was Archbishop Fénélon. The *dévôts* criticized Colbert's preoccupation with material advantage and his strategy of appealing to individual and sectional self-interest. They were Christian Agrarians, who distrusted the values current in urban life and among those concerned primarily with profit. Their belief that only agricultural pursuits created real wealth, and that all luxury trades and production subverted moral values, was linked to a fear that the artificial expansion of trade and industry would cause irreparable social disruption.[42]

The French critiques were mostly based explicitly on Catholic principles. By contrast many of the English critics of the influence acquired and exercised by the Financial Interest in the decades after 1688 were heavily influenced by Machiavellian principles. For them the Financial Interest represented a new form of corruption. Using the wealth increasingly concentrated in a small oligarchy of parvenus significantly reduced the ability of the individual to participate in public affairs, when he had the right to do so. Money was nakedly be-

coming the source of power and influence, undermining the essential
principles on which honest and effective representative government
must be based.[43]

The Financial Interest and the Balance of
the Constitution

The threats to English liberties which the legislation of 1689 sought
to ensure would never again be made were direct and blatant—laws
being set aside arbitrarily, an army being used to overawe the nation,
the suspension of the property rights of bankers (and their deposi-
tors), and the campaign to pack a subservient Parliament. By contrast,
after 1688 the dangers that threatened the free and legal operation
of the processes of representative government and consequently the
liberties of all individual subjects were more subtle, more difficult to
identify and therefore to defeat.

These dangers stemmed from developments—which nobody had
envisaged or consciously desired during the Revolution of 1688—that
made the possession of money, and notably money and wealth in new
forms, the predominant source of political power and influence. The
Financial Interest of bankers and rentiers, which in the past had been
condemned as auxiliaries whom the king could use to make himself financially independent, now seemed in the view of the Country
opposition to be moving into a position in which its leading members could dominate the most essential processes of government.
And whereas participation in the wars of 1689–97 and 1702–13 put
the utmost strain on the finances of the government and the productive economy of the country, members of the Financial Interest were
visibly increasing their wealth in spectacular fashion.

Expenditure on the war greatly exceeded revenue during the 1690s
and reliance on short-term loans was also failing to provide an assured and regular source of finance.[44] Long-term loans required much
greater security. But by institutionalizing those providing long-term
finance in the Bank of England Parliament effectively tied the hands
of later Parliaments and administrations. The Bank of England was
a privileged entity which had an obvious and permanent concern

to perpetuate its own existence and to maximize the profits which it made from government loan operations, and it could mobilize on its behalf an increasingly formidable political interest of shareholders, connections, and dependents.[45] By the terms of the 1694 statute which established it the Bank could have been allowed to expire in 1706, and the additional Act of 1697 (which gave it a monopoly) extended the term only to 1711.[46] In constitutional theory another statute could have been enacted at any time to suspend or reduce the interest due on the loans that had been contracted: unlike Charles II's suspensory action in the 1672 Stop of the Exchequer, any statutory action would by definition be legal and constitutional. The lenders would not have been able to obtain a remedy by an action in the common law courts because, from a legal perspective, there were no limits to what a statute could achieve. Until Britain became a member of a supra-national body, the European Community, and subscribed to international conventions on human rights, statute retained an omnipotent, Hobbesian authority: no mechanisms existed to invalidate a statute, however oppressive or defective its provisions.

Constitutional developments in the last decades of the seventeenth century demonstrated this omnicompetent authority, disproving Sir Edward Coke's earlier contention that a statute could be judged invalid because it infringed customary rights and law.[47] The Bill of Rights and the Act of Settlement set aside the law of the succession, depriving all Catholic heirs of their rights.[48] Although the last of its kind, the Fenwick Attainder Act of 1697 deprived a subject of his life by exclusively legislative processes.[49] The Bill of Rights declared illegal the prerogative power claimed by Charles and James to suspend statutes, or dispense with their provisions.[50] The Roos Divorce Act of 1670 even overrode divine law by allowing remarriage, ignoring the objection that marriage is a sacrament and could not be altered by human action.[51] The effective limits to any statutory action against the Bank ran entirely counter to this trend. No Parliament could have seriously contemplated suspending interest payments or repudiating loans. Such action would have annihilated the credit of the existing administration and its successors. More widely still, it would have caused the collapse of all credit for trade and industry and disrupted the whole economy.

The French wars made the Bank and the Financial Interest indispensable and put practical limits on the action the Parliament could undertake, even by statute. A Jacobite restoration also became less likely. Hostile polemicists naturally exaggerated the damage to sovereignty inflicted by the indispensability of the Financial Interest: Jonathan Swift asked rhetorically, "must our laws from henceforward pass the Bank or the East India Company, or have *their* Royal Assent before they are in force?"[52] A grain of truth underlaid this hyperbole. In 1702 the great Whig lawyer Sir John Holt, now lord chief justice, refused legal recognition to promissory notes with the tart observation that they were "a new sort of speciality unknown to the Common Law, and invented in Lombard Street [the site of the Bank] to give laws to Westminster Hall" [where the High Courts sat]. In law he may have been right, but Westminster (meaning Parliament) had to override him by a statute in 1705–6.[53]

The same effective limits on the action that Parliament could actually undertake applied to the army in time of war, and eventually in peacetime as well. The Bill of Rights in 1689 made the consent of Parliament necessary for the maintenance of a standing army in peacetime, but during the war of 1689–97 the largest-ever army had to be raised to deal with multiple enemy threats. In theory the Commons could have rejected the number of men the administration thought were needed, but by doing so it would incur responsibility for any failures and defeats: as a veteran Country MP complained in 1691, "this sort of proceeding by naming a sum takes away our liberty." Those who took part in the Revolution of 1688 had not foreseen the consequence that England would have to abandon its quasi-isolationist stance in foreign affairs and become involved as a principal contender in great power politics. Moreover it was the commitment with which William saddled England to maintain a large army and contingents of mercenaries in land warfare on the Continent that made it necessary to incur large and long-term loan obligations.[54]

A strong section of the Tory party opposed this commitment and tried to resist its renewal in 1702 under Anne. Tory leaders, especially the earls of Rochester and Nottingham, denied that the interest of England demanded large-scale continental campaigning. Instead they wished to concentrate on naval and colonial campaigns which, they claimed, would bring long-term benefits to the economy and substantial short-term gains to offset the costs. Consequently they claimed that the war could be financed exclusively by taxes and limited short-term borrowing.[55] Tory polemicists contended that continental campaigning was unnecessary and therefore there would be no need for further long-term loans. They went so far as to assert that the covert reason for engaging in expensive (and in their view inevitably inconclusive) continental campaigns was that it served the selfish interest of sectional groups. The Whig chiefs, the so-called Junto, exploited the patronage that an enlarged army brought them and the influence of the Financial Interest, for whose rise they were themselves responsible through the creation of the Bank. The Whigs might talk of fighting to defend the liberties of Europe, but by imposing heavy taxes and saddling future generations with an impossible burden of debt they were actually subverting the liberties of Englishmen.[56]

When peace was concluded in 1697 parliamentary consent became necessary for the maintenance of the army, and the critics of William's Whig administration could discuss the issue entirely in terms of domestic politics and constitutional principles. Country peers and MPs pressed for the disbanding of all but a cadre, treating the matter as a first and crucial test of what were known as Revolution principles.[57] Ideologists and particularly Andrew Fletcher and John Trenchard were opposed in principle to the very notion of a "mercenary" army, that is one in which the officers and soldiers served for money. They considered that active citizenship involved a personal obligation to serve under arms to ensure the defense of the community. Fletcher followed Machiavelli in arguing that defense should be entrusted to a citizen militia composed of those who possessed the franchise, the freeholders in the counties. Such men would contrast sharply with the human material used by the standing army, most of whose "common" soldiers were conscripted in wartime from the poor, but one of the purposes of Fletcher's proposals was educative. Military service would inculcate high forms of civic responsibility. But he went to ludicrous extremes of contemporary political correctness by suggesting that militia soldiers should not be permitted to hear sermons and should confine their drinking to a mutiny-inducing concoction of vinegar and water (with occasional brandies).[58] This nonsense underlines the fact that the kind of militia advocated in the anti-army pamphlets would have no military value: Fletcher, Trenchard, and the others simply ignored all the new techniques of warfare developed during the previous half century. Parliament did not give serious consideration to alternatives to the standing army which in 1697–99 it cut down to a minimum size: bills introduced to improve the militia made no progress. Its debates were related not to problems of national security and still less to the preservation of a balance of power in Europe but to preserving a balance in terms of the distribution of powers within the constitution.[59]

For Country MPs and writers only an excessively large army made it necessary to raise the large long-term loans that gave the Financial Interest its influence. Each formed a new sectional interest which had to be supported by the rest of the nation. This could not be consistent with the public good, especially as it resulted in a concentration of power in the hands of those ministers who controlled army and navy patronage and were associated with the Financial Interest.

This concentration threatened to unbalance the constitution. Obviously a greater risk of instability exists in a balanced constitution than in a rigidly authoritarian regime (such as that of Louis XIV) which invoked divine institution and sanction for its political and social structures. In England the traditional interpretation of the reasons why there had been so much instability since the death of Elizabeth centered on the destructive ambition and greed for power or wealth by individuals: in the Country view the dangers stemmed from "evil ministers" and a corrupt Court; in the interpretation advanced by the earl of Clarendon they came from scheming politicians and demagogues.[60] Such attitudes still colored post-1688 attacks on the Whig Junto and on Marlborough and Godolphin, but at the heart of the attacks on the Financial Interest lay a more sophisticated explanation which attributed political instability to large-scale changes in the ownership of landed property. James Harrington's thesis that political power and influence were directly related to the ownership of land, and that changes in the one were certain to produce changes in the other (and in both directions), gave the enemies of the Financial Interest their main line of attack.[61]

In general terms the danger was that the emergence of a new form of property, and one that was artificial—the creation of ministers and a parliamentary majority—would lead to a fundamental and in time irreversible shift in the distribution of power. Henry VIII's dissolution of the monasteries had had the unintended consequence of releasing large amounts of property to create an active land market which eventually meant that the gentry owned more landed property than did the aristocracy, the Crown, and the Church. The creation of the Bank of England had the consequence of giving investments in its stock and subscriptions to government loans at least as much security as the ownership of land conferred, with the bonuses of greater flexibility in acquisition and disposal and virtual immunity from taxation. According to what may be called neo-Harringtonian principles an adjustment to the balance of the constitution was certain to follow, and because of the close and mutually beneficial interconnections between ministers of the Crown and its bankers this would result in an access of influence and power for the executive. Independent landed gentlemen would be weakened in their ability to check the growth of ministerial patronage in both Lords and Commons. The Act of 1710 which required all MPs to be in possssion of substantial amounts of landed property put the situation clearly: it was enacted "for the better preserving the Constitution and Freedom of Parliament."[62] Otherwise all elections would be decided by bribery and corruption, and dependent MPs installed by wealthy patrons would legislate as they were told.

The best informed of the critics of the Financial Interest, Charles D'Avenant, substantiated a formidable case showing how both ministers and bankers were using the government's need for more revenue and long-term loans to entrench their influence.[63] His arguments were based on the use of political arithmetic, which he defined as "reasoning by figures, upon things relating to government."[64] But he also justified the Country MPs and peers who even for wrong-headed reasons—prejudice and instinctive hostility to innovations—forced the disbandment of most of William's army and maintained a vigilant watch on fiscal policies and the increase in governmental indebtedness. They did not deserve the opprobious name of faction when they acted to correct errors and watched "that no invasion may be made on liberty." But he warned landed MPs against seeing as a solution a shift of the burden of taxes onto the consumer by high general ex-

cises. These, he saw, would require an expansion of the fiscal bureaucracy whose officers could be used "to master the landed man in his
own corporation," that is his parliamentary constituency.[65]

≺ IV ≻

"Legal Tyranny" Avoided

Electoral manipulation represented a specific and open threat which
provoked legislation to disqualify government contractors, victuallers, and fiscal officers (but not army and navy officers) who were
assumed to be under governmental influence and whose numbers
could be arbitrarily increased.[66] There was, however, a more insidious
danger that although the forms of the constitution were apparently
respected, a ministry with a parliamentary majority would use the
power to legislate in order to establish a "legal tyranny," one that
would receive general acquiescence. Just as James II had expected to
induce a new form of passive obedience based on the people becoming
absorbed in the peaceful pursuit of their own interests and religious
toleration, so "the rich, the fearful, the lazy . . . all those whose livelihood depends on the quiet posture of affairs" would accept an absolute authority which "made a show of ruling by law, but with an awed
and corrupted Senate."[67] An exact example existed in Augustus's
transformation of the reality of authority in the Roman Republic.

Although opponents of Sir Robert Walpole in the 1720s and 1730s
depicted him as the architect of a legal tyranny, the changes brought
about by the consolidation of the Financial Interest's power and influence and the expansion of the governmental bureaucracy did not
unbalance the constitution. But whereas in France, Denmark, and
Prussia aggressive foreign policies and frequent involvement in war
required a concentration of authority that reduced representative
institutions to subservience, in Britain the role of Parliament was
actually enhanced. The key to this divergence lay in the exclusive
control over taxation exercised by the Commons. Expansion of the
machinery of state *followed* the crucial innovation of 1689 which
alone made such expansion politically acceptable. In the financial
settlement for William and Mary which followed the Revolution the
Crown was not voted the customary revenue for life calculated to

give the king or queen sufficient income to meet all the ordinary costs of government, including the maintenance of the navy (but not an army). Instead William and Mary received only a civil list income for life, enough to finance household and some customary administrative expenditure. Even if there had been no war against France they would have had to go regularly to Parliament for additional grants of supply.[68]

The wars and the servicing of the debts incurred during them made the Crown totally dependent on Parliament. Annual sessions became inescapable. Moreover most ministers before Walpole sat in the Lords, which had no power to initiate, amend, or reject money bills; the Commons had the greater political leverage. These bills were examined and debated in the Committee of the Whole House: the process enabled a number of MPs to develop a specialized expertise in financial matters comparable to that of Treasury spokesmen. The Public Accounts Committee, chosen by a secret ballot of MPs, expertly scrutinized all areas of governmental expenditure.[69] Similarly the presence of numerous army and navy officers, past as well as serving, enabled the Commons to conduct knowledgeable debates on administrative and financial as well as strategic aspects of wartime operations. Each year the administration had to submit a detailed "state" of the army and navy, itemizing the number, size, and type of military units and ships for the next campaign, with costings. Although the Commons rarely made substantial alterations— as it could have done, forcing a change in strategy—its approval could never be taken for granted, and all proposals had to be drafted in a form that was judged likely to be acceptable.

The consequence was that ultimate control over the size and composition of the army and navy, in wartime as much as in peace, had to be shared between the executive and the legislative. In no other European monarchy of first class status did a representative assembly (or civilians) exercise any effective control over the armed forces. The other crucial difference between Britain and the Old Regime monarchical states of Europe which made the new fiscal-military state entirely compatible with the constitution and liberties was the different character of the British landowning class, or rather of its leading elements. British gentlemen never tired of emphasizing that many of them were far richer, more respected, and more influential than most of the hereditary European aristocracy. As they diversified their sources of income into mining, real estate development, and investment in government and commercial stock the division between the Landed and Financial Interests ceased to be clear-cut. It was mostly those who lacked the capital, opportunities, or personality to grasp investment opportunities who saw bankers and rentiers as their enemies, accepting uncritically the propaganda of Jonathan Swift and other polemicists.

In its first years a relatively small number of people made investments in the Bank, and most of the stock holdings were large; but with time the number of persons connected with the Bank and other joint-stock companies increased considerably. The direction of the Bank remained in the hands of a London-based financial oligarchy, but the failure of this oligarchy to dictate national policy revealed the limitations of the influence the oligarchy could exert. Sir Gilbert Heathcote, its dominant figure, had the effrontery to warn Anne personally against changing her ministry in 1710: she ignored him.[70] And by careful preplanning Robert Harley, who came into the Treasury on the change of ministry, checkmated Heathcote's efforts to blackmail the new administration by withdrawing the Bank's financial cooperation. Harley succeeded in assembling an alternative group of City financiers, and later encouraged and gave official recognition to the South Sea Company in order to offset the Bank.[71]

In order to propitiate the Tory gentlemen on whom his administration had to depend Harley adjusted the incidence of taxation so as to reduce the amounts levied by means of the Land tax, and compensate with more revenue from excises. But over the decades after 1688 the Land tax was not as unpopular as this decision would suggest. Because it was paid almost exclusively by members of the political nation, that is by people possessing the parliamentary franchise and wielding political influence, the Land tax was treated by successive administrations as a sensitive matter. The commissioners responsible for its assessment and collection were appointed by Parliament, not the ministers, and their number was extremely small. Admittedly a price had to be paid for this parliamentary control: the north, south-west and Wales—all over-represented in the Commons—received light assessments, and their MPs could block any upward adjustment, whereas the more developed regions of England had to carry the main burden of the tax.[72]

Walpole, like Harley, also tried to levy the Land tax at the lowest practicable rate; this formed a part of his managerial strategy. However his attempt to reorganize the excise was undermined by a storm of cleverly stimulated and organized protest: whatever its technical merits his scheme was successfully depicted as oppressive and ruthlessly inquisitorial and had to be abandoned as politically damaging.[73] In this strategic retreat on a fiscal matter is to be found one of the principles that governed the relations between government and governed in post-Revolution Britain—though not in its dependent overseas colonies (including Ireland). Although forms of political bargaining were often crude an approximate balance was established between the various interests that had claims on government, and ministers and politicians alike recognized that constant adjustments were necessary to maintain this balance. As the failure of Walpole's excise scheme showed, there were limits which even a powerful and confident minister possessing a secure parliamentary majority and a continuing ability to manage elections could not overstep. Recognizing their essential interdependence, all sections of the political nation—with the obvious exception of the Jacobites—knew that they had to respect each other's essential interests. Only those excluded from this network of mutuality had a motive to alter the system— the Jacobites, the small groups of political radicals who claimed to speak on behalf of the excluded masses and, eventually when provoked, the colonial assemblies of North America.

Relations between the interdependent interests that made up the eighteenth-century British political nation required a degree of confidence in government that had been totally lacking before 1688. Authority no longer clearly derived from God and divine laws. Every sovereign's right after the Revolution depended on statute, and their heirs could (and still can) lose their right if by becoming Catholics they infringed the provisions of the Bill of Rights. The Indulgence Act of 1689 deprived the Church of England of its authority over religious dissenters.[74] Traditional legal restraints on charging interest on loans (usury) and raising food prices, based on biblical texts and patristic teaching, were replaced by laissez-faire attitudes resting on the belief in the operation of impersonal economic laws.

The Bill of Rights of 1689 stipulated that all actions by ministers and their officials must be within the law, but it did not contain the elaborate and detailed provisions that a written constitution would have added to ensure that they did not break the law. In every respect the assumption that underlaid the working of government was that those entrusted with powers and duties could confidently be expected to exercise them according to the law. In 1701, by the Act of Settlement, judges received security of tenure, with commissions to continue during their good behavior and with assured salaries: but they could be dismissed if both Houses of Parliament jointly became convinced of wrongdoing on their part.[75] Ministers had to retain the confidence of both the sovereign and Parliament: as recently as 1979 a Labor administration had to resign after a vote of no-confidence passed in the Commons (by one vote). There is no law to prevent an administration clinging to office in the face of no-confidence votes but such a defiance of a leading convention of the constitution, informal as it is, would effectively destroy the consensus on which the British constitution has rested since 1688.

The achievement of such a consensus, totally lacking before 1688, was a precondition for the establishment of political stability and the creation of a fiscal-military state that did not involve the invasion of liberties and property. The concept of a balanced constitution and a government with powers limited by law depended on a general confidence that each branch of government could be expected to remain content with its legal powers. It was the charge that this confidence had been misplaced that gave Dunning's celebrated resolution of 6 April 1780 its force: that "the influence of the Crown has increased, is increasing, and ought to be diminished," indicated a need for a restoration of the balance.[76]

The consequences of the establishment of a consensus, a general belief that those engaged at all levels of public affairs accepted the principle of a balanced constitution, were immense. A burden of taxation heavier than that borne by the subjects of European absolutist monarchies was voluntarily, if grudgingly, accepted as being necessary. It rested on the belief that governments were trying, if often mistakenly, to further or protect the interests of the nation, and that public servants were either basically honest or were compelled by supervision and regulation (as in the excise service) to behave honestly. The press—certainly the freest and most scurrilous in Europe—was quick to expose malpractices. And when evidence showed that public confidence had been abused very strong reactions were experienced, as with the hysteria directed against the directors of the South Sea Company and its imitative joint stock companies when the Bubble burst, and with the prolonged impeachment of Warren Hastings for extortion in India. Marlborough was the most successful general in British history, and from 1704 to 1710 the most important man in Europe, yet he became discredited by charges that he had been misappropriating army funds.

The emergence of confidence as the principle governing the working of the constitution represented the adoption by politicians of a principle which originated in commercial and entrepreneurial life: this could perhaps be described as the decisive step in the *embourgoisement* of British politics. Merchants and manufacturers had to be creditworthy; bills drawn on them and their correspondents largely formed the financial medium for their operations. The reputation of a merchant largely determined the extent of his success and prosperity: individual integrity formed an important part of his stock in trade and "good will" became a marketable commodity. Similarly after 1688 it became necessary to possess (or manufacture) a reputation at Westminster, to display for the eyes of the public qualities and attributes that testified to one's honesty and desire to serve the public interest, while opponents systematically engaged in character assassination.

Probably the most dishonest thing in public life before 1688 was the circulating silver currency. It was inadequate in quantity and defective in quality. Forgers deprived coins of much of their intrinsic value by the techniques of sweating and clipping. As a result, by the operation of Gresham's law, good quality coins were hoarded or exported. Foreign coins of many kinds and uncertain value and, at the local level, tradesmen's tokens, had to be used. Now coins of the realm were symbols of the king's sovereignty, and it was appropriate that the reform of a degraded and heterogeneous coinage should follow the Revolution of 1688.

Although the practical and political difficulties of restoring an honest and reliable currency were immense, the task was undertaken despite, and in the middle of, the financial and economic depression caused by the war against France. Under the provisions of the Coinage Act of 1696—not by prerogative act of the sovereign—the defective currency was called in to be replaced by a new and reliable but severely contracted one, which deepened the depression. Many of the details of the complex act, and the methods of its implementation, ran counter to the advice of contemporary economists and it was condemned by spokesmen of the mercantile interest as intended to benefit creditors in general, and bankers in particular, at the expense of merchants, manufacturers, tenants, and lessees.[77]

Whatever its economic defects the Coinage Act revealed great political courage and administrative resourcefulness among those who got it through Parliament and implemented its provisions. The act also possessed great symbolic importance. For the ordinary person coin of the realm, bearing the image of the king, represented the face of sovereignty. Before 1696 it lied to him or her, its face value bearing little relation to its intrinsic worth. By the act a degraded currency, in which no one had faith, was replaced by an honest (if scarcer) currency in which he or she could have confidence because it was regulated by statutory standards.

After early doubts investors developed confidence in the Bank of England. This confidence depended on a judgment that the Williamite regime would survive, and that the treasury would be able to pay interest regularly and eventually repay the capital advanced. It also represented a predictive judgment that in the next hundred years all future administrations would continue to honor these obligations entered into by predecessors long before their own time. Even more generally this confidence reflected an assumption that the economy in the future would have no difficulty in bearing the burden of these obligations.

Mutual trust and confidence were the preconditions for the large-scale investments on which the expansion of trade and industry depended, and without faith in the stability of government these would not be made. As Sir William Temple had written:

as Trade cannot live without mutual trust among private men, so it cannot grow or thrive to any great degree without a confidence both of public and private safety, and consequently a trust in the Government from an opinion of its strength, wisdom and justice.[78]

When he wrote this in 1672, the year of the Stop of the Exchequer, what he said was true of the government of his subject, the Dutch Republic, but emphatically not of England. Only after 1688 did this confidence and trust come into existence, and it was this that enabled

England to withstand the superior power of France. As D'Avenant concluded, after the first and most desperate of the series of wars that were to continue until 1815:

nothing but liberty, our interest in the laws and property, could have made us willing to endure such a heavy war, and able to bear its expense . . . the rights and liberties of a free people are chiefly what we have to oppose against the numbers, wealth, economy and military skill of France.[79]

Fiscal Crises and Constitutional Freedom in the Netherlands, 1450-1795

AUGUSTUS J. VEENENDAAL JR.

BETWEEN THE END of the sixteenth and the end of the eighteenth century, the Dutch Republic was seen by friend and foe alike as one of the most free and most stable governments in Europe. For a long time it was a major force in European politics, and its political influence drew sustenance from its remarkable economic strength. Taxation was considered higher than anywhere else in the world; yet it seemed that the high taxes were willingly paid. Fiscal crises, which seemed to be regularly occurring phenomena in surrounding countries, such as France, were apparently completely unknown.

This chapter will address a number of questions. How can this remarkable financial and fiscal stability be explained? Did the political and constitutional institutions have any influence on this stability, and vice versa? And did taxation influence the growth or decline of the Dutch economy? To answer these questions it will be necessary to examine the structure of taxation in the Netherlands under the Burgundian and Habsburg princes and the influence of taxation on the revolt, as well as the consequences this revolution had for the constitutional structure of the Dutch Republic and its system of taxation.

＜ I ＞

The Netherlands Under the Habsburgs

The original Netherlands were the lands of the delta formed by the great rivers of Europe—the Rhine (Rijn), the Meuse (Maas), and the Scheldt (Schelde, Escaut). Most of these lands formed the westerly reaches of the great Holy Roman Empire of the Germanic Nation; a few of them were originally fiefs of the kings of France. This chapter will, for the most part, concern what later became the Dutch Republic (or the Republic of the Seven United Netherlands, to give it its full title); but the origins of the Republic cannot be separated from the full seventeen Netherlands that once formed one conglomerate of territories—loosely knit together, it is true—under the rule of one monarch.

After a long and complex process of amalgamation, most of these seventeen Netherlands, roughly comprising the present states of Belgium, the Netherlands, and Luxemburg, came into the hands of the Habsburgs.[1] The power of the Habsburg rulers was not unlimited: some forms of regional independence dating back to a very early period continued in force, and with the granting of the Grand Privilege of 1477 these traditional liberties were officially confirmed by the prince. Under Charles V, German emperor and king of Spain, all seventeen Netherlands became united in one hand. And when on 25 October 1555 Charles laid down all his dignities and titles in the Netherlands in favor of his son Philip II, deputies from the seventeen Netherlands swore allegiance to their new prince. He thereby became duke of Brabant, Limburg, Luxembourg, and Gelders; count of Flanders, Artois, Hainaut, Holland, Zeeland, and Namur; and lord of Lille, Douai and Orchies (Walloon Flanders), Tournai, Mechelen (Malines), Friesland, Utrecht, Overijssel, and Groningen. But that is getting ahead of the story.

The tremendous multiplicity of institutions, offices, and office holders in the Netherlands precludes a detailed description. Briefly, however, the prince, in Brussels, occupied the central place; he was seconded by a variety of councils and institutions. Despite this centralistic tendency, most of the territories kept their own government, consisting of a stadholder or lieutenant as representative of the prince, assisted by a council of local nobles and sometimes even commoners. These were the three estates (*staten* in Dutch, *etats* in French) of nobility, clergy, and towns. In time these provincial estates came to be looked upon as the representatives of the people and the medium through which the interests of the people were maintained and protected against abuse of power by the prince. The Estates General comprised deputies from all the provincial estates.

In the Netherlands the influence of the second estate, the clergy, had never been very strong, and in some places—Holland—even completely absent. The nobility were the oldest of the three estates, and their economic influence was great during the early Middle Ages. They were at first the only ones to be consulted by the prince in important matters. Later, in territories like Flanders, Brabant, and Holland, where the towns were growing in importance, the burghers were consulted as well, at first in a haphazard way, depending on the occasion, but soon in established and regular procedures. In the fourteenth century the *Dagvaart,* or summons to appear at the court of the prince, included at least the larger towns.[2] Sometimes the towns also met on their own, without being convened by the prince at all, a proof of their growing independence.

   One of the more important duties of the estates, and therefore the increasingly frequent reason for a summons, was consenting to the "bede," the regular contribution of the several territories to the cost of the household of the lord and to the expenses arising from his foreign policy. Originally, of course, the prince had been expected to live by his own means. He travelled around and consumed the harvests of his Crown lands, which lay scattered through the territories. Income was supposed to come from the princely rights in the wilderness and public waters. He could sell the right to fish and hunt in these domains, and he had the right to establish tolls on the many rivers and charge shipping for using these waters. But income from these sources was small and could suffice only as long as the needs of the princes were small. The growing tasks of a more centralized form of government made a larger regular income necessary.

   The bede was to provide the needed income. The Dutch word *bede* literally means request, and the lord had to request his subjects to help him—to provide him with financial aids. Bedes were differentiated between ordinary and extraordinary ones.[3] Soon the ordinary aid was converted into a form of land rent, paid twice a year. Extraordinary aid was requested only on extraordinary occasions, when a pressing situation necessitated a special effort. In Holland for instance, the count made the round of the towns and asked in person for the bede. The magistrates of the towns concerned promised him the amount to be paid, generally to be taken from the towns' treasuries. The villages in the countryside were taxed according to their *riemtalen,* originally the number of oars every village had to contribute to the count's fleet. This aid in kind was soon converted into a contribution in cash, with every oar being represented with a certain fixed sum.

This system of taxation worked as long as the Netherlands remained relatively isolated from European politics. But when the Burgundian dukes got involved in costly wars with the French king or the emperor, the constant drain on the central treasury demanded a better and more regular system. Early in the fifteenth century the bede was gradually converted into a taxation on landed property. Despite strong opposition from groups traditionally exempted, such as the church and the nobility, the new method of taxation was grudgingly accepted after some years. The system slowly evolved into a more regular taxation: long term bedes, running for ten or twelve years, were periodically granted by the towns and the countryside.[4] Every town and village was taxed for a certain sum and no one was to be exempted. Nobility and church, however, while officially included in the assessment of the property tax, managed to stay exempt most of the time.

The aids the prince asked for had to be negotiated. He summoned his towns to appear before him and he outlined his financial needs to them. After a long process of give and take, an agreement was generally reached whereby the towns agreed to pay a fixed sum in return for certain privileges, small or large, depending on the position and the needs of the prince at the time. Thus the power of towns and nobles in Holland and other strongly urbanized provinces continued to grow, despite the process of centralization of government into the hands of the Burgundian dukes. To overcome the strong particularism shown by the several provincial estates, Philip the Good (1419–67) had introduced the practice of convening the Estates General. He aimed to speed up decisions in matters of taxation, but now and then he also asked for advice in political and dynastic matters. The Estates General under Philip and under Charles the Bold (1467–77) regularly granted the aids; otherwise they had little power, could not make decisions in political matters, and could only convene when the duke asked them to. After the death of Charles the Bold the absence of a strong central government caused the provincial estates, as always jealous of their own independence, to define the power of the Estates General only in the most vague and general terms. But the latter body continued to exist, and continued to play a role, albeit small, in the unifying process among the territories. And because the provincial estates considered themselves representatives—at least in theory— of the people, the Estates General could maintain a position of representing all subjects of the prince.

The long sequence of wars under Charles V necessitated additional revenues. The crude and somewhat haphazard system of assessment used to establish the just share of every town and village was replaced in 1514—at least in Holland—by a new way of assessment. Although much more efficient than before, it was still not enough to meet the needs of the central government. The deficit mounted continuously and new ways of gathering the already established taxes had to be found. The sale of heritable annuities (*losrenten*) yielding some 6.25 percent, or of lifetime annuities (*lijfrenten*) at a slightly higher rate, could realize a sizeable sum at short notice. These annuities were secured by the ordinary aid and soon became a cheap and quick way to collect at least part of the funds that had been consented to.[5] Because the Habsburgs' government was apparently considered a high-risk party, bankers' loans to the government in Antwerp or Bruges carried a rate of interest between 12 and 22 percent; the annuities, by contrast, carried a much lower rate of interest, because they were backed by the provincial estates and generally considered a safe investment. The sum of all the annuities sold constituted a consolidated debt, and although it was originally intended to redeem this debt as soon as possible, it became customary to leave a large portion of the outstanding debt unredeemed. A consequence of this policy was of course that an ever increasing portion of the regular income had to be used to pay the interest on the *losrenten*. Thus in 1531, only 36.8 percent of the annual ordinary aid in Holland was spendable and could be considered net income. It was clear that this system could not last. In 1542 the total accumulated debt of the central government in Brussels had mounted to such a staggering sum that the Estates General had to be convened to discuss matters and to accept new means of levying new taxes.[6]

The proposals of the government were revolutionary in the eyes of the provincial representatives. The first new tax was to be a hundredth penny (1 percent) on all goods exported; second was a tenth penny on the income from real property (including annuities); and third, a tenth penny on income from commerce. No government had ever tried to levy taxes along these lines and the reception of the proposals was only lukewarm. The commercial provinces feared the export tax most, as it was playing into the hands of the competitors outside the Netherlands. The estates of Holland refused to assent and in the end the export duty had to be imposed upon them by the central government. The tax on income from commerce was also contested by the Hollanders, and collection was slow and the result meager. Only the tenth penny on income from real estate was successful and a reasonable sum raised.

Soon it became clear that the enormous deficit of the government could not be reduced in this way. It was also evident that the ordinary aid could not be used to secure more annuities. In 1542 the government proposed that the provincial estates sell new annuities, to be funded by the estates themselves in whatever way they saw appropriate. A land tax or provincial excises could be used for this purpose, but the estates were free to think of other expedients. After some hesitation, most provincial estates accepted these proposals; in Holland new annuities were secured by a new provincial duty on beer and wine in the cities, and by a kind of land tax in the countryside. This new system of funding the *losrenten* meant a shift in the positions of the several receivers: the receiver of the prince became less influential, while the provincial receiver saw more and more money pass through his hands. Moreover, the provincial estates could use the surplus of this income for other purposes, if need be, and it enlarged their independence to some extent. The new kind of *renten* was regularly redeemed by the estates, in contrast to the earlier kind secured by the ordinary aid, and this feature made them popular with citizens, so enhancing the credit of the provincial estates. In this way an important step was taken in laying the foundations of the credit of the estates, which was to play such a large part in the fiscal and financial stability of the Netherlands after their independence from Spain.

The last years of Charles V were years of almost continuous warfare, plunging the government deeper and deeper into debt. The new ruler Philip II found a deficit of almost 4,000,000 pounds Flemish, which continued to grow until it had reached the staggering figure of more than 7,000,000 pounds in 1557. And this already enormous sum would have been even higher if Philip had not transferred huge sums (estimated at 10,000,000 pounds Flemish) from his Castilian treasury to the Netherlands.[7] Income from taxation had grown considerably in these same years but had not kept pace with the growth of expenditure. In the provinces there was a different story. Between 1552 and 1560 Holland had raised 1,236,401 pounds through sale of *renten,* funded by a provincial wine excise and land tax. Moreover during these same years 572,032 pounds Flemish were collected by way of the tax on income from real estate.[8] These figures show an enormous increase in tax income over the decades before. Apparently much more money could be squeezed out of the more affluent provinces, but only through an increased measure of independence of the provincial estates. Only when they were left to organize the collecting of taxes by themselves were the estates willing and able to raise their tax income substantially.

Thus, while the financial position of the central government in Brussels fell from bad to worse, the position of the estates of Holland slowly became better. Their credit standing was such that it was relatively easy to sell new annuities, pay off older debts, and use the surplus income for their own purposes.

≺ II ≻

The Dutch Revolt

During the reign of the Habsburgs it seemed that the seventeen Netherlands were on their way towards a more unified state, a movement reflecting the general development elsewhere. Despite the tenacious way the provincial estates and local governments clung to their traditional rights, the central government in Brussels was slowly encroaching upon their privileges. The revolt that broke out in 1566 destroyed the whole structure and caused a lasting division among the Netherlands.

A multitude of reasons lay behind the Dutch revolt.[9] The economy was affected by the almost continuous state of war in western Europe. In the 1550s the unsettling protestant movement, Calvinism, entered from France; it proved to have a strong appeal, quickly catching on in the Flemish industrial towns and spreading its revolutionary creed and church organization from there to the north. Meanwhile, the nobility felt that their position was endangered by the influx of a new generation of professional administrators, mostly foreigners from France, Italy, or Spain. The gentry, strongly dependent on the income from their landed property, were impoverished by several years of bad harvests, floods, and other acts of God, and not least by the already burdensome taxation. The presence of foreign troops, Spanish and Italian, was hated; the absence of the king, who was in far away Spain, made the people feel they were living in a colony, subjected to heavy taxation to finance wars in distant lands that were of no advantage to their own good.

The pent up anger and frustration seemingly was spent in the one single flash of the iconoclastic movement of 1566. Starting in the south, it petered out in the end of the year in Friesland. Though impressive in its fury, the movement had few practical results. Most of the nobles backed out; the wealthier classes—always afraid of mob violence—sided with law and order; and only a handful of Calvinists and other discontented groups persisted in their resistance. However, Philip II decided to take strong measures to end the unrest in his Netherlands once and for all; to reorganize the central government along modern lines, eradicate all forms of heresy, and make the territories contribute a larger share to the treasury of the Spanish empire. He dispatched the duke of Alba, whom he entrusted with far-reaching authority, and an army of seasoned Spanish veterans to execute these orders.

While the Spanish treasury had provided more than 3 million florins in 1567, Alba needed much more for his military operations. He therefore proposed a host of new taxes: a 1 percent levy on all property (the hundredth penny), a 5 percent duty on the sale of real estate (the twentieth penny), and an excise of 10 percent on all sales of goods and exports (the tenth penny).[10] This last was to be the most controversial. The Estates General were convened at Brussels just for one day (21 March 1569), to hear Alba's proposals, not to discuss them. The hundredth penny on all property was to be non-recurring, the other two were to be permanent. The deputies were told that they had to consent to the new proposals within a fortnight.

The one percent property tax encountered little opposition and was soon in operation everywhere. Despite some problems in the collection, the total yield was more than 3.5 million florins during 1570 and 1571. The twentieth penny on sales of real estate provoked more opposition in the provincial estates; and the tenth penny released a tremendous storm of protest from the mercantile provinces such as Flanders, Zeeland, and Holland. A tax along these lines, inspired no doubt by the Spanish *alcabala*, was considered so oppressive that it would drive trade and industry out of the country and into the Hanseatic towns and England. It would have taxed every step in the production process and every action in shipping or storing of goods, adding materially to the production or transport costs and thereby driving up prices. The estates kept protesting, and Alba, his treasury again empty, declared himself willing to compromise. By the summer of 1569 a compromise was reached: both the twentieth and tenth pennies were to be suspended and in return the Netherlands would pay a sum of 2 million florins annually during a period of six years. Most of the provincial estates eventually accepted this compromise, but only after the term of six years had been limited to two. Still, it took a very long time before the first installments of the redemption money reached the duke's treasury. Although the direct results may have disappointed the king, one important step had been taken: the provincial estates had recognized the king's right to levy taxes at will on a permanent footing.[11]

At the end of the two year period of suspension of the tenth and twentieth pennies, in the summer of 1571, Alba decided that the time for leniency and discussion was over. At that point only small sums of the annual 2 million florins had been paid into the treasury and he needed money desperately. He ordered that both new taxes be introduced at once, despite loud protests from everyone concerned. The provincial estates sent their delegates to Brussels to explain the destructive results of such a tax to their trade and industry.

Despite Alba's near despotic powers, protests against the new taxation could not be silenced and became ever more widespread. A war of propaganda was started against the proposals, cleverly fanned by William of Nassau-Orange, former royal stadholder of Holland and Zeeland and large landowner in the Netherlands, who had become the central figure in the resistance against Spanish rule. Obstruction was another weapon used; strikes and protest meetings were organized even under Alba's nose in Brussels. Outright sabotage by the local magistrates became common. Certain provincial estates decided to send delegations to the king in Madrid, although Alba in vain tried to dissuade them from this step. In Holland, Zeeland, and the other northern provinces events moved more quickly, changing the struggle against Alba from civil disobedience into open warfare. Inspired by the taking of Den Briel (The Brill) by the Sea Beggars (the privateers operating against Spanish and loyal shipping in the name of the prince of Orange) on the first of April 1572, most towns of Holland and Zeeland declared themselves for the prince of Orange, now the generally recognized leader of the revolt against Alba. In the north the new tenth penny was collected only in the few places where the Spanish still kept garrisons.

It is hard to describe the exact influence of the new taxation on the revolt in the Netherlands. Judged only by their merits, the new taxes promised to be fair by spreading the load more evenly over towns and countryside. At the same time church and nobility would have found it hard to be exempted. But most of the opposition against the tenth penny centered on the supposed ill effects on the economy. The economic situation was already bad enough, because of general unemployment and high food prices caused by the Swedish-Danish war and the resulting closure of the Sound. The tenth penny would certainly have pushed prices up still higher, both on exports and on domestic consumer goods. As the tenth penny was not collected anywhere before 1572, its direct influence on the economy can only have been slight; but its psychological effect was very important. The prospect of new and oppressive taxes, coming on top of all other ills, was enough to give merchants and industrialists the idea of emigrating and stimulated the revolutionary mood of the people. Alba's successor, Requesens, regarded the tenth penny as the foremost cause of the 1572 rebellion and requested its abolition most urgently.[12] Others considered the factors of religion and political freedom supreme, but the whole issue of taxation may very well have rallied all these different groups to the cause of the rebellion. That these taxes were to be levied in perpetuity and by the central government represented an important infraction of the traditional liberties and privileges of the Netherlands. Until now the estates had always been able in some measure to grant new taxes and to supervise the spending of the money collected. Now they were threatened to be pushed aside by the king and his governor-general, and their interests were clearly going to be subordinated to the global interests of the Spanish Empire. While in most countries the tendencies towards greater centralization of governmental power grew stronger and stronger, a clean break may be seen in the northern Netherlands, where a return to the traditional liberties of the estates was to be the outcome of the armed conflict.

Under the leadership of William of Orange, Holland and Zeeland succeeded in freeing themselves of Spanish troops. Many factors contributed to this success: the geographic situation of the waterlogged territories; the international political situation where Spanish interests in other theaters caused important diversions of manpower and money away from the Netherlands; the brilliant military leadership of the sons of William of Orange, Maurice and Frederick Henry; and last but not least the miraculous economic strength of Holland and Zeeland. On 23 January 1579 the Union of Utrecht was signed by delegates from Holland, Zeeland, Utrecht, and some of the southern provinces; and by Count John of Nassau, brother of William of Orange. Count John was the chief architect of this "closer union" as it was called, designed to strengthen the defense of Holland and Zeeland by co-operating more closely with Utrecht and Gelderland, the gateway by which Holland could be invaded from the east. At the same time this union established the preponderance of Calvinism in the north. Although certainly not meant as such, the Union of Utrecht became the "constitution" of the Dutch Republic, not because its framework was appropriate for that purpose, but simply because it was never replaced with something better. It had to serve practically unaltered until the end of the Republic in 1795.[13]

So far, at least in theory, the revolt had not been against the king but against his bad advisers. But in 1581 a truly revolutionary step was taken when the rebellious provinces deposed the king officially, in the Act of Deposition. Calvinist revolutionary thinking played an important role in this step, which was only gradually recognized to have been a step of immense historical importance. Never before had a God-given ruler been deposed because of serious misconduct towards his subjects. The new theory held that there existed an unwritten contract between the ruler and his people, whereby the former had to protect the latter as a shepherd of his flock. Now that the ruler had behaved as a tyrant and thus broken the contract unilaterally, his people were fully justified in deposing him. Junius Brutus's *Vindiciae contra Tyrannos* (1579) gave a multitude of reasons for rebelling against such a tyrant. One of the most compelling was spelled out neatly in a Dutch pamphlet of 1586: "the king, prince or lord of the country has no power to pledge or still less to sell the provinces, nor may he tax his subjects without the express consent of the States as co-rulers of the country"—a succinct statement of the principle underlying the general Dutch opinion on taxation.[14] After having deposed their king, the estates at first tried to interest the French king and the queen of England in protecting them. After some disappointments with troops sent by these foreign princes, the estates in the end decided to do without a ruler at all and took the sovereignty firmly into their own hands.

≺ III ≻

The Netherlands after the Revolt

The Republic of the Seven United Netherlands that emerged during the seventies and eighties of the sixteenth century always retained the constitutional structure that it had acquired at its birth. This cumbersome machine worked after a fashion, grinding to a standstill only in the late eighteenth century. Looking back it may be considered a miracle that it worked at all, and for such a length of time too. Politicians recognized its faults, but only once or twice did they make a serious attempt to improve the governmental system and to eliminate the most glaring defects. The results of their attempts were less than meager, and the governmental machine remained the same in all its essentials until the French invasion in 1795.[15]

The Union of Utrecht actually was meant to be no more than an alliance between a number of the provinces to enable them to withstand the common enemy. Members of the union continued to co-operate in the Estates General with non-members Brabant and Flanders, as they had done before. Only the fortunes of war caused the later defection of the southern provinces. When the union was signed, Philip II was of course still considered the lawful lord of the Netherlands; but after his deposition the remaining free Netherlands became their own sovereigns. Sovereignty was then vested in the estates of the several provinces.

With the deposition of Philip II the office of stadholder or lieutenant should have lost its function. However, William the Silent of Orange, formerly royal stadholder of Holland and Zeeland, was re-appointed as such after the revolt, but this time by the now sovereign estates themselves. The new office of stadholder was ill-defined.[16] Though he was the highest office holder in the provinces that had appointed him, his commission was very much restricted. Every province appointed its own stadholder, but in practice Holland, Zeeland, Utrecht, Gelderland, and Overijssel appointed the same person from the house of Nassau-Orange (until 1702), while Friesland and Groningen traditionally had a stadholder from another branch of the Nassau family. Stadholders could become very powerful and achieve almost monarchical status, but they never went as far as to overthrow the republican form of government. Part of the considerable influence the stadholders wielded derived from their traditional office of captain- and admiral-general, or commander-in-chief, of all armed forces. As such, the stadholder appointed all officers, and the almost unlimited patronage this right gave him played an important role in enhancing his position.

The assembly of the Estates General, meeting in The Hague since 1588, in reality was more a congress of envoys of the seven allies than a legislative and executive body. It could only discuss matters that touched the common welfare; sovereignty remained with the constituents, the estates of the provinces. Every province could send as many envoys as it pleased, but each province had only one vote. On most issues unanimity of votes was required; only in a handful of less important matters would a simple majority suffice. One of the great advantages of the system was, of course, that no single province could bully the others into submission or override otherwise unanimous decisions. A strong province such as Holland could not simply impose its will upon the weaker members of the union, but had to resort to persuasion—sometimes even outright bribery—to reach its goals. The rights of all provinces and their inhabitants were well protected, and the arrangement that the chairmanship rotated among the seven also helped to provide equality. No one had the authority over the others to decide what matters were to be discussed. The hard-fought sovereignty was jealously guarded by each of the seven provinces, and none of them was willing to cede even a small part of its authority to others.

Such a government offered obvious protection against the sort of mercantilist taxation common in France or Spain. It would be difficult, for example, to impose a tariff that would burden a particular province severely if the tariff required the assent of all the provinces. A stipulation in the Union of Utrecht that no province could tax residents of other provinces more heavily than it taxed its own had the same effect. As a result, tariff barriers were set very low, and the low tariffs encouraged foreign trade. Low tariffs remained the official policy of the Estates General during the entire life of the Republic. Although the staple market of Holland and Zeeland was protected as much as possible, the policy of safeguarding this staple market was not consistently pursued. Pragmatism and opportunism became the leading principles, and ultimately it was agreed that the best way to foster foreign trade was to avoid meddling in commercial affairs.

The system thus had its advantages in protecting the provinces against each other but also had severe drawbacks. For important decisions, deputies to the Estates General, before casting their votes, often had to return home to consult their provincial masters and hear their resolutions. The working of the Estates General therefore was desperately slow in times of crisis, and the system also could be used effectively to avoid taking decisions. A machine like this could only function when a strong leader was present to urge the members into action. To speed things in urgent matters, most important questions were well prepared by a small circle of influential members before being introduced in the assembly, giving much more impetus to the decision making.

In each province the estates were the supreme legislative and executive power, checked by no one except their own many headed assembly. Yet their government was seldom tyrannical, because their power was divided among so many regents, as the burgomasters and other city officials were commonly called. In Holland, the estates were composed of 19 members: the nobility and 18 towns. In other provinces the role of the nobility was somewhat more important, but everywhere the towns had strong influence. The town councils therefore were the real bases of power for the regents class. This group originally was undefined and open; rich merchants and industrialists, as long as they were members of the Dutch Reformed Church, could and did enter the council during the early years of independence. But soon a process of "aristocratization" set in; the town councils became closed to newcomers and the established regents set about to restrict the membership—and the accompanying spoils—to a small group. In the eighteenth century this restriction led to a serious shortage of eligible candidates for the several posts available and to a generally ossified state of affairs. Yet the rule of this regent caste was mostly benevolent and successful. And it was unique in Europe: nowhere else could there be seen such a "collective social dictatorship," instinctively hostile to dynasticism and autocracy.[17]

Among the changing deputies to the various estates and government bodies, the few officers who were appointed for long terms of office or even for life soon rose to positions of preeminence. They were not bound to the interests of their home town, as most deputies were, and could consider the current issues from a truly national point of view. The two most important of these office holders or ministers were the grand pensionary of Holland and the secretary of the Estates General.[18]

Holland was the most important province of the seven, and its grand pensionary had a number of important duties. He opened the incoming correspondence of the estates of Holland, drafted the resolutions, and chaired the assembly of that body. He was the only permanent deputy of Holland in the Estates General and he had the right to correspond with Dutch diplomats in other countries and with foreign diplomats in The Hague, which could make him one of the best informed men in the government. Although he was only the highest officer of the estates of Holland, he became the undisputed leader of Dutch foreign policy. But his room for maneuvering was limited; the town governments did not like to be governed by others than themselves, and the only instruments available to a grand pensionary were consultation and persuasion.

Duties of the secretary, or *greffier*, of the Estates General included opening the correspondence of the Estates General, drafting the resolutions, and holding membership on all special committees. In the hands of a capable man like François Fagel, who held office from 1690 to 1744, the position of secretary was nearly as important as that of grand pensionary of Holland.

As might be expected, the legal system of the Dutch Republic reflects the fragmentation of the political system.[19] Holland and Zeeland shared a court; every other province had a court of its own. But whatever political power and influence the courts had before the revolt was soon removed by the provincial estates, jealous of their newly won sovereignty and unwilling to have outsiders meddling in their business.

In Holland and Zeeland, for example, the courts of the first instance were the boards of aldermen in the cities and the bailiffs and sheriffs in the countryside, which judged both civil and criminal cases. Appeal could be made to the shared court of Holland and Zeeland. However, suits in matters of taxation, which were decided by the aldermen of the cities concerned, could only be appealed to the delegated councilors, the small permanent body that ran the day to day business when the estates of Holland were not assembled. Cases concerning the convoy and license duties had to be brought before the admiralty board and they too could only be appealed to the delegated councilors. This meant, of course, that all questions about taxation were taken out of the hands of the judiciary and were only decided by the provincial estates themselves.

The other five provinces had similar judicial systems though without supreme courts of appeal. All this may sound like a serious lack of protection of the common citizen, but in practice it had little meaning. Almost all judicial decisions were taken by lower authorities such as city magistrates, and citizens could protest to the provincial estates against unlawful decisions of these lower government bodies and often did so succesfully. There was, however, no judicial challenge to the provincial estates' right to tax at will. The provincial estates were the sovereigns, and they were recognized as the lawful authority, rightfully vested with power of taxation. The lack of conflict over taxation reflected the links between the provincial estates and merchants in the cities. The ties between the provincial estates and the merchants rapidly forged a compromise between the sovereign's need for money and the subjects' need for freedom from oppressive taxation.

In a mercantile and industrial society like the Netherlands, property rights were all important. Most medieval city ordinances explicitly protected the property rights of citizens and visiting merchants and provided for legal procedures to arbitrate commercial disputes. Confiscation by the prince, once a common penalty for many crimes, was gradually limited to a small number of well-defined criminal cases. Claims of creditors always came first, although confiscation by private creditors and government alike was sometimes prohibited, especially in charters of cities of Holland.[20] It was thus not surprising that Alba's indiscriminate confiscation raised such an outcry. After independence it was generally considered to be one of the first duties of government to protect the property rights of all inhabitants, including foreigners.[21]

Contracts were also considered sacred. During the Habsburg period, and even earlier, contracts concerning commercial operations, wills, insurances, transfers of property, and such were drawn up by notaries public; they carried absolute force of law and could be upheld in court if necessary. In the great mercantile cities a host of notaries was available, more often than not specialized in particular lines of business, so as to ensure a smooth and rapid drawing up of the necessary documents. In the period of the Republic this system was further perfected and notaries public became an important factor in the phenomenal growth of Dutch commerce and shipping.[22] The state backed up the private contracts: during the debate over a stamp duty in the 1620s, for example, the opponents of the new tax measure argued that stamped paper was of no use because the state was bound to uphold all contracts, wills, and other documents whether they were written on stamped paper or not.

≺ IV ≻

Liberty in the Dutch Republic

In such a highly complex structure of government, the notion of liberty took on different meanings.[23] In religion, a common denominator was the quest for freedom of conscience, one of the founding principles of the Union of Utrecht, which had its roots deep in the humanist principles of Erasmus and Coornhert. Perhaps one sign of the attachment to freedom of conscience came as soon as the rebellion was successful: the established authorities immediately took steps to curb the political power of the church and they made sure that church and state were separated. It is true that Reformed ministers were paid by the state and that office-holding was limited to members of the Reformed Church. But the state predominated even in church matters and it let freedom of conscience develop.

Freedom of conscience was of course not the same as freedom of worship. It was William of Orange's ideal to see Roman Catholics and Protestants worshipping side by side, but this proved impossible. As a concession to the victorious Calvinists, public worship by other communions was soon officially forbidden in the north, despite provisions made to the contrary when towns declared themselves for the prince of Orange, and at least in theory, non-Reformed worship was a criminal offense. It did not take long, however, before liberal notions—or at least liberal practices—came to the fore again. Worship by Lutherans, Mennonites, and other harmless protestant denominations was again openly allowed, and even the Roman Catholics could have their places of worship tolerated, albeit at a certain cost. Practical reasons may have played an important role here. Even if the city regents were not endowed with the sense of toleration that historians once supposed, they would have found it difficult to deny churches and clergy to the Roman Catholics, who formed perhaps one-third of the population in Holland alone.[24] The Portuguese Jews, many of them prosperous merchants, were even allowed to build their splendid synagogue in a very conspicuous place in Amsterdam, with full approval of the city fathers. In other towns there was much the same kind of openness.

Dutch "toleration" certainly had its limits, but it was highly unusual in the early modern world. In religious matters the letter of the law may have been as strict as elsewhere in Europe; but due to the high degree of fragmentation of the government, it was usually possible to circumvent its harshness. The history of Dutch printing makes clear that even the most outrageous books and broadsheets could be printed and published, despite sometimes draconian measures of prevention by the estates of Holland. Printers were penalized now and then, but mostly only after great pressure by bodies such as the Calvinist church or even by foreign potentates, who had to be humored because of the political situation of the moment. And bands of foreign fugitives, fleeing from religious persecution in their home countries, regularly found a safe haven in the Dutch Republic as long as they kept quiet and did not pose a danger to the government.

In political matters, freedom, or liberty, also had different meanings. Most common was the sense of opposition against foreign, despotic rule. After the revolt this notion soon passed into history and acquired a somewhat mythical value as "Batavian liberty," exemplified by the revolt of the Batavians under Claudius Civilis against the Romans. In the political nation, liberty was generally interpreted in a much narrower sense as the right of not being overruled by others: in the Estates General, in the estates of Holland, or anywhere. This sense was a throwback to medieval traditions and a return to older concepts of government, running against the general tide in Europe. And such "true liberty" could sometimes lead to anarchy, threatening to loosen all existing bonds among the seven provinces, all the more so during the periods when no stadholder could counteract these centrifugal forces.[25]

Most historians now agree that the Dutch revolt was fought mainly not for any abstract "liberty" but for "liberties," meaning the privileges that towns and provinces had obtained from the prince over the centuries. Several kinds may be distinguished.[26] The first were those held by some towns at the cost of others, such as the medieval staple rights of Dordrecht and Groningen. They were very common and were jealously guarded. After independence, towns suffering from this kind of privilege tried to abolish these ancient rights, but to little avail. Because of the delicate balance of power in the Dutch Republic, no single town could overrule another, and no one could force a town to give up acquired rights. The stalemate was an obvious result of the shortcomings in the constitution, but the balance of power also protected against new restrictive legislation that threatened to hinder trade and industry. It meant that after the Revolt privileges were not granted to one town at the expense of other towns' interests. In this respect the Dutch Republic was certainly different from most other countries of Europe.

A second kind of privilege, more general and thus more acceptable to everyone concerned, granted towns and provinces their own local or regional government and administration of justice. Such privileges usually took the form of charters wrested from princes in moments of extreme financial trouble. They limited the power of the prince and they were widely used as a justification of the revolt: because the prince had failed to uphold the contract, his subjects were justified in resisting the violation of their rights, if necessary by force.

A third kind of privilege, which acquired almost mythical proportions in later years, was that granting the burghers influence in municipal government. The burghers' rights were mostly vested in the guilds and civic guards, as spokesmen of the common people, but they were hardly ever written down in legal documents. The guards did play a decisive role now and then, as when they forced an unwilling government to open the gates of Amsterdam to the troops of the prince of Orange in 1578. Their influence was short lived, however, for in 1581 the estates of Holland passed a resolution forbidding the consultation of guards and guilds in matters of state.[27] In times of severe crisis, as in 1672 and again in 1747, civic guards played some role; but their political power remained very much limited because neither the stadholders nor the regents really wanted them to meddle in politics.

It would be fair to say that in practice (if not in theory) liberty in the Dutch Republic probably comes closer to the modern notion of liberty than anything else at the time. One provision, though, has to be made: Dutch liberty or liberties applied to a relatively small section of the population, the regent families. But throughout the seventeenth century, even the majority had rights that were not to be violated. Oppression by the authorities of the non-political part of the nation grew during the next century, when abuse of power spread more widely and generally. Eventually the disadvantages of government by a small group of powerful regents clearly showed and, in the second half of the eighteenth century, gave birth to the political ideas of the so-called Patriot movement, with its democratic overtones.

≺ V ≻

Taxation in the Dutch Republic

When levying taxes and excise duties, each of the seven provinces remained totally independent, although a certain uniformity did emerge despite the different names of all the taxes. The Estates General drew its income from several sources: the provinces' direct contribution, known as the quota; the convoy and license duties; the income from former royal domains; taxation in conquered lands governed directly by the Estates General; and contributions levied in enemy country during wars.

The procedure for obtaining the quota from the provinces was

this: the Council of State—a chief executive organ acting under
orders of the Estates General—annually issued a "general petition"
requesting the provincial estates to pay their share of the Estates
General's total budget.[28] In this general petition, the precise sums
needed were not specified, and only the money that was necessary for
the carrying on of business was requested. A special petition might
also be issued, requesting extra money for special occasions, military
as well as civilian. To give somewhat more substance to this rather
vague petition, a *staat van oorlog* (state of war) was soon added, giving
more particulars about the distribution of the cost of the army over
the provinces. This "state of war" could remain in force for years, as
long as no fundamental changes had to be made; the one issued in
1621 remained valid until the Peace of Westphalia in 1648. The first
states of war listed only military personnel and fortresses; in the first
decades of the seventeenth century other items were added, such as
diplomatic service, the officers of the secretariat of the Estates General, and the pensions paid to royal persons and highly placed foreigners. But even with these additions the general petition and the
state of war were never a complete annual budget, with income and
expenditure neatly set side by side. Important sources of income were
never mentioned, and expenses never explained. Thus it is almost
impossible to get a clear picture of the Estates General's finances.

During the second half of the seventeenth century the relation
between the state of war and the general petition shifted again: the
state of war became annual, and it more and more resembled a modern budget, though it was still incomplete. As for the general petition, it gradually began to explain the sums mentioned in the states
of war. Although in theory the provinces were free to consent to the
general petition, in practice this freedom meant little. Because every
province had its vote in the Council of State, all details had been
hammered out in accordance with the wishes and resources of every
province beforehand, ensuring the acceptance of the petition by the
provincial estates.

To ensure a regular payment of the troops, the state of war contained a detailed list of all companies together with the province
that acted as paymaster for each company. A very elaborate system
of distribution, the *repartitie*, was worked out over the years, to ensure that each province paid its appropriate share in the total cost.

Generally the system worked, although it could cause a division of command, with every province giving directions to its own troops, sometimes in disregard of the central command. The great advantage of the system was the short distance between paymaster and treasury. Money from a provincial treasury went directly to the paymaster of the troops that were assigned to the province, bypassing the receiver general of the Council of State, who had little actual money flowing through his hands.

The distribution of the quota over the several provinces took some time to crystallize into a more or less solid form, but during the twelve years truce with Spain (1609–21), and after much bickering among the partners, a system was established. Roughly speaking, Holland paid 58 percent of the total annual budget; Friesland 11; Zeeland 9; Gelderland, Utrecht, and Groningen 5 each; and Overijssel 3 percent. These figures show the significant place of Holland among the seven provinces. And, moreover, Holland was the only one of those which regularly paid its share; others were always in arrears. Despite recurrent complaints from most provinces about their quota, the system was not fundamentally altered until 1792, when Holland's share was increased to 62 percent, with Friesland paying 9 percent, Gelderland 6, Groningen 5, Utrecht 4, and Overijssel and Zeeland 3 percent. The rest of the quota was paid by Drenthe (not one of the seven provinces) and the Estates General itself, using its own revenues such as the taxes levied in conquered lands and enemy territory.

Every province, it should be stressed, was free to choose its own method of taxation, provided that the tax did not violate the articles of the Union of Utrecht. As long as a province contributed its established share to the annual budget, each province could impose the taxes it wanted, and the others could not meddle in its affairs. As a result, each province could arrange its taxes so as to minimize the deleterious consequences for its commerce and industry. Economic competition was of course strong among the seven, and each was trying to avoid driving trade elsewhere.

Among the important taxes were the convoy duties, which had their origins in the era before the rebellion, when a duty was collected on all seagoing ships to protect against privateering and enemy attacks. During the revolt, Zeeland and then Holland started levying license duties on trade with the enemy. Continued by the revolutionary government, the duties were lumped together as *middelen te water*, or "means for maritime affairs."[29] They soon developed into a tax on all imports and exports, in peacetime as well as in war, regardless of country of origin or destination, with the same rates prevailing throughout the Dutch Republic. The task of collecting the duties fell to the five admiralties, each of which covered a portion of the Republic. The admiralties established collection offices in the sea ports, in all inland river ports, and in other places through which trade passed; and they drew up a tariff schedule for the duties. The admiralties collected the proceeds and used them to build and equip the warships necessary for the protection of merchant shipping. Not a penny of the convoy and license duties flowed into the central treasury.

This complex of convoy and other duties was received by direct collection, rather than by the farming out common with most other taxes. The reason was the general belief that trade could only be taxed to a limited extent. If the officially published tariff was strictly adhered to, it was generally feared that trade would probably find other, and cheaper, channels to pass through. By keeping the collection in their own hands, the admiralty boards, themselves closely linked to the mercantile circles in their home towns, could at least make sure that the trade of their cities was not unduly hurt. The competition between the Holland admiralties and the Zeeland admiralty was intense in this respect. In Zeeland it was said that some 80 percent of all goods evaded taxation, while in Holland these figures were thought to be between 30 and 40 per cent. The custom officers who collected the duties were under orders not to intervene unless the tax evasion was large—over one-sixth of the value of the goods.[30]

Greater differences in fact were often tolerated, and the higher authorities, always afraid of chasing trade away from their home ports, closed their eyes to it. When the authorities briefly experimented with farming out the convoy duties in 1687, the proceeds increased enormously; but complaints from the mercantile groups grew so loud that they swiftly returned to direct collection. Trade, they felt, simply could not survive if the tariff was strictly enforced.

It is thus highly unlikely that the convoy duties contributed much to the decline of Dutch trade during the eighteenth century: enforcement was too lax and evasion too prevalent. It is true that a substantial reduction in the duties was proposed in the 1750s, and one might take the proposal as a sign that they were bearing down too heavily on the economy. But the same proposal involved strict enforcement of the convoy duties, and strict enforcement would in all likelihood have canceled out the rate reduction. In the end, the changes discussed in the 1750s would have left the effective tax the same.

The remaining sources of income of the Estates General may be treated succinctly. The royal domains, sequestrated after the deposition of the king in 1581, were originally meant to be administered by the Estates General. But some provinces, notably Holland, had already taken these domains into their own hands and even sold some of them, when money was badly needed. It was in the end decided to leave all the former royal domains, and their revenues, in the hands of the provincial estates. Only those domains that were situated in the conquered parts of Brabant and Flanders were governed by the Estates General or through them by the Council of State. The taxes levied in these lands mostly served for paying the local magistrates, and not much remained in the central treasury. The contributions levied in enemy country in wartime and other temporary revenues were generally used for war expenses. Moreover they formed no regular source of income, but fluctuated with the fortunes of war.

<< VI >>

Taxation in Holland

The provincial estates were sovereign in the field of taxation—as they were in most respects. They were free to tax their subjects at will. Here we will survey the taxes in Holland as representative; in most other provinces the system did not materially differ from the one in Holland, despite different names and customs.

Nearly every object was taxed. Sir William Temple, the famous English ambassador in The Hague, speaking of the excises tells us: "The first is so great and so general, that I have heard it observed at Amsterdam, that when in a tavern a certain dish of fish is eaten with the usual sauce, above thirty several excises are paid, for what is necessary to that small service."[31] In Holland, as elsewhere in the Netherlands, the unrelenting demand for tax money made taxation the provincial estates' greatest concern. That much is clear if one reads the printed resolutions of Holland's estates; but the importance of taxation becomes overwhelming if one examines the private minutes kept by some of the delegates. Hardly a day passed without a discussion of finance or taxation, discussion that could drag on for months.[32]

The taxes in Holland may be subdivided into direct and indirect levies.[33] Of the direct taxes the *verponding*, a tax on real estate based on the rentable value, was the most important one. It was collected by receivers, who were appointed in each tax district by the regents of the city that was the district center. The receiver kept an assessment register, *kohier*, that indicated the value of rental property, agricultural land, dwellings, factories, or warehouses, with a list of the owners. From the 1620s on the tax rate stood at some 20 percent of the rents of agricultural land and some 12 percent of the rents of houses and other buildings. In addition to the *verponding*, there was also a tax on fireplaces or chimneys. First levied in Holland in the early 1600s, it soon extended over buildings without fireplaces, such as warehouses and barns. Whenever the need was pressing, an extra tax on real estate could be imposed for short periods, after which a return was made to the usual tax rates.

Indirect taxes or excises provided by far the largest part of the regular income of the estates of Holland. Beer and wines were among the first articles subject to the excise, but it soon applied to other consumer goods and services as well, such as grain, flour and beans, salt, soap, beef, cattle.[34] An excise on the *rondemaat*, that is everything measured by volume, not weight, was introduced in 1600, followed by imposts on woolen cloth, horses, luxury cloth, fruit, candles, firewood, peat, and coal; for these fuels a lower rate was applied for industrial use. In 1621, at the end of the Twelve Years Truce, when war with Spain was resumed and the need for money was pressing, new excises were imposed on oil, fish, tobacco, shoes and boots, and several other articles. Some indirect taxes were assessed according to estimated consumption. Excises on wines, salt, and flour were levied in Holland in this way beginning in the 1680s, and the practice became more common during the eighteenth century.

The collection of excises was regularly parceled out in very small parts to tax farmers.[35] The estates of Holland were always reluctant to do business with big contractors, although these sometimes offered very favorable terms. In the seventeenth century tax farmers hardly ever contracted for sums of more than 10,000 guilders. Contracts were for six months generally and had to be renewed at the end of that period. The system was open to fraud, as every system of taxation will be. An innkeeper could buy his beer and spirits in a neighboring district and agree on a lower rate with the tax farmer of that district, who was eager for more business than expected. Other businessmen did the same and they could thereby pressure their local tax farmer to lower his rates. Should the local tax farmer attempt an appeal to the judicial authorities, he faced a bench staffed by local regents eager to protect their peers.[36]

In general, however, farming out the excises did seem to work. As soon as the contracts with the tax farmers had been drawn up, the estates' annual income could be safely anticipated. Because the collection of excises was parceled out in small lots, an occasional default by one tax farmer did not threaten the estates' entire income. The estates tried earnestly to make the system as fair and efficient as possible.[37]

Altogether, the combined excises pressed heavily on the food prices for the common people, making the relatively high wages paid in Holland a sheer necessity for survival. The high labor costs caused a flight of some industries to cheaper areas, such as States Brabant, where the excises were generally much lower than in Holland. Entrepreneurs in the Leyden textiles industry set up shops in Tilburg and environs, profiting from the cheaper labor.

The estates of Holland also derived income from the duties on all kinds of services, such as weddings and burials; and from the so-called "small seal," a stamp duty on paper used for requests and the like. This small seal was a Dutch invention, introduced in 1624 and soon applied widely.[38] The duties on marriage and burial met with much objection from the populace; the outcome was a serious riot in Amsterdam in 1696, which was only quelled by calling out the civic guard.[39]

The real estate tax, the excise duties, the imposts on weddings and burials, and the stamp duty were called the ordinary means of the estates. High though they were, they were insufficient to cover the staggering costs of war. During emergencies, the estates of Holland (and of other provinces as well) introduced special, temporary taxes to avoid deficits. When the key fortress of Bergen-op-Zoom was threatened by the Spanish in 1622, for example, an extra taxation was found via the so-called *hoofdgeld*, or capitation. Every householder was required to register himself, his wife and children, his domestic servants, and other dependents.[40] He then paid a tax according to the size of his household. This *hoofdgeld* remained an exception though, for the emergency taxes usually took the form of a levy on real and personal property at a rate of between 1 and 0.1 percent (a hundredth or thousandth penny).[41] Unfortunately, the fiscal emergencies were all too common. Indeed, only a few years passed without such special taxes being imposed by the estates of Holland. In some years—1672 (three times, a half percent), 1677 (four times, a half percent), or 1708 (four times, one percent)—the demands were almost too severe.[42] Between 1672 and 1677, 65 million guilders were squeezed out of Holland in the form of extra property and income taxes.[43] After 1722 these extra property taxes were still consented to now and again, but less frequently than before.

If all this was still not enough, permanent extra taxes were assessed on the number of housemaids and other domestic personnel per household; and on carriages and yachts, except when used for business purposes. A new duty was levied on offices, the *ambtgeld*. In 1716 all office holders were pressed to buy 4 percent state bonds to a total of more than 1.5 million guilders. The same procedure was followed in 1727, but now with 3 percent bonds to a total amount of more than 2 million guilders. Twenty years later the same sum was squeezed out of the office holders in Holland once more.[44] In 1750 every civil servant was even required to pay a quarter of the income from his office for a period of four years.[45]

After the outbreak of the War of the Austrian Succession in 1740 the situation became so desperate that a new tax was introduced, the personal *quotisation* of 1742, meant as an income tax. Assessment lists of all inhabitants of the cities were drawn up, and all income was included. Incomes below 600 guilders a year remained outside the new tax, while incomes above that figure were assigned various rates. The highest was for incomes over 50,000 guilders, on which 2.25 percent tax had to be paid; the smallest taxable incomes paid 1 percent. Here, for the first time in Holland, was the modern element of progressive taxation.[46]

≺ VII ≻

Government Borrowing

When all the ordinary and extraordinary means proved to be insufficient, the deficit could be made up by loans. Loans in the form of life annuities had been a regular source of income for the estates during the Habsburg days, and the Republic continued to rely on this cheaper system of annuities and on straight bond issues with a fixed rate of interest. Originally the rate for life annuities was some 8.3 percent, and for other redeemable loans somewhat less.[47] Paying this interest proved to be difficult, particularly during the turbulent years of the revolt. In 1575 the estates of Holland even suspended all payments of interest because of other more pressing needs. Soon, though, the payment was resumed, and in 1598 the last arrears had been eliminated.[48]

In general, the young Republic, and especially Holland, was considered a low-risk borrower by its own citizens. It was therefore able to tap the wealth of its mercantile circles by borrowing on easy terms. Of the total national debt, almost all was held in the country itself.

During the early years of the seventeenth century small amounts of annuities or bond issues were sold, bringing the total bonded debt of Holland in 1609 to almost 4.5 million guilders. The sum rose to 5.2 million in 1616, despite the fact that the war with Spain had been suspended since 1609. Renewal of the war in 1621 brought new needs, and more money was borrowed. Yet despite the increased borrowing, Holland's credit rating remained high, and it proved to be possible to lower the rate of interest gradually, as private rates slackened. Public interest rates had stood at 8.3 percent in 1599 but had fallen to 7.15 percent in 1606 and to 6.25 only two years later. Rates of interest on commercial and private loans also continued to fall; and because the estates of Holland remained creditworthy, in 1611 they converted all existing annuities and bond issues to the 6.25 level. The rate of interest of life annuities shows the same picture, decreasing by a third in this period.

Despite the lower public interest rates, the total amount paid as interest was growing rapidly because of the enormous increase in the size of the public debt. After long discussions it was decided in 1640 to redeem all outstanding loans by converting them into new loans of 5 percent. A special fund was established at the same time to redeem the bonds and annuities whose owners would not agree to the conversion.[49]

The wars with England and in the north to safeguard the free passage of the Sound brought a new increase in the burden, but at the end of the second war with England (1667), the total public debt of Holland stood no higher than it had in 1648. This almost miraculous achievement was largely the work of grand pensionary John de Witt, who was not only a great politician but also a financier and mathematician of note. Apart from the introduction of new extraordinary taxes De Witt also recommended a further lowering of the interest to 4 percent, possible because rates of interest, both public and private, continued to fall. Holland's creditworthiness remained unshaken after the end of the first war with England, and in 1655 De Witt managed to get the estates' consent for his proposal. With Holland's total debt amounting to some 140 million guilders in 1655, De Witt's reduction of interest rates saved 1.4 million guilders a year in interest payments.[50] The measures De Witt favored should not be confused with a default: bondowners were free to opt for continuing the old loan at a lower rate of interest, or for redemption of their loans at par. Most chose the first option.

Despite the millions needed to support a fleet during the second English war, Holland's debt amounted to only 132 million guilders in 1667, thanks to De Witt's policy. When considering the annual sum to be paid as interest the picture is even brighter: in 1652 interest payments were only 7 million, and in 1667 they were a little less than 6 million.[51] New wars meant new loans, however, and from 1672 enormous sums had to be negotiated to keep Holland afloat. At the time of the peace of Nijmegen the debt had increased by some 33.6 million. Generally it proved to be no problem to raise the necessary loans in Holland at the usual 4 percent interest, although Holland's credit did suffer during the War of the Spanish Succession. The Dutch also managed to raise money for foreign princes who were their allies during the war. The foreign princes generally paid more than the 4 percent Holland did, and their loans were often guaranteed by the estates of Holland or the Estates General, because the princes had to be kept in a friendly mood during the war. The resulting drain on Dutch capital was looked upon with disfavor by contemporaries; but for obvious political reasons, little could be done to end the practice.

The growth of the sums needed for servicing the public debt continued, with some ups and downs, during the rest of the eighteenth century, despite a further reduction of the rate of interest to 3 percent in 1723.[52] By 1795 the public bonded debt of Holland as a whole had grown to the gigantic sum of 420 million guilders.

≺ VIII ≻

The Eighteenth Century: Fiscal Crises Narrowly Averted

Despite the growth of government debt in the Dutch Republic, a real fiscal crisis—one that would seriously affect political life—never occurred. Time and again the point seemed to be reached when expenditure had outgrown revenue to such an extent that crisis was imminent. Yet on every occasion measures were taken to remain afloat and avert disaster. The events that caused these near-crises were always wars with powerful neighbors, jealous of the economic and political power of the Republic during the seventeenth century. Because of its great creditworthiness and the enormous wealth of its citizens, the Republic managed to borrow the necessary money in emergencies. The solvency of the Republic, especially of Holland, was never really in doubt; and the merchant-capitalists, coming from the same families that filled the town and state assemblies, willingly put up their own money for Holland's long term loans, which gave them a modest but ultimately acceptable return on their savings.

These capitalists-regents made up the government themselves, especially in Holland and Zeeland; and their chief interest lay in continuing the existing structure, which protected them and their commercial and financial interests. A complete breakdown of the state could only mean the increase of the power of the stadholders to the detriment of the regents' influence, not to speak of even worse things, such as foreign intervention or democratic movements from within. So whenever the government machine threatened to seize up because of lack of financial lubrication, the regents, sometimes grudgingly, provided the money for new loans, loans that were safe because the regents themselves decided how the state's debts were to be serviced. They could do so easily, for they controlled both public expenditure and tax collection, and they could further the public interest together with their own. Nor was there a shortage of capital for government loans. Money was drawn elsewhere in the economy—it went to drain inland lakes and to feed the East and West India Companies—but these investments could hardly exhaust the enormous accumulation of savings during the seventeenth and eighteenth centuries. The amount saved was so great that much of it had to spill over into government loans. Loans to cities, to the estates of Holland and other provinces, and, to a lesser extent, to the Estates General or other institutions actually became the most popular form of investing surplus capital. The rate of return may have been mediocre, but the investment was completely safe. Regular payment of interest may have been in jeopardy once or twice, but the public debt of the Dutch Republic or of its constituent bodies was never repudiated during its existence. Moreover, bonds and other stocks were generally not taxed to the same degree as was landed property or real estate, making these loans even more attractive.[53]

Loans to foreign governments that borrowed in the Netherlands generally carried a higher rate of interest, and they were considered riskier unless they were guaranteed by the Estates General as part of the effort to maintain a network of allies. In times of acute need, when borrowing was exceptionally heavy, more incentives were sometimes needed, such as lotteries or tax exemptions; but the rate of interest on domestic public loans never rose. On the contrary, it dropped gradually, from roughly 8 percent in the early seventeenth century to 3 percent in the mid-eighteenth century. That was below the going rate for private business loans, which in the mid-eighteenth century ran between 3.2 and 3.4 percent. The public loans were evidently safer than the private ones, an unusual achievement in early modern Europe. Despite the enormous burden of public debt in Holland, the Dutch state was always a good risk.[54]

The danger of the gargantuan public debt was, of course, the cost of servicing it, despite the low rate of interest. Ideally new loans were to be accompanied by tax measures to ensure the necessary extra revenue for servicing, but tax increases were not always possible in an already overtaxed Holland. New levies were introduced on occasion, and other, "temporary," taxes were extended over longer periods than originally intended; but more often than not new debts were contracted without the necessary guarantee of revenue to cover the cost of servicing them. This lack of security apparently did not unduly disturb Dutch capitalists, but there were responsible statesmen and economists who warned repeatedly against such practice and who advocated some kind of constitutional and fiscal reform.

The need for some kind of reform came to the fore during the last years of the war with Spain. Holland's debt alone stood at some 140,000,000 guilders; and the annual interest, despite the reduction from 6.25 to 5 percent, laid a too large claim upon the revenue. Holland convened the so-called "Great Assembly" in 1651 to decide on the future political system of the Republic. This turned out to be a grave disappointment. Although the regents decided to do without a stadholder (except for Friesland and Groningen), there was no fundamental reorganization of the system of government, and provincial independence was only reinforced. General measures in the sphere of taxation or public debt were not taken, but left to the initiative of the provinces.

The War of Spanish Succession, which ended with the peace of Utrecht in 1713, almost completely exhausted the Dutch Republic. Maintaining an army of more than 100,000 men, paying for all the siege artillery and equipment, providing large subsidies to allied princes, meant that almost nothing was left for the fleet—in a country strongly dependent on its overseas trade. The admiralties could not equip the ships necessary for convoy duties, unless helped by considerable subsidies from the Estates General or the estates of Holland.[55] Emergency measures, such as the introduction of new, temporary taxes or loans from the East India Company, lotteries, and even loans from the Swiss canton of Bern, were needed to stay afloat. The situation grew desperate early in 1712 when the British defected from the alliance and the Estates General took over all foreign troops hitherto in the pay of England. The peace treaty came just in time, and even before the official signing at Utrecht the army was pared down in size. The public debt was staggering, taxation was already too high, and in 1715 the tellers at the general office of the Estates General had to stop paying interest on the outstanding debts because there was no money left in the till.

The suspension of payments may have sounded worse than it actually was. The loans in the name of the Estates General constituted only a minor part of the Republic's total public debt, most loans being in the name of the provinces or towns. But the temporary moratorium on the servicing of even that small part of the debt did make a profound impression everywhere: the financial plight of the Republic was all too clear to the world. After nine months the payment of interest was resumed, now at a rate reduced from 4 to 3 percent as a consequence of the general downward trend in the commercial rate. Although the provinces themselves did not default—they did not even temporarily stop the interest payment on their loans—most were hard up for money and far behind in paying their consented contributions.

Holland, always having been able to advance the necessary cash for the others in the last resort, was itself in serious trouble and could not continue to help the others. Its debt had increased by almost 120,000,000 guilders since 1702, and the total interest paid annually amounted to some 14,000,000 guilders.[56] As the total annual revenue could not cover such debt service, the deficit was still 1,600,000 guilders in 1719, even though the armed forces had been reduced and extraordinary war taxation continued. The situation was desperate: high taxation and excises were driving up wages and thereby weakening the ability to compete with surrounding countries.[57] Still, private wealth, albeit in a limited circle, was enormous and even growing, and money could be had at a very low rate of interest. But Holland simply could not increase its debt, nor could it further tax its already overburdened population. The tax system itself was at fault, because every town was inclined to be lenient in collecting imposts from its citizens out of fear of driving them to an even more lenient neighboring town. The lesson to other countries was that wealth and riches alone did not guarantee state power.[58]

While domestic matters were less affected by the financial problems, the foreign policy of the Dutch Republic certainly was seriously hampered by the lack of money. The difficulties of maintaining a large fleet forced the Dutch to withdraw from international affairs.[59] The center of diplomatic activity shifted away from The Hague to London and Paris and the Dutch Republic became a quiet backwater. That did not mean that its economic power suddenly disappeared altogether. When compared to the growth of the economies in surrounding countries, the Dutch Republic had ground almost to a standstill; in absolute figures, however, the decline was much less noticeable.[60] The Amsterdam money market remained throughout the century one of the most important financial centers of the world. Despite the domestic problems, private wealth was still enormous, and this accumulated capital was available to the world at reasonable rates. There was hardly a government in the world that did not borrow regularly in Amsterdam.[61]

A second "Great Assembly" was convened in The Hague in 1716 to make an inventory of all defects in the constitution and propose the necessary improvements. The secretary of the Council of State, Simon van Slingelandt, drew up a number of documents, clearly summing up the existing faults and indicating the way to improvement. But as in 1651, nothing was achieved, because of the deeply rooted distrust of all attempts to reduce the traditional independence of the sovereign provinces. Everything remained as before.

Most provinces succeeded in improving their financial situation during the 1720s by cutting down expenses as much as possible, while an economic upswing was of a considerable help. Holland initiated a sale of public domains, but still it only barely managed to balance revenue and expenses. When the international situation in the early 1730s necessitated a new expansion of the army, the annual deficit grew again, to one million guilders.[62] The only way to meet the extra expenses was to float new loans, which in the eyes of many was a sure way of getting into deeper trouble sooner or later. In 1740 the servicing of the outstanding debts needed almost 12 million guilders, 62 percent of the total tax revenue.[63] As these latter figures cover only the southern quarter of Holland, which made up between 80 and 90 percent of the province of Holland, the figures for Holland as a whole must have been even higher. Instead of the evil being attacked at its roots, the "personal quotisation" was introduced in 1742.

Large-scale rioting against the system of taxation did break out in several provinces in 1747–48, when the Republic was invaded by French armies, and led to the only fundamental change in the system of tax collecting during the existence of the Dutch Republic. The necessary changes in the political institutions, hoped for by large segments of the population, came to nothing in the end, but at the time the popular revolt was seen as an almost overwhelming threat to the structure of government by those who were interested in retaining the system as it was. Tax riots were of course nothing new, having broken out now and again as popular protests against the high level of the excises. The common people, sometimes led by a few interested persons, now and then protested violently against a proposed higher excise or new forms of weighing or measuring taxable products. Yet these riots remained local in character and were easily suppressed. They had no permanent results, although some measures were withdrawn or altered until the unrest subsided. Sir William Temple's view of the willingness of the population to pay taxes may have been too rosy in the 1670s, when he wrote: "And the great simplicity and modesty in the common port or living of their chiefest ministers, without which the absoluteness of the Senates in each town and the immensity of taxes throughout the whole State, would never be endured by the people with any patience, being both of them greater than in many of those governments which are esteemed most arbitrary among their neighbours."[64] By 1747 the people's patience had certainly disappeared.

The riots of 1748, however, were not just fiscal but also political.[65] They were political because the populace held that only an Orange prince could save the Republic from destruction now that the French had invaded its territory. The Republic had been drawn unwillingly into this war, and the almost total neglect of the armed forces now made itself felt, when the French easily overran the barrier in the southern (Austrian) Netherlands and even laid siege to the fortress of Bergen-op-Zoom in Dutch Brabant. The stadholder of Friesland and Groningen was raised to the stadholdership in the other provinces as William IV. Of course he could do little to turn the tide at such a short notice, but fortunately the peace of Aix-la-Chapelle in the spring of 1748 put an end to the hostilities and restored the former frontiers. The enormous extra expenses of expanding the army were met by a "liberal gift," an extra property tax that was consented to in September 1747.

Popular hopes for the new stadholder were unlimited. He was expected to end all political abuse, restore the economic position of the country, and give the hard pressed middle classes breathing space. The common target for all popular feelings was found in the structure of taxation. The "liberal gift" had only given the screw one more turn, without promising any solution to the problems in the long run. The public sale of all offices was proposed by the Orangist party, but the stadholder showed himself averse to such a drastic step. The provincial and local magistrates felt so insecure that they agreed to some measures to remove some of the most glaring abuse of power by the regent classes. Popular feeling was not sufficiently placated, however, and it now turned against the tax farmers.

This movement started in the north but soon spread to Holland as well. Its first aim was the redress of the system of taxation, but it was very much mixed with demands for more popular influence upon the government. The middle classes—shopkeepers, artisans, small merchants, and intellectuals—felt excluded by the growing contraction of the regent classes, and they saw their opportunity now. The movement caught on in Holland, and in the summer and fall of 1748 riots developed in a number of cities like Haarlem and Leyden, where unemployment was high.[66] The houses and offices of tax farmers were looted and the civic guards refused to protect them, hated as they were. The local magistrates could do nothing but abolish the system of tax farming; later the stadholder advised the estates of Holland to do likewise. The result was that no taxes at all were collected, for a new system had not yet been worked out. To fill the gap in Holland (some 10,000,000 guilders) a provisional tax measure was introduced for one year originally, but was renewed several times. It involved replacing the excise taxes with assessments based on estimates of how much taxpayers would have spent on goods formerly subject to the excise. As these assessments had to be drawn up quickly, they provoked complaints about the haphazard way in which the city fathers had raised the necessary sums.[67] Other provinces, such as Zeeland and Gelderland, continued the system of farming out the collection of imposts as before.

The results of this year of high hopes proved to be disappointing. True, some abuses had been abolished, the hated system of farming out the taxes had been replaced in Holland by a system that might be better, but the structure of taxation itself had not been touched at all.[68] The popular movement petered out, because the stadholder, who abhorred democratic experiments, had only used it to strengthen his own position. Measures of real reform were not taken, the public debt rose higher than ever, and the old machine labored on, though manned with new personnel here and there. There was a far-sighted proposal in 1751 for establishing a limited system of freeports, in order to bolster the old function of the staple market. It would have lowered excises and convoy duties, while strictly enforcing those lower rates. It provoked discussions for some years but was withdrawn in 1755. Once more opposition from the vested interests had proved to be too great.[69]

Despite the lack of reform, trade actually revived after 1748 and Holland succeeded in refunding or redeeming part of its public debt, while new loans proved unnecessary. In the years between 1755 and 1780 Holland's revenues regularly exceeded its expenses, making the redemption of older loans and lotteries possible. In 1780 the total burden of debt of the southern quarter of Holland was about the same as in 1740, but general income was much higher. However, the outbreak of war with England in December 1780 plunged the Republic into financial abyss once more. Trade came almost to a halt and income declined dramatically, while the cost of equipping fleets soared. The only way to meet the emergency was to ask for new loans, undoing everything that had been accomplished since 1740.

Yet high as the financial burden may have been, fiscal problems did not cause the collapse of the Dutch Republic. The Republic suffered from constitutional deadlock and institutional impotence, particularly during the last half of the eighteenth century. No one in power was willing to undertake a thorough reform by breaking up old class structures and privileges. Not even the stadholder, who after 1748 wielded almost despotic power, wished to overthrow the system of which he was a part.[70]

Such paralysis was not unique. In other countries too, political and social structures had frozen hard; in France, it took a revolution to change things fundamentally. In the Dutch Republic the demand for thorough reform was long advocated by certain political theorists, but it only came to fruition when it was taken up by the so-called "patriot" party, a group of democratic thinkers and anti-stadholder regents. With French help, they succeeded in overthrowing the old structures in 1795. But even the new regime they established could not manage to maintain the heavy debt burden. In 1805–6 it resorted to a heavy-handed repudiation of two-thirds of the Dutch debt.

≺ IX ≻

Conclusion

When considering the financial history of the Dutch Republic, one is struck by its exceptional stability. While almost every neighboring ruler at times hovered on the brink of financial disaster or even had to declare bankruptcy occasionally, the Dutch Republic presented a picture of almost unbelievable financial stability. During its existence as an independent state no real fiscal crisis occurred, not even in 1747–48, when the fiscal policy of the estates was seriously questioned.

There had been a real fiscal crisis before independence, during the time of the revolt against Spain; and this crisis did influence the later shape of constitutional government in the Republic considerably. Although certainly not the only cause of the revolt, the duke of Alba's oppressive fiscal policy was one of the contributing factors to the tenacious resistance in the Netherlands, the leading fiscal principle behind the revolt being the belief that the prince could not tax his subjects at will without their consent.

After they won their independence from the Spanish king, the new leaders made sure that such oppression could never happen again. To do so they used institutions that went back to the times long before the revolt, but with some fundamental changes. The merchants' state of the late sixteenth and seventeenth centuries could not bear oppressive and stifling taxation at home, yet on the other hand it also needed protection from threats by foreign potentates, necessitating at least some form of central authority. The first aim was attained by placing the power to tax in the hands of the provincial and even local authorities. The provincial estates, now sovereign, and the city boards of aldermen and burgomasters were made up from the class of people who held the greatest interest in trade and industry, and they made sure that the policy—fiscal policy included—of the estates did not threaten these two pillars of their economic strength. They considered their republican form of government the true aristocracy, in the original meaning of the word: "rule by the best." This body politic may have been small, but relatively it was probably larger than its like elsewhere in Europe at the time. Moreover, being sovereigns themselves, they had no need to share their power with a prince, although some stadholders did wield almost autocratic power, sometimes because of their own forceful personality, sometimes because of the exigencies of the times.

The necessary protection against foreign threats was provided by the Estates General; but when redefining the authority of this ancient body, the new leaders made sure that no single province could take over this central authority for purposes of its own. The principle of one province one vote safeguarded the interests of every province against a richer and more influential neighbor, and the requirement of unanimity on matters of war and peace and other important questions also contributed to the stability of the system. And because the provincial delegates to the Estates General came from the same group of people that filled the benches of the city boards and provincial government, the mercantile and industrial interests were always protected. The antagonism between ruler and representative bodies so common elsewhere in Europe was completely absent in the Dutch Republic, because the representative bodies had taken the place of the ruler.

The system presented numerous occasions for the ruling classes to enrich themselves by oppressing the mass of the people. Yet there are few instances of large-scale frauds or tax evasions—and these only towards the end of the Dutch Republic. On the contrary, the leaders of the new state were well aware of their great responsibility to the people, partly from motives of Christian charity and partly also from the need of keeping the common people docile. As long as the economy was booming this proved to be no real difficulty, but during times of decline the problems became almost insurmountable.

The absence of real fiscal crises since the 1560s may be attributed firstly to the economic strength of the new Republic, and secondly, after this strength diminished in the eighteenth century, to the interest that the ruling classes had in maintaining the financial stability of the state. As the principal lenders to the government they were naturally bent on avoiding bankruptcy, which would only have meant disaster for themselves. As long as the economy could bear heavy taxation and as long as capital was abundant, no real problems arose in financing the state and in servicing its debt.

Fiscal policy in the Dutch Republic was attuned to the needs of the economy and the economic growth in turn made possible the relatively high wages, necessary in a country of high excises. Only during its economic decline did this system cease to function, when high unemployment made large masses of the population extremely vulnerable to, for example, even slight fluctuations in food prices.

It is not easy to fathom the influence of the system of taxation on the growth or decline of the Dutch economy. It is true that the fiscal system as it evolved was considered well suited to trade, but evasion of the convoy and license duties—taxes directly affecting trade— thoroughly complicates any analysis of the fisc's effect on the mercantile economy. After all, the evasion was so much a part of the convoy and license duties that we cannot easily measure their influence on the growth or decline of trade. As for the excise taxes, their heavy burden was invoked by eighteenth century economists as the principal reason why industry fled Holland and Zeeland: their argument was that the heavy excises on foodstuffs drove wages too high. The alternative to the excise taxes—some form of income taxes—was of course little favored by the ruling classes, who would have borne the brunt of an income tax. Ideally, one would like to resolve the issue by comparing tax burdens in the Dutch Republic with those elsewhere in Europe. If the tax burden were heavier in the Netherlands, particularly in Holland, then one might be able to argue that taxes caused the Dutch economy to stagnate in the eighteenth century. Unfortunately, the evidence needed for such a calculation is meager and riddled with almost impossible uncertainties, both for the Netherlands and for other countries. If we simply ignore the difficulties and use what little evidence exists, then it does seem that Holland was overtaxed in the eighteenth century. Measured in terms of wheat—if one can trust such dubious calculations—the tax burden in Holland in 1721 was much higher than in England or France. But the same was also true back in 1650, when the Dutch economy was thriving.[71] Moreover, even if the tax burden in Holland were higher, it might not be a cause of economic stagnation, for it could simply reflect the great wealth that the Dutch had accumulated.

In any event, it is certain that the lack of reform of the fiscal system in the eighteenth century influenced the foreign policy of the Estates General. After the near crisis of 1715 and the almost complete financial exhaustion of the government, the Netherlands' active role in world politics had to be given up. Without sweeping reforms of the fiscal system, the estates could never accumulate enough revenue to equip the armies and fleets necessary for such a role. Now and then the estates were drawn into European conflicts against their will, and the financial needs of such moments could only be met by new borrowing. Yet high as the financial need may have been, fiscal problems did not cause the eventual collapse of the Republic: constitutional deadlock, combined with invasion by foreign armies, finally accomplished the necessary sweeping reforms in the structure of government.

In its time the Dutch Republic had been the symbol of freedom, with little oppression by the authorities and even less police supervision. Because of its decentralized structure, its delicate internal system of checks and balances, and its international character, common to small mercantile countries, its inhabitants enjoyed a degree of liberty unknown elsewhere in the world, only spoiled to a certain extent by a degree of taxation unheard of elsewhere in Europe.

≺ APPENDIX 1 ≻

Some Figures For Comparison

Solid figures of revenue and expenditure of the Estates General are almost impossible to come by. The only official who was supposed to keep records of all income and expenditure was the receiver general, and his records were destroyed in the nineteenth century. Even if his records had been preserved, however, they would have to be used with the utmost care, as many items— both revenue and expenditure—were never listed at all. It almost seems as if the financial administration of the Dutch Republic was made as chaotic as possible on purpose, to make sure that no one was able to get a complete survey, not even the highest officials themselves.[72] Yet some figures may be given on Holland and will provide some insight at least into the finances of that province. Holland's revenue from the imposts, the "general means," seems to have been pretty stable over the years: it stood at 8,404,533 guilders in 1650 and had climbed to 9,280,129 fifty years later. For 1721 the figures are more specified: "general means," 10,633,155 guilders; the real estate tax (*verponding*), 2,694,331; and the "extraordinary means," 6,394,897, making a grand total of 19,722,383 guilders revenue.[73] To this should be added the yield of the convoy and license duties, 1,166,660 for the three Holland admiralties.[74] The grand total of revenue for Holland in 1721 was 20,889,043 guilders.

For expenditure, figures are more difficult to come by. For 1720, one year earlier than the figures for revenue, total expenditure of Holland has been given as 19,800,000 guilders, of which 13,700,000 went to the payment of interest and 5,500,000 for defense, including naval equipment.[75] This all for a population (Holland only) of some 800,000. Expenditure in 1720 was about the lowest of the eighteenth century, and it grew to a high total of 44,700,000 in 1794. Revenue also grew, but at a much slower rate, until a high of 28,200,000 was reached in 1758, afterwards dropping down to 21,400,000 guilders in 1794. All these figures mentioned apply to the province of Holland only, but with Holland's share in the total budget of the generality standing at 58 percent, they give some indication of the total annual budget of the Estates General. Obviously, it is impossible to measure the tax burden in the Netherlands as a whole, and nearly impossible to do so in Holland. All we can do is to take the meager evidence for Holland—itself subject to considerable uncertainty—and use it to estimate the tax burden. The resulting figures permit comparison with England, France, and Spain, but they must be used with the greatest of caution.

‹ APPENDIX 2 ›

The Burgundian and Habsburg Lords of the Netherlands

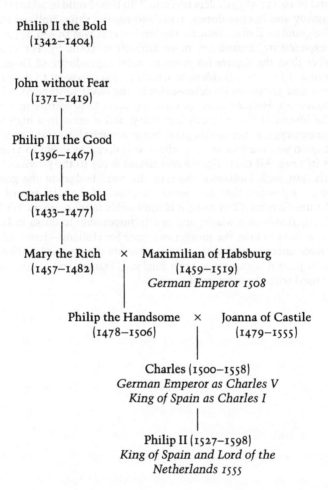

Philip II the Bold
(1342–1404)

John without Fear
(1371–1419)

Philip III the Good
(1396–1467)

Charles the Bold
(1433–1477)

Mary the Rich   ×   Maximilian of Habsburg
(1457–1482)   (1459–1519)
                        German Emperor 1508

Philip the Handsome   ×   Joanna of Castile
(1478–1506)   (1479–1555)

Charles (1500–1558)
German Emperor as Charles V
King of Spain as Charles I

Philip II (1527–1598)
King of Spain and Lord of the
Netherlands 1555

≺ APPENDIX 3 ≻

Stadholders from the House of Nassau-Orange

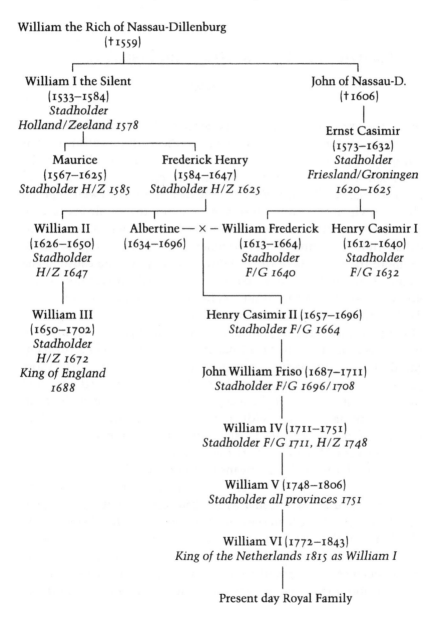

William the Rich of Nassau-Dillenburg
(†1559)

William I the Silent
(1533–1584)
Stadholder
Holland/Zeeland 1578

John of Nassau-D.
(†1606)

Ernst Casimir
(1573–1632)
Stadholder
Friesland/Groningen
1620–1625

Maurice
(1567–1625)
Stadholder H/Z 1585

Frederick Henry
(1584–1647)
Stadholder H/Z 1625

William II
(1626–1650)
Stadholder
H/Z 1647

Albertine — × — William Frederick
(1634–1696)   (1613–1664)
                            Stadholder
                            F/G 1640

Henry Casimir I
(1612–1640)
Stadholder
F/G 1632

William III
(1650–1702)
Stadholder
H/Z 1672
King of England
1688

Henry Casimir II (1657–1696)
Stadholder F/G 1664

John William Friso (1687–1711)
Stadholder F/G 1696/1708

William IV (1711–1751)
Stadholder F/G 1711, H/Z 1748

William V (1748–1806)
Stadholder all provinces 1751

William VI (1772–1843)
King of the Netherlands 1815 as William I

Present day Royal Family

Castile: Polity, Fiscality, and Fiscal Crisis

I. A. A. THOMPSON

FOR 150 YEARS, from the early sixteenth to the middle of the seven-teenth century, the king of Spain was the most powerful ruler in Europe. His empire stretched from the Low Countries, Milan, Sicily, and Naples to Mexico, Peru, and the Philippines in the west; and from Portugal to Goa and Macao in the east. His armies were reputed almost invincible, and his resources, notably the shiploads of gold and silver from the mines of Central and South America, seemed in-exhaustible. To maintain his hegemony, to protect his empire, and to promote the interests of the Habsburg dynasty and the cause of the Roman Church, the "Catholic King," as by Papal entitlement he was known, was engaged in almost continuous warfare. The Ottoman Turks and the Moslem states of north Africa, the Protestant princes of Germany, the king of France, the queen of England, and his own rebellious subjects in the Low Countries, Catalonia, and Portugal en-gaged him in a succession of military conflicts fought for the most part overseas, in Italy, Flanders, the Mediterranean, the Atlantic, and the Caribbean. Not until the recognition of Dutch independence in 1648, a humiliating peace with France in 1659, and the definitive loss of Portugal in 1668 was the constant pressure of war on the resources of the Spanish Monarchy, as the empire was always known, some-what relaxed, though by no means totally removed.

Early-modern Spain was a plurality, an aggregate of different con-stitutional and fiscal systems which had separate but not indepen-dent histories—Castile in the center; Aragon, including Valencia and Catalonia, in the east; and, from 1580 to 1640, Portugal in the west. Within this plurality, Castile had both the political and the economic preponderance. Size, population, wealth, history, perhaps even her constitution, made her the central pillar of the Monarchy. Castile had two-thirds of the territory of the Peninsula, three-quarters of the people, and the highest density of population; it was the residence of the king and the seat of government. It was, therefore, Castile and her American dependencies that provided the bulk of the resources needed to sustain the king of Spain's international position. Whilst the contributions of Flanders and the states of Italy to their own defense were far from negligible, it was only Castile that regularly exported millions of ducats in specie and credit to finance military activity in other parts of the Monarchy. Eighty percent or more of the money received by the military paymasters in the Netherlands between 1567 and 1659 was sent from Castile.[1]

The ability of the king to mobilize funds on such a scale was, of course, related to the enormous resources of his realms; but it is also often said to have been a function of the unlimited authority he was able to exercise in Castile. In the Crown of Aragon public finances were subject to parliamentary control, and consequently Catalonia, Aragon, and Valencia contributed next to nothing to the imperial budget. In Castile, on the other hand, royal absolutism, the bullion from America, and the defeat of the great revolt of the Comunero cities in 1521 are said to have freed the king from financial controls and destroyed the capacity of the Castilian parliament, the Cortes, to protect the country from an international policy which subordinated national interests to dynastic ends. Except for some fifteen years during the ministry of Olivares (1622–43), when the exhaustion of Castile forced Philip IV's government to try to extend its revenue base to Aragon and Portugal, it was Castile almost alone of the Spanish kingdoms which suffered the repercussions of the fiscal crises of the monarchy.

The connection between fiscality and absolutism has had a prominent place in the historiography of imperial Spain, as in that of other European countries. It was because they believed he had vast independent revenues, could tax at will, and was not beholden to his parliaments, that so many foreigners at the time held the view that the king of Spain had the power "Turk-like" to tread under his feet all the natural and fundamental laws, privileges, and ancient rights of his subjects. Yet not only is such a view now widely challenged by most recent historical scholarship; it would also have been in every respect totally at odds with the perceptions of contemporary Spaniards.

≺ I ≻

Liberty, Law, and Polity in Post-Reconquest Castile

Castile in the Middle Ages was, it can be claimed, the freest society in Europe.[2] A frontier society, its institutions and liberties were formed during the long process of reconquest and settlement which began in the eighth century and was not completed until the fall of the last Moorish kingdom of Granada in 1492. As the Visigothic peoples who survived the Islamic invasion of Spain in 711 began to push the enemy back, the need was to resettle the successive layers of reconquered territory and to organize the defense of the unconsolidated frontier. A new population had to be attracted by allowing them personal liberty and allocating lands to them on favorable terms, and charters of privileges and self-government (*fueros*) had to be granted to the new towns. Along the rolling military frontier between the two faiths the municipalities emerged, together with the lords, the church, and the great, crusading military orders, as essential pieces in the organization of resettlement and defense, and in the government of the countryside. The urban militias, composed of commoners and "villein knights" given the privileges and exemptions of nobility for as long as they maintained themselves with horse and arms, provided a vital counterbalance to the power of the great nobility.[3] Like corporate lordships, the greater cities of Castile governed extensive districts (*tierras*) and dominated sometimes scores of subordinate towns and villages, appointing their judges, controlling their finances, apportioning their military contributions, and supervising their justice.[4] Castile was "a great community composed of many cities," an aggregate of barely articulated city states, held together by the coordinating power of the monarchy.

At the same time, the Reconquest reinforced the supreme authority of the Crown. As a crusade it gave the nation a sacred purpose, and the monarchy emerged as the embodiment and director, but also as the instrument of that purpose. The traditions of centralism, unity, and community characteristic of the Visigothic monarchy were thus combined in the monarchy of the Reconquest with Christian providentialism and, from the thirteenth and fourteenth centuries, with a reinvigorated Roman law which reinforced both the idea of royal sovereignty (*soberanía*) and the Roman concept of *imperium* as public office. In accordance with Roman law precepts the vast tracts of empty and lordless territory which were acquired by war belonged to the king. Consequently, all grants of lands, jurisdiction, and privilege were seen as temporary and revocable cessions of the king's sovereign and inalienable jurisdiction. Even in periods of royal weakness in the late Middle Ages, it was accepted that the king had no superior in temporal affairs, was the source of all authority within his kingdom, exercised supreme jurisdiction, made and unmade the laws, and was the fount of all civil honors and offices.[5]

But if the king had an "absolute royal power" ("poderío real absoluto") to dispense with laws, by-pass ordinary channels of government, override property rights, do injustice to individuals, even abrogate his own contracts, that power was justified only by necessity and the common good. The common good was the absolute measure of the legitimacy of the prince's actions, as it was of the justness of the laws themselves. The monarchy was to serve the interests and wellbeing of the community. The king was the minister, the "mercenary" of his people, subject to the law and the common good.[6] Hence the personal and communal liberties that the kings had themselves granted were perceived as threatened not by the authority of the Crown, but by the usurpations of the great and the powerful. The danger to liberty came not from royal power, but from royal weakness, or the dependence of royal power on baronial faction; and the cities in the later Middle Ages, in perpetual conflict with their aristocratic neighbors over land rights and jurisdiction, were in general the keenest defenders of the king's supremacy, which was the guarantee of their own independence from baronial domination.

The medieval Castilian enjoyed both personal liberty and communal liberties. Personal liberties implied the direct vassalage of every man to the king; equality before the law and access to the king's sovereign justice; and the right to bail, to the safety of his home, and to a legal value on his life. Castile was a society of freemen. Feudalism never developed fully: there was no serfdom; the peasant was not subjected to personal labor services; he was free to leave the land, to dispose of his holdings at will, and even on occasion to choose his own lord. Lordship was, in the main, separated from landownership and was primarily a matter of jurisdiction.[7] The Castilian's life, labor, and goods were his own, properties of which he was not to be deprived without his consent, except for the common good as established by due process.[8] Communal liberties meant both the right of a community to be its own lord, and so to enjoy independent jurisdiction and self-government under the Crown; and the benefits associated with the particular customs, privileges, and ordinances of the municipality in which the individual lived, or the estate to which he belonged. These included the right to be judged in accordance with special laws and by special justices; to participate in local government by means of open meetings of the commune, the election of the town's governing body, or popular representation on the town's council; to have access to the municipality's often extensive communal lands and pastures; and to share in the fiscal privileges of the community or group of which he was a member. Liberty meant to be the citizen of a self-governing municipality, because it was only through its judicial autonomy that those benefits could be defended.

In practice, universal rights, like those of property, though not ignored, were not as central to the definition of liberty in Castile as they were in England, for example. Liberty in Castile was as much a social as an individual concept, expressed less in universal terms than in terms of particular, and often conflicting, rights and privileges, originally granted by the king, and thus more suitably defended juridically than politically, through the justice of the king's courts rather than through the representative assembly of the kingdom.[9] The profound belief in individual liberty as a supreme good that pervades Castilian political thought[10] was qualified, therefore, by the recognition that the exercise of that liberty had ultimately to be subordinated to the common good of the community. The absolute priority given to the common good was one of the key differences between the political cultures of Castile and England in the early-modern period. There is no sense in Castile that the common good might be inseparable from the private good of every individual. "Truly, for the common good private individuals may, and must suffer, even guiltlessly," declared Dr. Alvaro de Villegas in the Royal Council.[11]

What was in the common good, it was accepted, was for the king to determine in the light of reason and counsel; but, perhaps because there was no history of bondage, there seems to have been neither that obsessive fear for personal liberty, nor that anomic subservience that is found elsewhere. Freedom from tyrannical rule was maintained in theory by an instrumentalist view of government, the indefeasibility of property rights, and the autonomous subjection of the individual to the rule of law. Concretely, it was defended by the specific institutional forms which gave those ideas expression; the monarchy conceived as a public office, the assembly of the realm as the necessary agency for consenting to taxation, and the collected laws of the kingdom as the measure of the legitimacy of government action.

The freedom of the individual in his person and property was conceived as surrendered conditionally only for a specific purpose and in accordance with an implied contract of government between king and kingdom. A declaration by a representative of the city of Toledo in 1599 sets out the common understanding of the principles on which that contract was based:

It is a clear and proven fact, as the experts in divine and natural law teach, that king and kingdom, in temporal and secular affairs, are like a mystical body and its head. Thus there has to be understood between king and kingdom, as between monarch and monarchy, an agreement and pact by which the king undertook and bound himself to preserve his kingdom in peace and justice and to defend its inhabitants and their property on land and sea; and the kingdom bound itself to maintain its king and head properly as king, and to give him the wherewithal for the port and splendour of a king and the nerves for war and arms, which is money. And so, the obligation of the king, as of the kingdom, is one of justice and of conscience.[12]

The institutional expression of that contract and of the liberty of the Castilian not to be deprived of his goods and property without his consent was the Cortes, the representative assembly of the realm.

The Cortes had emerged as an institution in the late-twelfth and thirteenth centuries as kings sought to mobilize the political and financial resources of an expanding urban sector.[13] By the fourteenth century they had become an assembly to which normally only the towns were summoned. At one time the proctors (*procuradores*) of over 100 cities and towns were present, but during the fifteenth century the right of representation came to be concentrated in only eighteen cities, each of which sent two deputies. Somehow, and the process is not at all clear, those cities had come, through the administrative arrangements made for the allocation and collection of the "services" the Cortes granted, to establish themselves as the administrative capitals of eighteen fiscal provinces. The proctors of

the eighteen cities with a vote in the Cortes ("ciudades de voto en
Cortes") claimed, therefore, to speak for the entire body of the realm,
the *Reino*, but only as the agents of the capitals of eighteen discrete
territorial units. For this reason, and because of the small numbers
involved, it could be said that the voice of the realm resided properly
not with the proctors assembled in the Cortes, "el Reino junto en
Cortes," but with their principals, the individual "ciudades de voto
en Cortes" whose powers they bore. The cities were thus the real pro-
tagonists in a political system which was fragmented, localized, and
particularist. The Cortes were only a sort of negotiating committee
mediating the demands of the king and the separate interests of the
cities. The *Reino* was, therefore, an ambiguous concept; ultimate authority in practice lay with the "ciudades de voto" and the Cortes
were never the undisputed voice of the realm in quite the way Parliament was in England.[14]

The influence of the Cortes on government was limited by their
lack of legislative powers. The Cortes did not make law and were not
necessary for the making of laws, nor after the end of the fifteenth
century, with the advent of printing and codification, for their promulgation. The complaints of the Cortes that laws were being made,
or revoked, during sessions of the Cortes without their knowledge
were not claims that their authority was needed for the promulgation
of laws, only that, if the laws were to be well-considered, it was ad-
visable that they be consulted and that the king be fully informed of
their views.[15] The petitions presented to the king at the end of every
Cortes could with royal approval become the basis for new legislation; but the Cortes never made the grant of supply dependent on a
favorable response to those petitions, which often remained unan-
swered for years on end. The king could, therefore, rule without the
Cortes, which had no existence without his summons, met to do his
service, and were dissolved at his will. The requirement enshrined in
the *Nueva Recopilación*, the great collection of the laws of the kingdom published by Philip II in 1567, that the king consult the estates
of the realm to discuss "great and difficult matters," was too general
and undefined to be prescriptive in any particular situation.[16]

In effect, the influence of the Cortes derived almost entirely from
their fiscal prerogatives. The *Nueva Recopilación* declared that "no
impositions, contributions, or other taxes are to be imposed on the

whole Kingdom without the Cortes being summoned and without their being granted by the *procuradores*."[17] Yet that requirement was held to apply only to the "extraordinary" services granted by the Cortes, and not to a wide range of so-called *regalías* (customs duties, the *quintos* of the mines, coinage, the salt and other monopolies, expedients like the sale of royal graces), nor even, from the early fifteenth century, to the sales tax, the *alcabala*. Moreover, the need for the consent of the Cortes could be glossed not only to limit it solely to new, general, and permanent imposts, but also to argue that consent could not justly be withheld if the demand were just, the justice of the demand being a matter of which the Cortes could not be the sole judge. Indeed, on at least one occasion the king's prosecutor instituted a criminal suit in the Royal Council against the *procuradores de Cortes* for unjustly refusing their consent to a royal request.[18] But if the Cortes were not to be the arbiter of the king's need, what was not disputed was that it was for the *Reino* to determine how that need was to be met.

In the medieval Cortes the clergy and the nobility had participated sporadically as separate estates, but after the nobility led the resistance to the taxation proposed in the Cortes of 1538 neither of the privileged orders was again summoned. From 1539 until 1664, when the last Cortes of Castile to meet in the Habsburg period were dissolved, the Cortes comprised a single chamber in which individual aristocrats might sit, but only as representatives of the "ciudades de voto." One effect of the separation of clergy and aristocracy from the Cortes, a process actually beginning long before 1539, was to diminish the importance of the conciliar role of the Cortes, which was so important an element in the political power of Parliament in England. In Castile the function of counsel was largely absorbed by the development of the Royal Council, or Council of Castile, during the late fourteenth century.[19] It was the Royal Council, composed of men learned in the law, which took over the role of guardian of legality and of intermediary between king and kingdom. In England, on the other hand, the king's council never had the mythic respect that was accorded to the Council of Castile and was never recognized as having the same constitutional role, perhaps because the natural counsellors of the king, the lords and bishops, also had their voice in Parliament through the House of Lords. Whereas in England the determination of what was in the common good was something that Parliament never accepted as pertaining to the Crown alone, in Castile it was the Council, not the Cortes, by whose advice or concurrence the "common good" was authenticated, and by whose legal judgments the personal and communal liberties of Castilians were upheld.

That neither the consent nor the participation of the Cortes was necessary for the making of law was a crucial element in the power of the Crown in Castile. That power was reinforced by the revival of Roman civil law from the mid-thirteenth century. Its presumption that all law was legislation, unless there was concrete proof to the contrary, weakened the force of custom and of any rights not emanating from some royal act of grace or compact. Old prescriptions were gradually transformed into royal codes and ordinances. By the sixteenth century the great legal code of Alfonso X, the *Siete Partidas*, and the *Nueva Recopilación* of Philip II had come to acquire something of the standing of a written constitution, to which the Crown no less than the subject appealed repeatedly as authoritative "laws of the kingdom" (*Leyes del Reino*).[20] The laws of the kingdom, therefore, provided the basis for both redress and coercion, for appeal by the subject to the royal courts, and for the prosecution of the subject on charges of disobedience. They defined the relationship between the governor and the governed in the terms of concrete, legal injunctions and, therefore, in judicial rather than in political terms, terms to be regulated not by the Cortes, but by the courts.

Although legislation was the prerogative of the king alone, strict canons determined the legitimate form and substance of royal decrees and how they were to be received. The *Partidas* and the *Recopilación* laid down that royal commands contrary to divine and natural law; or against conscience, the church, or the faith; or uttered in anger were of no force. Commands contrary to established law and legal principles, to privileges, to the common good, or to specific laws, unless expressly excepted, were not to be obeyed until confirmed. Commands prejudicial to any individual not cited or heard in law were invalid, even with express clauses of derogation. In such cases there was recognized in the famous formula, "Obedézcase, pero no se cumpla" ("to be obeyed, but not put into effect"), a right, indeed a duty, of supplication to the king and the Royal Council.[21] Supplication did not nullify the royal order, it merely imposed a temporary suspension of its operation until the reasons for it had been heard and the order rescinded, or reiterated. The practice of supplication did, however, maintain the principle that legality was to be defended even against the intervention of the king himself, and that the king's orders were to be weighed against external standards of justice and public policy.[22]

The appeal against unacceptable royal commands was made to the king in his council. The Royal Council, as the highest judicial tribunal in the kingdom, was inclined to see itself as having a responsibility to the law that was independent of the king. Some even held that it was the vestige of the popular origin of royal power and in that sense "represented" the people. It certainly had pretensions to being an "intermediary" between king and people, the guarantor of the legitimacy and respectability of royal resolutions; and it claimed a right of remonstrance (*replicar*) reminiscent of that of the French parlements. The Council of Castile stood for legalism and due process against arbitrariness, and for a judicialist as against an administrative or executive mode of government, actively resisting any recourse to extraordinary or irregular procedures and consistently defending established rights and contractual obligations.[23]

The Royal Council was part of a system of councils through which the Spanish Monarchy was governed. Institutional expressions of the requirement that the king must take counsel and heed reason, they were not, however, merely advisory bodies. Each of the twelve principal councils in the capital represented a particular jurisdiction, or franchise; a form of procedure; and a separate, competing institutional interest. Conflicts of jurisdiction among the councils were systemic. They expressed fundamental differences of professional formation and political mentality, between legist and lay councils, law and prerogative, due process and pragmatism. Because a royal decree was never solely an order of the king, but also the expression of a council's competence in a particular area of business, these conflicts at the center were echoed in the field by the denial of the validity of royal decrees by recipients who belonged to a competing jurisdiction. Administratively this was a serious nuisance. Politically it provided a way for local resistance to play off the central tribunals against each other and so find legitimate means to thwart the execution of royal policies.[24] Thus the conciliar system itself served as a sort of official,

internal opposition, a channel for the expression of grievances, and
a protection for individual and corporate rights, as well as a buffer
deflecting any legal challenge away from the king's authority and
against the council which was implementing it.

It is important to stress the central role of the machinery of law
and administration in the defense of liberty in Castile, because so
often the history of freedom is seen as inseparable from the history of
parliaments. However, the relevance of the Anglo-Saxon, liberal, par-
liamentarist vision for the history of liberty in early-modern Castile
has surely to be questioned. The Cortes were neither the only institutional constraint on arbitrary rule, nor necessarily the best defenders
of "liberty." The demise of parliamentary institutions in Castile did
not therefore mean the demise of either personal or even (in the
broadest sense) political liberties. We need to think of liberty not just
in terms of modern parliamentary democracy but, as most contemporary political writers believed, as something which was not totally
incompatible with "absolute monarchy," and which, in some of its
personal and communal aspects, was actually promoted by the very
absolutism of the monarchical regime. Liberty was a question not
only of the relationship between the state and the subject but, no less
importantly, of the relationship between one subject and another. If
that was recognized much more clearly then than it is in our own
age, it is no doubt because the early-modern state was only one (and
not always the most oppressive) of the powers which impinged on
individual and communal freedoms.

< II >

The Finances of the Monarchy

The king's revenues were dependent, more or less directly, on the
economy. In the grossest terms, the Castilian economy was in a phase
of expansion from the later fifteenth century to the later sixteenth
century and then in a phase of recession until the later seventeenth
century. From the 1530s to the early 1590s, demographic growth was
of the order of 50 percent, from about four and a half million to something over six and a half million. In Old Castile, in the north, that
growth may have peaked between 1540 and 1570; further south it

may have continued somewhat longer, but the 1580s seem to have been a turning point in many, though not all, areas. A plateau in the early seventeenth century was followed by a period of sharp recession, troughing in the 1640s or 1650s, and then by a stuttering and unspectacular recovery from the 1660s or so.[25]

The wealth of Castile, like that of almost everywhere else in 1500, was preponderantly agrarian. Agricultural production probably contributed 70 percent or more to Castile's gross domestic product and, although it varied greatly from place to place and year to year, overall probably 70 to 80 percent of that production was grain, with lesser, but important, contributions from wine and sheep. Agricultural production followed a path roughly parallel to that of population. In the diocese of Segovia the wheat tithe peaked in the 1580s, was down by a quarter in the 1590s, and bottomed out in 1630–59 at 70 percent of 1570–99.[26] The land and the product of the land were not taxed directly, except for the two-ninths of the tithe paid to the Crown as the *tercias reales*.[27] This meant that by far the greater part of Castile's wealth remained outside the reach of the fisc. The result was that the Crown's revenues were extracted overwhelmingly from the market sector of the economy, and within that sector from sales of non-cereal foodstuffs and manufactured goods. On the evidence of Cordoba and Segovia, the two most important cloth centers in Castile, the 1580s were a turning point for manufacturing output and for trade as well as for agriculture. Cloth production in both cities reached a ceiling in the 1580s and then fell, though in Segovia, and perhaps in some of the smaller centers as well, it did not collapse until the 1620s.[28] In compensation, the historically important wool trade, which from the 1560s had been badly hit by taxation, war, and piracy, recovered somewhat from a low point in the 1580s and held up reasonably well until the second half of the seventeenth century.[29] The Indies trade, on the other hand, reached its peak around 1610, but its center, Seville, was already showing signs of weakness. By the 1630s registered tonnage engaged in the trade was only half of what it had been twenty years before, and by the 1650s only a quarter. However, bullion imports, crucially important for the Crown's international payments, after reaching record levels in the 1590s may not have fallen as much as once was thought, until the 1640s.[30]

The key phenomenon of the period was the general rise in prices, which in terms of silver approximately doubled in each fifty years of the sixteenth century. These remained comparatively stable after 1610, but nominal prices continued to rise. By mid century grain prices were 20 percent higher in Old Castile, 60 percent higher in Andalusia, and 90 percent higher in New Castile than they had been in the 1590s.[31] The significant feature of the seventeenth century was the disparity between silver and *vellón* (copper or copper-mix) price movements and the consequent devaluation of the *vellón* coinage relative to the silver. After 1625 the premium for converting *vellón* into silver never fell below 15 percent and rose on occasions to exceed 50 and even 100 percent (1626–28, 1640–42, 1650). As international payments by the Crown were required to be made in silver and domestic revenues were received almost entirely in *vellón*, the added strain on the fiscal system was considerable.[32]

In general the south of Castile was wealthier and more urbanized than the north, and towns wealthier than the country.[33] The disparity between north and south, which was probably widening throughout the period, but particularly from the 1560s onwards, meant that the north was always disadvantaged relative to the south by flat-rate taxation, which became a feature of the Castilian fiscal system after 1600 just at the moment when the economy of the north was in full retreat.[34] Widespread deurbanization throughout Castile in the seventeenth century and a regression to nonspecialized, subsistence production in much of Castilian agriculture also contributed negatively to a fiscal account which had to be paid in specie and in which revenue from trade was of prime importance. The changes that were taking place in the Spanish economy in the later sixteenth and seventeenth centuries therefore had fundamental effects not only on overall returns to the treasury, but also on the incidence of taxation and on fiscal policy. The decline of the cities and a contraction of the domestic market made it essential to find ways of tapping, directly or indirectly, coercively or voluntarily, noncommercialized rural production and noncirculating, hoarded wealth. Together with the need to expand the revenue base to include the privileged orders of society and those provinces whose constitutions had hitherto protected them from the fisc, these were the key considerations which underlay financial policy in the seventeenth century.

The fiscal system which this economy supported consisted of two parts, conventionally classified as "ordinary" and "extraordinary." The "ordinary rents" were essentially the creations or re-creations of the fourteenth century. They mark the shift, as the Reconquest drew to its close, from a fiscal system dependent on a military aristocracy and the profits of war to "a new fiscality of the state," based on economic development and the growth of trade.[35]

The period 1338–1406, from Alfonso XI to Henry III, was characterized by new financial institutions, the replacement of tax collection by the municipalities themselves with tax-farming, and new revenue sources derived almost entirely from trade.[36] The *alcabala*, nominally a 10 percent sales tax, originally granted on a temporary basis to Alfonso XI but perpetuated as a regalian right during the reign of Henry III, was much the most important, making up 80 percent of the "ordinary rents." Other prerogative revenues levied at the king's discretion: customs duties, the levy on sheep movements, and the salt monopoly, made up the rest. By the fifteenth century the system was well established, but as the new state expanded into new foreign involvements it was less and less adequate for royal requirements. This led to the increasing importance of "extraordinary" revenues, which by the death of Isabella in 1504 amounted to two-thirds of the "ordinary rents."[37] The "extraordinary" revenues were essentially income of two sorts. First, there were regalian rights of a casual or erratic nature (the *quinto* from the American mines, for example) and ad hoc expedients (*arbitrios*) pertaining to the *regalía* (the financial exploitation of the royal prerogative of grace through the sale of offices, the alienation of jurisdictions and rents, and so on). Second, there were concessionary grants by the Papacy (Cruzada Bulls, *Maestrazgos*) and by the Cortes, the *servicios*, which were in principle an imposition only on the *pechero* (the tax-paying commoner) and hence a mark of ignoble status, the clergy and nobility being exempt by right from direct, personal levies. The *servicios* were not taxes, properly speaking, but fixed grants made voluntarily by the *Reino* in response to a specific royal need and on specific terms, either through the Cortes or directly by the cities represented in the Cortes.[38]

Both the "royal rents" and the "services" of the *Reino* were "public" revenues. The king of Spain was exceptional in having virtually no private patrimony of any financial significance, no domain, manors, or estates that pertained to the king as a private individual, apart from the various royal palaces and his rights of justice. The notion that the king should "live of his own" was not, therefore, a strong one in Castile. What was reinforced was the concept of the king as a "public" figure, dependent on his subjects for his maintenance. Taxation, therefore, was not so much an exceptional, and exceptionable, imposition as the expression of the bond between king and kingdom, a condition of the compact between them, the dowry the king received for husbanding his country, or the salary the king was paid for doing his office.[39]

The distinction between "ordinary" and "extraordinary" revenues was an important one for contemporary accounting because it separated sources which could be permanently applied to known, permanent expenditures from those uncertain revenues which could be used only on the current account. The "ordinary rents" were, therefore, the essential foundation for the consolidation of debt, and it was their availability which determined the size of that debt. Consequently from the time Ferdinand and Isabella (1474–1504) instituted the bulk sale of interest-bearing bonds, or *juros* as they were known, as instruments of long-term credit, the "ordinary rents" were increasingly hypothecated at source to the payment of interest without passing through the central treasury at all. In 1522 one-third of the ordinary revenues was allocated to *juro* payments; by 1560, the entire ordinary revenue was insufficient for the obligations consigned against it.[40]

"Ordinary" and "extraordinary" are not, however, the best criteria for the analysis of the fiscal system. From the constitutional point of view, the distinction between the "royal rents," regalian revenues which were the king's by right and which he could exploit autonomously; "services," concessionary revenues which required the consent of the Cortes or the approval of the Pope; and "transactional" revenues, which involved a voluntary exchange, is crucial. From the administrative point of view, rents could be put into *administración*, that is collected directly by ministers of the Crown; farmed out (*arrendadas*) for an agreed figure to private financiers who collected the revenues by means of their own agents or sub-contractors; or compounded for a lump sum (*encabezadas*), raised and collected by the tax payers themselves, by the methods, at the rates, and on the commodities that best suited them. In general, the direct administration of revenues was avoided by the Crown as costly, inefficient, and uncertain in its returns, and unwelcome to the country as inflexible and intrusive. Tax-farming and *encabezamiento* (compounding) agreements relieved the Crown of the burden of administration, for which it lacked both the personnel and the expertise. They also had the advantage of promising fixed sums which could be offered as collateral for government loans, or of requiring the contractors themselves to make anticipations against their farms. Different methods of tax collection, therefore, produced different credit facilities, different degrees of control over abuse and corruption, and different political responses. The privatization of the administration tended to confuse public revenue with private interest but at the same time helped distance the king and his government from much of the hostility levelled against the exactions of the fisc.[41] From the economic point of view, the distinction between fixed revenues, insulated from the movement of the economy, and product revenues, which responded automatically to economic fluctuations, also had important political and constitutional repercussions.

These different lines of demarcation cut through the fiscal system in different ways. By and large the "ordinary" income was composed of permanent, regalian, product revenues, collected by tax-farmers and uniform in incidence; the "extraordinary" revenue was in large part concessionary, a fixed sum, granted for a set term and a stated purpose, and administered directly by the grantor according to a variety of local methods. There was a tendency, therefore, for the Crown to want to transform "extraordinary" into "ordinary," and for the *Reino* to seek the reverse. Crown policy was, however, somewhat ambivalent. Its goal was a national tax-based fiscal system that would be uniform, permanent, unhypothecated, and socially equitable. On the other hand, the administrative convenience of the *encabezamiento* and the budgetary certainty which made it a more reliable source of credit meant that the Crown was prepared in the last resort to settle for the sort of fiscal system that was the goal of the Cortes and the cities, a system based on "services," concessionary grants voted on a once-for-all basis and for a specific purpose, with their resourcing, incidence, and administration locally determined; a system, in other words, that was heterogeneous, decentralized, and subject to manipulation in the interests of the urban capitals and their ruling groups.

The outcome was a sort of fiscal entente reached between 1495 and 1536 by which the *Reino* agreed to a single composition for the whole of the *alcabalas* and *tercias*, the *encabezamiento general*. The *alcabala*, much the most important of all royal revenues, though theoretically a regalian right, now became in effect an "ordinary" *servicio*, fixed in sum for a given number of years, administered locally at rates far below the notional 10 percent and in a wide variety of ways which frequently altered its original nature as a sales tax. At the same time the *servicios* of the Cortes doubled in size and became a regular, triennial grant (actually called the *servicio ordinario*), also locally administered, often in ways which did not distinguish between the legally exempt *hidalgo* and the tax-paying *pechero*. The king thus got more money, but the *Reino* was left with the independent administration of the *servicios* and *encabezamientos* it voted; the Cortes, or in their absence, after 1525, their permanent standing-committee, the *Diputación*, having control over the general administration of the grants and the cities and towns the power to determine locally how they would be levied.[42]

The starting point for the analysis of early-modern Spanish finance is not income, however, but expenditure. Expenditure was determined in the first instance by priorities (personal and political) not immediately related to the calculation of available revenues. Those priorities were overwhelmingly military. According to a treasury account of the twenty years 1621–40, 47 percent of expenditure was spent on war; 45 percent on servicing the funded debt, itself contracted largely to finance war; and only 8 percent on government and household expenses combined.[43] There is no reason to believe that those proportions would be vastly different for any other decade of the period.

Treasury data, however, are merely expressions of the limited functions of the early-modern "state." Most government was local, private, or self-financing, and there is no doubt that the cost weighed much more heavily on the governed than is revealed in the official record. Monopoly rights, tax-farming, and corruption all imposed hidden, but probably very substantial, charges. Finance ministers and tax reformers asserted that only one-third, one-quarter, even one-fifth of what the country paid ever reached the king. It is impossible to know. What matters is that in that gap between payment and receipt, there seemed to many, and not least to the government itself,

TABLE I

Nominal Crown Income and Expenditure in Castile, 1504–1674

Total income (ducats)					
1504	1,450,000	1559	3,000,000	1607	12,500,000
1532/4	1,430,000	1565	5,600,000	1621–40	av. 17,100,000
1546	2,600,000	1577	8,700,000	1640s/50s	20,000,000
1555	2,300,000	1588	9,500,000	1674	23,000,000

Index Nos.	Expenditure	Income	Exp/Inc
1504	100	100	1.00
1532/4	106.3	98.6	1.08
1559	308.4	206.9	1.49
1565	482.1	386.2	1.25
1577	616.8	600.0	1.00
1588	1104.2	655.2	1.69
1601	1255.8	866.2	1.45
1607	1139.5	862.1	1.32
1621–40	2000.0	1179.3	1.70

SOURCES: M. A. Ladero Quesada, *La hacienda real de Castilla en el siglo XV* (La Laguna, Tenerife, 1973); J. A. Llorens, "Spanish Royal Finances in the Sixteenth Century," (Ph.D. diss., Harvard, 1951); R. Carande, *Carlos V y sus banqueros 2, La Hacienda Real de Castilla* (Madrid, 1949); M. Ulloa, *La hacienda real de Castilla en el reinado de Felipe II*, 2d ed. (Madrid, 1977); A. Domínguez Ortiz, *Política y Hacienda de Felipe IV* (Madrid, 1960); M. Artola, *La hacienda del Antiguo Régimen* (Madrid, 1982). Figures for 1559–1621 tabulated in I. A. A. Thompson, *War and Government in Habsburg Spain, 1560–1620* (London, 1976), table A, 288; for 1600, *ACC* 18:629; for 1674, C. Viñas Mey, *Imperio y Estado en la España del Siglo de Oro* (Madrid, 1941), 20. Partial expenditure figures in A. Castillo Pintado, "Mecanismos de base de la hacienda de Felipe IV," in *Historia de España Ramón Menéndez Pidal*, ed. J. M. Jover Zamora, vol. 25, *La España de Felipe IV* (Madrid, 1982), 217–55, at 247.

to be scope for a reform of the fiscal system which could, at one and the same time, fill the king's coffers, relieve the burden on his subjects, and restore administrative probity.

All the figures we have for total expenditure and income pose major problems of interpretation. The reconstruction of expenditure is particularly problematic on account of the great variation year by year in extraordinary military expenses, about which we are very poorly informed. Expenditure estimates can almost always be regarded as minimum figures; income figures are almost always nominal, and in the seventeenth century they become progressively more unrealistic. Nevertheless, it looks as if between the start of the sixteenth and the later part of the seventeenth century, total royal expenditure in Spain increased over twenty fold, from less than one million ducats at the death of Isabella (1504) to about 24 million ducats at the death of Philip IV (1665). It did not rise again until the eighteenth

century and may even have fallen back to a nominal figure of around
20 million ducats during the reign of Charles II (1665–1700). Until
the mid 1530s the increase was slight; but by the 1570s, and allowing
for the general inflation of prices, expenditure had quadrupled. It increased by 25 percent by 1600, and by a further 40 percent between
the 1620s and the 1640s. Table 1 represents the approximate pattern
of the growth of both expenditure and income.

≺ III ≻

Fiscal Crisis

Income growth consistently lagged behind expenditure. This was
most marked in the periods 1539–59, 1566–88, and 1618–32; but from
the mid 1530s, with a new anti-Ottoman offensive in the Mediterranean coterminous with the shift of the European battlefront from
Italy to Provence, Flanders, and Germany after the renewal of hostilities with Francis I, there were only brief periods when the problem
of balancing income and expenditure did not seem to be critical. If
by "fiscal crisis" we simply mean an unbridgeable gap between unavoidable expenditure and disposable income, then the Spanish Monarchy was in an almost continuous fiscal crisis. From the accession
of Philip II in 1556 to that of Charles III two hundred years later, not
a single king of Spain came to the throne without his revenues mortgaged for years ahead.[44]

It was not, of course, either necessary or possible for expenditure to be met out of current income. Expenditure was erratic; and
its peaks did not necessarily follow the trend lines. The problem for
the financing of the Spanish Monarchy was not to balance an annual
budget, but to be able to borrow however much was needed for immediate needs by anticipating future income, and to have the money
delivered to whichever part of the Monarchy it was required in an
acceptable medium. Credit was, therefore, the first, not the last, response to the pull of expenditure. As an anonymous memorialist put
it, "of all wealth the greatest that there is is credit."[45]

The king of Spain's superior access to credit was one of the major
factors which gave him the advantage over his international rivals.
From the time the Fuggers of Augsburg underwrote the election of

Charles V as Holy Roman Emperor in 1519, the king of Spain was able to rely on the services of the greatest banking houses of Europe to operate the international payments mechanism without which it would have been impossible to employ the resources of the Castilian empire to finance expenditure in Italy and the Netherlands. Short-term loan and exchange transactions (*asientos*), backed by the assignment of anticipated revenues from American silver or Castilian rents and guaranteed by the issue of security bonds (*juros de resguardo*) that could be sold on even before the credit had been supplied, were negotiated with the German bankers who dominated Spain's international finances during the reign of Charles V, with the Genoese, who took over the lead until the reign of Philip IV, and with the Portuguese, whose importance really begins in the 1620s.[46] The ability of the Spanish Crown to replace creditors worn out by its own defalcations with a succession of fresh opportunistic lenders, and thus to draw on the capital generated and then released by the progressive stages through which the world economy was passing in the sixteenth and seventeenth centuries, was the benefit it derived from heading a world empire and the secret of its survival during the critical decades of the 1550s and the 1620s.

However, after the 1640s, the Portuguese, cut off from new capital generation by the loss to the Dutch of the profits of the Far East and Brazil trades, were unable to continue to finance the Monarchy.[47] The weakening of Spain's monopoly over the Indies trade and the consequent diversion of American silver to France and the Netherlands, together with the separation of Portugal in 1640 and increased pressure from the Inquisition against crypto-judaizers, led many of the most important Portuguese financiers, almost all of whom were Jews, to abandon the service of Spain. With their departure the Jewish financial network which had linked Madrid, Lisbon, and Amsterdam ceased to function.[48] The Crown's credit was being de-internationalized, and as registered bullion imports from the Americas fell and domestic silver stocks were depleted by the overvaluation of base monies, Spain was being cut out of the silver circuit. That can be clearly seen from the budgetary shortfalls on the silver account, compared with those in *vellón*,[49] and from the desperate, and sometimes arbitrary, expedients employed to try to solve the silver shortage. The repeated manipulation of the *vellón* coinage, which called into question in some quarters the royal prerogative over money; the use of the sale of privileges as a way of destocking, by requiring a portion to be paid in silver; the attempt through the *erarios* (a scheme in 1622 to establish a network of low-interest, rural loan banks) to create an alternative capital market for borrowing, were all ways of trying to mobilize domestic specie stocks.[50]

With an insufficiency of internationally negotiable silver, credit was having to become increasingly internalized and decentralized. Although the difficulty of raising silver for external expenditure was acute, the *vellón* which sufficed for internal needs could be procured from Castilian financiers by advanced payments from tax-farms and by a shift from state credit to municipal and private credit as "donatives" and the myriad government transactions with communities and individuals were in effect financed by loans taken locally and serviced by entailed estate revenues and municipal rents and excises (*censos*). By making the local authorities, the lords and the city oligarchies, the pivots of royal fiscality, the Spanish Crown was able to maintain its domestic expenditure from domestic credit, but only at the expense of allowing these local authorities the freedom to control and manipulate the local economy and local revenues.[51]

Conventionally, the series of Crown "bankruptcies"—1557, 1560, 1575, 1596, 1607, 1627, 1647, 1652, 1660, 1662—though not all of the same order or kind, have been taken as an indicator of the persistence and the periodicity of fiscal crisis.[52] However, this very periodicity, until the end of Philip IV's reign an almost rhythmic recurrence, suggests that, rather than manifestations of "crisis," these "bankruptcies" were an integral part of the financial system of the Monarchy.[53] The term "bankruptcy" can be misleading. These events were bankruptcies insofar as they were a rescheduling of debts, but they did not mean that the Crown was without resources. Determined unilaterally by the Crown, they did not involve any legal process, nor any sequestration of the Crown's assets; neither did they stop the Crown taking on more loans. They were in some respects more like new rights issues. Until their nature changed in the second half of Philip IV's reign—perhaps the *real* mark of "crisis"—they were paradoxically symptoms of the Crown's creditworthiness. They involved two steps: first the *decreto*, the unilateral suspension of payments on the short-term and floating debt, usually on the grounds that these payments were usurious; second, the *medio general*, an agreement with the Crown's creditors, sometimes after prolonged and rancorous negotiations, to consolidate the floating debt at a lower rate of interest by substituting *juros* for the revenues previously pledged to its repayment, and to accept the revenues thus released as collateral for new short-term loans. The bankers were authorized in turn to repay their own creditors with the *juros* they had been allocated. The more powerful of them, and some key figures were always exempted from the full terms of the *decreto*, were thus not only able to negotiate private terms with the Crown, including the partial reassignment of their debt, but also able to profit from the discount market in *juros* at the expense of their own creditors and other weaker firms who could not or would not lock themselves into another cycle of high-interest, high-risk loans.[54]

The consolidation of the debt was the key to the long-term ability of the Spanish Monarchy to live beyond its immediate means, for it made possible a continuous renewal of the cycle of borrowing in advance of progressively retreating and hence progressively less attractive incomes. The *juro al quitar*, a negotiable, undated bond assigned against a specific source of "ordinary" revenue at a fixed, nominal rate of interest, usually about 7 percent from the mid sixteenth century, 5 percent from 1621, was the instrument which made possible that consolidation.[55] The *juro* enabled the Crown to mobilize for its credit the idle wealth of a large proportion of the rentier classes of society—the clergy, the nobility, the urban gentry, the upper bureaucracy, and their widows; as well as of religious and charitable institutions and endowments, almost all of which had some investment in *juros*, and in some cases depended on them for their entire incomes. The bankers were the principal mediators in this process. When the firm of Vitoria was caught in the suspension decree of 1596 it owed in excess of a million ducats to over 600 persons, at least 400 of whom were "friars, monasteries, almshouses, widows and orphans, and other such people who are not in business."[56] Between 1504 and 1667 the annual interest owed to the holders of *juros* increased thirty fold. Table 2 gives the figures in ducats.

By the mid seventeenth century, the nominal capital invested in *juros* probably exceeded 150 million ducats. To a greater or lesser degree practically the whole of the political nation must have had some

TABLE 2
Juro Interest Obligations 1504–1667

1504	300,000	1594	3,915,000
1529	621,000	1598	4,635,000
1554	877,000	1623	5,600,000
1560	1,668,000	1637	6,400,000
1573	2,752,000	1667	9,100,000

SOURCES: F. Ruiz Martín, "Crédito y banca, comercio y transportes en la etapa del capitalismo mercantil," La documentación notarial y la historia, Actas del II Coloquio de Metodología Histórica Aplicada 2 (Santiago, 1984): 725–49, at 739; A. Castillo Pintado, "Los juros de Castilla. Apogeo y fin de un instrumento de crédito," Hispania 23 (1963), 60.

involvement in the public debt. In the north Castilian city of Burgos, with a population of only 800 families or so in 1650, there were some 120 juro-holders with a nominal investment approaching two million ducats, all but two or three of them from the caballero elite which ran the city.[57] The juro, therefore, committed the city oligarchies to the fiscal system from which their interest was paid, but it also made them resistant to any fundamental reform of that system and hostile to the king's international creditors whose preferential treatment was encumbering their revenue assignments and whose rapacity was draining away the country's wealth.

Each "bankruptcy" was necessarily associated with new, compensatory juro issues, which the bankers then sold on, and therefore with some package of permanent revenue increases on which those juros could be assigned. In terms of their resourcing, these "bankruptcies" differ in kind and consequently in their political implications. Three phases can be distinguished. Until the medio general of Philip's III's reign (1608) the "bankruptcy" settlements were financed by the natural growth of "product revenues."[58] These were private arrangements between the king and his creditors in which the Cortes had no direct part, though the popularity of the decretos gave them some political value in helping to lever tax concessions out of the Cortes. With the cessation of the natural growth of the "ordinary" revenues it became necessary to seek to apply "extraordinary" revenues to the funding of juro payments, and this meant the direct involvement of the Cortes. This was done, in the first instance, by getting the Cortes to apply some proportion of their concessionary grants to the release of the "ordinary rents" through a sort of sinking fund. The involvement of the Cortes in such a release, or *desempeño* as it was called, had been proposed on a number of occasions since the 1550s, but not until the reign of Philip III was agreement reached. As a result, the "bankruptcy" of 1607 was resourced not by the Crown but by the *Reino*, the Cortes taking upon themselves the securing of 12 million ducats at 5 percent to repay the bankers and free revenues, pledged in some cases as far ahead as 1614. In return the king ceded one million ducats a year of the existing grants the Cortes had voted, 600,000 to service the principal and the remaining 400,000 ducats for the sinking fund to begin the *desempeño*.[59] The political consequences for the Crown were serious. With a contractual responsibility for the royal debt, the Cortes, always inveterate enemies of the international banking interest, insisted on having a supervision of new royal borrowing and controlling dealings with the bankers who were the mainstay of the Crown's financial independence.[60]

The best alternative for the Crown was to secure the consent of the Cortes to the simple perpetuation of their extraordinary grants, so that they could then be alienated to purchasers of new *juros*. This happened for the first time in 1626, the year before Philip IV's first "bankruptcy," when the Cortes gave their consent to the sale of 500,000 ducats of rent on the grant known as the *millones* at 5 percent. By the end of Philip IV's reign, 1,370,000 ducats of the 4 million ducats of the *millones*, all four extensions of the *alcabalas*, known as the *cientos*, and 345,000 ducats on the *servicios* had been alienated in this way. To that extent the renewal of existing parliamentary grants became a formality, an inexcusable obligation to the *juro* holders, among whom the elites of the cities represented in the Cortes were perhaps the single largest group.

A second device which avoided the intervention of the Cortes in the Crown's business with its bankers was the direct release of the revenues assigned to the *juros*—first by the general reduction of the rate of return in 1621, and then, from the 1630s, by the retention of substantial proportions of *juro* payments, supposedly against compensation with other *juros*.[61] In effect, this meant the compulsory reinvestment of *juro* rents in further purchases of *juros*, which now not only were returning one-half, one-third, or one-quarter of their par rate, but also were effectively unassigned. To sh re up the discredited structure of the *juro* market, there was cons uc ed a complicated scaffolding of priority assignments, discounts, exemptions, reservations, and non-revenue compensations which sustained some measure of negotiability for the *juros*, especially where administrative or political influence could be brought to bear, but which was incapable of preserving the viability of the *juro* as a long-term instrument of government credit.

The "bankruptcy," therefore, was a viable extension of credit so long as there was a sufficient flow of additional, permanent revenue sources on which to assign the new issues, and so long as confidence in the *juro* remained strong. When that ceased the *juro* and the suspension decrees simply became arbitrary exactions. Depending on the consistency of the revenue source on which they were assigned, the *juros* were holding up reasonably well overall and still trading near par into the 1590s. But in Philip III's reign they were already being widely discounted. However, the 1630s was probably the crucial decade, with 16 million ducats of interest payments held back by the Crown after 1633. By the 1680s, even the best *juros* were said to be saleable for only five or six times their nominal rental value, an interest rate of 16 to 20 percent.[62]

Philip IV sold more *juros* than any other ruler; he was the first king to make their purchase obligatory, and he was the last to issue them.[63] With the *juro*, the "bankruptcy," and the *asiento* the Spanish Monarchy was sustained by the most advanced credit system in sixteenth- and seventeenth-century Europe, enabling it to maintain both an international multilateral payments system and a permanent state debt, which mobilized a substantial proportion of domestic savings. The ending of the regime of the *juro* was, therefore, decisive, for it put a strict limit on the public borrowing power of the Crown. The ultimate fiscal crisis was not simply an inability to balance the budget, nor a failure of the Crown to repay its short-term debts, but a cessation of credit, an inability to prolong the cycle of income anticipations because of the impossibility of further consolidation of the floating debt. It was at this stage that expenditure, and hence policy, became contingent upon income.

There were only two definitive responses to fiscal crisis: to increase income, by fiscal measures or by borrowing; and to reduce outgoings, by expenditure cuts, administrative reform, or default. A secular phase of economic expansion facilitated income growth and

TABLE 3

Distribution of Income by Type, 1517–1674

(in percentages)

	1517	1560	1572	1577	1601	1621	1640	1674
Product Revenues	26.0	44.6	46.3	41.6	35.8	33.5	20.1	34.9
Concessionary Revenues	63.7	30.5	26.3	36.8	50.3	50.6	43.4	48.0
Expedients		10.4	8.8	7.4	2.4	2.4	24.8	8.9
Papal Graces	10.3	13.3	17.5	14.2	11.5	13.6	10.9	7.9

SOURCES: See Sources, Table 1.

royal fiscal autonomy. During the upswing the traditional, product-based, regalian rights were readily expandable, either by natural increase or by the independent action of the Crown, and a buoyant market helped boost the voluntary taxation of the *arbitrios*. Domestic reaction diminished rapidly as the real burden of any increase was eroded. The reversal of the secular trend, on the other hand, brought with it the end of "easy taxation." Product-based revenues stagnated or fell; *arbitrios* were more difficult to dispose of; and the Crown had to request, or demand from the realm, "services" and "donatives" which, fixed in quantity and falling on a reduced and impoverished population, were more resented, less productive, and (because their administration was subject to negotiation) potentially, at any rate, constitutionally limiting. The growth of income, therefore, took place in a series of distinct phases, each marked by the predominance of different types of revenue, and hence of different political relationships (see Table 3).

In the first phase, from the 1490s to about 1540, "concessionary" revenues predominated. By the death of Henry IV in 1474, decades of aristocratic usurpations had brought the royal fiscal system to the edge of dissolution; but during the 1480s the Catholic Kings succeeded in doubling their income and restoring the ordinary revenues to the best levels of the early fifteenth century. Unlike their predecessors, they were thus able for much of their reign to ignore the Cortes as a source of extraordinary supply. The succession wars and the conquest of Granada were sustained by military and financial contributions from the nobility and from the cities associated in the league of the *Santa Hermandad*, and by indulgences sold for the crusade by Papal grant. From 1480 to 1498 no Cortes at all were summoned. Foreign wars after 1495, however, could not so readily be financed by those means. New extraordinary supplies were needed and the Cortes had to be recalled. Faced now by strong monarchs, firmly on the throne, the Cortes dropped the pretensions to control the spending of "services" that they had so aggressively pursued in the fifteenth century, and subsidies were voted at the demand of the monarchs without any limitations on their use. In return, the Cortes cities were allowed a greater involvement in fiscal administration, the allocation of quotas for the *servicios* being done by the capitals of provinces and sub-districts (*partidos*), and the detailed assessment and collection by the local councils. A parallel development was the transfer of the administration of the *alcabalas* to the cities through local composition agreements, the *encabezamientos*, which committed the individual cities to paying a fixed sum in lieu of the variable amounts the sales taxes would have realized if they had been left to the market, but which also enabled them to determine on what and at what rates the taxes would be levied.[64]

The consequence of this accommodation was that after the death of Isabella (1504) the revenues stagnated. With the accession of Charles V in 1516, the demands of imperial policy led the young king's ministers to attempt to secure both extra supply and firmer control over the Castilian fiscal system. The establishment of a Council of Finance on the Flemish model, in 1523, and of a single office of record, in 1517 (reorganized in 1543), were major steps towards a more coherent central administration.[65] However, the attempt in 1519 to end the decentralized, local administration of the *alcabalas* (the single most important source of royal revenue) by putting their collection into the hands of tax-farmers was abandoned as part of the rapprochement with the cities after their revolt in 1520–21 against the Emperor's unprecedented financial demands. The outcome was the restoration of the *encabezamiento* on a permanent and general basis in 1536 and as a result the virtual petrification of the *alcabalas* for the rest of the reign.[66] An attempt in 1538 to establish a new general excise on foodstuffs (the *sisa*) to be imposed indiscriminately on all social groups and conceived perhaps as a means both to tax the fiscally privileged and to liberate the Crown from dependence on the traditional *servicios*, granted by the Cortes every three years and paid (in theory, at any rate) only by commoners, was also a failure. It ended with the final separation of the nobility and the clergy from the Cortes and a quid pro quo with the cities, as a result of which the *sisa* was withdrawn and a new ceiling, at more than double the previous sum, agreed for the *servicios*. They were to remain at that level for the rest of the Old Regime.[67]

The result of the agreements of 1536 and 1539 was that the *alcabalas*, though in theory a regalian right, took on the form of a "service," and the Cortes and the cities effectively controlled both the grant and the administration of the two items which together made up some 60 percent of royal revenue. What this meant was that whereas Charles V's government had not succeeded in tying royal income to the growth of the economy, and consequently in freeing the Crown from the Cortes, the Cortes cities had successfully defended the economy against the fisc, and local interests against central control. Indeed, until the 1560s the cities were not uncommonly in surplus on their *encabezamientos* and able to offset other local or central government charges against them.[68]

Having failed to put his finances on a new footing in 1538, Charles V chose to avoid further conflict with the cities. After 1539 concessionary revenues from Castile stagnated. During a reign in which the general price index rose over 70 percent, royal income increased by little more than half, and the real value of parliamentary grants fell by one-sixth. Charles V's campaigns in the 1540s and 1550s were financed, without extra aid from the cities, by borrowing on the international market on a massive scale and on progressively more exorbitant terms.[69] Those loans were underwritten partly by the first substantial returns of bullion from the New World, which between 1536 and 1555 brought in for the Crown on average five times more than they did in each of the previous ten years; and partly by the exploitation of traditional regalian rights through a series of ad hoc expedients (*arbitrios*) for which the consent of the Cortes was not required. Some of these were transactional: sales of such things as lordships, towns of the Military Orders, jurisdictional independence, waste lands, municipal offices, patents of nobility, rights to *alcabalas*, and licenses to ride mules. Others were arbitrary, like the sequestration of private bullion from the Indies.[70] Though mitigated by the corruption and evasions allowed by officials on the spot, the special consideration given to the Indies traders and the great international merchants by the government, and the *juros* given in compensation for the confiscated silver, the repeated seizures of private bullion during the 1550s resulted in acute crises of liquidity in Seville and caused serious dislocation of Atlantic commerce.[71] Despite their effects on the economy, such expedients were henceforth to be permanent standbys of royal fiscality and almost the first recourse in moments of crisis throughout Philip II's reign, and again under Philip IV.

Charles V's legacy to his son, therefore, was a nonconfrontational policy toward the cities, the alienation of the royal patrimony, stagnant revenues, and enormous debts. At his accession, Philip II's short-term debts amounted to 7 million ducats, and the prospects of refinancing were greatly diminished by a sharp drop in bullion imports, down by 60 per cent in 1556–60, and by the refusal of Paul IV to renew permission to tax the clergy. For only half the necessary repayments were there disposable funds until the end of 1562, and *juro* obligations substantially exceeded the "ordinary rents" on which they were assigned.[72] The "bankruptcies" of 1557 and 1560 were the price Philip had to pay for the failure of Charles V's political nerve after 1520.

The fiscal effect of the two debt conversions of 1557 and 1560 was to add 1,220,000 ducats to the annual obligations against the Crown's "ordinary rents." Philip II, therefore, had no choice but to begin his reign by seeking substantial increases in regular taxation. Economic growth enabled him to do this largely by the independent exercise of his rights over "product" revenues. His reign can be seen as a continuous attempt by the fisc to take its full share of the profits of growth. By creating new trade taxes, increasing tariffs, re-incorporating alienated duties into the royal domain, asserting royal monopoly rights, and getting the cities to accept a new fifteen-year *encabezamiento general* from 1562, 37 percent higher than that which had run since 1536, Philip increased his ordinary revenues by nearly 1,500,000 ducats, or some 50 percent, by the mid 1560s. Furthermore, the renewal of the *subsidio* for the maintenance of the galleys in the Mediterranean and the *cruzada* for the war against the heretic in 1560, and the addition of the *excusado* in 1567 to help finance the suppression of the revolt in the Netherlands, marked a new relationship between the Catholic King and the Counter-Reformation Papacy. The "three graces," as the *subsidio, cruzada,* and *excusado* were known, were to increase steadily in value to over 1,600,000 ducats a year in the 1590s. At some 15 percent or so of total income they were a major extraordinary source of supply largely independent of domestic, if not international, political implications.[73] The "three graces," the increase in product revenues, the doubling and redoubling of American bullion returns from the later 1560s, and the recurrent resort to transactional expedients saw Philip through a decade of spectacular military and civil expenditure without the need for further parliamentary grants. By 1575, however, the Crown again had short-term debts of more than 15 million ducats.[74] With foreseeable extraordinary revenues pledged in advance and the financial and military position in the Netherlands falling apart, the collateral for new *asientos* had to be released by another debt conversion, and that could only be done if ordinary rents were available on which to assign the new *juro* issue. With foreign trade affected by the war in the Netherlands, Philip was unable to raise customs duties as he had at his accession, and a domestic economy, which, paying the *alcabala* at an effective rate of only 2 to 2½ percent, was in real terms 20 percent less burdened than it had been half a century before, seemed a fair target for extra demands.[75] Philip's proposals for new taxation, either on flour or from a higher sales tax, would, like Charles V's *sisa*, have given the Crown a permanent source of income that would fall universally on all social groups and would not constantly need renewal in the Cortes. Failing to get the agreement of the Cortes cities, the king unilaterally abrogated the existing *encabezamiento* contract in 1575 and tripled the *alcabalas*, to 3,700,000 ducats. The refusal of the cities to compound at the new rate and the inability of the administrators collecting the tax directly for the king to reach their targets, or indeed in some cases even to match the levels of the previous *encabezamiento*, forced Philip to settle from 1578 for a new, short, four-year contract of 2,700,000 ducats, still one and a half million ducats more than the previous one, but administered by the *Reino* and negotiated in the same way as a "service."[76]

Fleet reductions in the Mediterranean, an extra million ducats a year from American silver, and a massive wave of short-term borrowing enabled Philip to finance his wars in Portugal, the Netherlands, France, and England between 1579 and 1588 without additional taxation in Castile, or new "services" from the Cortes, but only by resorting to transactional expedients and *arbitrios* to an unprecedented degree. More than half of all the *baldíos* (waste lands) and nearly a third of the *alcabalas* sold by Philip II were disposed of in the 1580s.[77]

The years from 1539 to 1588 were thus a period of "regalist" fiscality characterized by the predominance of "product" and "transactional" revenues. Throughout the period virtually all new royal revenue was derived from trade taxes, mining rights, expedients, and grants from the Papacy paid either per capita (*cruzada*) or from the product of clerical rents (*excusado*). In the third quarter of the sixteenth century independent "regalian" sources, which did not depend on parliamentary grant and, where appropriate, were administered for the Crown by contracts with private tax-farmers (port and customs duties, pasture rights, monopolies), made up well over half of all royal revenues. Even including the *alcabala* increases, technically part of the *regalía*, parliamentary sources accounted for only one-quarter of all revenue growth between 1539 and 1588.

However, the scale of military spending in these years was such that the period from 1577 to 1588 saw the sharpest jump in the expenditure to income ratio throughout the entire sixteenth and seventeenth centuries. The consequence was that in October 1588 Philip II was forced to appeal to the Cortes for an immediate subvention in order to rebuild the Armada and continue the crusade against England. The cities agreed to an extraordinary grant of 8 million ducats to be paid over six years from 1590 and to be raised at their own individual discretions. Known thereafter as the *millones*, this was the first, new, parliamentary grant for fifty years. It was the start of a new period of "concessionary" fiscality.

The reversal of the long phase of economic growth brought with it the end of easy taxation. By the 1590s product revenues had reached a ceiling, and in some cases were already beginning to turn. A decade later the decline was general. The market for *arbitrios* was collapsing. The market had been flooded, the best buys had gone, and the opposition of the Cortes to the sale of offices and the alienation of the royal patrimony had to be heeded whilst delicate negotiations on the *millones* were in progress. By the 1590s all the standard expedients had dried up. Municipal offices could not be sold and their prices were stagnating; the *baldíos* sold in the 1590s amounted to not much more than a third of the figure of the previous decade, and *alcabalas* were selling for 25 percent less than in the 1550s.[78] By the start of the seventeenth century the American trade was also ceasing to be an unstanchable fountain of wealth. Royal silver returns in the first five years of the seventeenth century were only 54 percent (and by 1616–20 less than 40 percent) of those of the last five years of the sixteenth, and the take from the *alcabalas* and customs duties of Seville had begun to falter.[79]

With the cessation of growth of the "regalian rents," the Crown again became dependent on the "services" of the Cortes and had to face increasing political pressure to cut expenditure, stop the *asientos*, and reform inequities and abuses. From 1590 parliamentary grants become progressively more important; by 1601 they once again made up more than 50 percent of royal revenue, and by the middle of Philip IV's reign they had regained the levels of the early sixteenth century. By the time of their dissolution in 1664, the Cortes were granting on a recurrent basis a nominal total of around 15 million ducats a year.[80]

In the sixteenth century Crown policy had been to shift the balance of fiscality from fixed "services" to taxes that were responsive to the favorable economic conjuncture; in the seventeenth century regalian rents and product taxes were having to be transformed into "services" in order to fix them against the falling trend. Royal monopolies, like salt, tobacco, chocolate, ice, brandy, were incorporated as elements of the various *millones* grants. The *millones* themselves, in 1601 a variable, product revenue granted in the form of standard taxes on certain comestibles to be collected directly by the cities, by 1611 were underperforming so badly that they were changed into fixed, local commitments (*repartimientos*), even though that meant accepting a 20 percent reduction in the sum agreed.[81]

The collapse of the market also led to an attempt, not always successful, to shift the incidence of taxation from trade to consumption and wealth, from manufactures to agriculture, and from town to country. The excises on wine, meat, and oil, introduced in the *millones* agreement of 1601 and to remain the nominal basis of the tax system throughout the century, locked on to precisely those elements of agrarian production which were the most buoyant in the seventeenth century, just as the *medias anatas* (a new levy on the first year's income of offices and pensions), and the various "donatives" levied on ministers and officials in central and local govern-

ment were mulcting the one group in Castilian society that was in-
dubitably prospering. Despite the failure of the attempt to tax the
subsistence economy by collecting at the point of production rather
than at the point of sale, the *millones* and the *sisas*, which funded
most of the municipal "donatives" and *arbitrios*, still fell more nearly
in proportion to population than did the *alcabalas* and other market
taxes of the sixteenth century and so did something to redistribute
the burden of taxation from the declining town to the countryside.[82]
The *sisas*, charged initially by cutting standard wine and oil measures rather than by increasing the price, were also a way of getting
round the lack of cash in the economy and did something to mitigate
the sensitivity of the populace to higher taxation.

The highpoint of the "contractualist" phase that had begun in
1590, characterized by a series of formal contracts between the king
and the *Reino* setting out the terms and conditions on which the various "services" were granted, was probably reached during the Cortes
of 1638–43. From 1643 there followed a twelve-year period without
new parliamentary grants. More important, during the 1640s the in-
capacity of Castile to bear the fiscal burdens that had been heaped
upon her was revealed in a general collapse of tax returns. By 1649
the *millones* and other "services" of the Cortes, totalling a nominal 9.6 million ducats, were bringing in only 3.1 million, and it was
calculated that Castile as a whole owed the king in excess of 36 million ducats in tax arrears. Additional general taxation was patently
counter productive.[83]

As recession deepened, from the 1620s, the Crown was led to
employ an increasingly arbitrary and coercive fiscality in order to
buck the trend of economic depression. The *medias anatas*, retentions of interest on *juros*, compulsory purchases of *juros*, compulsory "donatives," revisions of land titles and alienated *alcabalas*,
bullion seizures, even the appropriation of funds deposited for pious
and charitable effects were characteristic fiscal devices of the 1620s
and 1630s. These measures in effect amounted to a massive erosion
of the fiscal exemptions of the privileged classes in Castile. At the
same time, Philip IV's great reforming minister, the count-duke of
Olivares, began his assault on the exemptions of the privileged kingdoms of the Crown of Aragon and extended the measures applied in

Castile to Portugal and the provinces in Italy. Though Olivares's great scheme for mutual military cooperation projected in the Union of Arms never became a reality, his success in increasing the military and financial contributions of these areas should not be underestimated. The Monarchy was able to fight on in the dark middle third of the century in part because of a real, if not spectacular, shift in the burden of empire away from Castile.[84] The political reaction in those kingdoms, however, led to revolts which, breaking out almost simultaneously in Catalonia and Portugal in 1640, were to drain even more of Castile's resources for wars which now were being fought within Spain itself. Thus the revitalization of the royal finances, to which the Union of Arms and the domestic expenditure cuts, also a central feature of Olivares's program, were intended to contribute, was not achievable either by constitutional change or by an economic reform, which was in the main both budgetarily and politically unsuccessful.[85] The treasury kept afloat only by default and by the devolution of spending functions.

Ironically it was when government was localized that its burdens were felt most acutely. By the 1640s, with the Crown defaulting on its bills, its subjects defaulting on their taxes, and the fiscal system in virtual collapse, the protracted war now being fought on Spanish soil made possible a new phase of what might be called "barter fiscality." The narrowing of the market sector and the chronic shortage of specie in the country could now be offset by a reversion to a sort of non-monetary fiscality, with demands for direct, local contributions of men, hay, and transport for the wars, and billeting, wage, victualling, and provender costs for troops in frontier provinces offset against tax obligations.[86] In these circumstances general taxes had little value, and the Cortes of Castile as an institution for the authorization of general taxation no useful function.

The collapse of general taxation led to a shift of emphasis from a national to a devolved, decentralized, or localized fiscality. This was characterized not only by the imposition of direct burdens in money, men, and kind on individual cities, towns, and villages for the support of the military on their local front; but also by towns and cities taking on the farming of their own taxes, a sort of *encabezamiento* on a piecemeal basis;[87] and by the development of the "donative," the supposedly "voluntary" contribution, into what was virtually an alternative revenue system. Used occasionally in the past, during Olivares's ministry "donatives" were demanded with growing frequency, thirteen million ducats being raised from them between 1625 and 1635. But it was only from the 1640s and 1650s that they became regular events. There were at least four in the 1650s, three in the 1660s, four in the 1670s, usually of one or two million ducats a time. Because it was theoretically a free, personal gift and not a general levy, the donative could be demanded of communities and individuals on the basis of wealth without detriment to status or exemption, and without the consent of the Cortes. It was, however, a fiscal device the very resort to which revealed the weakness of the "tax state." Each community and private individual negotiated his contribution separately, together with the means to be employed to raise it, thus effectively undermining the donative's potential equitableness. The consequence was the fragmentation of fiscal space and the weakening of the sense of the *Reino* as a politically active whole.[88]

Peace with Portugal in 1668 opened the way finally to a "reformist" response to economic collapse and fiscal saturation, which implemented, through a program of tax cuts and administrative simplification, at least some of the ideas that had been common coin for half a century. In some places taxes were cut by 30 percent. *Juro* payments were drastically curtailed and old *juros* annulled. The "ordinary rents," in some cases carrying nearly double the *juro* commitments on them that they were worth, were disencumbered by a draconian system of priority payments guaranteeing that the needs of the Crown would be met first.[89] Some progress was also made towards a partial simplification of local, fiscal administration, bringing the "rentas reales" and the "servicios del Reino" (the *alcabalas, cientos,* and *millones*) together under a single head at the level of the province. The *encabezamiento general* was brought to an end and the general administration of the *alcabalas* and *tercias* taken over by the Crown and out of the hands of the *Diputación* of the Cortes, where it had been since 1525.[90] The effect was to subject the cities in financial matters to the supervision of a royal minister, and to centralize the control of the revenues in the king's Council of Finance. This was a process which had already been going on for a long time, in the case of

the *millones* from the 1630s, in that of the *alcabalas* from the end of
the sixteenth century.[91] There was, however, no increase in the level
of the *alcabalas* and it does not seem that their *local* administration
was much affected. Nor was the centralist direction of administrative
change necessarily irreversible. A number of different administrative
solutions were attempted during the course of the reign: the appointment of provincial *superintendentes generales*; the transfer of responsibility for all the revenues in his district to the *corregidor*, the royal
governor in the cities; agreements with the towns for the general *encabezamiento* of all their rents. It is clear from these repeated changes
that none of them worked, but equally that there was no irreducible
objection in principle to allowing the cities to administer their revenues themselves had that turned out to be financially satisfactory.
Indeed, the main motive for ending the *encabezamiento general* and
farming the *alcabalas* was not a desire for centralization, as such,
but the need for the credit that the tax farmers would advance.[92] The
reign of Charles II was a reign without Cortes, without new taxation,
and without new *juros*; it could be reformist precisely because it no
longer sought the means of maintaining Spain's great-power pretensions, did not have to make political compromises in return for new
revenues, and was helped by a slowly, if erratically, improving economy.[93] Charles II's ministers, Medinaceli, Oropesa, and Los Vélez, did
not solve the fiscal problems of the Monarchy, which were as acute in
the 1680s and 1690s as ever they had been; but they did clear some of
the ground for the centralized fiscality of the eighteenth century.[94]

≺ IV ≻

The Tyranny of the Fisc

Royal income from the Crown of Castile more or less tripled in
nominal terms from 1575 to the 1660s. Between those two dates the
population of Castile had fallen by perhaps a quarter, but prices and
money wages had doubled. In real terms, therefore, the per capita tax
burden had also roughly doubled—though, it should be said, from a
level that was somewhat lower than it had been in the 1520s.[95]

For what they are worth, the best estimates suggest that in the last quarter of the sixteenth century average income per household (*vecino*) was in the region of 60 to 70 ducats a year, giving a national figure of 80 to 90 million ducats. In that case, royal taxes would have come to something like 8 percent of national income in the 1580s and 12 percent in the 1660s—probably not much more than in France, but perhaps four or five times as much as in England at the same time.[96] Moreover, the increased burden would have seemed all the more heavy for being more apparent. Almost the entire increase came from taxes that were paid directly on personal consumption or by levy, excises, sales taxes, and *repartimientos*, whereas the customs and wholesale trade taxes paid by the merchants at the ports remained virtually stationary. In Segovia, for example, the *servicios*, *alcabalas*, and *millones* increased more than six-fold over the period, a per capita increase in real terms of over 350 percent.[97]

In reality the attempt to estimate the overall burden of taxation in this way makes little sense. In the first place, the actual tax-take was very much less than the sums that had been granted. In view of the shortfall in receipts, the enormous backlog of unpaid taxes, much of it irrecoverable, and the widespread evasion practiced under the cloak of clerical and aristocratic privilege, it is likely that by the 1640s only 30 to 60 percent of expected revenue was actually reaching the treasury.[98] In 1660 the kingdom of Murcia owed over one million ducats in back taxes for the years 1642–58. Only 150,000 could be recovered; the rest had to be written off.[99] On the other hand, the country was certainly paying far more than was officially being received, three times as much according to some contemporary calculations, five times as much according to others; the surplus lined the pockets of the tax collectors and receivers, the rich, the powerful, and the producers. In the second place, it is impossible to make general statements with any confidence about how these taxes were collected, or on whom and on what they fell. The disparity even between neighboring villages could be enormous.[100] The *alcabalas* and the *millones*, which should have been paid from taxes on sales and comestibles, seem in many places, particularly in villages where the market was weak and trade insufficient to meet the agreed quota, to have been raised by borrowing, serviced by local taxes on consumption or by rents from communal properties.[101] For this reason it is logically impossible to separate local and central government taxation, or, except in specific instances, to calculate the total tax burden, or its incidence, especially when it was in effect met from the loss of communal amenities. No less important in evaluating the impact of the fisc on the local economy is the question of the recirculation of tax revenues. It is too often forgotten that the *juro* was a means of channeling taxes back into the community that paid them, and for most parts of Castile the only means of doing so, and hence retaining scarce specie and spending power within the locality. The returns did not, of course, go directly to the same people that paid the taxes, nor in the same quantities. Sixteenth-century Valladolid, for example, received more in *juro* payments every year than it paid in taxes. In Burgos in 1650, the interest due to the *juro* holders amounted to the equivalent of about 250 days of labor for every family in the city.[102] The over-commitment of the *juro* assignments by the seventeenth century and the regular retention of 50 or even 75 percent of the payments due on them from the 1630s must, therefore, have had a devastating effect on the local economies, concentrating more and more wealth in Madrid. The explosion of fraud, contraband, and tax evasion that becomes apparent in the seventeenth century was one way of counteracting the damage to the local economy from high taxation and the loss of purchasing power. To what extent the effects of the tax system were mitigated by these means it is impossible to know. By the 1680s, with taxes possibly doubling the cost of meat and wine, the problem of contraband had become so serious and so widespread that a special *Junta de Fraudes* was established to combat it, with spectacular results. Within six months it was claimed that the proceeds from the meat tax in the provinces of Cordoba and Seville had risen by two-thirds.[103]

The real burden of complaint was directed less against the actual level of taxation than against the chaotic multiplicity of revenues and the inflated and vexatious administration that collected them.[104] Given its inability to get agreement on a more simple tax structure, it was to the advantage of the government to create new taxes unencumbered by *juros* rather than to increase rates on existing ones. The consequence was the proliferation of taxes each with its separate administration, farmed or sub-farmed at the level of the province, the district, or the town, with receivers, accountants, notaries, and treasurers for each; and the generation of what seemed to contemporary critics a vast army of taxmen.[105] Furthermore, every administrator, tax-farmer, or financier with an assignment against a particular source of revenue might be authorized to enforce payment through his own separate executors or bailiffs. The costs of collection and enforcement were said, probably with some truth, vastly to exceed the tax itself.[106] In the city of Murcia, in 1618, there were seventeen bailiffs trying to collect a mere 3,000 ducats. In the district of Arjona, there were in 1647 no less than 70 bailiffs, some of whom had been there over four years; their salaries were costing 40,000 ducats a year. Rather than against taxation per se, it was against their "esclavonia" to the private profiteers of the public purse that Castilians complained; and against the "saqueo general" of the bailiffs, executors, and tax collectors, entering houses to check on contraband, demanding bonds pending judicial settlement of disputes, distraining property, or compelling the public sale of household goods for debt.[107] Liberty was to be "free from such continuous slavery to these multiplying bloodsuckers, swarming, ruinous locusts, as that to which these suffering vassals are subjected."[108] When Castilians talked about "tyranny" in the seventeenth century, it was invariably some immediate, local, private oppression that they had in mind. The vital political issue in seventeenth-century Castile was not the constitution, but the administration.

At the core of this volume is the proposition that fiscal crises brought about adjustments to power relations in the early-modern state that led to forms of government, more or less absolute, or more or less limited, which in varying degrees hindered or advanced the progress of liberty. Fiscal crisis may itself be generated by political and constitutional limitations on the fisc; or attempts to overcome the crisis may lead to a restructuring of the polity, either affirming or breaking down such limitations. Financial crises may then induce administrative changes leading to more or less centralization, more or less intrusive methods of assessment and collection, or more or less equity and participation. They may also generate a variety of fiscal expedients which have as their consequence the cracking of traditional social and economic rigidities, freeing tied communal lands, entailed capital, and mobility blockages; alternatively they may lead to the creation of new economic and social obstacles. To assess the applicability of these propositions to Castile we have had to examine the structure of the fiscal system, the nature of the fiscal crises, and the range of financial and administrative measures taken in response to those crises. However, our purpose has not been to treat of the fiscal system for its own sake, but to focus on the impact that fiscal crises and the changes they imposed on the structure of the revenue system had on those two concepts of liberty, the political and the private. The former can be defined negatively as the ability to restrain arbitrary government, and positively in terms of the participation of the governed in their own government; the latter involved both the enjoyment of particular privileges and liberties, and the extension of freedom of access to those liberties. The political impact of fiscal crisis as it affected the relationship between the Crown and the representative assembly of the realm and the relationship between fiscal crises and liberty in its wider constitutional, governmental, and social dimensions are the subjects of the next chapter.

≺ APPENDIX ≻

The Burden of Taxation in Castile 1557–1664

1557   tax revenues 2.5 million ducats (937.5 million *maravedís*)
       (*servicios, alcabalas/tercias, tres gracias, rentas arrendadas*)
       population c. 6 million
       wheat (New Castile 1554–62 [six years])
       284 *mrs/fanega* (= 55.5 litres)
       wages (Valladolid building craftsmen 1551–60) 56 *mrs*/day

1664   tax revenues 20 million ducats (7,500 million *maravedís*)
       (*servicios, alcabalas/tercias/cientos, tres gracias, rentas
       arrendadas, millones, nueve millones plata, quiebras, dos
       millones y medio, ocho mil soldados, lanzas, papel sellado,
       pasa, donativos, nuevas sisas*)
       population c. 5 million
       wheat (New Castile 1656–65 [10 years])
       870 *mrs/fanega*
       wages (Valladolid building craftsmen 1661–65) c. 220 *mrs*/day

Taxation *per capita*

1557	1664	1664/1557	
156	1,500	9.62	*maravedis*
0.31	0.96	3.14	hectolitres wheat
2.8	6.8	2.44	days labor[109]

Castile: Absolutism, Constitutionalism, and Liberty

I. A. A. THOMPSON

IN THE CLASSIC Whig tradition the history of freedom has been inseparable from the history of parliaments. According to that view the propensity of monarchical regimes to absolutism was checked only where the continued vitality of the estates enabled them to deny kings the right to tax at will and make and unmake laws at their own discretion. It was the ultimate predominance of representative institutions within the state which not only guaranteed the civil rights of property and the person but was itself the very essence of modern political freedom. Thus the assumed debility of the Castilian Cortes, crudely portrayed as a supine tax-voting machine composed of venal and complaisant self-servers, has led to a perception of Castile as a country without political liberties, ruled by an all-powerful prince whose financial independence released him from the need to compromise with his subjects and under whom there was neither personal freedom nor security of property.

So long as historians believed that the Cortes of Castile no longer had any political significance in the sixteenth century, the relevance of fiscal crises to the development of representative government and political and personal liberty was not an issue. The recurrent fiscal crises into which their wars led the Spanish Habsburgs were seen solely as problems in the relations between the Crown and its creditors, not as occasions for the renegotiation of the political balance between the king and his kingdom. In the last few years, however, a revision of the history of the Castilian Cortes, at least as profound in its implications as that which has occurred in the history of the Tudor and Stuart Parliament in England, has been taking place.[1] What is now patently clear is that there was no such thing as "fiscal absolutism" in Castile. The king was not free to tax at will, and although he had a number of important financial resources which were his of right, these "royal rents" were over the long term secondary to the aid that had to be sought from the kingdom. The rehabilitation of the Cortes as a major actor in the political history of Habsburg Castile has given a new constitutional dimension to fiscal crisis. The demonstration that from the reign of Charles V through that of Philip IV (1516–1665) the Castilian Cortes, far from being an impotent irrelevance, were of continuing and, indeed, of increasing importance, now gives an enquiry into the connection between fiscal crises, the vitality of representative institutions, and the history of liberty in Castile a validity which it could not previously have had. It also raises a question which is central to the western constitutionalist concept of liberty; namely, why was it that the Cortes failed in the end to establish themselves as an indispensable instrument of national government in Castile in the way Parliament succeeded in doing in England.

≺ I ≻

Crown, Cities, and Cortes 1520–1621

At the end of the fifteenth century the Cortes of Castile appeared to be in terminal decline. The attempts of the Crown to pack the Cortes and to use them as political tools in the civil and succession wars had made them suspect with the cities for whom they were never anything more than a glorified negotiating committee. For eighteen years between 1480 and 1498 no Cortes were summoned; instead, the Catholic Kings dealt directly with the cities through the Santa Hermandad. The revival of the Cortes, which were to meet nine times in the next eighteen years, was related not only to the Crown's need for subsidies for its foreign wars and the more secure position of royal authority in Castile, but also to the concessions made to the cities in the matter of fiscal administration. This entente with the cities was undermined after the death of Isabella (1504) by a series of policies damaging to the cities' interests, notably by the Crown's support for aristocratic usurpations of municipal rights and its threat to abrogate the local encabezamientos in favor of tax farming.[2] At the same time confidence in the independence of the Cortes waned. There were bitter complaints of undue interference by the Crown and denunciations of the venality of the *procuradores*, who were for the most part not elected but chosen by lot from within the quasi-hereditary, municipal ruling oligarchies.

In the spring of 1520 the surrender of the Cortes to the unprecedented "services" demanded by a foreign king, the Habsburg Charles V, to sustain his ambitions as newly-elected Holy Roman Emperor triggered an uprising that swept across Castile. From the viewpoint of municipal politics, the Comunidades or Revolt of the Comuneros, as it is known, was both a civic reaction against the Crown policies that had alienated the cities after 1504 and a popular reaction against the "Court" factions in the ruling oligarchies of the cities and the unrepresentative Cortes with which those oligarchies were associated. The program of the *Junta* of the Comunero cities, submitted to the Emperor in the so-called "Project for a Perpetual Law" of October 1520, would have established a reformed, responsible, and incorruptible Cortes as the guardian of the constitution. Deputies, elected without royal interference by local assemblies of each estate, would be subject to strict and inviolable mandates and, debating and voting free from ministerial supervision and constraint, would be accountable to their cities at the end of every Cortes. The Cortes would meet every three years with or without the king's summons to ensure the government's adherence to the terms of the "Perpetual Law." In its broad aims the Comunero program looked back both to the pretensions of the late-fourteenth and fifteenth-century Cortes and to the medieval conception of a monarchy limited by the law and by the prescriptive rights of the society of orders. Without pre-judging its potential for developing in the direction of "modern freedoms," and it has been considered by some to be "a first modern revolution,"[3] we can say that the Comunero program marked the limits of what "medieval liberties" aspired to. The "Project for a Perpetual Law" never contemplated the extension of the proprietary representation of the eighteen cities in the Cortes into a truly national representation, nor did it seek for the Cortes anything but a passive role in government. It wanted for the Cortes the right not to govern but to monitor, not to legislate but to counsel; but most of all it wanted the Cortes to be responsible to the cities. The Cortes would not even have been allowed to vote new revenues; both the Cortes and the state were to be kept in their places.[4]

Much of the future history of the Cortes can be seen to have been

a playing out of the issues of the Comunero Revolt. Though decisively defeated the revolt served as a warning both to the Crown and,
because of its social content, to the governing bodies of the cities.
Rather than crushing municipal independence, it had in many ways
precisely the opposite effect.[5] The Crown was tentative in pushing
too hard against the resistance of the cities in areas in which law
and custom were plainly on their side. For their part the cities were
doubly suspicious of the loyalties of their unelected *procuradores*,
extra sensitive to popular pressures, yet astute enough to use the
threat of popular disturbance in their dealings with the Crown and
its *corregidores*. When faced with determined resistance to its fiscal
proposals the Crown compromised, or even backed down. Whilst the
economy was buoyant the Crown could find alternative and independent sources of supply. The loss of the *sisa* in 1539, for example, was
followed by a massive exploitation of *arbitrios* in the 1540s and 50s.

The consequence was that the Cortes became marginalized; without the lords they were irrelevant to the politics of the Court, and
their financial contribution was of declining importance. The monies
they voted, even including the massive increase in the *encabezamiento general* in 1577, amounted to not much more than one-third
of total royal revenues. When, as in the 1550s and 1560s, weightier
matters were put to the *procuradores*, a request for an extraordinary
"service," or for the *desempeño* of the royal revenues, they referred
the matter back to their cities. Until the 1570s Cortes were frequent
but brief: twenty Cortes met between 1518 and 1571; only two lasted
more than seven months.

In the 1570s things were beginning to change. The average of the
six Cortes between 1573 and 1590 is nearly twice as long as the long-
est ever previously recorded. There is a clear association here with
the acute financial problems of the middle years of the decade and
with a new attempt by the Crown to treat the Cortes rather than the
cities as the real (and more manageable) representatives of the *Reino*.
The control of the Cortes was again becoming a serious issue. There
were complaints about the Cortes being packed with royal servants.
The *ex gratia* payments given each *procurador* by the king increased
in value, to 200 ducats in 1573 and 1,000 ducats in 1579. Communi-
cation between the Cortes and the cities without royal authority was
forbidden. In response there was a general movement by the cities

to reassert control over their *procuradores* through the restriction of their "powers" (*poderes*), and the imposition of instructions and oaths of obedience. Against this background the 1576 Cortes, fronting the resistance of the cities to the great *alcabala* increase, were peculiarly contentious and have been argued to be a turning point in relations between the Crown and the *Reino*.[6]

Nonetheless, taken as a whole, the period from the 1520s to the 1580s was one of equilibrium and compromise. If the Crown failed during that time to secure a fundamental revision of the fiscal system, or of the place of the Cortes and the cities in that system, it nevertheless succeeded in quadrupling its income in real terms without compromising its authority and was also moving toward securing greater central control over administration.[7] The Cortes, for their part, made no headway with any of their fiscal grievances. They were unable either to get a reduction of the *encabezamiento* or to have it made perpetual, and their repeated denunciation of the regalian trade taxes imposed by Philip II at his accession without their consent proved unavailing. No more successful was their attempt to vindicate their non-fiscal, constitutional claims: direct access to the king, direct access to the records of previous Cortes, a view of legislation enacted or revoked during Cortes, the resolution of their petitions and grievances before they voted supply or before they were dissolved. If in 1577, after two years of resistance by the cities, Philip II had to accept an *encabezamiento* increase one million ducats less than he had demanded, that increase came without any strings attached. Moreover, in this case, the king was constrained not so much by the constitutional power of the Cortes to hold back the *servicios*, as by the overestimation of returns from the direct administration of the new *alcabala* and by the need for a settlement with his bankers. The bankers, it should not be forgotten, contributed to the financial independence of the Crown only within the limits of constitutionality. It was repeatedly their insistence that their promised collateral be properly voted before committing their funds that compelled the Crown to summon the Cortes to renew the "services."[8]

This balance between king and kingdom was disturbed during the 1590s by the involvement of Spain in new and expensive warfare in the Atlantic and by the oncoming of economic recession.[9] The widening gap between income and expenditure and the impossibility of bridging it by means of the existing fiscal prerogatives of the Crown meant that it was now impossible to get by without a direct appeal to the kingdom and without making the concessions over fiscal policy necessary to gain the good will of the Cortes cities. The *millones* of 1590 was the first *new* "service" offered by the *Reino* for fifty years. In return the king had to accept a number of private conditions imposed severally by the individual cities. By the time the *millones* came up for renewal in 1596, these local conditions had been formulated by the Cortes into a formal contract between king and kingdom the conditional nature of which was unambiguous—"this service is granted by the *Reino* for as long as the conditions of this contract are observed, and if any of them are broken it shall *ipso facto* cease, and the *Reino* will have no obligation to continue with it."[10] This first *millones* contract, only finally ratified and published in 1601, served as the model that was repeated, subject to renewal and revision, at each successive regrant of the *millones* and every time a new "service" was introduced.

The private conditions imposed by the cities in 1590 and the formal contract with the *Reino* in 1601 now made explicit the contractualism implicit in the concept of the "mystical body" and ingrained in the Castilian political tradition. The notion of a fiscal contract was, of course, inherent in the *encabezamientos generales* of the *alcabalas* going back to 1536; but the *millones* contracts went far beyond their predecessors not only in being concerned with the administration of the "service" itself, but also in specifying the purposes to which the money was to be applied and in making the grant conditional on the promulgation of a large number of general measures deemed to be for the common good of the kingdom. The conditions of the *millones*, more than one hundred in some contracts, were concerned with all aspects of the government of the country: economic regulation, the administration of justice, social policy, even the organization of defense—all the matters, in fact, which before had been put to the king as *petitions* in the *capítulos generales* submitted at the end of each Cortes. What had previously been petitions were now made express *conditions* of the *millones*, or other "services," dispensation from which required the specific consent of the Cortes. From 1601, therefore, the relationship between Crown and

Cortes had been put onto a formally contractual basis, not totally dissimilar from the "pactismo" usually associated with the Cortes of the Crown of Aragon.

The *millones* not only initiated a new compactualism between king and kingdom; they also led to a formal definition of the constitutionally ambiguous relationship between the Cortes and the cities. When the request for a new aid was put to the Cortes in October 1588, the *procuradores* would only proceed on the understanding that they would discuss means but "neither concede nor determine without informing their cities and without having their consent for each and every part," and they insisted that the cities each be allowed to select the measures to be used to raise the money. This procedure was repeated when the *millones* came up for renewal in the next Cortes, but this time the cities refused to ratify what their *procuradores* had granted. The same thing had happened in 1539 and in 1573 over the "sisa" and the flour tax, but it was not until the late 1590s, with the appearance of the terms "voto decisivo" and "voto consultivo," that new constitutional concepts emerged to give formal expression to the subordination of the Cortes to the will of their cities. That subordination was given constitutional status in a formal "protestation" made by the first Cortes of Philip III in 1599, and thereafter prior to every major vote until 1629, expressly reserving the final decision on any "service" voted by the *procuradores* to the governing bodies of the Cortes cities. Though in practice this is what had happened in the sixteenth century when extraordinary matters arose, from the theoretical point of view the "protestation" was a new and unambiguous statement that the Cortes were the voice of the cities and not of the kingdom, that the *Reino* was not represented by the Cortes but by the cities represented in the Cortes.[11]

The formal recognition of the cities' right to the "decisivo" in no way diminished the deliberative or administrative functions of the Cortes, particularly after 1601 when the *millones* became a system of general taxation levied on specified items of consumption, rather than a series of separate agreements with the cities. The "Reino junto en Cortes" remained the only legitimate agency for the formal concession of services, and it was in the Cortes that the measures were initially proposed, the conditions and "supplications" drawn up, dispensations from the conditions granted, and the form of administration worked out, before being submitted to the cities for their ratification.

Between 1590 and 1621 the Cortes and the eighteen cities with a vote in Cortes secured a position in the state such as they had not had since the end of the fourteenth century. The regime of the *millones* gave the Cortes the exclusive administration, some say in the appropriation of the grants and, through the conditions imposed, some voice in legislation and some restraint on the king's use of the *regalía*. By making supply dependent upon the promised redress of grievances, expressed in the form of conditions and hence appealable to the law, the Cortes had succeeded in vindicating their long-standing demand that the king respond promptly to their petitions, and thus in overcoming one of the principal theoretical weaknesses that historians have attributed to them. The promulgation of the conditions in the form of royal decrees which were to have the same force of law as if included in the *Recopilación* of the Laws of the Kingdom, in effect gave the Cortes the power of legislation. In addition, the formal consent of the Cortes, or the cities with the vote in Cortes, was required for practically the entire gamut of expedients that properly speaking pertained to the *regalía*, but which were now expressly prohibited by the conditions of the grants.

Adding to their role in the administration of the *servicios* and the *alcabalas*, the *millones* contracts now gave the Cortes, in the name of the *Reino*, a great part of the financial administration of the state. In each town the *millones* were administered by a special commission consisting of the royal justice and two *regidores* (city councilmen) appointed by the town council—a function all the more valuable in that whereas the *alcabalas* were assigned at source to *juro*-holders, the *millones* were free and therefore profitably liquid in the hands of their collectors. From them a hierarchy of supervision and appeal led finally and definitively to the Cortes and their *Diputación* or, from 1611, their *Comisión de Millones*, to the express exclusion of the royal Council of Finance. The Cortes were thus established as the "verdadero administrador" of the *millones*, "administrators general . . . and judges for His Majesty over all that pertains and is dependent upon them."[12]

Also written into the *millones* contracts was the hypothecation of specified sums to predetermined expenses (frontier defenses, the fleets, the royal household and administration), and the control of the Cortes over the administration and distribution of the *millones* made it possible to prevent these being raided for other purposes. More and more the grants made by the Cortes to Philip III and Philip IV came to follow this pattern, tying (in theory) a large proportion of royal revenues to approved charges.

The regime of the *millones*, therefore, meant the acceptance by the Crown of almost all the fiscal priorities of the cities. Although the shift from a purely locally determined "service" in 1590 to a universal, tax-based agreement in 1601 was an important step towards the creation of a uniform, Castilian fiscal space, the *millones* were temporal, conditional, and politically and administratively rather "hacienda del Reino" than "hacienda del Rey"—revenues of the kingdom rather than revenues of the king.[13]

Though we should not assume that what we have here is a "struggle for the constitution" between king and parliament, neither should we be led too far along the recent paths of revisionism into accepting at face value the prophylactic and sanitized language of harmony in which the king's subjects wrapped their opposition. There is an increasing self-importance and pretentiousness in the Cortes in these years, an insistence on defending "the authority and reputation" of "that which must be the intermediary between king and kingdom." The king's ministers certainly believed that the Cortes— or important elements within the Cortes—were obstructive, suspicious of the government, inveterately oppositional, and perhaps even a real threat to the authority of the Crown. There were even some *procuradores* arguing against making any fixed, perpetual grant in order that the king should always be dependent on having to call the Cortes. The 1607 Cortes not only made it one of their conditions that the Cortes be summoned every three years but also required the king to swear on oath to observe those conditions, which, had he agreed, would have made him liable to excommunication in the event of their breach.[14]

The intervention of the Cortes in financial administration, their insistence on approving *asientos*, viewing accounts, allocating supply, and controlling the incidence and collection of taxation, "as if they were its real owner," was condemned by ministers as a usurpation of the functions of the royal councils and offensive to the "sobe-rana regalía" of the king. The administration of the *millones* by the Cortes and the cities was condemned as corrupt and incompetent. The Council of Finance, deprived of its jurisdiction, could do nothing to prevent the city bosses from holding on to the money they collected for their own profit, defrauding the treasury and leaving the assignees of the revenue over a million ducats short. The attempt to remedy this by committing the cities to a fixed *repartimiento* simply helped undermine the regime of the *millones* as a universal system of *taxation*, and so ultimately left the cities with even more discretion in the administration of the revenues.[15]

By the time Philip III died in 1621 the Cortes and the Cortes cities had acquired a formidable position. It was acknowledged that there could be no new "services" without the vote of the Cortes and that there could be no vote of the Cortes without the prior consent of a majority of the cities. The possibility of independent revenue increases was drastically curtailed by the state of the economy; and the conditions of the *millones* themselves, forbidding alienations from the royal patrimony, sales of privileges and offices, and exemptions from jurisdictions, limited the scope for the usual exploitation of regalian rights. The issue of *vellón* coin in 1599–1603, 1617, and 1621, the reduction of the interest on some *juros*, and the occasional sale of offices were the only major sources of new, extra-parliamentary revenue during the reign. That is one reason why such measures, especially the manipulation of the coinage, and the *arbitristas* who proposed them were so vehemently denounced by "constitutional-ists" of the stamp of the Jesuit Juan de Mariana, and why in turn he and his *De mutatione monetae* were condemned by the Council and the Inquisition as seditious.[16] It was necessary for the Court now to secure the acquiescence of both the *procuradores* of the Cortes and the *regidores* of the cities in the Crown's fiscal demands and in its requests for dispensations from the conditions of the *millones*, an acquiescence which was costing more in money, time, and trouble than ever before. Assenting votes had to be won by protracted negotiation and the constant distribution of presents and promises. The result was an expensive and dilatory Cortes, whose six sessions are said to have cost Philip III two million ducats;[17] an unsatisfactory revenue administration in which it was not possible to intervene; and, at the same time, progressively less generous grants—three million ducats a year in 1600, two and a half million in 1608, two million in 1611. By the time of his death Philip III's total income was only 80 percent or so of what it had been twenty years earlier.

<< II >>

Cortes, or Cities? 1621–1667

It was against the position the *Reino* had won in the 1590–1620 period that the new government in 1621 directed itself. Indeed, the reign of Philip IV was characterized by a concerted effort by the Crown to recover its freedom of action and to assert its control over the machinery of consent and the administration of the finances. This was a policy made necessary by the fall in royal revenues, but justified and made possible by the inability of the *Reino* to produce the sums for which it had contracted. In effect the failure of "service" fiscality was to undermine the compactualism of the *millones*.

Philip IV succeeded first of all in breaking the control of the Cortes and the cities over the administration of the *millones*. In the absence of an adequate study of seventeenth-century financial administration, it is not yet clear in every detail how and when this was done. One aspect was a gradual take-over of the *Comisión de Millones*, the permanent committee of the Cortes responsible for *millones* administration, which resulted in the Cortes consenting in 1658 to the incorporation of the committee into the Council of Finance. Finally, in 1694, the *Diputación*, the permanent committee responsible for the administration of the *alcabalas*, was abolished and subsumed into what was now the *Sala de Millones* of the Council of Finance, though four commissioners elected by the cities retained their position in that tribunal.[18] Another aspect was the intrusion of royal "administrators" into the *millones* administration. Initially the Cortes consented to the king's being able to appoint "administrators general" in six districts only, in order to offset the growing arrears in the 1630s. In 1655 "administrators" were appointed by the king to all fiscal districts. It seems clear from the complaints of the cities that by this time the king had taken over the administration of the *millones* completely (though not that of the supplementary grants), sometimes collecting the proceeds through special administrators, sometimes through the *corregidores*, sometimes through tax-farmers; and that the local commissions for *millones*, consisting of the *corregidor* and two city councillors, had largely ceased to function.[19]

Philip IV also succeeded in evading many of the inhibitions on royal action imposed by the *millones* contracts by requiring the Cortes and, in their absence, the cities to consent to dispensations from specific conditions for specific purposes. Such dispensations had been given in the previous reign also, but now they became so frequent and the demands so peremptory and so taken for granted that they systematically undermined the effectiveness of the contracts. These dispensations did not always come free, nor were they always uncontested or undiluted; and they remained conditional in form and, therefore, legally—if not always politically—enforceable; but there is no doubt that the king got, and got in a technically legitimate way, almost everything he wanted.

The most important coup achieved by Philip IV, however, was to reverse the constitutional subordination of the Cortes to the cities, formalized in the *millones* regime. Having previously been unsuccessful first in attempting to by-pass the Cortes by appealing directly to the cities for support for a program of financial and governmental reform (1622), and then in attempting to shift the basis of the tax system from Cortes grants to the *regalía* by replacing the *millones* with a perpetual salt tax (1631),[20] in 1632 the Crown reverted to the earlier policy of centralizing consent in a Cortes that would be independent of the cities. By dint of unrelenting moral, financial, and sometimes physical pressure on the city councils, it succeeded in getting the cities to send their *procuradores* with full powers "to vote decisively, without referring to them anything at all concerning the Cortes." Despite bitter and protracted opposition in the cities, which persisted in some cases on the occasion of every writ of summons until 1665, this strategy worked. The cities were separated from the Cortes and reduced to mere executive agents of Cortes' decisions. After 1632 every Cortes operated independently of and without reference to the cities, up to and including the moment of decision.[21]

The significance of 1632 does not lie primarily in any change in the balance of power between king and kingdom. Meetings of the Cortes continued to be protracted, costly, difficult, and not always as productive as was hoped. Nor was it possible in practice to dispense with the consent of the cities, not only for the issuing of the "poderes decisivos" at each summons, but also for any dispensation the Crown wanted from the conditions of the *millones* during gaps between Cortes, and for an ever widening range of "voluntary" donatives and military contributions which did not fall within the purview of the Cortes and which were becoming more and more frequent under the pressures of internal war after 1640. In 1643 the policy of 1632 was reversed, and the king reverted to what had been tried unsuccessfully in 1622, a direct appeal to the Cortes cities. This time the policy was a notable success. Not only were the cities remarkably amenable, but the king saved 200,000 ducats in costs to boot.[22]

The direct appeal to the cities between 1643 and 1645 was designed expressly to avoid having to deal with the Cortes. It was a measure of political decentralization appropriate to the insecure leadership of the immediately post-Olivares period and for a tax policy particularly sensitive to the dangers of popular disturbance. As long as the need to ask for *new* taxes could be avoided, it was possible to govern without the almost continuous presence of the Cortes which had characterized Olivares's ministry. Whilst the Cortes had been in session for 202 months between 1621 and 1643, between 1643 and 1655 they were in session for no more than 40 months, solely to renew existing grants.

It was a position impossible to maintain in the 1650s. Between 1655 and the end of the reign the Cortes were to be in session for eight out of the ten years. The Cortes summoned for April 1655 marked a complete reversal of the financial policies of the post-Olivares era. The grants they made were the first new, general imposts voted in Castile since 1642.[23] These new taxes, perhaps precisely because of this gap, generated a wave of local tax riots right across the country. None of these disturbances appears to have been of any great seriousness, but they were unique in manifesting the most widespread popular resistance to taxation in Castile since the Comuneros. They were perhaps a further indication of the loss of authority of the Cortes as a tax-granting institution.

The collapse of the revenues, however, made it essential not only to raise new taxes, but, even more important, to adopt fundamental measures of fiscal reform that would render them more productive than they had been in the past. How that was to be done was to be the central political issue of the last ten years of the reign. What the Crown wanted was a general reform of the entire tax system, but neither taxation nor reform was possible without the Cortes. The Cortes of 1655 were summoned, therefore, to seek "a universal remedy (*medio universal*) which will weigh in equal proportion on those who have wealth and will not fall on the mendicant pauper, the workman, the artisan, and others who support themselves solely by the labour of their persons."[24]

The idea of a single, unified tax, a "medio grande universal," to replace the *millones* and the mass of other existing taxes, each supporting its own separate administration, had inspired many proposals in the past. However, any such "medio universal" not only threw into question the future of all the *juros* situated on existing revenues, it also threatened to provide the king with a source of income independent of the consent of the Cortes and uncontrolled by the *comisiones de millones* of the *Reino* and the "ciudades de voto." The Cortes, therefore, if nothing else the political voice of the *juro*-holders, wanted not tax reform, but the reduction of expenditure and the reform of the administration, a reform which would give them and their principals a supervisory role in the management of the finances. What was at issue, therefore, was the place of the Cortes in the government of Castile; and neither the Cortes of 1655 nor those of 1660 were prepared to consent to a long-term reconstruction of the finances without the revenues they voted being hypothecated to specific expenditures and administered by the Cortes cities.

For their part, the Cortes returned to the schemes for a disencumbering of the revenues which they themselves would control, claiming that otherwise "any service that the *Reino* makes [the King], will be alienated into the hands of his creditors the very day it is granted." In addition, they demanded that they should be allowed to examine the accounts of the royal revenues and all the assignments and audits of the bankers, "in order that the *Reino* assembled in Cortes, as it is this day, may participate in the *desempeño*." They may even have gone so far as to offer to take over the administration of the entire royal revenue.[25] The third extra one percent on the *alcabala*, granted in 1656, was perpetuated, and a fourth *ciento* granted in 1664, both to be applied to the disencumbering of rents assigned to the financiers;

but the *desempeño* folded. Once the income had been perpetuated, without administrative control there was no way the Cortes could enforce its appropriation, and it was soon clear that the war against Portugal was going to have absolute priority over the restoration of the finances.

The Cortes of 1660–64 were the last to meet in the Habsburg period and the last Cortes with more than a ceremonial function to meet under the Old Regime. But it was not on account of their own weakness, as is too commonly believed, that the Cortes of Castile passed away. It was the weakness of the Regency government, with the accession of the four-year old Charles II in 1665, which made it not dare risk recalling the Cortes, fearing the renewal of their attempts to control the administration of the finances and their historic claims to a role in government during a royal minority. Neither, of course, did the functions of the Cortes cease with them. From 1667, and throughout the following century, the grants that had previously been made by the Cortes continued to be made directly by the cities which had been represented in the Cortes, the *millones* and other "services" being prorogued every six years for the same sums and on the same terms as they had last been conceded. It was the cities also that were called upon to consent to dispensations of conditions of the *millones* contracts, as they had done before in the gaps between Cortes.[26]

After 1667, therefore, the constitutional position replicates that of 1643–45, when the king had appealed directly to the cities rather than recall the Cortes. The cities negotiated individually and made their own contracts with the Crown. Madrid, for example, required that the private conditions it imposed for the regrant of the *millones* in 1667 "have the force of contract, mutual, reciprocal and binding between His Majesty and this Town."[27] It was, in essence, a reversion to the identification of the *Reino* with the cities which had prevailed prior to 1632. The centralized structure of the *Reino* had broken up. The functions of advice and consent were exercised locally, and the permanent representatives of the cities in the *Sala de Millones* and the *Diputación* became part of the Court's central financial administration.

Not until the accession of the new Bourbon dynasty in 1700 were the Cortes again summoned in Castile. By then their absence from

the political scene for a generation and the assumption of their consultative and consensual functions by other bodies, namely the city
councils and the permanent committees at Court, meant that they
were no longer capable of serving as the representation of the kingdom against a regime that had established itself by force and that
was embued with the absolutizing convictions of its French parent-
age. The history of liberty in Spain did not come to a halt in 1700
but, until the end of the Old Regime in the nineteenth century, arbitrary government was to be restrained not by the contractual rights
of the kingdom, but by the traditional institutions of the law and the
administration.

If the old view of the Cortes of Castile as an ineffectual cipher
is no longer tenable, how is it to be explained that they failed to
maintain the position they had acquired between 1590 and 1620 and
ultimately ceased to have any effective role in the Castilian constitution? On the one side, the recovery of the initiative by the Crown
was essentially a matter of necessity and of will. Philip IV and Olivares had no instruments available to them, either legal or physical,
which had not been available to their predecessors. The packing of
the Cortes and the city councils, the inducements given to the *procuradores* and *regidores* for their votes, the role of the *corregidores*
in managing their cities, the arguments from the Laws of Castile and
from custom and practice had all been current under Philip II, and
no doubt long before. It is the political tone of Philip IV's reign that
is so different from that of Philip II's or Philip III's, in their different ways. The debates in the city councils give the impression that a
more "absolutist" position was being expressed by the *corregidores*
and their supporters. However, the difference is most marked in the
brutality of the language employed in royal orders to the cities in the
1630s and 1640s. Under Philip II the *corregidores* were repeatedly instructed to withdraw coercive and violent measures, like the fining
and imprisonment of *regidores*, and enjoined to "blandura" ("emol-
lience"); under Philip IV they were condemned for compromise and
moderation. The issue of the "poder decisivo" is indicative of the way
a determined political will; persistence; a tough line by the *corregidores*; the unblushing application of threats, bribery, patronage, and
gerrymander; a conviction of rightness; and a shrewd assessment of
how far legal arguments could be pushed in the direction of arbitrari-

ness, enabled a custom and practice to be overturned without any explicit change in legal niceties.

But the fact that from the mid 1630s the war was being fought on Spanish soil was also crucial in determining the climate in which the king's demands were received. With the outbreak of war with France in 1635, the invasions of Roussillon and Guipúzcoa in 1637, the revolutions in Catalonia and Portugal in 1640, Spain itself was under threat and the integrity of the Monarchy in jeopardy. There could be no question but that the demands were just and that to accede to them was a necessity of survival as well as conscience. The notorious "Then let them be damned" response to the Dutch war in the Cortes in 1593 was not an appropriate attitude in the 1640s.

The other side of the equation was the apparent willingness of Castile to do without its Cortes. The almost total lack of contemporary writings about the Castilian Cortes in the sixteenth and seventeenth centuries, compared for example with those on the Cortes of the Crown of Aragon, is not only an indication of indifference; it also prevented the growth of informed public awareness. Such was the degree of local ignorance about the Cortes that even some quite large towns of 3,000 and 4,000 people did not know which city spoke for them in the Cortes.[28] Neither in 1643–45, nor for many years after 1665, was there any great agitation in the cities for a recall of the Cortes, or any condemnation of the *form* of the sexennial "prorogations" of the *millones*. With no more than a handful of exceptions, what 1643 and 1665 reveal is a Castile largely indifferent to the fate of its Cortes.

The Cortes suffered from serious limitations as a representative institution. They were geographically unrepresentative. Thirty-six (later forty) *procuradores* from eighteen (later twenty-two) cities spoke for the whole kingdom. They were also socially unrepresentative, both in that there was no separate clerical or aristocratic representation, and because of the exclusion of the lower classes. Neither was there any direct representation of rural or seigniorial populations, as such, although there was always a certain number of the *procuradores* who were "lords of vassals," or even titled nobility. The overwhelming majority of the *procuradores*, however, were rentiers and *juro*-holders, members of the *caballero* city patriciates, drawn by lot from among the *regidores* who governed the cities.

The narrow basis of representation in the Cortes meant that they neither had the support of the most powerful elements in society nor were they a popular institution. The program of the Comuneros in 1520 was only one example of demands for a widening of participation coming from excluded groups. Those regions and cities without their own *procuradores*, their sense of exploitation sharpened by the greatly increased importance the *millones* gave to the eighteen Cortes cities in local, financial administration from the 1590s, were in continuous conflict with their capitals—Galicia with Zamora, Oviedo with León, Palencia with Toro, Logroño with Burgos, Andújar and Alcalá la Real with Jaén.

Outside the cities with a vote in Cortes and, indeed, outside the ruling bodies of those cities, there is no evidence of any widespread support for the Cortes as an institution. On the contrary, contemporary comment is uniformly critical of the Cortes as defenders of the public good and unanimous in castigating the self-interest and venality of the *procuradores*. The patrimonial nature of the *procuración* meant that, rightly or wrongly, the Cortes tended to be seen as an instrument for the furtherance of the private interests of the *procuradores*. A whole string of commentators, ministers, even participants conformed with the sentiments of President Acevedo that "nothing moves them but their own interest."[29] Such criticisms are not necessarily to be taken at face value, but they reveal, and no doubt also propagated, a common, negative perception of the Cortes which was a fact relevant to the way the public, the government, and even the *procuradores* themselves responded.[30]

The arguments in the city councils against granting the "poder decisivo" to their *procuradores*, at a time when "services" were being demanded of the Cortes as never before, clearly reveal the extent to which the *procuradores* were no longer seen to be representative of their cities. Those debates express a widespread concern to change the basis of the *procuración* by making the *procuradores* responsible to the cities at the point of election. More radically, the centralization of consent in the Cortes led a number of *regidores* to evoke the ancient precept of "quod omnes tangit," asserting that it was proper that all who bore the burdens should have a voice in the decision. Reformers, like Lisón y Biedma, called for the proper election of *procuradores* by popular assemblies, just as the Comuneros had in 1520;

and there were elements even within the city oligarchies in the 1630s, 1640s, and 1650s looking to a widening of political participation by giving clergy, nobility, and commonalty a vote in the decisions of the councils.[31]

It needs to be asked, therefore, for whose liberties did the Cortes of Castile speak, and whether after 1632 those liberties were not better defended outside the Cortes than inside them. In the seventeenth century, the Cortes had been coming more and more to stand for general and uniform solutions to the needs of the Monarchy, even against the particular interests of the cities and provinces.[32] The appeal against the "voto decisivo" of the Cortes to the "voto decisivo de toda la comunidad" (Don Francisco de Angulo in the city council of Valladolid, 8 January 1649) can thus be seen as the expression of a generalized localist reaction, a disaffection of the local community from the center, which brought into question the acceptability of the Cortes as a national institution. The traditional principle that no new services were legitimate unless granted by the "Reino junto en Cortes," which the cities had been happy to insist upon in October 1622 and in the *millones* contracts, they were now equally happy to jettison. In its place they sought to distinguish between renewals of existing services, which they were prepared for the Cortes to decide on, and new grants, which they wanted reserved for the decision of the cities. Some tried to ignore the "decisivo" of the Cortes; others to trade off centralized consent against localized administration, accepting the "decisivo" in the Cortes but leaving the cities with the power to select their own financial measures. But in practical terms there was little they could do. As long as there was a Cortes the interests of the cities and their provinces could only be defended by their presence in the Cortes. An independent Cortes, purporting to speak for the *Reino* as a whole, was not, however, the kind of Cortes that the cities wanted. Their responses to the decision of the government to bypass the Cortes in 1643–45 stand in sharp contrast to their responses in 1622 when the same maneuver had been tried. In 1622 at least twelve cities had demanded the recall of the Cortes; in 1643–45 in most of the cities there was hardly a voice that even mentioned the Cortes. By freeing their *poderes* and breaking the link that bound the *procuradores* to their cities, the Crown had cut off the Cortes from their last support in the country and destroyed their viability as a representative institution. The failure to call the Cortes after 1665 was greeted, just as the events of 1643–45 had been, with almost total acquiescence—after all, what it meant to the cities was the restoration of their "voto decisivo" and of all the benefits, both the corporate concessions and the private *mercedes*, that went with it.

Taking the long view, the importance of the Cortes can be seen to have been closely related to the economic conjuncture. When the trend was upward, the variable regalian revenues were buoyant and royal fiscality was independent and reasonably self-sustaining; when the trend reversed, the Crown had to turn to the *Reino*, not only for new sources of revenue, but also to guarantee sums fixed against the falling trend. By the reign of Philip III political and economic conditions and the collapse of "regalist" fiscality were providing the opportunity for the *Reino* to establish for itself a dominant role in the control and administration of the finances, and hence a decisive influence in government. Indeed, it went a long way along that path, but a permanent readjustment of the political balance was prevented by the internal competition between the Cortes and the cities and by the inability of the cities to act cohesively outside the Cortes.

As long as the Cortes remained subordinated to the cities the concept of national representativeness, propounded by the Crown and its ministers in the Cortes, was unable to develop as against a particularist, community-centered view of representation. When in 1632 the tension between the Cortes and the cities was formally resolved, it was by fiat from above imposing a national form of consent on the cities just at the moment when the collapse of the economy and the ravages of war were making local self-preservation the predominant instinct and eroding the value of the taxes the Cortes voted. Because in those conditions a national system of taxation proved to be unviable, the Crown was driven to adopt forms of exaction which made a national system of representation and consent redundant. The Cortes lacked the power to sanction legislation and their participation in government was entirely dependent on their fiscal-administrative functions. Once alternative ways were found of carrying out those functions, or once they had ceased to be able to exercise them effectively, the Cortes were dispensable.

The abandonment of the Cortes was of profound significance on several different planes. Constitutionally, it signified the victory of a federal over a national principle of representation; politically, the failure of royal authoritarianism to effectively conciliarize the Cortes by turning them into a mere instrument of government. From the administrative point of view, it was one aspect of a more general decentralization of government, reversing, if only temporarily, some of the most important administrative changes made by Philip IV in the 1650s;[33] from the fiscal perspective, it marked the acceptance of a permanent restraint on royal expenditure, freezing taxation in the forms and at the levels of 1664 and making it impossible to fund any increase in the long-term debt, or to maintain anything more than a minimalist position towards military and foreign policy commitments. The end of the Cortes thus signaled the end of centralizing absolutist government in Castile and the end of great-power status in Europe.

<< III >>

Constitutionalism in Castile

In view of the enormous disparity between the contributions of the Crowns of Castile and Aragon to the finances of the Monarchy, the question arises whether the Cortes of Castile were constitutionally less capable of defending the liberties of Castile than were the Cortes of the more privileged kingdoms of Aragon and Navarre. The contrast between Aragonese "constitutionalism" and Castilian "absolutism" has been a commonplace of Spanish political historiography.[34] In the Crown of Aragon neither taxation nor legislation was lawful without the unanimous consent of all the estates, and the irremovable *Justicia Mayor* had absolute jurisdiction over all cases in which a breach of the kingdom's privileges was alleged. Leaving aside the new skepticism concerning the reality and the generality of those liberties in the Crown of Aragon, it could be argued that the *millones* contracts with their "nullity clauses" put the Cortes of Castile in at least as strong a position in law as that which their separate laws, customs, and practices gave to the Cortes of the other kingdoms.[35] The difference between the various Cortes was less a matter of constitutional forms than a matter of the different meanings these representative institutions had for their electorates and the different positions those kingdoms had in the political geography of the Spanish Monarchy. The continuous pressure that could be exerted by the Court on the Cortes in Madrid was not possible in Aragon unless the king was prepared to spend long periods in residence there, at great expense and inconvenience, for returns which in view of the relative size and wealth of the territories could hardly be justified. In Castile the king also had a very much more powerful presence in local government than was available to him elsewhere. The Castilian Cortes did not lack a nationalist sense of defending Castile against foreign profiteers and against the inequitable distribution of the burdens of the Monarchy, but after the middle of the sixteenth century Castile was much more closely identified than were the other kingdoms with a king who was born in Castile, resident in Castile, and regarded by outsiders as Castilian, and with a Monarchy which was widely seen as an instrument of Castilian hegemony. Castile's "common good" was, therefore, less affronted by the Crown's financial and military demands. The legitimacy of the causes for which Castile was having to bear the burden—the defense of the Catholic religion, the Spanish Monarchy, and the Castilian homeland—was rarely questioned in the seventeenth century. How important this was is clear from the very different response to Charles V's demands in 1518–20. The attitudes of the Castile of the Comuneros, with its sense of being exploited in the interests of an empire to which it had no commitment, closely paralleled those of the Catalans and the Portuguese in 1640. Nonetheless, it should not be forgotten that the privileges of the regions could not save any of them from the consequences of war on their own soil, or on their borders. Aragon and Valencia from 1626, Catalonia, Navarre, and Vizcaya from the 1630s, submitted to substantial and repeated contributions of men and money for the front. Nor did those privileges enable the Cortes of the Crown of Aragon to survive any longer than the Cortes of Castile. There were no Cortes in Catalonia after 1653, none in Valencia after 1645, and only two meetings of the Cortes of Aragon in the second half of the seventeenth century. Only the Cortes of the small Pyrenean kingdom of Navarre, loyal supporters of the Bourbons, continued uninterruptedly into the nineteenth century.

That is not to say that, simply in a fiscal role, the Cortes and cities of Castile were totally lacking in achievement. On a number of occasions they were able to reject, or reduce, the demands being made of the kingdom—the *sisa* in 1539; the aid for the Algiers campaign in

1563; the tripling of the *alcabala* in 1575; the *millones* in 1589, paid over a six-year rather than a four- or five-year term; the "500 *Cuentos*" in 1596; the successive reductions in the *millones* from three to two million ducats between 1601 and 1611; the 72 million ducat package of 1624; the 13 millions of 1636; the extra 2 percent sales tax of 1655 and 1660—though their successes in this respect are often obscured by the fact that the political variable was not usually the sum demanded, but the period over which it was to be paid. However, it was not so much the extent of the fiscal burden that they were able to determine, as the nature of the fiscal system—what would be taxed, how, and at what rates. Even more important, they were able to determine what would not be taxed. The most notable achievements of the Cortes and the cities were to block a whole series of proposals regarded by the Crown as crucial to the reform of the inequitable and inefficient tax-structure—the rural banks scheme of 1622, the "medio universal" of 1655, repeated attempts to establish a single tax on flour—as well as to have dropped, modified, or emasculated many lesser tax proposals and fiscal devices which did not conform to their own view of what was in the best interests of the kingdom.

But perhaps there were other and more fundamental achievements. The contractual view of the relationship *Rey-Reino*, which, overshadowed by Alfonsine "absolutist" formulations in the thirteenth and fourteenth centuries, had developed late in Castile,[36] was given a legally-binding, instrumental form in the seventeenth century in the contracts for the *millones* and other Cortes grants. Historians have been rather dismissive of these contracts, and the Cortes themselves complained repeatedly of their infraction. However, the majority of infractions were administrative actions by tribunals and ministers against which redress was available through the courts, or directly from the king. In Philip III's reign the conditions of the *millones* were by and large adhered to, as is evidenced by the condemnation of the financial and administrative consequences of those conditions by the president and the Council of Finance. Under Philip IV, it is true, the *millones* contracts were undermined in a more systematic way. The important thing, however, is that this was done not by arbitrary action, but through the legitimate channels of parliamentary consent, with dispensations voted by the Cortes or the cities. So, whether the terms of the contracts were in practice enforceable (as in the case of the successful appeal to the Council of Castile in 1647 against both the incorporation of the *Comisión de Millones* into the Council of Finance and the over-selling of offices and jurisdictions)[37] or not, the crucial thing from the constitutional point of view is that the *millones* contracts set the parameters within which *Rey* and *Reino* related throughout the seventeenth century. Every renewal of the *millones* and every subsequent service in a similar form repeated the explicit acceptance by the king of his subjection to the principles of the civil law of contract and the implicit right of his subjects to impose terms and conditions upon him.

The fiscal issues which arose between king and Cortes also generated a revival and a propagation of neo-Thomist fiscal theory, with its clearly defined requirements for the justification of royal demands for new services on the basis of "just cause" and "just form," and its acceptance of the advisability of, if not the moral necessity for, the consent of the kingdom, as best informed about how and on what such demands could least burdensomely be met.[38] That theory was instrumental in guiding the advice of lawyers, theologians, and confessors and the responses of the *procuradores* and the *regidores* of the cities. It compelled government spokesmen to present their case within the framework of "rationalist" rather than "absolutist" argument. It was government propaganda itself, therefore, which emphasized the depersonalization of kingship, the separation between the legitimate demands of the king insofar as he was acting in the common good for the defense of religion and his people and the illegitimate demands of the king acting simply as a man for his own private interests, in order that it could insist that consent to the just demands of the king was an obligation which in law and conscience could not be refused.[39] The apparent willingness of the Crown to put that principle to the test of the courts shows how far the monarchy in Castile was from asserting anything like a "fiscal absolutism" which would have made taxation depend solely on the royal command. Even those who publicly argued the royalist case that the king was not obliged to get the consent of the kingdom did so hesitantly and totally within the framework of traditional theory, allowing taxation without consent only in the case of a need so incontestable and of such extreme urgency that it could not wait upon the summoning of a Cortes.[40]

The Crown having got at least tacit acceptance of its claim that the consent of the kingdom was no more than a concession of the generosity of past kings to be exercised only in respect of the secondary issue of "just form,"[41] the requirement that consent was needed for new taxation, established both in the practice of centuries and in a series of royal decrees enshrined as Laws of the Kingdom in the *Nueva Recopilación*, was never in principle repudiated. Indeed, not only were no new, general taxes imposed in the absence of the Cortes after 1664,[42] but in the seventeenth century consent was sought for a wider range of measures than ever before, and even for many that had hitherto always been regarded as independent regalian rights. The remarkable thing in the seventeenth century is the absorption of the *regalía* into the "services" granted by the kingdom, as regalian rights over trade taxes, monopolies, the sale of honors and offices were allocated to the payment of specific "services," or made dependent on formal dispensations by the Cortes, or the cities, from the conditions of the *millones*. The "donative," remaining in form voluntary, in incidence particular, and in quantity negotiable, marked the limit of the claims of the late-seventeenth century Castilian "tax-state."

The keynote of the fiscality of the seventeenth century was universality of contribution. The extension of the burden of taxation and a greater equality of distribution were at the heart of practically all reform projects, public and private. The *millones* were intended from the start, as much by the cities as by the king, to be a universal "service" to which all would contribute regardless of status; they have been described as "the first important step towards equality of taxation."[43] The *cientos* recognized none of the exemptions enjoyed from the *alcabalas* of which they were formally an extension; the *medias anatas* and the retentions of *juros* were something like a partial income tax; and the "donatives" were in intention, if not always in effect, direct levies on wealth.[44] It was the privileged and the wealthy who were in many ways the immediate (though not necessarily the ultimate) victims of the fiscal arbitrariness that was at its height during the ministry of Olivares. It could be that as much as 60 percent of the 140 million ducats, or so, of new royal income raised between 1621 and 1640 came from the pockets of the upper classes.[45] As one of the bitterest opponents of the Olivares regime complained, the Crown was in effect depriving the nobility of its fiscal immunity: "Nobles and villeins, the great and the humble, all paid and were taxed at whatever sums were asked of them, or they were assessed for. That was done with the full rigour of the law, sequestrating their property and sending bailiffs against them in the same way as against the most ordinary husbandman."[46]

It has been suggested that we are here at the dawn of a modern type of impersonal tax-state which ignored both status and honor.[47] Fiscal privilege was undoubtedly worth less in the mid-seventeenth century than it had been sixty years before; and so consequently was mere nobility, to whom it seemed that it was "noble" wealth (pensions, offices, *juros*) that was being taxed, and merchant wealth that was privileged.[48] There was a shift in the reality of fiscal exemption from privilege to power that was part of a long process in which nobility was to become plutocratized and inseparable from the wealth needed to sustain it. There was, however, no challenge to the concept of privilege as such. On the contrary, the forms of personal exemption were strictly preserved, by the fiction of the "voluntary" donative, by the compensation promised for the *medias anatas* and retentions of *juros*, and, most important, by the depersonalization of fiscal demands by mediating them through unprivileged institutional and corporate bodies, councils, tribunals, municipal corporations, and so on. The voting in the municipal councils shows the city nobility intransigent in their opposition to forms of contribution that risked confusing social distinctions or derogating their status, particularly any kind of *personal* capitation, but by no means necessarily averse to accepting measures which hit them solely in their pockets—*juro* deductions, for example.[49]

The belief that because the Castilian nobility enjoyed the immunity of the *hidalgo* from the *personal* taxation of the *servicios* they were unaffected by taxes on consumption and wealth and as a result indifferent to the demands the Crown was making of the Cortes and the country is, therefore, wrong. There was a serious aristocratic and gentry opposition to the regime in the reign of Philip IV, to which the various exactions of the fisc made a substantial contribution; but it was directed not against the royal prerogative but against the usurpation of that prerogative by the king's chief minister, or *valido*, Olivares. The *valido*, by enabling the king to be distanced from decisions, made it possible for discontent to be absorbed in the politics of the Court rather than turned towards more fundamental constitutional issues. Indeed, because, in contrast to the English Lords, the aristocracy in Castile no longer had an institutional voice in the Cortes, as it had had in 1538, it was only through the Court that its opposition could be politicized. The Cortes, therefore, did not become involved in the political struggle, as Parliament did in England; and financial issues remained financial issues and never became transformed into political or constitutional issues. The separation between payment and privilege; the redistribution of power and wealth in favor of the nobility effected by the centralization of "feudal rent" through the medium of royal offices, pensions, and honors; their participation in the dismemberment of the royal domain; their dependence on the Crown for access to their entails and on the royal courts for defense against their creditors and their vassals, were among the reasons why the nobility did not see the crisis fiscality of the seventeenth century in constitutionalist terms as they had done at the time of the *sisa* in 1538.

That was not true, however, of the other privileged order, the clergy. The clergy not only held a strong conviction of the moral and practical rightness of its corporate privileges; it had the intellectual and ideological armory with which to defend them, a public platform for its propaganda, an institutional forum in which to organize, and powerful external encouragement from Rome. The clergy retained its own representative institution, the *Congregación del Clero de Castilla y León*, throughout the seventeenth century, as the body through which the contributions authorized by the Papal briefs were renegotiated, always downwards, and reallocated. If the brief was late, or in improper form, the clergy simply refused to pay. Conflict was endemic, and more often than not the clergy won. Despite a number of semi-official attacks on the appropriateness of clerical immunities in fiscal and jurisdictional matters, the willingness of the clergy to defend themselves—frequently backed by the Nuncio and the Pope—against city governments and royal ministers by the ready deployment of interdict and excommunication, the consequent reluctance of the laity to act against them, and the general ethos of the Catholic Monarchy kept ecclesiastical liberties intact until the eighteenth century.[50]

That is not to say that the clergy was not made to contribute very heavily to the costs of the Monarchy, either by Papal grace or by royal

distraint of the incomes of vacant sees, grants of pensions against
episcopal revenues, donatives, and levies of troops and provisions. Indeed, the Castilian clergy claimed that it was being bled white, and
it is clerics who are generally found spearheading local resistance to
taxation by their preaching and popular agitation.

The clergy's defense of its immunities was, of course, particularist; but it was more than that. At the grass roots level, the clergy's
opposition to taxation voiced a criticism of the extravagance, waste,
and corruption of the Court that was populist in social terms, puri-
tanical in moral terms, and hawkish in religious terms.[51] At the theological level, although the prelates generally acted as apologists of
royal policy and pedagogues of obedience in their cities, the royal confessors and divines, who were consulted on the justice of specific proposals, were the theological guardians of the king's fiscal conscience,
as the Council was the guardian of his legal conscience. Their negative verdicts were instrumental in the withdrawal of a number of
fiscal measures.[52] By applying practical and moral considerations of
justice to the letter of the law, the theologians helped preserve something of the reality of the kingdom's free consent to the granting of
taxation.

≺ IV ≻

Liberty for a Price

The Cortes may, however, not be the right place to look for the preservation or extension of liberty. If by "liberty" we are really thinking of "liberties," both in the communal sense in which they would
have been understood in the seventeenth century and in the individual sense in which nineteenth century liberal philosophy would
have understood them, the connection with "fiscal crisis" is to be
found less at the national than at the local and individual level and is
not mediated through the Cortes, which were predominantly a bastion of established rights and incorrigibly resistant to the extension
of those rights to other parties, so much as through the direct operations of the royal fisc. It was through the exercise of the royal "grace"
that Galicia, Extremadura, and Palencia were able to buy seats in the
Cortes and their freedom, respectively, from Zamora in 1623, Sala-

manca in 1655, and Toro in 1666. It was by similar means that such places as Huete, Vélez Málaga, Andújar, or Utiel were set up as separate *corregimientos*, and a host of towns and villages were able to buy judicial independence, township status, or the ownership of their own taxes, "liberating" themselves by such means (the expression is their own) from the administrative supervision and jurisdiction of their provincial or district capitals (*cabezas de partido*), and bringing themselves under the direct authority of the royal courts. The continuous sale of jurisdictional exemptions in the Habsburg period, which was the direct outcome of the Crown's financial necessities, extended the municipal autonomy that in the classic Castilian liberal tradition has been regarded as "a sure barometer for measuring the development of public liberties," and "the true basis of political liberty," to one in two of previously subordinate villages.[53]

All such exemptions were fiercely opposed by the Cortes, in principle, and by cities like Cordoba and Cuenca, in particular, who for years, bid by bid, were fighting off the bids of subordinate towns and villages to escape their control. Ironically, it was only when Cuenca was itself over 40,000 ducats in debt, largely as a result of these efforts and the burdens of royal taxation, that it sought permission to sell off the jurisdiction of Mezquita and to give township status to two of its own villages.[54]

The purchase of "liberty" was not necessarily sound business. The mortgages taken out to pay for it frequently turned out to be financial albatrosses from which the only release was to resell the "liberty" that had so recently been bought. Nonetheless, when one considers that Bujalance, for example, was prepared to pay 80,000 ducats to become an independent city with a royal *corregidor* and a *comisión de millones* of its own to administer its taxes, or that the citizens of Logroño voted the equivalent of 200 days of labor for each family in order to replace its ruling oligarchy with an elected council, there can be no doubt what meaning "liberty" had for the ordinary man and how he thought it was to be achieved. Success in "liberating" themselves from "slavery" to their capitals was greeted by spontaneous celebrations, dancing in the streets, bell ringing, processions, and fiestas.[55] There was thus considerable grassroots support for the prerogative powers of the Crown against the opposition in the Cortes and the city councils. Faced in 1621 with the objections of Zamora

and twelve other cities to her new seat in the Cortes, Galicia denounced her opponents for something close to *lèse majesté*, arguing
that "one could almost say that they are committing an offense in
this instance, since their objection amounts to denying the right and
authority that His Majesty has to grant *mercedes* and to increase or
reduce 'votos,' the one and the other consisting solely in his will,
being an act of his prerogative alone."[56]

The royal *arbitrios* in a similar way offered a means for individual
advance in social status and local influence, and for the privatization
of communal resources. The sale of peerages, knighthoods of the military orders, patents of nobility, baronies, town councilorships—all
crisis measures—extended in different degrees the channels of social
mobility. Fiscal crisis also made possible the commutation of archaic
and socially derogatory obligations, like those of the *caballero de
cuantía* in Andalusia and Murcia. The repeated, block sale of offices
in the cities contributed to the breakdown of the old family clans,
the *linajes*, and their transformation into more associational groupings, if only by accelerating a process already under way. The sale
of the government of towns and villages to private individuals and
the control this gave over the exploitation of communal properties
and common pastures; the sale of *baldíos*, often confirming existing
illicit use, thereby defining previously uncertain property rights; and
the permission given to municipalities to raise their services and tax
quotas by selling or renting out their communal properties, all helped
promote a shift, though by no means a complete one, from a commu-
nalist to an individualist agrarian economy. Given the limited extent
of a free land market in Castile, the access to land resources through
administrative and judicial channels was extremely important. There
was in all this an element of "modernization," the harmonizing of
wealth, power, and status, which is an essential component of the
concept of modern freedom. All these *arbitrios* were opposed by the
Cortes and prohibited by the conditions of the *millones* in the interests of social and economic stability, though after 1629 repeated dispensations greatly mitigated the effects of that opposition and made
the reign of Philip IV an age, perhaps not of great social change in
itself, but of the ratification of the social changes of previous generations.[57]

However, if liberty could be bought, so too could domination.

Seville in the sixteenth century and Madrid in the seventeenth were each enabled to extend their jurisdictions or to prevent escape from them, by their willingness to underwrite large loans to the king; and it was open to any town or city to overbid any attempt to buy exemption from its *tierra*, or to suppress the creation of new offices or new *hidalgos*.[58] It does seem, however, that by the 1630s, after repeated waves of such creations, the elements resisting change were becoming too financially exhausted to hold out or compete further. Between the 1540s and the 1660s something like 8,000 voting offices in local government were sold by the Crown in recurrent waves, and from the time of Philip III those offices had become full, freehold properties. The nineteenth-century idealization of the democratic Castilian municipality was a simplistic myth even in the Middle Ages. By the mid seventeenth century, all the towns and cities, and many of the villages, where previously the councils had been elected every year were governed by a narrow oligarchy of hereditary and venal aldermen. Even the "liberation" of a town or village from a superior jurisdiction was often merely a device by which, at the cost of the commons, the local "poderosos" rid themselves of external constraints on their domination of the village.[59]

It is commonly argued that this resolution of the fiscal-constitutional problem was in effect a deal between the Crown and the ruling classes, the lords and the municipal oligarchies, over the control and redistribution of the surplus product of the local economy. The shift from tax-based revenues to assessed *repartimientos* opened up opportunities for the political manipulation of the fiscal system by the governments of the provincial and district capitals which were less available when duties were centrally determined and collected at the point of production or sale. These assessments, paid as lump-sum advances, were financed by *censos* and *arbitrios* funded by local excises (*sisas*) and by the commercialization of municipal *propios* (grazing rights, communal fields, grain stores, woods) managed by the town councils in the interests of the dominant classes and at the expense of the urban poor and the peasantry of their subject *tierras*. Such was the almost unanimous view of contemporary ministers and reformers, even in the 1680s—showing, incidentally, how little the resumption of the administration of the *millones* and *alcabalas* by the Crown really affected what went on on the ground. It is an argument with some force, and it offers one explanation for the complaisance of the Cortes and the cities towards royal tax demands.[60] A paper by the king's chaplain, Dr Alexandro Parenti, in 1669, made this point precisely: "The officials, the aldermen and the propertied in the towns and villages remain exempt and unaffected, and for that reason care nothing that there are so many taxes. Not only do they in many cases pay none of them, but they are often of profit to them by way of what sticks to them of the quotas they allocate over and above what Your Majesty should get."[61] The liberty of the towns and cities was clearly not the liberty of all their citizens.

Yet it is too easy to reject the alternative vision of the civic "republica." There certainly does not seem to have been any obvious, widespread breakdown in the "moral economy" of urban society. As far as the limited work that has been done in this area indicates, levels of public disorder in the towns and cities of Castile between the 1660s and the 1760s were remarkably low, and in the countryside scarcely recordable. It may be that, as Pegerto Saavedra's study of Mondoñedo suggests, the devolved fiscality of the second half of the seventeenth century was frequently more responsive to local needs, in which after all the city governors also had an interest, than we have hitherto chosen to believe. It may also be that the localization of fiscal administration, by dissolving and denaturizing centrally imposed "universal" taxes into a variety of local forms, helped keep open the "flight" option and left markets, capital, and individuals with the opportunity to seek out the fiscal regimen that best advantaged them.[62]

Fiscal issues may also have had the effect of broadening the consultative process in Castile. There is evidence of attempts to take the debate out of the oligarchic city councils to a wider public at the time of the "decisivo" issue, and earlier, in the 1570s and the 1590s, at the time of the *alcabala* increase and the *millones*. Interestingly enough, in Valladolid in 1539 and in Murcia in 1576 it was the *corregidor* who threatened to appeal to groups outside the city council in order to overcome the resistance of the *regidores*. In Granada a *junta* of "caballeros comisarios" was set up "at the request of the citizens" to consider whether the city should compound for its *millones*, and in Orense the city council voted to agree to the proposition of the *procurador del común* to consult the opinions of representatives of the rural parishes on the same matter.[63] It has been argued that in rural areas where taxes were usually paid by individual assessment, the financial demands of the Crown revitalized the local village assemblies. The allocation of quotas and the collection and despatch of the proceeds to the district capital were a community enterprise, carried out by the selectmen of the village, cheap to run, and on the evidence of the Mondoñedo province of Galicia, a much more equitable system than is often imagined, reflecting a "genuine fiscal solidarity."[64] With the recurrent waves of sales and resales of offices, exemptions, and jurisdictions, it was legally necessary, if the community as a whole was to be committed to the cost, for public meetings of the whole town to be summoned to decide on a course of action. Although in practice this requirement was not always carried out to the letter, meetings in which nearly every male villager was present and voting were in fact frequently convoked, reviving what had once been a widespread tradition of popular consultative assemblies.[65] The local survival of these assemblies and other forms of democratic expression into the early modern period is still largely uninvestigated, but the belief that by the seventeenth century they were largely moribund is clearly far from the truth, and it may be that they helped both to preserve an active sense of the local community and to reinforce the tendency towards the fragmentation of the Castilian polity in the seventeenth century. To that extent, and to the extent that the centralization of representation and decision making in the Cortes limited the scope for the local voice, it may be that we have here another element in the relocation of "liberty" in early-modern Castile.

≺ V ≻

Fiscal Crisis and Arbitrary Rule

Fiscal crisis may have generated *arbitrios*, but it also generated arbitrariness. A string of fiscal exactions was imposed on Castile, particularly in the 1550s and from the 1630s to the 1660s, many of them formally prohibited by the conditions of the *millones*. Donatives and loans were requested under the pressure of personal visits from ministers and *corregidores*, with house arrest for the recalcitrant, and the cost of the armed guards posted at the door to be paid for as well.[66] The interest due on *juros* was cut or held back by royal fiat; private

bullion and plate were seized; "quo warranto" proceedings were instituted over *alcabalas* and other privately held royal rents; offices once
sold were resold or renegotiated; promises, paid for with good money,
that "never again, in perpetuity for all time" would membership of a
town's governing body be put up for sale or its villages alienated, reneged upon two, three, or four times. Though restrained by the legal
punctiliousness of the councils, measures like *juro* retentions, forced
loans, and the sequestration of private bullion affected all levels of
society: courtiers, nobles, ecclesiastics, religious and charitable institutions, widows, merchants, even the wills of the deceased.[67]

What is surprising is that this fiscal arbitrariness does not seem to
have provoked any sort of debate about royal authority, nor apparently
any real concern that Castile was being threatened with monarchical
tyranny. Whether these measures really signified an arbitrary extension of royal authority at the expense of the rights of the individual
or the community, therefore, needs more consideration than it has
been given. It may simply be our ignorance of the political culture
of the seventeenth century that makes it seem so. Even the captious
Don Francisco Antonio de Alarcón, a by no means uncritical treasury minister in the Olivares regime, insisted in 1643 that "none of
these measures can be regarded as unjust."[68] The legal basis for these
measures was not usually made explicit, but neither do they seem
to have elicited a legal response. Except in cases which contravened
the conditions of the *millones*, it does not seem that the legality of
the Crown's demands was ever challenged in the courts, though ap-
peals for financial relief were made to the Council and lawsuits were
instituted against the actions of royal ministers and against the private beneficiaries of royal grants. Many of the measures in question
were, in fact, properly voted by the Cortes and the cities; others were
accepted regalian rights, frequently also reinforced by grants of the
Cortes and the cities, or by dispensations from the conditions of the
millones, and thus absorbed into the politics of consent. What then
was at issue was not so much the authority of the Crown as the
legitimacy of the consent, and that was an issue between the Cortes
and the cities.[69] Even when real infractions of the conditions of the
millones were involved, the Cortes responded as parties to an agreement rather than as guardians of the constitution. Issues were thus

reduced from matters of constitutional principle to mere civil actions for breach of contract.

That is not to say that there was not a good deal of opposition to the fiscal *arbitrios* of the Crown. Even some of the *corregidores* seem to have felt a certain unease at the way they were expected to conduct the exaction of forced loans, and the newsletters of the day express something of the outrage such measures aroused.[70] Minor tax riots, threats against local councillors, attacks on tax officials, even their murder, are reported in the chronicles, particularly in the mid 1630s and 1650s, inspired by the increase in the wine excise and the stamped-paper duty, currency manipulations, and compulsory purchases of *juros*. Nevertheless, they remained isolated and local incidents, directed against immediate targets and (except perhaps in the case of clerical opposition) against the economic effects of the impositions rather than their legality, not in any way bringing the king's authority into question. None of the Crown's fiscal measures ever generated a legal-constitutional crisis such as occurred on more than one occasion in Stuart England. There are no great constitutional cases in seventeenth-century Castile, and no great constitutional martyrs. Why that should have been so is not easy to say. The Crown seems to have been able to prevent resistance from becoming a national issue, partly no doubt because coercion did not always have to take place in the full publicity of the capital. The failure of the Council of Castile or the regional appeal courts, the *Chancillerías*, to explain the legal basis of their decisions may also be important. It meant that there was no judgment, only sentence, and therefore no ground for precedent and no public discussion of principle. But it may also be that the Crown was operating within the accepted framework of the law, applying well-known principles of the private, civil law, as well as accepted prerogative rights to its operations as a public body. It was by virtue of the dispensing power inherent in the "poderío real absoluto" that the *fueros* of the great municipalities were breached and their seigniorial rights abrogated. The principles of the inalienability of the royal patrimony[71] and of "el engaño en más de la mitad del justo precio" (fraud in excess of half the just price) provided grounds for the revocation of sales and alienations.[72] The right of compulsory purchase for the royal service, with due compensation, justified the seizure of private bullion, for example; and the legal moratorium available to a grantor incapable of effecting his donation sanctioned the withholding of pensions, salaries, or *juros*.[73] The question of usury apart, the right of the king to refuse payments to his creditors in the event of need was accepted, indeed recommended, by those most critical of royal fiscal demands, for whom the bankers were no more than bloodsuckers, responsible for the bleeding of Spain and the exhaustion of the treasury.[74] Similarly, many of the apparently arbitrary exactions imposed on the privileged orders were in fact revivals or commutations of the ancient feudal obligations which were the bases of their privileges, or, like the *medias anatas* and retentions of *juros*, were technically subventions for which compensation was due, and ultimately given, often in the form of credits in part payment for purchases of offices, rents, or jurisdictions.[75]

Whether or not royal action was seen to be arbitrary or legal was also related to which one of the two crucially distinct areas of the prerogative, *gracia* or *justicia*, was operative in any particular instance. Favors granted by the royal grace were dependent upon the king's pleasure alone. Fiscal crises, however, tended to make relations between the Crown and its subjects (whether we are talking about the Cortes, the cities, or even individuals, with whom royal ministers were negotiating donatives, contributions, and sales on an *ad hominem* basis), increasingly transactional. Favors were given as one side of a deal, the *quid pro quo* for some specific "service." This had the effect of transforming what had been a royal grace into an obligation of justice, subject to the principles of equity and contract.[76] That justice was enforceable in the law by due legal process. Indeed, it was to the Council of Castile that the Cortes appealed for the defense of their own contractual rights, and it was in the Cámara that the contractual obligations of the king to the Cortes were most insistently reaffirmed. In 1624 the king summoned a joint assembly of the Councils of State and Castile to seek their advice on whether he could, by virtue of his "absolute power," levy the *millones* voted by the Cortes notwithstanding the refusal of the "ciudades de voto" to ratify the grant, and in future do without the Cortes altogether. The councilors declared that the cities could not be deprived of their "statutes and customs," and the king was told (as the English ambassador reported), "that it is neyther convenient for him to take that course, neyther cann his Majestie putt it in execution without injustice and tirany."[77] It is with the judicial system, and not least with the royal councils, which were at the summit of that system, and with their defense of a "judicialist" concept of the monarchy, rather than with representative institutions, that the history of liberty in Castile should be associated.

≺ VI ≻

Conclusion: Fiscality and Polity

When the Habsburg regime came to an end in 1700, the balance of political and social forces was significantly different from that two hundred years before. The Catholic Kings had embarked upon the restoration of royal authority after the civil wars of Henry IV's reign by concentrating political power in their own hands, reasserting the supremacy of royal justice and legislation, and strengthening central controls over local government at the expense both of municipal autonomy and of the powerful aristocratic factions that had opposed them. This movement in the direction of a centralized, absolutist polity was checked by the crisis fiscality of their Habsburg successors. "The finances," as Olivares once observed, "are the nerves of authority."[78] With the collapse of their finances the Habsburgs had no recourse but to liquidate their authority, by selling their jurisdiction, vassals, offices, and rents.

The chronic degeneration of effective state power, the symptoms of which were already apparent in the later sixteenth century, reached its culmination in the reign of Charles II. Throughout the last decades of the seventeenth century contemporary observers were all but unanimous in their view that the king had only the shadow of authority over the country. If the polity remained monarchical in form, and often authoritarian in tone, it was decentralized in structure and privatized or seigniorialized in operation. As the ambassador of Lucca reported in 1674, "The government has come to be and proceeds more in the manner of a Republic than a Monarchy."[79]

The control of the Crown over the apparatus of the state was weakened by the progressive privatization of the administration. This process, apparent in the last decades of Philip II, was accelerated in the seventeenth century by the spread of venality in officeholding, particularly in fiscal administration, and by an increasing reliance on private contractors, notably in branches of military administration previously managed directly by royal ministers, as the Crown proved incapable of providing the necessary flow of funds to conduct those activities itself and had little option but to rely on the concealed credit the contractors and entrepreneurs were prepared to advance. Although these procedures offered immediate practical and financial advantages to the Crown, they were politically regressive, alienating functions of government, jurisdiction over the king's subjects, and control over finances. Worse, the terms and conditions of these contracts were becoming more onerous, requiring licenses for the uncontrolled export of bullion; penalties, regularly amounting to 20 percent *per annum* for late payment; the handing over of the administration of specific royal revenues as security; the appointment of private judges for their causes; even personal indemnities for tax evasion. The acceptance of such terms was excused by the Crown in the teeth of the protests of the Council of Castile, "considering that the calamitous state of the times and our lack of money are reason for us to make use of every means possible."[80]

The privatization of the administration was one aspect of a more general devolution of state functions. By the second half of the seventeenth century the hold of the central agencies of the Crown on the government of the country had been fragmented and diffused across a multitude of local authorities, seigniorial and municipal. The transfer of fiscal and military-administrative functions to the provincial and district capitals, burdensome as they might be for the community as a whole, represented a real acquisition of power and influence for the local ruling elites. By 1658, the senior *regidor* of Cuenca could claim to have been involved in the voting of "services" of more than 60 million ducats.[81] This made the commercialization and the patrimonialization of local government, effected by the mass sale of offices in the municipal councils and in local financial administration, a matter that had serious implications for local government and administration. Philip III, prevented by the conditions of the *millones* from creating new *regimientos*, thereupon sold existing *regidores* the right to make their offices legally hereditary, thus depriving the Crown of its ability to intervene in the transfer of offices from one holder to another. The renewed sale of perpetual *regimientos* by Philip IV swelled the numbers in the town councils and reinforced the venal and patrimonial nature of an inflated municipal ruling group profiteering from its control of the local market, municipal taxation, and the exploitation of communal rents and properties.[82] Moreover, by selling immunities and pardons, even for murder, and by making the post of *corregidor* a cheap reward for complaisant *procuradores*, the Crown was undermining the very judicial and institutional sanctions designed to check such misgovernment. In 1639, the local magistrates and other officials of the forty-four *concejos* of the province of Seville bought exemption from judicial review by the city for 115,875 ducats. They were offered the same privilege again in 1652, by which time they had gone twelve years without visitation.[83] The effect was to increase the operational independence of local government and its irresponsibility from external supervision and effective central control.

This fragmentation of authority vis à vis Madrid was paralleled by the fragmentation of authority at the local level as well. The district capitals in 1636 were made independent of the capitals of their provinces in the administration of the *alcabalas* and *sisas*; the sale of exemptions from the jurisdiction of the cities and the sale of *regimientos* in the villages undermined the control of the cities over their *tierras*. By the middle of the seventeenth century many of the great, medieval, municipal *señoríos* had crumbled, broken up by the wave of exemptions, as the devolution of administration cascaded from the provincial capitals down to the district capitals, and then to the towns.[84] The entire chain of authority in Castile was being ruptured from top to bottom, between Madrid and the localities, between the provincial capitals and their provinces, between the cities and the towns and villages of their *tierras*. As the Council of Castile complained in 1654, government and justice had become a babel of voices.[85] No reform program proved capable of checking the disintegration of government in Castile. On the contrary, it was only by promoting that disintegration that even a reformer like Olivares was able to achieve success in his priority duties as a finance minister.

A parallel development was the extension and the reinforcement of the seigniorial regime, a process that some historians have termed "refeudalization" or "seigniorialization."[86] Between 1625 and 1668 alone, at least 169 new lordships or baronies, each with primary and secondary jurisdiction and the right to appoint village magistrates and officials, had been created by grant from the Crown, and some 80,000 families, perhaps 15 percent of the population under the immediate jurisdiction of the Crown, had been sold out of the royal domain into seigniorial jurisdiction.[87] Lords were enabled to buy extensions of their powers over justice and patronage, new lands with independent jurisdiction, and the sales taxes and other royal rents of their villages. By 1637, in excess of 3,600 places, with one-third or more of the population, were paying their *alcabalas* to their lords, and the alienations were continuing apace.[88] In addition the sale of woods, wastes, pastures, and offices in adjacent villages offered lords the opportunity to round off control of their estates. When this resulted in conflict between the lord and his vassals, as in the case of the purchase by the duke of Arcos in 1635 of woods in the Serranía de Villaluenga, the inclination of the Crown, "mindful of the duke's loyalty, his many and signal services, and the needs of war," was to support the lord.[89] Alienation from the royal domain was generally much resisted and, if they could afford it, often reversed by the populations concerned, for whom "liberty" meant being vassals of no one but the king. Nonetheless, successive waves of privatizations (royal jurisdictions in the later fourteenth and fifteenth centuries, those of the military orders and the church under Charles V and Philip II, and the royal domain again under Philip III and Philip IV) meant that by the mid seventeenth century the political balance in local government was markedly different from the situation even 100 years before.[90]

What was of supreme political importance was that the contraction of royal justice, the issue of "cédulas de suspensión" to prorogue judicial processes, the sale of independent offices in seigniorial estates, the transfer of fiscal rights, and the reliance on the lords for the organization of compulsory recruiting and other military quotas were subjecting the seigniorial vassal to the authority of his lord over a greatly extended range of activities, whilst simultaneously cutting him off from ready judicial recourse in the royal courts.[91] At the same time, the increased reliance on the military and military-administrative services of the lords was seriously affecting the king's ability to act decisively within the state. This was recognized clearly enough by Philip IV in 1646 when considering the fate of the marquis of Ayamonte, condemned for treason: "Such are the times, for my sins, that it is necessary not to offend the nobility, rather it is best to gratify them in every way possible."[92] Crown and aristocracy were enmeshed in a web of mutual dependence, but after the grandees forced the dismissal of Olivares in 1643, there was no doubt in the minds of contemporary observers of what the aristocracy was capable when it felt its interests and its honor to be seriously threatened. "Though this be a great monarchy," wrote the English ambassador in 1691, "yet it has at present much aristocracy in it, where every Grandee is a sort of prince."[93]

The direct attempt to restructure the Monarchy from the center, notably during the ministry of Olivares, failed, therefore, not only with respect to the proposals for a greater integration of the various provinces of the Monarchy, but also within Castile itself. The Crown was unable to alter the balance of the constitution between *Rey* and *Reino*, or between Cortes and cities. The end of the Cortes represents, therefore, a victory for the traditional constitution as a community of communities, and with it the end of the wholesale restructuring of local power that had been going on during the previous 100 years. With the end of the Cortes, there was a stop to the sale of new municipal offices and a drastic reduction both in the number of exemptions from municipal jurisdiction and in the number of alienations of lands, vassals, and rents. A new stasis emerges in the 1660s.[94] Thereafter the structure of local government and local power relations remains fixed until the reforms of the 1760s.

The crisis fiscality of the sixteenth and seventeenth centuries, constrained by the deep-rooted particularisms embedded in the institutions and the political cultures not only of Aragon and the other privileged kingdoms, but of the kingdom of Castile as well, hindered rather than advanced the development of the tax-state in Spain. The king, whose very titles expressed the ideology of particularism,[95] was ultimately incapable of destroying those "liberties" on the defense of which the justification for his monarchy depended. It was only with the end of the fiscal crises specific to the Habsburg system of credit—fiscal crises engineered by the need to facilitate new *asiento* borrowing rather than to "balance the budget"—that some progress began to be made with the unification of the tax system by integrating the various rents into a single administrative structure under *superinten-*

dentes generales de provincias, who were responsible for both *rentas reales* and *servicios del Reino* (the new *rentas provinciales*) on a common centralized basis. These changes foreshadowed in the 1680s were to form the basis of the fiscal system of the eighteenth century. By then the institutions which had represented the communal, contractual liberties of the medieval body politic had lost their vitality or, in Aragon, Valencia, and Catalonia, had forfeited their autonomy by rebellion.[96]

The Bourbon conquest is a real divide in the history of Spain. That is not to say that economic and administrative recovery had not begun before 1700, nor that there are not real continuities between Habsburg and Bourbon Spain, but rather that the political ideology of the eighteenth century is sensibly different from that of the seventeenth. The Bourbon regime was ideologically absolutist and regalist; its government regulated by administrative priorities rather than judicialist principles; centralizing, uniformist, and statist with respect to administrative processes; utilitarian and universalist in its social and economic reformism. In such a climate, the ideological and institutional defenses of "medieval" liberties were of little weight. Indeed, it was surely the very inability to protect and preserve particularist liberties that helped promote the crucial conceptual transformation of liberty into a universal right. The old Cortes of Castile had been the bastion of particular liberties; the new liberty that emerged as a real political force in the nineteenth century out of the ashes of the Peninsular War needed to create a new Cortes and a new constitution to defend it.

I should like to thank Mark Steele, Charles Jago, Pauline Croft, and Mía Rodríguez Salgado for generously giving of their time to read and comment on earlier drafts of this and the preceding chapter.

≺ GLOSSARY, CHAPTERS 4 AND 5 ≻

administración direct administration by ministers of the Crown, e.g. tax collection, provisioning
alcabala a sales tax, nominally 10 percent, in practice usually compounded for a fixed sum at a much lower rate

arbitrios ad hoc fiscal devices and expedients pertaining to the royal prerogative

arbitristas "projectors," writers of treatises on economic and fiscal reform

arrendamiento (rentas arrendadas) tax-farming (farmed taxes)

asiento a government contract to supply goods or advance money, a short-term loan and exchange transaction with financiers

baldíos waste lands without title of ownership

caballero gentleman; originally a knight serving on horseback

caballero de cuantía property-owners of a certain level in Andalusia and Murcia, obliged to serve with horse and arms when summoned, and to attend two inspections a year

cabezas de partido capitals of fiscal sub-districts

Cámara de Castilla a sister body to the Council of Castile responsible for advising on administrative law and on appointments and personal royal grants and favors

capítulos generales the petitions of the Cortes submitted to the king at the end of the session

censo a private or municipal mortgage serviced from local rents and excises, or from entailed estate revenues

Chancillerías the regional high courts in Valladolid and Granada subordinate only to the Council of Castile

cientos the four one-percent extensions of the *alcabala* voted by the Cortes successively in 1639, 1642, 1656, and 1663

ciudades de voto en Cortes the cities with the right to send proctors to the Cortes (Avila, Burgos, Córdoba, Cuenca, Guadalajara, Jaén, León, Madrid, Murcia, Salamanca, Segovia, Sevilla, Soria, Toledo, Toro, Valladolid, Zamora, plus Granada from 1498, Galicia from 1623, Extremadura from 1655, Palencia from 1666)

Comisión de Millones the permanent committee of the Cortes responsible for the administration of the *millones*

concejos the ruling bodies of the towns and villages

Congregación del Clero the convocation of the clergy of the thirty-six dioceses of Castile and León

consultivo vote (*voto*) or authority to vote (*poder*) of purely advisory force; as opposed to *decisivo* = conclusive

corregidor the chief royal agent in the cities; he had judicial, military, and executive functions, and presided over the city council ("ayuntamiento"); *corregimiento*, the district controlled by the *corregidor*

cruzada see *Tres Gracias*

cuento one million maravedís; the 500 *Cuentos* (1⅓ million ducats) was the "service" proposed in the Cortes as the continuation of the first *millones* which expired in 1596

decisivo see *consultivo*

decreto the royal decree of "bankruptcy," suspending payment on the short-term and floating debt

desempeño a sinking-fund for disencumbering the revenues of the Crown
    assigned to servicing the debt
Diputación de las Cortes the permanent committee responsible for the ad-
    ministration of the *encabezamiento general*
encabezamiento the composition of a variable revenue for a lump-sum; *ren-
    tas encabezadas* revenues so compounded
encabezamiento general del Reino the general composition agreement for
    the *alcabalas* and *tercias* made by the Cortes for the kingdom as a whole
erarios a scheme proposed to the cities in 1622 to establish a network of local
    banks lending at low interest capital raised from a 5 percent levy on wealth
excusado see *Tres Gracias*
extraordinario irregular, discretionary, not permanent
fueros charters of rights and privileges
gracia the royal "grace" (as in "grace and favor"); a grant made at the will of
    the king as a favor without "consideration" and therefore without obliga-
    tion; as opposed to *justicia*, the obligation in justice deriving from such
    "consideration"
Hermandad, Santa a league of towns for mutual defense and the mainte-
    nance of order, reorganized under the auspices of the Crown in 1476
hidalguía noble status; *hidalgo*, a person with noble status and exemption
    from personal taxation
hombres de negocios business men, financiers of national and international
    standing
juro a negotiable bond assigned on a specific source of "ordinary" royal reve-
    nue at a fixed nominal rate of interest (see chap. 4 n. 55)
juros de resguardo juros temporarily assigned to financiers as security for
    their loans
Justicia Mayor high official of Aragon with the duty of defending the king-
    dom's liberties
Leyes del Reino the Laws of the Kingdom inscribed in the *Nueva Recopila-
    ción* (qv)
Maestrazgos revenues of the Masterships of the three Military Orders of
    Alcántara, Calatrava, and Santiago, pertaining to the Crown and leased to
    the German banking house of Fugger
maravedí unit of account: 34 = 1 *real*; 375 = 1 ducat
medias anatas a levy on the first year's income of offices and pensions intro-
    duced in 1631
medio general agreement with the king's creditors affected by the *decreto*
    (qv) to consolidate their short-term loans into *juros* (qv) at lower rates of
    interest
mercedes royal grants or favors
millones name given to the extraordinary grant of 8 million ducats over six
    years made by the *Reino* in 1589, and to subsequent renewals from 1601
Nueva Recopilación the collection of the Laws of the Kingdom first pub-
    lished in 1567
partido a fiscal sub-district

pechero a tax payer, a commoner (cf *hidalgo*)

poder the "power" (as in power of attorney), or mandate by virtue of which the proctors acted for their cities in the Cortes; see *consultivo/decisivo*

poderoso a man of power, a local boss, a Mr Big

procurador de Cortes proctor, or deputy of the cities in the Cortes; *procuración*, the office of *procurador*

procurador del común an elected official representing the interests of the commonalty in municipal councils

propios communal properties and revenues administered by the municipalities

quinto the royal right to a fifth of precious metals mined

regalía the royal prerogative

regidor a municipal councilman

regimiento a municipal corporation; the office of *regidor*; in villages usually elected; in most cities and towns, proprietary, venal, and in the 1600s hereditary

Reino the Realm, or antonomastically the Cortes (see chap. 4 n. 14)

rentas reales royal rents, non-concessionary revenues pertaining to the king by regalian right

repartimiento quota, assessment of tax contribution among districts or individuals

Sala de Millones section of the Council of Finance formed by the incorporation of the *Comisión de Millones* in 1658

señorío lordship, barony

servicio grant of aid by the *Reino* to the king on specific terms and for a fixed period

servicio ordinario/extraordinario a triennial grant by the Cortes renewed continuously after 1539 at 304 and 150 *cuentos* respectively

Siete Partidas the great legal code of Alfonso X, dating from the 1260s

sisa an excise, a local tax on foodstuffs

subsidio see *Tres Gracias*

superintendente general the royal fiscal supremo in the provinces

tercias reales the two-ninths of the ecclesiastical tithe paid to the Crown by Papal grant and collected with the *alcabalas* as part of the *encabezamiento general*

tierra the territory of a municipality's jurisdiction

Tres Gracias the Three Papal Graces: the *cruzada*, the Papal grant of an issue of indulgences, originally to finance the war against the Moors; the *excusado*, the most valuable tithe in each parish, granted by the Pope in 1567 for the war in the Netherlands; the *subsidio*, a direct tax on the clergy granted for the upkeep of the Mediterranean galley fleet

vecino household (as a demographic unit)

vellón copper, or copper-mix coin

voto a vote, or opinion in Cortes; *voto consultivo, voto decisivo*, see *consultivo/decisivo*

Early Modern France, 1450-1700

PHILIP T. HOFFMAN

IT IS ALWAYS SAID," observed Richelieu in his *Testament politique*, "that money forms the sinews of the state."[1] Most historians of early modern France would agree. "Absolutism was, in large part, the child of the fisc," notes one influential essay on early modern France, and a chorus of recent works repeats the same refrain.[2] Fiscal crises, it seems, provoked nearly every change in the French political system from the Hundred Years War to the Revolution; and the tax system brings into sharper focus than any other facet of the French state both the limits of absolutism and the peculiar nature of liberty in France.

To speak of the limits of absolutism may of course seem self contradictory, particularly in the case of the kings of France, who have usually been considered models of unconstrained power, able to judge, to legislate, and to tax at will. But in practice absolutism was hemmed in on all sides. To begin with, any king, even a Louis XIV, could only tax the wealth available in his country: he could not take what his subjects did not have. In France the wealth available was by and large land—some 464,000 square kilometers at the end of the sixteenth century, and 514,000 a century later. The king's subjects— roughly 8 million in 1440, 16 million in 1560 and 1600, and 27 million at the end of the Old Regime—by and large tilled the soil. It is estimated that 73 percent of them worked in agriculture in 1500, a figure that fell only slightly in the next two centuries: to 69 percent in 1600 and to 63 percent in 1700. In England and the Netherlands, by contrast, a smaller fraction of the population seems to have been engaged in agriculture, at least by 1700. In that year, only 55 percent of the English farmed and only 40 percent of the Dutch did so. The gap was even wider in the late eighteenth century.[3] The difference reflected lower agricultural productivity in France, a different crop mix, and less urbanization; and it squeezed state finances, for with a smaller fraction of the population involved in trade, the fisc had to lean more heavily on the land. In the first half of the seventeenth century, for instance, before Colbert's fiscal reforms, taxes on trade provided less than 26 percent of the monarch's revenue, and the figure could drop to 16 percent during periods of war.[4]

Other, more daunting obstacles also restricted the revenue from the taxation of trade. Urban tax exemptions, we shall see, allowed powerful merchants to escape taxation; and even in the absence of exemptions merchants were generally entitled to secrecy in their business dealings, so that their income remained hidden and difficult to tax. At the same time, the dispersion and the diversity of French commerce made excises and tariffs costly to levy. Paris after all did not dominate the kingdom's economy as London did England's, and even wine was not a staple as was English wool. Finally, the atomization of the French economy restricted economic growth and reduced the amount of trade that could be taxed. France lacked highly developed internal waterways and the sort of interlinked network of cities one found in the Low Countries, and at least before the eighteenth century the economy resembled a congeries of lilliputian markets, each one primitive and isolated, as though the regions the markets served were separate countries.[5]

As one might expect from such an economy, the French polity was splintered as well, with the fragmentation of the kingdom marking the limits of royal political power. The kings of France had assembled their realm by a process of accretion, adding provinces and cities from the Middle Ages into the eighteenth century. As they yoked territories to the kingdom, they confirmed traditional liberties and even conceded new privileges in order to win over a province or a city. When the strategic port of Bordeaux returned to French rule in the last stages of the Hundred Years War, for example, Charles VII granted the inhabitants tax exemptions and considerable local political autonomy. The Crown gave equally generous privileges to organized elites, such as the nobility, whose political support remained essential; and it granted still others—assigning a municipal guild a local monopoly, for example—in order to facilitate the task of tax collection.[6] The liberties that a king had granted or confirmed might later be circumvented, but even the most rapacious ruler would hesitate before revoking customary privileges, particularly when he risked the wrath of mighty subjects.

Powerful organizations also checked the monarch's powers. In over a dozen provinces, estates voted on taxes; and everywhere sovereign law courts (among them were the parlements, the most important one being the Parlement of Paris) could bend the king's will by refusing to register a royal edict. A court's refusal deprived an edict of legality and made it difficult to enforce. The Crown could force registration, but it then faced delays, ill will among the court's magistrates, and the obstruction of other legislation. Even a powerful king such as Louis XIV, who curtailed registration during the years 1673–1715, did not really ride roughshod over the parlements.[7]

The autonomy of royal agents further limited the king's freedom of action. By the beginning of the seventeenth century, judges and financial officials by and large owned their own offices, which they could buy and sell like private property. Many appointments thus escaped royal control. The governors, the Crown's provincial military commanders, also wielded considerable power over regional appointments. They could name army officers and royal officials, and they often pursued their own interests independently of the king. To lay a firmer hand on regional affairs, particularly those of the army and finances, the monarchy began to dispatch to the provinces a set of more reliable agents—the intendants. Sent out with revocable commissions, the intendants possessed extraordinary judicial and executive powers. The practice was systematized in the seventeenth century, but despite their powers the intendants still had to seek the cooperation of local office holders and powerful elites.

To eighteenth-century observers, and to many a modern historian, such a system of governance has appeared a hopeless muddle. Seemingly outmoded institutions—the parlements, the provincial estates, and a host of corporate groups—survived alongside the sleek new body of intendants. Despite the absolute monarchy at the center, each region possessed its own particularistic laws and customs, which the Crown itself had confirmed. Yet it would be a mistake to think that the hoary corporate institutions and the particularistic customs were merely vestigial survivals that the king ought to have swept away. They were integral to French political history, for to win the cooperation of powerful provincial elites, the Crown had granted them corporate institutions—a Parlement, for example, or provincial estates—and confirmed their privileges and local customs. To maintain their cooperation, the Crown showered them with additional favors: pensions, patronage, discretion over government spending, or the favorable treatment of a legal appeal to the king's council. In a sense, the Crown became the dispenser of spoils and the sole arbiter of the frequent differences among the privileged groups, who gained more by cooperating with the monarch than by resisting or by setting out on their own.[8]

< I >

The Fiscal System

The fiscal system provides the best illustration of how this curious polity worked and of what the limits to royal absolutism were. From an early date the tax system teemed with regional exceptions and privileges and spoils for elites. Consider, for example, the French nobility. When regular annual taxes not tied to a state of outright war began to be collected in France in the middle of the fourteenth century, nobles had no exemption. They paid as everyone else paid, although perhaps not so heavily. By the end of the century, however, they had escaped from taxation. During the reign of the weak and intermittently insane Charles VI, the Crown had to make concessions to powerful noble factions, and among the concessions was the exemption from a new direct tax granted to nobles in 1388. In 1393 the nobles got freedom from excise taxes levied on the produce from their own properties. The next king, Charles VII, was in no position to antagonize the nobles and so he reaffirmed their exemptions.[9] They also benefited from the military employment that the taxes supported, and certain magnates pocketed a large share of royal taxation directly.

Nor were the nobles unique. As the fisc grew, exemptions spread to all sorts of privileged individuals: magistrates, royal officers, and wealthy residents of cities. Only peasants and artisans—a majority of the population but unorganized and powerless—were not spared. Whole regions, as we noted above, escaped certain taxes by virtue of privileges that were accorded (or confirmed) upon their entry into the realm. The list of the elites fattening at the public trough also grew. Besides the nobility, who benefited from military employment, pensions, and control of patronage, there were the holders of government annuities (*rentes*); the owners of government offices, whose inflated salaries (*gages*) depended on taxation; the financial officers, who battened on the rights they had to a share of the taxes they collected; and, mingling with them all, the semi-public financiers, who thrived by providing services for the fisc and by mobilizing the savings of the wealthy for the Crown.[10]

The complexities of the fiscal system almost defy description, particularly since it changed considerably between the fourteenth and the seventeenth centuries. But at the risk of oversimplification, one can say that the French taxpayers paid direct taxes levied chiefly on land and income from land, although initially the direct taxes may have simply been a fixed sum per hearth. The best known of the direct taxes was the *taille*, but there were other related levies, such as the *taillon*, the *crues*, and the *capitation*. Taxpayers also owed indirect taxes: excise taxes on a bewildering variety of items, most notably wine; transit taxes for goods passing from one region of the kingdom to another; and a salt tax (the *gabelle*).

Rights to collect a considerable portion of indirect taxes were sold to private tax farmers. The other taxes (chiefly direct taxation) were collected by the provincial estates or by royal officials known as *élus*. In certain provinces—in Languedoc, for example—the estates not only voted and collected taxes but also determined their form.[11] In other provinces, estates voted the taxes but the *élus* collected them. And in the areas that had long been part of the kingdom, the Crown imposed taxes without any vote by estates and the *élus* collected them.

If we consider the Crown's problems in the abstract, we can perhaps make sense of certain features of the tax system, which many historians dismiss as irrational and incomprehensible.[12] First, as we already know, the Crown had to make concessions to powerful elites and to new provinces. Hence the widespread exemptions in the tax system and the lack of uniformity. Hence too the elites' capturing the lion's share of tax revenues. In 1677 fully 33 percent of the taxes collected in Languedoc passed directly to local notables, and another 19 percent was spent under their direction.[13]

A second problem stemmed from the high cost of assessing wealth in a country where few could read and where much of the wealth was in land and spread out over an enormous countryside. The military engineer and tax reformer Vauban complained of the difficulties of judging the value of land and assessing a land tax at the beginning of the eighteenth century, and the obstacles were undoubtedly more severe in the fourteenth and fifteenth centuries.[14] Because commerce was dispersed and heterogeneous, similar problems arose with levying excise and transit taxes. Widespread exemptions only aggravated matters: how did one stop cheap, untaxed salt from being smuggled into areas that paid a high price for salt because of the *gabelle*?[15] Wealth, be it in land or in commerce, was therefore costly to assess; and taxes, both direct and indirect, were expensive to collect. And monitoring financial officials—to detect cheating, for example— proved arduous. It was hard to determine whether a tax receiver was in arrears because of corruption or simply because a late harvest had delayed collections.[16]

In a vast country with primitive transportation and an atomized economy, the Crown also confronted the laborious task of moving money from place to place. Shipping coins to Paris was so costly that it was only attempted for provinces near Paris, and even then only a fraction was sent. In 1609, for example, only 20 percent of direct taxes collected were carted to Paris, and most of the shipments came from nearby Normandy. The distant *généralité* of Riom sent only 0.7 percent of its take.[17] Most tax revenues were therefore spent locally. The king typically earmarked certain tax revenues for local salaries; in Languedoc, for example, he used the *gabelle* to pay the magistrates of the Parlement of Toulouse.[18] Other revenues were committed to regional military expenses or went to pay pensions to neighborhood magnates. Such local disbursements (known as *assignations*) were in fact the most common way for the Crown to pay all of its bills.[19] And since so much tax revenue was spent in the provinces, the monarchy had to wrestle control over its funds from local elites, who had their own ideas about how the money should be spent.[20] The result was to reduce the portion of tax revenues at the king's disposal.

When the Crown actually had to make payments in bullion— when it had to support troops abroad, for example—it relied upon skilled bankers able to carry out the transfer of funds. Even here, though, the bankers strived, whenever possible, to avoid the cumbersome shipment of coin by using paper instruments such as bills of exchange. That bills of exchange did not always suffice to pay armies abroad helps explain why accumulating bullion often obsessed the French kings. For them it was a strategic good, a weapon essential for war.[21]

The difficulties the Crown encountered in assessing wealth and in moving money from place to place help explain the fisc's predilection for farming out the indirect taxes. Confiding the indirect taxes to a centralized bureaucracy would have raised horrendous problems, given the diversity and dispersion of French trade and the widespread exemptions. Each local office would have been obliged to levy taxes on different items, at different rates, and on trade that fluctuated wildly. The task would have been far more daunting than collecting the *taille*, for year in and year out the *taille* struck the same resource, the comparatively stolid revenues from land. The complexities and uncertainties are perhaps one reason why the rights to collect the indirect taxes were generally auctioned off. The auctions attracted the individuals who knew best how to collect a particular tax and got them to reveal what the tax was worth. The tax farmers who bought the auctioned rights also helped make disbursements, by paying salaries or covering *assignations* with the money they had gathered.[22]

The final and most serious dilemma the king faced—one that merits detailed attention because of its political consequences—was the necessity of borrowing. War, as we shall see, inflated the king's expenses grotesquely, while the ravages of fighting depressed the economy and caused tax revenues to fall. The solution was to borrow, but the Crown remained a notoriously poor credit risk. The king repeatedly broke his agreements with lenders, particularly when the immediate needs of war pushed him to desperation; only when it was in his "interest to do so," as one historian has observed, were his promises to his creditors kept. The king might conclude a contract with one of the *traitants*, who furnished him with short term loans, and then break it almost before the ink was dry. Or he could engage in something far worse—full scale default and debt repudiation. Lenders were therefore loath to extend him credit, except on the dearest of terms. "The king," as Colbert said, "has no credit; one deals with him only with the expectation that he is to go bankrupt."[23]

In the sixteenth century, it is true, the monarchy did briefly seem to have fashioned the beginnings of a system of public credit. In 1522 the Crown gained access to long term credit by having the city government of Paris issue perpetual annuities (*rentes sur l'hôtel de ville*) backed by royal tax revenues that the Crown placed under the city's control. Having the city government administer the annuities reassured the rente holders, who would have hesitated to lend to the king directly. The rente holders—most of them Parisians—knew that the city and its powerful allies in the Parlement of Paris would protect their interests. The city served as a financial intermediary for the issue of *rentes* again in 1536, and the same reassuring practice was soon regularized and swiftly extended to other cities, among them Lyon, at the time the financial capital of France. There the Crown also managed to tap the vibrant short-term commercial money market of the local fairs by borrowing regularly from a syndicate of bankers known as the *grand parti*.

But the king could not be trusted. In Lyon the Crown defaulted on its debts, seized tax revenues that it had pledged for short- and for long-term credit, and employed force to extort loans from city councilors. The *grand parti* collapsed with a bankruptcy in 1558, and afterwards the only money that Lyon advanced came from personal loans that city councilors contracted, often under duress. In Paris, the *rentes sur l'hôtel de ville* also degenerated into forced loans. By the end of the sixteenth century, public credit had largely disappeared, and the monarchy was reduced to the medieval practice of having the king's councilors take out loans in their own name.[24]

Thereafter lending to the king continued to be risky. Default by the Crown was common, usually punctuated by the establishment of an extraordinary royal tribunal—a *chambre de justice*—to threaten lenders and frighten them into renegotiating loans. One can count at least fourteen *chambres de justice* in the sixteenth, seventeenth, and eighteenth centuries. The members of the *chambres de justice* were handpicked by the Crown, and at least in theory they had the power to send financiers to the gallows. Although death penalties were extremely rare (usually the *chambre de justice* did nothing more than impose fines, after which the king declared an amnesty so as not to frighten away lenders), the losses from defaults, late payments, and renegotiated loans drove many a financier into bankruptcy.[25] It is hardly surprising, then, that the Crown had to pay enormous interest rates to attract lenders, at least in moments of crisis when the risk of default ran high. During the difficult years of the 1640s and 1650s, for example, the Crown paid 10, 15, or even 25 percent interest, at a time when private parties borrowed at about 6 percent.[26]

Tax farming and the sale of government offices, which survived longer in France than in England, provided the government with expedients to attract wary lenders; as a result, much of the monarchy's credit was advanced by tax farmers and office holders. The tax farmers loaned money to the Crown and then arranged for repayment out of the taxes they collected. Their tax farms protected them (at least to a certain degree) from a government default because they had a fairly secure claim to government revenue: after all, the taxes they took in were in their hands, not in the king's. Moreover, the Crown might hesitate before defaulting on their loans because it would have to go to the trouble of installing new tax collectors. In a sense, their tax farms served as collateral for their loans.[27]

Selling a government office, which amounted to a loan by the office purchaser, protected the lender in much the same way, for he had a prior claim on the revenues and other benefits attached to the office. The benefits could include not just the revenues of the office, but power, honor, tax exemptions, and other privileges. By the late seventeenth century, government borrowing via the sale of offices was highly developed; and it had transformed the office holders into financial intermediaries, who provided the government with a limited but relatively cheap source of long-term loans. Under law, offices were deemed real property, and prospective purchasers could borrow from private parties to acquire an office, using its value as collateral. The government apparatus that administered the system—the *parties casuelles*—kept track of the title to each office and of the liens by the private lenders who had financed its purchase. The private lenders could sue the office holder if their loan was not paid; and like the holder of a modern mortgage, they were assured of a first claim on the value of the office. Since they did not have to worry about the office holder's other financial dealings and since the value of the office that backed their loan was readily ascertained, they were willing to advance money to purchase offices at market rates of interest. And since the office holder himself could readily finance his office at market rates, and since his liability in the affair was essentially limited to the value of the office itself, he would demand less of a premium in the form of the benefits and revenues attached to the office. The result was that the government could raise private capital at relatively low cost, particularly since some of the benefits accorded office holders—power, tax exemptions, and other privileges—were non-pecuniary.[28]

The Crown could also borrow from existing office holders by promising increased revenues in return for an additional loan. The value of the offices involved would then rise; and by using the increased value of the posts as collateral, the office holders could raise capital privately to finance the sum they advanced to the Crown. In the first half of the seventeenth century, it is true, such transactions frequently masked forced loans extorted from the office holders, but by the eighteenth century the process was usually voluntary. It began with negotiations between the Crown and an organized corporation of existing office holders—negotiations conducted efficiently with an agent of the office holders' corporation—and it concluded with an agreement that had to be approved by a majority vote of the members of the corporation. The whole system made it more difficult for the king to default on the payments due the officer holders. Not only did they have a prior claim on the benefits of the office, but tampering with the payments due them could provoke the ire of powerful, organized corporations.[29]

None of these devices, of course, afforded perfect protection to those who advanced money to the Crown. The king repudiated agreements with tax farmers, and he withheld payments to office holders as well. These expedients and others like them did not eliminate all the dangers of lending to the Crown, nor did they permit the Crown to do all of its borrowing at private market rates: the king continued to pay a substantial premium on many of his debts, at least during times of crisis. The expedients did, however, attract lenders to do business with a horribly unreliable client. That the king resorted to such practices was thus understandable, and we can see why he did not simply sweep them away, even though in the long run they ate away at his power. The sale of offices, after all, cost the king control over officials and encouraged the granting of privileges and immunities to corporations of office holders. So did loans made by existing

office holders. So too did yet another fiscal expedient: having a corporate body like the Estates of Languedoc use its good credit rating
to borrow for the Crown. When the corporate body borrowed for the
Crown voluntarily, it usually received something in return, such as
stronger privileges or discretion over some of the king's revenue.[30]
The loss of power that such corporate borrowing or the sale of offices
entailed might be a small price to pay, though, if it permitted the
king to raise cash in a moment of crisis.

Here the theoretically minded reader might wonder why the king
did not sell more offices and thereby dilute the office holders' share
of power. Or why not aggressively play one group of officers against
another to achieve the same goal? Either maneuver would eliminate
obstructive officials, and the monarchy was certainly not above stoop-
ing to such tactics—indeed, it employed them before and during the
revolt known as the Fronde. The problem was that it could not push
such tactics too far. Multiplying the number of offices or unleashing
cutthroat battles among the holders would eventually diminish the
value of the offices that served as collateral for the king's loans. Not
only would the king lose the backing of officials whose support he
needed but he would reduce his ability to borrow. Perhaps that is one
reason why Louis XIV took steps to limit access to the elite: ultimately it strengthened the fisc.[31]

Exactly how much money the French fiscal system put at the
king's disposal is nearly impossible to say; the system was so riddled
with privileges, corporate influence, and other peculiarities that it
condemns to futility any effort to determine the Crown's spendable
income precisely. In the first place, we generally do not know what
funds lay under the control of the king and what belonged to privileged elites.[32] Worse, the tax figures we do have—numbers gathered
in the first half of the eighteenth century by Jean-Roland Mallet
and François Forbonnais—are by and large incomplete. They are derived from the archives of the central treasury, and unfortunately
the central treasury did not record everything the government collected. The treasury accounts omitted from tax receipts large sums
that were spent locally on assessment and collection costs, salaries
and military expenses, and certain disbursements and *assignations*.
The amounts excluded loomed large in the budget, and in some instances the feeble receipts in the treasury documents formed only a
fourth of what was actually collected.[33]

One might assume that the central treasury numbers represented the fraction of tax receipts under the king's control—the king's spendable income. Nothing, though, could be more misleading. The sums missing from the treasury accounts included royal surtaxes hidden under the rubric of collection costs, large payments to royal troops posted in or traveling through the provinces, and politically sensitive disbursements that the king wanted paid secretly—all clearly items under royal control. The expense figures in the central treasury accounts are equally misleading. And the fact that the accounts mix in a bewildering fashion both tax receipts and money advanced in the form of loans only compounds the difficulty, particularly during times of crisis, when taxes fell into arrears and loans mounted.[34]

The best we can do is to construct a series of guesses, beginning with the central treasury figures (Table 1). Given their shortcomings, all we can hope is that they yield a trend. Although they cannot reveal the precise level of tax receipts or of the king's spendable income, we might reasonably expect them to run roughly parallel to the king's income. The figures themselves are fairly certain, at least after about 1600, and the trend stands out fairly clearly for the seventeenth century. If we convert the monetary figures to a commodity such as wheat or to man-days of labor, then we see that both real tax revenue and real per-capita taxes rose abruptly in the 1630s, receded slightly in the 1660s, climbed again during the wars of Louis XIV's reign, and then reached even higher levels in the eighteenth century. It would be reasonable to assume that the king's spendable income did the same.[35]

To overcome the limitations of the central treasury records, we can use some rough estimates assembled by James Collins for the period up to 1640 (see Table 2). His figures attempt to account for revenue that was spent locally and that never appeared in the central treasury records. They concern regular taxes only (here meaning traditional direct and indirect taxes), and hence they exclude a bewildering variety of expedients that the monarchy resorted to in times of crisis, particularly during the 1630s and 1640s. The expedients, ranging from forced loans and temporary taxes on officers to every imaginable sort of borrowing, raised, at least temporarily, the money at the Crown's disposal; and since they permitted France to wage war against the Habsburgs, their importance cannot be denied. But ulti-

TABLE I

Central Treasury Receipts, 1560s to 1780s

Decade	Average annual receipts nominal[a]	Grain equiv.[b]	Labor equiv.[c]	Per capita receipts nominal[d]	Per capita grain equiv.[e]	Per capita labor equiv.[f]
1560/69	10.22	2.56	33.83	0.63	0.16	2.10
1570/79	20.97	3.73	42.81	1.29	0.23	2.64
1580/89	30.39	4.43	54.70	1.88	0.27	3.39
1590/99	21.26	2.04	41.34	1.30	0.13	2.53
1600/09	24.30	3.94	48.97	1.53	0.24	3.00
1610/19	30.68	4.63	48.58	1.71	0.26	2.72
1620/29	43.11	5.07	74.80	2.41	0.28	4.18
1630/39	92.35	10.48	153.92	5.16	0.59	8.60
1640/49	114.98	11.15	159.06	6.58	0.64	9.11
1650/59	126.86	10.53	154.11	7.26	0.60	8.83
1660/69	91.72	8.63	107.86	5.00	0.47	5.87
1670/79	108.95	13.57	139.21	5.25	0.65	6.71
1680/89	119.28	13.83	155.32	5.52	0.64	7.19
1690/99	145.83	12.62	184.82	7.25	0.63	9.19
1700/09	117.99	11.42	142.28	5.87	0.57	7.08
1710/19	130.82	10.48	147.65	6.19	0.50	6.99
1720/29	197.18	15.18	201.92	9.29	0.72	9.51
1730/39	213.00	19.78	234.57	9.50	0.88	10.46
1740/49	289.39	24.97	302.69	12.45	1.07	13.02
1750/59	273.38	22.59	262.31	11.34	0.94	10.88
1760/69	343.80	25.83	331.82	13.53	1.02	13.05
1770/79	362.00	21.62	320.27	13.72	0.82	12.14
1780/89	421.50	29.50	328.71	15.46	1.08	12.06

SOURCES: Central Treasury receipts for the 1560s, 1580s, 1660s–1710s, and 1770s come from Philip T. Hoffman, "Taxes and Agrarian Life in Early Modern France: Land Sales, 1550–1730," *JEH* 46 (1986): 46–47. Receipts for the period 1590–1659 come from Françoise Bayard, *Le monde des financiers au XVIIe siècle*, (Paris, 1988), 29, supplemented by the figures in Richard Bonney, *The King's Debts*, (Oxford, 1981), 304–5, when Bayard's figures for a year were lacking. Figures for the 1570s average those given by Hoffman and Bayard. Figures for the 1720s average those given by Hoffman and those in James C. Riley, "French Finances, 1727–1768," *JMH* 59 (1987): 209–43. The figures for the period 1730–69 come from Riley and those from the 1780s from Peter Mathias and Patrick O'Brien, "Taxation in Britain and France, 1715–1810," *JEEcH* 5 (1976): 601–50. Population figures were derived from Jacques Dupâquier, ed., *Histoire de la population francaise*, 4 vols. (Paris, 1988), 1:513–24, 2:64–68. Where Dupâquier gives low and high figures, I averaged the two and to correct Dupâquier's numbers for the size and contemporary frontiers (Dupâquier assumes fixed modern frontiers) I used evidence on the area of France in Roland Mousnier, *The Institutions of France Under the Absolute Monarchy, 1589–1789*, trans. Arthur Goldhammer and Brian Pearce, 2 vols. (Chicago, 1979–84), 1:682–86. The wheat equivalents were figured using a nine-year moving average of Paris wheat prices centered on the year in question; the wheat prices come from Micheline Baulant, "Les prix des grains à Paris de 1431 à 1788," *Annales* 23 (1968): 520–40. Labor equivalents were calculated using daily wages for unskilled Parisian laborers in Micheline Baulant, "Les salaires des ouvriers du bâtiment à Paris de 1400 à 1726," *Annales* 26 (1971): 463–83.

[a] Millions of livres.   [d] Livres.
[b] Millions of hectoliters of wheat.   [e] Hectoliters of wheat.
[c] Millions of man-days.   [f] Man-days.

TABLE 2

Gross Regular Tax Revenue, 1364–1640

Period	Direct taxes[a]	Total taxes[a]	Grain equiv. of total taxes[b]	Labor equiv. of total taxes[c]
Charles V (1364–80)		2.0		
Charles VI (1380–1422)	0.6–1.4	2.0		16.0
Charles VII (1422–61)	0.6–1.4	1.8–2.3	2.3–2.9	12.4–15.8
Louis XI (1461–83)				
Maximum for reign, in 1483	4.4	4.7	7.3	37.6
After reign	2.1	2.5		
	(1487)	(1484)		
Francis I (1515–47)				
Ca. 1523	4.8	8[d]	6.5	53.3
Avg. for reign		8–10	5.0–6.2	48.0–60.1
1549	6.6	8–9[d]	3.1–3.5	40.0–45.0
1581	7.3	31.6[e]	6.8	57.5
1607	17.9	30.4	5.0	60.8
1620	19.2	33.7	4.9	56.2
1634	38.9	63.2	7.5	105.3
1640	44.1	77.8	9.2	103.7

SOURCES: Tax figures come from James Collins, Fiscal Limits of Absolutism: Direct Taxation in Early Seventeenth-Century France (Berkeley, 1983), 48–55, 233–36. Grain equivalents and labor equivalents were calculated using figures in Micheline Baulant, "Les salaires des ouvriers du bâtiment à Paris de 1400 à 1726," Annales 26 (1971): 463–83 and "Les prix des grains à Paris de 1431 à 1788," Annales 23 (1968): 520–40.

NOTE: Regular taxation includes direct taxes, salt taxes, sale taxes, and transit taxes. Although the figures attempt to include sums levied and spent locally, certain local charges are omitted. For details, see Collins, Fiscal Limits of Absolutism, 48–55, 233–36. For each year of the table, the grain and labor equivalents were calculated by using the median of the average annual prices (or wages) for a nine-year period centered on the year in question. For the reigns of Charles VI, Charles VII, and Francis I (average for reign) the calculation used the following years: 1402, 1442, and 1531. Wages here are for unskilled labor and do not reflect the cost of skilled labor such as soldiers.

[a] Millions of livres.   [c] Millions of man-days.

[b] Millions of hectolitres.   [d] Certain taxes excluded.

[e] Includes loans and irregular tax revenue in addition to regular taxation; certain levies for local charges omitted.

mately it was the regular tax revenue, not the expedients, that defined the revenues at the monarch's disposal.[36]

Along with local tax series, Collins's estimates let us push the evolution of French taxes back into the fourteenth century. Once converted into grain or labor equivalents, his estimates confirm that real taxes shot up in the 1630s. They perhaps disclose an earlier increase as well, between the reigns of Louis XI and Francis I, although the size and durability of this increase depend on whether one prefers the labor or grain equivalents. Local tax records paint the same picture: spiraling real taxation in the seventeenth century, and perhaps in the late fifteenth or early sixteenth century as well. And the local series stretch back far enough to reveal the very first revolution in real tax levels: the jump that accompanied the initial imposition of permanent taxation during the Hundred Years War.[37]

The Role of Representative Institutions

The role that representative bodies played in providing and spending French taxes changed considerably during the early modern period. In the late fourteenth century, they seemed condemned to insignificance. This was true in particular of the Estates General, which had lost a magnificent opportunity to have a voice in taxation by the 1360s. Summoned thereafter at the king's will—and only when the Crown was weak—the Estates General would never become a regular organ of government and never exercise control over the purse. While in England the Parliament was convening better than three years out of four between 1327 and 1485, in France the Estates General did not meet even one year out of five during the same period, and thereafter their meetings became even more sporadic. The English Parliament meanwhile had become the arena for negotiation over taxes; in France, what negotiation there was took place in provincial estates and local assemblies, bypassing the Estates General altogether.[38]

The Estates General never wielded true legislative powers either. Although they influenced royal legislation through petitions and remonstrances, their role remained advisory, for it was the king who made the law and he was under no obligation to heed the opinion of the Estates. And even when the Estates General tried to assert themselves, the Crown easily overcame them by pitting off one interest against another or by ignoring their requests once they had been dissolved. At the Estates General of Tours in 1484, for example, it was suggested that all parts of France have provincial estates with rights to consent to taxation. The Crown persuaded deputies from regions that already had provincial estates not to support the proposal, and it was dropped from the cahier of remonstrances.[39] The same Estates General also asked for regular meetings of their body every two years to deliberate over taxation. The king's chancellor accepted the re-

quest; but once the Estates were dissolved, the Crown went on levying taxes without ever calling back the Estates. The Crown even
managed to get a vote in favor of dissolution by pitting region against
region in negotiations over regional tax shares.[40]

Like the Estates General, the provincial estates also fell into decline in the late fourteenth century. Even under a weak king—such
as the mad Charles VI—the monarchy was able to tax without their
consent, largely because important provincial elites (the nobility, government officers, influential city dwellers) had been bought off with
exemptions and a share of royal tax revenues. What did they care if
the local peasants and artisans shouldered the burden?[41]

Beginning about 1420, though, the provincial estates experienced
a revival. In much of France they met more frequently, gained royal
recognition for their right to consent to taxation, and developed a permanent corps of officials who assessed and levied the taxes they had
approved. A few of them faltered, but by the late sixteenth century
provincial estates voted taxation in over half the country. Their revival reflected, at least in part, the royal strategy of confirming local
privileges in order to yoke provinces to the Crown. What better way
was there to bind a region and its elites to the Crown than to confirm their right to assemble, to present remonstrances, and to consent to taxation? The provincial estates also facilitated the task of
negotiation between the Crown and the local elites. And finally, the
Crown came to rely upon them to assess and to collect local taxes—
a task that we know was both difficult and costly in France. While a
region with strong provincial estates—Languedoc for example—escaped with a somewhat lower tax burden thanks to the protection
they afforded, the king had less difficulty assessing, collecting, and
predicting his tax revenue when the estates were in charge.[42]

In the seventeenth century, the balance of power between the
king and the provincial estates shifted in the king's favor. The change
was particularly marked under Louis XIV. The Crown now had more
agents to collect taxes and to enforce the royal will than it did in
the sixteenth century.[43] More important, it could distribute greater
resources in order to make the provincial estates bend to the monarch's will. If the provincial estates resisted, if they hesitated to grant
the king's will or failed to meet his demands in their entirety, the
Crown could react summarily. It is thus not surprising that in the

seventeenth century the monarchy suppressed—or simply failed to summon—estates it considered dilatory or obstructive, so that by 1700 the area where the provincial estates voted taxes had fallen to only 30 percent of France.[44]

More frequently, however, the Crown resorted to rewards and to manipulation, methods that succeeded with even the strongest estates, such as those of Languedoc. Pensions, access to royal patronage, discretion over the spending of tax revenues, and outright bribery from the abundant royal coffers were all used to win the assent of particular estates. If such measures failed, the Crown interfered with elections, packed assemblies, manipulated agendas, and excluded obstructive members in order to get its way. Loyal servants of the Crown presided over meetings of the estates and reported on recalcitrant deputies who failed to heed the royal will. By the late seventeenth century, the royal tactics had rendered the remaining estates completely docile. As John Locke noted during his travels through France, even the estates of Languedoc dared not refuse the king's demands for higher taxes.[45]

≺ III ≻

Coping with Fiscal Crises

Although the king's expenses, like his tax revenues, are impossible to determine accurately, we know that the costs of war provoked nearly all of the tax increases and fiscal crises of early modern France. The Hundred Years War gave birth to permanent taxation in France; the Italian wars ushered in the tax increases under Francis I; and the wars of religion released a torrent of government debt. The Thirty Years War, the struggles against Spain, and the conflicts under Louis XIV caused the spiraling levies and the fiscal imbroglios of the seventeenth century. The reason was simple: armies ballooned in wartime, armies that had to be fed and outfitted. War required guns, horses, subsidies for allies, and increasingly costly defensive fortifications. The cost per soldier grew steadily and so did the size of the armies that had to be assembled. From a maximum of at most 12,000 men when mobilized in the thirteenth century, the French forces could be stretched up to 50,000 men during wartime in the sixteenth century, up to 150,000 or more in the 1630s, and up to 400,000 late in Louis XIV's reign. Although precise figures are impossible to assemble, it is clear that military expenses grew as well, in order to pay for the soldiers, their supplies, and the ever more expensive weaponry and fortifications.[46]

Taxes could not keep pace with the effort needed for mobilization; indeed, indirect taxes were likely to fall as war disturbed the economy.[47] The only way to meet the rocketing expenses was to borrow. Every war thus brought in its wake a flood of red ink and frantic attempts to procure loans. On top of the military costs themselves were piled the crushing rates of interest that the Crown had to pay, and it was during the fiscal crises provoked by war that the Crown turned to its most desperate financial expedients, the ones with the most striking political consequences.

The first half of the seventeenth century—the period from roughly the end of the Wars of Religion (1598) to the close of the war with Spain (1659)—witnessed several crises of this sort, crises with lasting political consequences. Throughout the period, the French fisc was racked by repeated difficulties, but three crises seem particularly revealing: the default on government *rentes* in 1602–4, the seizure of *droits aliénés* in 1634, and the reduction of payments due rentiers and office holders in 1648. The first occurred as Henri IV sought to mend the fiscal ills brought on by the Wars of Religion. The king had emerged from the wars burdened with enormous debts. Even if we ignore the large annual payments he owed office holders (their *gages*, which provided them with a return on their investment), Henri IV's debt service still amounted to over 11 million livres per year in 1607, some 35 or 40 percent of his tax revenue.[48]

To cope with the burden, Henri and his minister Sully undertook a number of reforms and repudiated part of the government debt by defaulting on a portion of the government *rentes* in the years 1602–4. Typically, the *rentes* were held by officers, who had to swallow the reduced return on them and the concomitant loss of capital. To placate them, and for other purposes as well, the monarchy granted the officers a considerable boon: absolute heredity for the offices they owned. In 1604 Henri removed the legal risks that hindered the transfer of offices and gave the officers the right to bequeath their posts to their heirs in return for the payment of an annual fee, the so-called *paulette*. Although their *rentes* had declined in value, they gained more secure title to their government posts, and the market value of their offices surged.

As for the Crown, not only did it placate the officers but it could now sell new offices at inflated prices—or in other words, borrow at a much lower interest rate. The Crown thus had a further reason to favor the *paulette*, its effect upon borrowing. Its consequences for patronage were probably appealing too, for it would undercut the control that the great noble families exercised over government posts. One may of course debate the relative importance of the various motives behind the *paulette*, as historians have, but it is clear that it was at least in part a fiscal expedient designed both to mollify the influential victims of a recent bankruptcy and to facilitate future borrowing. The price of the expedient was of course political, as contemporaries recognized. In the long run the *paulette* reinforced the autonomy of yet another privileged group and weakened the king's hold on what should have been his loyal agents.[49]

In the 1630s, a fiscal crisis again drove the monarchy toward expedients with lasting political consequences. Here the occasion was France's entry into the Thirty Years War. As French involvement grew, as the kingdom struggled against encirclement by the Habsburgs, the Crown sold not only hundreds of offices but also large numbers of *droits aliénés*, the rights to collect hefty new surtaxes, which sometimes dwarfed the *taille* itself. The sale of *droits aliénés*, which were usually purchased by the very financial officers who assessed and collected the surtaxes, was yet another form of government loan. Even these fiscal devices, though, did not make ends meet, and in 1634 the Crown went through what amounted to a partial bankruptcy: it confiscated the rights to the surtaxes (the surtaxes themselves were of course not abolished) and paid off the owners with *rentes* of lower value. The partial bankruptcy was a last-ditch expedient that saved the king 15 million livres a year in debt service, but it enraged the financial officers. Infuriated, they abetted tax revolts, blocked the collection of the surtaxes, or made no levies at all, thereby aiding the numerous peasants who beginning in the late 1630s simply refused to pay taxes.[50]

The monarchy's response was to dispatch the intendants, who took over the local tax system and deployed special military brigades to gather back taxes. The soldiers, though, who might better have been employed in the armies fighting the king's foreign wars, cost more than they collected. They devastated the villages they occupied and kept whatever money they seized for themselves. Clearly, the monarchy could not do without the financial officers' cooperation: it could not perform the difficult task of assessing and collecting taxes without their help. The Crown needed trustworthy tax agents but found itself instead at the mercy of yet another privileged group. Not until much later, on the eve of Colbert's fiscal reforms, did the intendants begin to work side by side with the financial officers. Only then did tax collection proceed smoothly.[51]

Admittedly, the monarchy had other reasons to send the intendants to the provinces: the decision to do so did not merely result from the bankruptcy of 1634. They were needed to suppress tax revolts, reform the army, and prevent the conspiracies fomented, so Richelieu feared, by France's foreign enemies. Nor should one exaggerate the importance of confiscating the *droits aliénés* in 1634. The financial officers—and office holders in general—had other grievances beyond the loss of their *droits aliénés*, and the crisis in 1634 was only the beginning of the chronic fiscal difficulties that plagued France throughout her involvement in the Thirty Years War. Still, the crisis was undeniably one of the factors that brought about the system of provincial intendants, a hallmark of Old Regime governance in France.[52]

In 1648 fiscal expedients once again provoked political upheaval, when they helped trigger the Fronde. The grievances that caused the revolt were complex, but prominent among them, at least at the outset, were the exactions the Crown had recourse to in its desperate attempt to fund the continuing war against the Habsburgs in the Empire and in Spain. To demonstrate to the Spanish negotiators that the French had the will to continue the war, the Crown borrowed heavily. By 1648 it had already anticipated tax revenues due in 1650 and 1651, and it was resorting to even more dire expedients. It diverted taxes earmarked for payments due on existing debt and used the revenue thus released to pay for new loans, contracted, at understandably high interest rates, from financiers. Among the payments cut were those due the owners of government offices and the holders of government *rentes*.[53]

The victims of this partial default included the magistrates of the sovereign law courts. Income from their offices had suffered severely; so had their investments in *rentes*. They were further outraged by a delay in the renewal of the *paulette*. Infuriated, the judges of the Paris Parlement refused to register new fiscal edicts; the Crown had to force them to do so, in a ceremony in which one of the magistrates, Omer Talon, declared that forced registration was improper and that the magistrates ought to be able vote freely on registration without royal interference. In the aftermath, the sovereign courts in Paris united in a joint assembly and demanded a program of reforms that included withdrawal of the royal intendants, financial reform, payment of sums due on *rentes* and offices, and the right to deliberate on financial edicts freely and without royal coercion.[54]

The Fronde raged on until 1653, enlisting the angry opposition of numerous social groups but never provoking any constitutional reorganization. Ultimately, the magistrates of Parlement retreated in horror when the Fronde veered toward fundamental change, and the interests arrayed against the Crown were in any case too diverse to effect a redefinition of the king's role. The precise course of these events need not detain us here; what is worth noting, though, is the way the Crown acted in the aftermath of the Fronde. Throughout the 1650s, when Mazarin was prime minister, the Crown feared that tampering with the *rentes* and the offices would rekindle the Fronde. Unfortunately, France remained at war with Spain until 1659, and the cost of the fighting forced the Crown to curtail payments due on *rentes* in the late 1650s. The Parlement of Paris again reacted, but this time the Crown managed to appease the magistrates of the Parlement by assuring that the *rentes* they held were paid. Giving priority in the payment of *rentes* to the magistrates split them from the other *rente* holders and prevented them from uniting with other opponents of the Crown in a reenactment of the Fronde.[55]

The same sensitivity to the political consequences of default persisted in the 1660s, when Mazarin was dead and Louis XIV had begun his personal rule. Writing in 1663, Colbert worried that *rentes* had fallen into the hands of magistrates from the sovereign courts and other politically influential persons. Such organized individuals could easily react to protect their interests; and Colbert found the situation so threatening that he urged a thorough overhaul of government credit, lest the monarchy and its policies fall hostages to influential creditors.[56]

During each of these seventeenth-century crises, the Crown's reactions fit a clear pattern. In each instance, the costs of warfare necessitated fiscal expedients, typically including some sort of default. But the expedients then unleashed surprising political consequences, whether the Crown tried to appease the debt holders or merely coped with their anger. The needs of the moment—what economists might call the ruler's high discount rate—undoubtedly justified defaulting on the *rentes* in 1602–4, seizing the *droits aliénés* in 1634, and cutting payments due rentiers and office holders in 1648. But the political consequences were considerable and not always predictable: the *paulette*, the intendants, the Fronde, and an enduring concern with the sensitive politics of government debt. If such seventeenth-century examples do not suffice, one only has to consider the decision to call the Estates General in 1789.

The long-run effect that wars and fiscal crises had on representative institutions, on the other hand, is more complex. Consider, for example, the Hundred Years War. After initially helping to advance the cause of the estates, it ushered in a long period of taxation without consent. Then, in the latter stages of the war, the Crown found it in its interest to negotiate with local assemblies, and the provincial estates revived. They gave the king an effective forum for dealing with local elites, particularly in farflung provinces where the Crown's hold was weak, and in return for spoils and privileges they helped the king assemble his realm from the wreckage of the Hundred Years War. Well into the sixteenth century most of the provincial estates thrived in cooperation with the monarchy and assisted the feeble bureaucracy in the fleecing of the common people.

In the seventeenth century, however, the balance of power, as we saw above, turned in favor of the Crown. To wage war against the Habsburgs, the monarchy pushed taxes far higher, particularly in the 1630s; and despite the tax revolts and the fiscal crises that repeatedly shook the country, the Crown in the end had greater resources at its disposal than ever before. It had larger armies, more servants, and larger sums of money to spend. The resources all served to reduce the provincial estates and other representative assemblies to docility.

It is important to recall here that the provincial estates were not

crushed by force. By and large, the members of the estates were bribed
and bought off, like other local notables throughout the realm. That
the king no longer needed the provincial estates as organizations
may well have reflected the fact that he could now use other channels to dispense spoils. The intendants were particularly effective at
distributing the king's favors, and they could also conduct negotiations between the Crown and local elites, supplanting the provincial
estates in this role. The estates survived only where they were too
deeply ingrained in local privileges to be uprooted or where they continued to aid the king in the difficult task of tax assessment and tax
collection. But even where they persisted, they never developed true
legislative powers and never formed a real forum for resistance to
the Crown.[57]

Given the weakened role of representative assemblies and the
structure of governance in France, it is hardly surprising that by
the seventeenth century French political thought did not necessarily
resonate with the same language one heard across the Channel.
Although Protestant and Catholic theorists in France had spoken of
resistance to the Crown during the Wars of Religion, the experience
of forty years of civil war created a powerful argument for a strong
monarchy and pushed French political thought toward firmer em-
brace with absolutism by the dawn of the seventeenth century. By the
time of the Fronde, we can thus have a crisis in which the abundant
pamphlet literature rarely raises fundamental constitutional issues,
since nearly all authors agree on the need for a strong monarchy. The
contrast with England, where pamphlets openly addressed constitutional limits to the king's powers, is striking.[58]

Not that the French considered themselves slaves. The most influential French political thinker of the late sixteenth century, Jean
Bodin, pointed the way toward absolutism by subjecting customary law to the king's authority. But for Bodin, the king's subjects
were "free." Because the king was to abide by the laws of nature,
his subjects, so Bodin maintained, enjoyed natural liberty and were
by no stretch of the imagination slaves. In much the same manner
did Charles Loyseau, an important legal theorist of absolutism in
the early seventeenth century, rule out any contradiction between
a strong monarchy and personal liberty. In traditional Aristotelian
fashion, Loyseau distinguished between absolute monarchy and des-

potism and argued that a monarch would respect property and contracts. For him and for most other French thinkers of the time, only a despot would violate personal liberty. Similar arguments were made even during moments of crisis. On the eve of the Fronde, when the magistrate Omer Talon declared his opposition to the forced registration of financial edicts, he acknowledged that the king was accountable to no one. Yet he too distinguished the king's absolutism from despotism and asserted that the king's subjects—to the king's glory—were free and not slaves.[59]

The problem with such an idea of freedom was that nothing backed it up. Bodin grounded his notion of the subject's freedom in a flimsy and highly theoretical notion of natural law, which the king was supposed to observe. Loyseau's guarantees of liberty were equally shaky. More telling than constitutional theory here, in a kingdom where theory was no guide to practice, was the reality of politics: in the seventeenth century there simply were no powerful countervailing forces that could guarantee liberties for all of the kingdom. No central organization could negotiate with the Crown and speak, even in theory, for the entire realm. In particular, no governmental organ could protect the average subject's property from arbitrary taxation. The Estates General had long been in decline, no doubt because they were ill suited to negotiation in a country as vast and diverse as France. The provincial estates survived, but they cooperated with the Crown, enjoyed its privileges, and helped collect its taxes. It was therefore unlikely that they would consistently defend peasants and artisans against royal taxation, and in any case their interests never extended beyond their provinces. As for the magistrates in the sovereign law courts, their offices gave them a stake in the system, and they were easily bought off with specific favors. Like the provincial estates, their interests tended to be narrow and particularistic. They might ask for a form of *habeas corpus*, as the sovereign courts in Paris did at the onset of the Fronde, but it would apply only to the magistrates themselves. Or in a provincial Parlement the magistrates might support resistance to the *taille* but not to the indirect taxes that provided the income due them from their offices.[60]

In practice then liberty amounted to nothing more than privilege, particularly when liberty meant securing property from arbitrary taxation. Without an Estates General or another broad organization that could prevail against the Crown, "resistance to taxation," as Jean Meuvret said long ago, could "only rely upon the provincial courts and estates; by that very fact the goal of tax resistance usually boiled down to the defense of particularistic privileges," and the "struggle for liberty" became little more than the protection of narrow advantage.[61] The privileges in question here were often disguised as medieval in origin, but as we have seen most were created by the early modern monarchy. As the monarchy pursued its fiscal and political goals, the privileges grew ever more tangled. It was never clear whether they were inalienable rights or revocable concessions, but what supported them was not constitutional theory but political power. Indeed, privileges under the Old Regime were a form of property secure only when backed by power; and power, like liberty, came down to defense of privilege.

Not that a more general notion of liberty was inconceivable. In 1664 the Cour des Aides of Paris (a sovereign court that handled tax cases) ruled against *taille* collectors who had searched notarial records to see if a taxpayer was underassessed. In its ruling, the court denounced the audacity of such an action and claimed that it violated the "public liberty of Frenchmen." Yet despite the invocation of a general principle of public liberty, what outraged the court was something very specific: the investigation of notarial records. By revealing the true wealth of families, such investigations undermined tax exemptions for the elite and could be used to mount an attack on privilege. They thus violated an unwritten covenant of late seventeenth-century politics, which protected the elite's property and strengthened their privileges. In the sixteenth and early seventeenth centuries, the elite's property and privileges had not always merited such respect; but by the personal reign of Louis XIV, their property was safe from attack, and their privileges, though sometimes investigated, were thoroughly reinforced. If the concern shown by the Cour des Aides was therefore understandable, the court's real fear was clearly the attack on privilege—the privilege of powerful elites. Even here "public liberty" masked something very narrow.[62]

The peculiar nature of liberty in France thus reflected the structure of the French state in the early modern period: a shifting coalition linking the Crown and various elites, who had given their allegiance to the monarchy in return for privileges and spoils. Long unstable, the coalition hardened and closed in the late seventeenth century. Politics in Old Regime France was the pursuit of privilege and the settlement of arguments among the elites within this coalition; but despite their frequent quarrels, the notables all agreed on the sovereignty of the Crown. Privileged and exempt from taxes, siphoning off a share of the government's revenues, they had little reason to question or to fear the authority of the king.

At the same time, the monarch's powers were hardly unlimited. The Crown depended on the privileged groups and could not survive without the allegiance of at least some of the notables. At various times it relied on the political support of the great magnates, the good will of the courts, or the credit of the financiers. And it always needed reliable agents to carry out its will—for example, the financial officers who collected taxes and advanced money. But the king's ultimate weakness was that he alone held the coalition together. No forum assembled his various supporters, and any decision that would require the elite's assent—for instance, the ending of fiscal exemptions and the imposition of taxes upon the privileged—would entangle the Crown in long and costly negotiations with each privileged group. It is no wonder then that the question of fundamental tax reform, when finally raised, paralyzed the entire polity.

The loss of freedom in the polity was born chiefly by those outside the realm of privilege, the peasants and artisans. The economy in particular suffered, since the property rights of those without influence were insecure and their taxes unpredictable. Privileges cut across the realm and could ensnarl any entrepreneurial undertaking—building a canal, creating a manufacture—in a thicket of litigation. The toll exacted on the economy awaits calculation, but at least in agriculture and transportation there are signs that it dampened trade and discouraged investment. Other sectors of commerce suffered as well since so much effort was devoted to the pursuit of privilege, a pursuit of redistribution that produced absolutely nothing. Banking in particular seems to have suffered grievous harm. Long before John Law, the Crown's actions shattered a nascent financial network in sixteenth-century Lyon, but even more damaging in the long run was the insidious appeal of the fisc. State finance siphoned away talent and capital that might otherwise have been mobilized for productive investment within France.[63]

There remains, though, a paradox within the tax system of early modern France. Shaken by numerous crises, a drag on the French economy, it nonetheless managed to survive until 1789. It muddled through, and the fisc coughed up enough in taxes and loans to fight war after war. Not that the tax system was fragile, as is sometimes supposed. What appeared to be fragility was merely the lack of hierarchy and of centralization, since tax administration under the Old Regime was decentralized—farmed out, auctioned off, or left to the care of local officials. The decentralization was in a sense the strength of the tax system. But having weathered so many crises, why did it founder in 1789? What was different about the final crisis of the Old Regime? Perhaps it was the political paralysis that tax reform provoked.

≺ APPENDIX ≻

The Cost of Government Borrowing

What it cost the Crown to borrow is a complex subject and a forbidding one for the non-specialist. In the first place, at any given time, the interest rate varied greatly from loan to loan depending on the guarantees and the collateral that the government offered. Interest rates on a given type of loan also varied over time, depending on the financial health of the monarchy and the prospects for repayment. In the late 1540s, for example, the Crown typically paid 4 percent per quarter for its short term debt at the Lyon fairs, whereas private merchants borrowed at only 2.5 to 3 percent per quarter. But the effective interest rate the government paid on this debt changed dramatically in response to news of war, peace, or financial difficulty. Evidence for such dramatic changes can be found in the secondary market for the Lyon fair debt, in which prices varied inversely with the effective interest rate or return. A reassuring amortization plan pushed the government debt in Lyon to 101.75 percent of its face value in 1555; the 1558 bankruptcy immediately drove it down to 70 percent of its face value and eventually to 38 percent of face value by 1564. The seventeenth century witnessed similar variations in the premium that the government had to pay lenders. Typically it was high during moments of crises, but it could come down during times of peace and when the finances were healthy. After Colbert righted government finances, for example, the monarchy's credit rating improved, so that by 1680 it contracted some loans at the going private rate of 5 percent. In the eighteenth century war again drove government interest rates up above the market rate during moments of crisis.[64]

The French Fiscal Crisis of 1788 and the Financial Origins of the Revolution of 1789

KATHRYN NORBERG

IN MARCH OF 1789, representatives from the villages, towns, and guilds of the bailiwick of Bar-le-Duc met to choose from among their numbers deputies to attend the Estates General. In accordance with royal decree, the Lorrainers elected their representatives and then drew up instructions to guide their deputies; they also included grievances to be presented to the king. This document, or *cahier*, began with protestations of devotion to the Crown: "The love of Louis XVI," the Lorrainers proclaimed, "is the only emotion of the French; the people of the countryside have forgotten their miseries and given themselves over to transports of generosity; a happy future is going to replace the days when the peasantry could only procure enough money to pay their taxes and buy coarse bread." The Lorrainers would remain loyal to their king, but their devotion had special terms and distinct conditions. They wanted the Estates General to vote by head; they asked that the "constitution of the government be established and ordered"; and they insisted that "the liberty of property and subjects also be under the safeguard of the laws." They also demanded that the Estates General meet periodically, for "no tax direct or indirect and no loan can be established without the free consent of the nation." The Lorrainers went on to explain that "all taxes whether for the king or the needs of the provinces are the price of the protection that each subject receives from the king."[1] A contract existed between king and people, which was sealed by taxes and directed toward the maintenance of freedom.

Over the course of the next decade, the French would witness a remarkable increase in civil and political liberty. In the spring of 1789, every village and town would meet for the first time in nearly two hundred years to elect representatives for the Estates General. By the fall of the same year, the Estates would have become the National Assembly, the sovereign authority in the land, and every Frenchman would have his civil liberties guaranteed by the Declaration of the Rights of Man and the Citizen. Approximately three years later, French subjects, now citizens, would have a written constitution, a limited monarchy, a regularly convened legislative assembly, and limited manhood suffrage. Many regimes would follow and many changes would occur, some of which enhanced freedom (the adoption of universal manhood suffrage), and some of which did not (the dictatorship of the Committee of Public Safety and, much worse, that of Napoleon Bonaparte). The revolutionaries did not always live up to the slogan "liberty, equality, and fraternity," but between 1789 and 1799 Frenchmen still enjoyed fuller political liberty than their contemporaries either on the Continent or, arguably, across the Channel. The years between 1789 and 1799 witnessed many political changes and a series of different political regimes, but most scholars would concede that overall the French Revolution occupies an important— if not key—place in the history of freedom.

What these same scholars would have considerably more trouble agreeing upon are forces which led to the Revolution. Few historical questions have exercised historians more than the causes of the French Revolution, and two hundred years after the event unanimity is far from being achieved on this issue. Still, all scholars agree that one circumstance immediately precipitated the Revolution and with it the emergence of modern freedom in France: the collapse of the royal finances. Government bankruptcy usually leads the list of "causes" attributed to the Revolution and "the death of credit" was recently once again invoked in a popular synthesis.[2] But in 1788, the French Crown was no stranger to fiscal difficulties. In 1715, 1722, 1759, 1763, and 1772 the Crown had declined to meet or had suspended its obligations. It had declared at least partial bankruptcy and faced, it appears, financial problems if not as serious at least as compelling as those of 1788. But at these times, no Revolution occurred. Only in 1788 did the fiscal difficulties of the Crown lead to a restructuring of the French polity along more democratic lines. What made the fiscal crisis of 1788 different from all the others that had preceded it? What made the fiscal difficulties of 1788—or at least their consequences—unique?

Indeed, what made the bankruptcy of 1788 the Revolution of 1789? This is the question that this chapter seeks to answer. The chapter begins by examining current scholarly explanations of the bankruptcy, all of which provide insights but none of which supplies an answer to the question posed here. In order to answer the question it will be useful first to ask what had *prevented* revolution during previous bankruptcies. The next two sections examine two other crucial moments in French fiscal history: 1720 when Law's system collapsed and 1763 when France faced bankruptcy thanks to the Seven Years War; both crises were contained and neither occasioned the political turmoil which followed the fiscal difficulties of 1788. We are then ready to see why the bankruptcy of 1788 was unique and why this financial crisis turned into the revolution of 1789.

The key here is politics. Decades of evolving political theory and bitter political struggle preceded and precipitated the revolution of 1789. Financial problems became entangled with political problems and a simple request for a loan involved liberty, sovereignty, and the natural law. The king's economic problems were problems of political economy, and a history of finances alone is not sufficient to explain the astonishing political event of 1788, the king's virtual bankruptcy. Financial problems certainly were relevant; but 1788 was different from 1720 or 1763 because the political situation—both practical and theoretical—was different.

< I >

The Background

An old and voluminous bibliography can help us elucidate the problems of the French fisc in 1788. Analyses, accounts, apologies, and libels explaining, excusing, and condemning the financial collapse appeared in 1788 and even before. Much of our data comes from contemporaries, men like finance ministers Necker, Calonne, and Loménie de Brienne.[3] But we must keep in mind that they were driven by self-justification, vindication, or outright revenge. The officals who followed these ill-fated ministers, the men of the revolutionary assemblies, are another source of information. In their attempt to cope with the problems they inherited from the Old Regime, they collected a vast amount of data; but they too allowed the political passions of the moment, often only distantly related to finance, to color their view of the Crown's fiscal policies.[4]

In the early twentieth century, some scholars, notably Schnerb, Braesch, Stourm, and of course the best known historian of French fiscal matters, Marion, produced vast tomes on state finance, in particular taxation and revenues.[5] Like contemporaries, these scholars tended to blame certain ministers (like Necker) for France's problems and extol others (like Calonne) for their enlightened but doomed attempts at reform. Such special pleading is not beyond even more recent works. The studies of J. R. Bosher, J. D. Harris, and James Riley also take individual ministers to task.[6] But generally these scholars, who possess a comparative perspective and a grounding in economic history, have promoted a broader view. They take into account administrative structure, interest rates, and economic growth; their research has done much to clear away "the tedium" and "obfuscation," to quote Lucien Febvre, that used to cloud the history of French finances in the Old Regime.[7] Even more enlightening has been the work of the economic historians Eugene White, David Weir, and François Velde, who bring to the study of French finances the theoretical insights of economics and force us to rethink accepted ideas about the crisis of 1788.[8] Our understanding of the Bourbon fisc has also been greatly increased by a virtual rebirth of eighteenth-century political history thanks to Keith Baker, Dale Van Kley, Bailey Stone, François Furet, and others.[9]

Despite this new work, virtually all textbooks and most historians still subscribe to Marcel Marion's interpretation, now some eighty years old. For Marion, the force which undermined French finances was privilege and those who enjoyed it, the nobility. "The Old Regime," Marion observed, "perished because its tax system struck only the inferior classes . . ."[10] Fiscal immunities, whether inherited or purchased, undermined French finances and put the king in the apparently ridiculous position of taxing those who had nothing to tax. They also made it impossible for the Crown to reform the fiscal system and render it more equitable and more efficient. Marion's interpretation has the great advantage of explaining not just the Crown's depleted finances, but also its inability to do anything about the situation. The nobility, the primary beneficiaries of fiscal immunities in Marion's mind, thwarted the attempts of a series of ministers, from Machault down to Loménie de Brienne, to institute equitable and profitable taxes. Fiscal privilege and its beneficiaries brought down the French fisc.

The history of relations between the king and his parlements in the eighteenth century appears to bear out this interpretation. Beginning in the 1720s but escalating in the 1750s and 1760s, the king and the magistrates repeatedly came to blows over fiscal edicts. The issue until the end of the reign was almost always the same—the *vingtième* tax, the only really new tax created in the eighteenth century. Unlike the old *taille*, which was a tax on land, the *vingtième* (at least in principle) constituted a levy on all income and one that struck both commoner and noble, both rich and poor alike. The *vingtième* bore a marked resemblance to Vauban's old reform tax, the *dixième*, which had been levied intermittently during the years 1710–16, 1733–37, and 1741–49, principally when France was at war. In 1749, the finance minister, Machault, performed the impressive feat of transforming the *dixième* into the *vingtième* and extending it into time of peace.[11] Machault successfully ran the gauntlet of the Parlement but his successors were not so lucky. Emboldened by their success in thwarting royal policy on Jansenism and the Gallican liberties, the sovereign courts, especially the Parlement of Paris, greeted each renewal of the *vingtième* and all attempts to apply surcharges, like the *sol pour livre*, with violent hostility.[12] The *vingtième*, which was the Crown's attempt to overcome fiscal immunities and tax privilege, was the issue that soured relations between the king and his parlements.

Privilege and the nobles' deep attachment to it appear to have brought down the French treasury. Marion and subsequent historians have been all too happy to "blame" the nobility, in particular venal office holders of the sovereign courts, for their egotistical opposition to reform. This is certainly how a series of reforming ministers (many themselves nobles) saw the situation; Calonne quite specifically painted the nobles as deeply attached to their fiscal privileges.[13] But on a merely political level, this interpretation poses several problems. First, the magistrates themselves rarely invoked fiscal immunity when opposing the king's edicts concerning the *vingtième*. Of course, one would not expect them to admit openly that self interest motivated their resistance. But they could have easily pointed to the immunities bestowed by the king on his provinces, on his clergy, or on other groups that formed a part of the French "constitution." They did not.[14] Furthermore, the French nobility offered to aban-

don its fiscal immunities in 1788 according to the lists of grievances
drawn up by assemblies of nobles throughout the provinces.[15] Here
is a fact which historians have been loath to recognize even though
the nobility's willingness to compromise on this point was described
and analyzed by Sieyès in his famous pamphlet, *What is the Third
Estate?*[16] Admittedly, one could construe this concession as nothing
more than a politically astute move. By the winter of 1789, it had become clear that the nobility would have to adopt a more conciliatory
stance if it were to save its political preeminence.[17] But even this interpretation suggests that the nobles had comparatively little to lose
when they lost their fiscal immunities.

The argument that the nobles received little material benefit from
their fiscal immunities was suggested by C. R. Behrens in a controversial article in 1962. Her argument is based upon the fallacious assumption that the king's *vingtième* tax actually worked as intended
and struck noble and commoner with equal ferocity.[18] Such was not
the case, as many chagrined ministers of finance repeatedly complained. The nobles did receive tax relief but not because they had
a legal right to it. As Guy Chaussinand-Nogaret has pointed out,
they did not need such a right. The nobles, he observes, benefited
from their status as powerful and important individuals to obtain tax
advantages from local collectors and even intendants. On the local
level, influential individuals could easily persuade, bludgeon, or pay
the tax assessor—or even the royal intendant—to ease their burden.
As the duke of Orleans explained to a friend during the Assembly of
the Notables, "as for my taxes, I always arrange things with the Intendant."[19] The nobles willingly abandoned their legal tax advantages
because power and influence, not ancient privileges or hoary tradition, secured tax immunities.

Moreover, the nobility was not the only group to enjoy tax advantages. Many commoners also benefited from tax breaks. The inhabitants of the *pays d'etat* like Brittany, Languedoc, and Burgundy, where
old provincial Estates still handled financial affairs, could depend
on these institutions to negotiate a relatively favorable levy with
the king.[20] City dwellers also escaped the *taille*, though excise taxes
or *aides* (especially those on markets) weighed more heavily upon
townspeople than upon rural folk.[21] Even within the same *élection*,
some parishes got off more easily than others. In the future depart-

ment of the Yonne, for example, Robert Schnerb found wild variations in the *taille* assessments of neighboring parishes, variations which had little to do with the parish's prosperity. Indeed, tax assessments were sometimes inversely related to wealth.[22]

Such variations appear to have been random, especially as regards the *taille*, which Lavoisier characterized as an "arbitrary imposition."[23] But the wealthy benefited from most of the loopholes. The great tenant farmers, or *fermiers*, who constituted the plutocracy of the rural world, often paid no tax at all. They kept their leases secret and when the tax collector appeared passed themselves off as mere farmhands, thereby benefiting from their noble landlord's tax exemption.[24] The wealthier and more influential segments of the rural world had yet other means of acquiring if not outright immunities then reduced tax assessments. Certainly, as James Collins has shown, the great landowners of any parish paid more than the poor peasant; but how much more?[25] Was this burden apportioned proportionally? Lack of good documentation makes this question hard to answer, but the system was certainly so devised as to make tax evasion easy for the rich and influential. The job of tax collector in many parishes fell to the richest members of the community or their creatures. The elite could therefore spare themselves and their families and cast a disproportionate tax burden on the weak or timorous.[26] They could also see to it that certain parcels of land were discreetly omitted from the *taille* roll. In 1817, officals in Seine-et-Oise discovered that over 2500 hectares of land had never been included in the tax rolls and never taxed.[27] One stipulation in particular constituted an extremely profitable tax immunity for the rich. Absentee landlords or owners of multiple estates had, as far as the *taille* was concerned, the option of choosing in which parish they would have their property assessed. Of course, they chose a community with low tax assessments, thereby securing a huge tax reduction. That this ruling constituted an abuse and a loss for the treasury was very clear to the Crown. In the 1750s and 1760s the king repeatedly tried to abrogate this regulation, only to meet with the entrenched resistance of the Parlement.[28] Here, the nobles, indeed the magistrates, clearly benefited from a fiscal immunity and clung to it tenaciously. But one did not have to be noble to escape taxation, for a variety of subterfuges—in addition to noble privilege—regularly deprived the Crown of revenue.

Just how much the treasury suffered is unclear. Though all historians believe that privilege deprived the Crown of income, no one, James Riley has observed, has actually tried to "test the hypothesis" and put a figure on the cost.[29] Riley himself has attempted to figure out what privilege cost the Crown in revenues. He demonstrates that the Crown that established quotas for the *taille* sought no increases in the tax over the course of the eighteenth century. Presumably the monarchy, well aware of the abuses which riddled this old tax, simply settled for a minimum and placed little pressure on this kind of imposition. French fiscal officers preferred to place pressure on the *vingtième*, which though far from perfect was a more equitable tax and less subject to immunities. Ministers, after wrestling with the sovereign courts, laid on additional *vingtièmes* and accessories or small additional charges. From 1756 to 1760, two *vingtièmes* were in force; from 1760 to 1763, three. Lapses would occur and new *vingitièmes* would be laid on for specified periods.[30] At the same time, the government chose to raise indirect taxes, whether internal customs duties or the *aides et droits*, which included taxes on legal documents. Consequently, the abuse-ridden *taille* constituted a smaller and smaller portion of French revenues—and from the subject's perspective, tax burdens—as the century wore on. Therefore, Riley concludes, "the proportion of revenues lost to privilege declined as more of the tax burden was shifted to the kind of levies raised by the Farm, which presented fewer opportunities for tax avoidance and as the direct taxes emphasized the *vingtième* over the *taille*." The "importance of privilege was shrinking," he observes, "because the relative scale of real benefits to privilege was declining with the relative weight of taxes open to privilege."[31]

This argument is borne out by the declining value of venal offices in the eighteenth century. Venality, historians have always believed, constituted a serious fiscal problem because virtually all offices entailed some kind of tax immunity. Indeed, some were purchased, it appears, for no other reason. Charges of *secrétaires du roi* for example, entailed no significant functions; but the position brought with it exemption from most *droits*. According to Marion, individuals acquired these offices before major purchases in order to avoid the taxes that could amount to as much as 10 percent of the purchase in question. The sale once concluded, the new secretary would quickly divest himself of his office.[32]

If venality deprived the treasury of revenue, it had, most historians argue, even more serious political consequences. Not only did it encourage fruitless rent seeking and the pursuit of hollow honors and perquisites; it also set up a class of individuals, principally judges or magistrates, who could not be removed and who defended their privileges, including tax privileges, tooth and nail. Certainly, the struggles between the king and his sovereign courts from 1750 to the revolutionary crisis itself seem to bear out this contention. The king would certainly have been better off without the officers of the parlements, the Cour des Aides, and a host of other corporate bodies.

Or would he have been? Historians have so long condemned venality that they have overlooked its significance within the context of French finances. Several recent articles by David Bien have helped us see the significance of the corporate bodies and venality in a new light.[33] The corporations (Estates, parlements, towns, guilds, and clergy) benefited the king and helped him fill his coffers. Venality and the corporate bodies that usually stemmed from it facilitated a task essential to the fisc: borrowing and taxing.

We are not apt to think of the venal office holders as a source of credit but this clearly was their most important function. Office holders purchased an office and in return received *gages* (literally wages) whether they performed any real function or not. The *gages* constituted interest on their loans. When the king was desperately in need of funds, he either created offices or better yet "refinanced" the old ones. Officeholders either could face a diminution in the value of their offices thanks to the creation of similar offices or could secure their own positions by purchasing the new offices. The king, in return, increased the officers' wages (*augmentation de gages*), thereby paying the officeholders interest for what was, in fact, a loan. Through venality, the king created, as James Riley has observed, "a captive group of creditors who could be pushed around."[34] These same creditors were themselves debtors so they helped soak up all the available credit and functioned as intermediaries between the Crown and its lenders.

Such was also the role on a much greater scale of the provincial

Estates, the Assembly of the Clergy, and many municipalities. Unable to float loans on its own, the Crown borrowed money through these more creditworthy corporate bodies. The loans constituted on the city of Paris, the famous *rentes* de l'Hôtel de Ville, were of this sort, with the municipal venal office holders of the city government serving as guarantors. Because the cities, like the provincial Estates, handled local and royal taxes, creditors considered these loans secure and would loan money at rates lower than those offered the Crown alone. So advantageous were these loans made through the corporate bodies that the Crown sought them consistently throughout the eighteenth century. Indeed, in 1787, Calonne and then his successor Loménie had floated huge loans on the Estates of Flanders, Brittany, Languedoc, Provence, and Burgundy as well as the city of Paris.[35] When this avenue of credit was exhausted or at least closed, as in 1787 when the Assembly of the Clergy refused to provide the subsidies demanded by Loménie de Brienne, total bankruptcy was imminent.

The corporate bodies, which could on occasion appear so obstructive, generally facilitated rather than blocked revenue collection. The provincial Estates, in particular, greatly facilitated the Crown's task for they offered the prospect of immediate revenue collected at little or no cost. The king engaged in what was essentially a "protection racket." He created new taxes, like the *vingtième* and its surcharges, and then asked the provincial Estates if they would like to "subscribe," that is pay a fee, rather than suffer the new impost. By such means, revenue entered the royal treasury quickly and cheaply. The provincial Estates provided the Crown—which had created many of them in the first place—with distinct fiscal advantages, such important advantages that the Crown never attempted to dissolve or supplant these institutions.

Of course such maneuvers had a hidden cost: in the long run, such subscriptions deprived the king of income for they always represented much lower sums than would have been otherwise collected. The king was worse off, but so too were the *pays d'élection*, those areas without provincial Estates, which consequently bore a heavier, disproportionate burden. Inequities in the system led to heavy taxation, particularly, some would maintain, of the peasantry. If the royal fisc went bankrupt it was because, the argument goes, the poor peasants could simply bear no more. Here is one of the oldest explanations of the financial crisis of 1788, one which owes a great deal to the magistrates of the Parlement of Paris who never tired of castigating the king for overtaxing his subjects. This explanation has been given new life in the twentieth century thanks to that wandering British agronomist Arthur Young. The interest in social and economic history in recent years has led to a rebirth of interest in Young's *Travels*, one of the most frequently cited sources on pre-revolutionary France.[36] So omnipresent is Young's book that few historians have thought to question it or underscore its bias. The "legend" of the destitute French peasant, as one expert on fiscal matters has observed, lives on.[37]

But it has been seriously challenged, and a handful of historians maintain that, far from being overburdened, the French peasantry enjoyed a relatively light tax load and one that was diminishing. In 1944, Ernest Labrousse argued persuasively that the eighteenth century witnessed a rise in prices and a decline in the value of money.[38] According to the Labroussian view, the tax burden actually eased throughout much of the eighteenth century, only to fall on the peasantry with crushing weight during the "mauvaise conjoncture" of the last years of the Old Regime. This short term disaster aside, however, the French peasant was less taxed than his ancestors.

Did the Crown run out of money because it had squeezed its poorest subjects dry? Or did the French peasantry, thanks to inflation and a decline in the real value of money, actually enjoy tax relief? Overtaxed or undertaxed—historians are divided between contradictory interpretations. On the surface, a substantial increase in taxation appears to have occurred. Net nominal revenues certainly grew in the eighteenth century: in 1726, the Crown collected 181,000,000 *livres*; in 1788, 471,600,000. The per capita tax burden grew in this period from 8.1 *livres* to 17 *livres*, or more than doubled.[39] But a closer look reveals that, in fact, the French peasant of 1788 was probably less troubled by the royal fisc than had been his great great grandfather of 1688. The rise in prices and concomitant decline in the value of money means that in real terms taxes probably declined. *Taille* assessments, for example, were fixed and so landowners saw their tax bill decline thanks to the inflation that characterized the period.

Arthur Young's picture of the overtaxed French peasantry has now been replaced with the notion of a relatively unburdened rural France. But some historians find this picture too optimistic. According to Mathias and O'Brien, tax revenues figured in grain amounted to about 20 million hectoliters in the 1730 and grew to 29.3 million in 1780.[40] Because everything depends on the coefficient one uses to change nominal to real money, it might be more accurate to figure tax receipts based upon wages. Michel Morineau calculates that in 1726 it would take the average Parisian 10 days to acquit his tax bill; in 1789 it would take him 14 or 15 days. If one makes calculations on a head of household rather than a per capita basis, the figures are more impressive. Again according to Morineau, the average Parisian head of household would need 40 days of work in 1726 and 50 in 1789 to pay his taxes.[41] Whether this constitutes a real or significant difference is debatable and Morineau's wage rates may not be representative. Still, virtually all historians agree that whatever the long term history of taxation, the last quarter of the eighteenth century saw an increase in royal impositions relative to incomes. A severe economic crisis occurred in the last years of the Old Regime which made it difficult for many subjects to pay their taxes. As Ernest Labrousse, the foremost student of this crisis, has said, "it was not so much that the fiscal charge increased, but that he who had to bear it weakened." The outcome was a "fiscal reaction," that is growing resentment of and resistance to taxation.[42]

The French of 1788 may have hated taxes but that does not mean that they could not pay taxes. Were the French really overtaxed? Did the royal fisc face the seemingly indissoluble problem of impoverished tax payers? Apparently not, for only a few years later the governments of the French revolution would exact huge sums from the French citizenry. After a slight drop in 1790, French budgets mushroomed with the advent of the war in 1792.[43] While the monetary woes of the period make it risky to compare pre- and postrevolutionary budgets, we can see that the constitutional monarchy demanded much more than the so-called "absolutist" monarchy. From approximately 471 million *livres* in 1789, the royal budget grew to 857 million in 1792 and then, with the advent of the war and the republic, to astronomical sums. Between October of 1792 and June of 1793, the Republic spent 1 billion *livres*. Republican accounting was as confused as its Old Regime predecessors, largely because of the constant state of emergency produced by the war and internal revolt. Still the trend is clear: Cambon estimated in September of 1793 that

6,244,000,000 *livres* had been spent since the opening of the Estates General in 1789. Had the old monarchy survived and Necker's last budget been enacted annually over a four year period, total expenditures would have come to only 3,685,539,000 *livres*. Revolutionary governments spent almost twice that much.[44] While the size of the revolutionary armies makes such figures credible, we must be skeptical. These statistics reflect only a nominal increase in taxes. If we use the figures for real tax receipts proposed by Mathias and O'Brien, we find that in grain equivalents tax revenues in 1785 amounted to 27 million while those in 1807–08 amounted to 35.5 million hectoliters.[45] The French could pay more taxes and during the Revolution they did.

Consequently, the king's bankruptcy does not reflect the bankruptcy of his subjects. They could and would pay more. France was a rich country, an exceedingly rich one by the standards of the time; it should have been able to pay the king's bills. One estimate is that had the *vingtième* truly been a levy of five percent on income, it would have returned 135 million in the 1760s. The short term difficulties of the 1780s should not have seriously undermined the royal revenue and in that decade income from this tax alone should have amounted to 255 million *livres*.[46] Instead, it brought in only 23 million. Something was wrong and it had less to do with the weight of taxation than with the manner of collection.

J. F. Bosher has argued in *French Finances, 1770–1795* that the problem did indeed lie in the fiscal administration, which he portrays as cumbersome, disorganized, and confusing. Indeed, Bosher may be the only individual since Necker to have understood the intricacies of the dozens of *caisses*, *receveurs*, and *payeurs* which constituted the Old Regime system for collecting and disbursing funds. The royal administration was exceedingly complex, contradictory, and scattered because the French monarchy traditionally relied upon others, be they semi-private corporations, venal office holders, or subordinate government bodies, to handle its financial affairs. The *fermes générales*, or farmers general, collected custom duties; the government's responsibility ended with the infamous lease negotiated at five year intervals. A *régie*, or semi-private corporation, collected the *aides* on legal documents. A host of *receveurs* (receivers) and *payeurs* (paymasters) who had purchased their offices collected and disbursed funds from the *taille* and the *vingtième*. Approximately 40 *trésoriers généraux* and *receveurs généraux* who also purchased their offices managed the central *caisses* into which all tax receipts poured. Except for the *régie*, which simply "managed" the tax collection operation, all of these advanced money to the Crown when necessary and issued *rescriptions* on future receipts. In addition, a host of other officials handled the *gabelle*, the tobacco monopoly, and the funds of the armed forces. If the king wanted to know how much money he had or how much he had spent, he would have to consult all of these individuals. Small wonder then that it took one of the chief financial officers of the realm, Calonne, two years to arrive at a relatively accurate appreciation of the kingdom's financial situation.[47]

Complexity rendered the treasury's operations confusing and the reformers' and revolutionaries' desire for a simple, single tax system is comprehensible. For Bosher, however, the problem was not so much complexity as the prevalence of venal office holders and individuals more interested in lining their pockets than in filling the king's coffers. Like revolutionary pamphleteers, he believes that the mingling of private and public brought down the Old Regime fisc. "The crown practically always relied upon the services of intermediaries," Bosher tells us, "to manage its financial business . . . (so) there were very few phases in the management of government funds which could be properly described as *public* finance."[48] The monarchy's penchant for farming out taxes and borrowing from its own tax collectors, its recourse to private individuals for revenue assessment and credit, its tendency to place public goods in private hands—here lay the downfall of the Old Regime. The lack of disinterested public servants, Bosher claims, was the "fundamental cause of the monarchy's financial ills."[49]

This is not a new idea. Contemporaries, be they Grub Street pamphleteers or magistrates of the Parlement of Paris, generally believed that tax collectors siphoned off huge amounts of government revenue, that the treasury's difficulties stemmed from greedy *traitants*. A change of personnel was all that was needed to solve the treasury's problems and ministers were certainly not above suspicion. Calonne's fall, for example, was hastened by rumors he peculated funds. Most suspect in the public eye were the tax farmers who the public believed enriched themselves at the expense of the public. The farmers general were not the plutocrats the public imagined nor were their fortunes rising in the eighteenth century. Nor could peculation alone account for the distress of the French fisc.[50] Still, Bosher's point deserves serious attention. The confusion of public and private may not have led to embezzling but it may well have led to exorbitant collection costs, which weighed down the treasury's operations.

While it is virtually impossible to figure out just how much the system of venal tax collectors and tax farms cost, we have some indication that the arrangement was not as detrimental to royal finances as Bosher thinks. George T. Matthews suggests that as far as taxes on consumption were concerned the system worked fairly well.[51] Levies came in quickly and the cost to the Crown was quite reasonable. Certainly, a disproportionate number of individuals appear to have been engaged in one capacity or another in the business of the king. But the Revolution, while reducing the numbers at the top through centralization, did not seriously diminish the numbers at the bottom—on the local district and department levels—engaged in tax collection. Moreover, individuals be they venal office holders or bureaucrats have to be paid for their services. In the Old Regime, officers of the fisc received a minuscule wage and the legal right to retain 2 to 5 percent of the funds they handled. In particularly difficult years the Crown might add incentives in the form of bounties.[52] To modern eyes, such maneuvers look faintly criminal, but they were neither illegal nor necessarily costly. A salaried bureaucracy could also be expensive: in 1798, the French treasury paid its employees 1,703,000 *livres* in wages and this sum does not take into account the salaries of district and department civil servants engaged in tax collection.[53] Comparisons between pre-revolutionary and revolutionary statistics always bring risks, but the results can be interesting. A. Vuhrer for example has estimated that in 1787, the cost of tax collection amounted to 7.35 percent of receipts; in 1885, it came to about 7.89 percent of revenues.[54] In other words, tax collection by venal officeholders may not have cost the king very much. In fact, in some instances, it may have saved him money. What some might call "farming out," others might consider "shifting the cost." For instance, the king levied taxes on villages collectively and then forced them to appoint a tax collector who would spend his time, energy, and (if the community could not pay) money doing the king's business.

By such means, the Crown limited its costs and maximized its revenue. Recent research by James Riley suggests that the French fiscal system worked remarkably well—that in the fiscal year 1752, for example, no more than 14 percent of the Crown's revenues went to pay the costs of collection.[55] In the *pays d'état*, collection costs amounted to 13 percent of revenues, once the expenses involved negotiating with the Estates—a charge incurred only once every four or five years—are deducted. Of the king's other imposts, the least expensive were the general farms (9 percent collection costs) and the *vingtième* (7 percent). When one bears in mind that the British who were held to have a more efficient and less costly fiscal apparatus paid 10 percent in collection costs the Old Regime fisc does not look so bad.[56] Historians' protestations notwithstanding, the fiscal machinery of Old Regime France worked fairly well and did so for over two hundred years.

But eventually the system failed. Using the informal budgets drawn up by the Crown's officers, Michel Morineau provides another explanation for France's chronic fiscal weakness—war. Starting with the "budget" of 1726, Morineau follows the fortunes—and misfortunes—of the French fisc. In that year, royal revenues came to 180 million *livres* and expenditures to 200 million *livres*, something close to equilibrium despite a debt of some 60 million *livres* inherited from Louis XIV. This fragile balance did not last long. In 1734, French expenditures had risen to 209 million *livres*, but expenses had also grown. The culprit is not hard to find: the War of the Polish Succession. Expenditures on the army and the navy rose from 38 million *livres* to 113 million *livres*. There appears to be a financial crisis of some scope. But disaster was avoided and the French fisc came out of the war without permanent scars. Between 1733 and 1736, the king sold life annuities (*rentes viagères*), extracted greater subsidies from the Assembly of the Clergy and the *pays d'état*, borrowed money from the *receveurs des finances*, and imposed a new tax on all kinds of wealth, the *dixième*. By 1740, most traces of the war had been erased and service on the national debt had been reduced.[57]

But again in 1741, the royal treasury confronted expenditures greater than its revenues. Expenditures now amounted to over 257 million *livres*, of which the army took the lion's share. By "extraordinary" means—that is by taxes other than the *taille* and the *aides*—

the Crown managed to finance the War of the Austrian Succession. The king imposed a new *dixième*, added to the *capitation*, or head tax, and instituted new excise taxes. The Crown had to borrow money, but in 1751 the percentage of the budget used to service the national debt had not changed and indeed looked as if it might decline.[58]

Such was not the case in the years after 1755. Here again, the culprit is not hard to find: the Seven Years War, which cost approximately 1 billion *livres*. Again the Crown had recourse to borrowing—this time at rates of as much as 10 percent.[59] The nefarious consequences of this new policy are evident in the "état" of 1775. Here, tax revenues were on the rise, but so too was spending: the royal household in particular had grown, after a period of retrenchment, to 50 million *livres*. Worse yet, the servicing of the national debt now absorbed two-fifths of the budget and perhaps as much as one-half if various indemnities, gratifications, and charges are included.[60] That the Seven Years War constituted a turning point became evident by 1782. French involvement in the American war of independence cost between 1000 and 1300 million *livres*, a sum not much greater than the amount of money spent on the Seven Years War. Similar too were the ways in which the two wars were funded. Necker like his predecessor relied upon loans, especially 100 million in new life annuities or *rentes viagères*. But he avoided the tax increases that had characterized the response to crisis in the past. The result was predictable: by 1788 the annual sum needed to service the debt was between 120 and 130 million, an increase of about two-fold over previous years.[61]

The stage was now set for the events of 1788. This brief account of fiscal policy points to one culprit, one force behind the financial crisis—war. The budgets of the navy and the army almost tripled in the years between 1726 and 1789. No other area of expenditure increased as quickly. Of course, royal revenues increased too and at about the same rate. But the expenditures for war came in bursts, leaving behind them a trail of debts that weighed down the budget. As Morineau observes, foreign policy, not fiscal incompetence, brought down the French Crown.[62]

But this comes as no surprise. When French authorities created new taxes, they carefully specified that the "extraordinary" levies were to last for the duration of the hostilities only. Under Louis XIV the *dixième* had been temporary and under Louis XV and even

Louis XVI the *vingtième* was also officially temporary. To be sure, Machault had carried off the feat of prolonging the *vingtième* into peace time.[63] But other ministers would find such maneuvers difficult if not virtually impossible. Once the hostilities ceased, the sovereign courts felt free to vent their wrath against the government for they would not be accused of a lack of patriotism during a royal emergency. Only by dogged perseverance did the government force the parlements to accept a peacetime *vingtième* in 1763, 1772, and 1781.[64] As one rather jaundiced contemporary, Thomas Paine, observed, "taxes were not raised to carry on wars, but wars raised to carry on taxes."[65]

Consequently, war had a more ambiguous impact upon the royal fisc than is first apparent. It created occasions for the extensions of the fisc and exerted enormous pressure on revenues at the same time. One wonders if war alone sufficed to bring down the Old Regime. After all, Louis XIV made war—and more often than his descendants; yet the monarchy survived. In the eighteenth century, one might object, France was not the only country in Europe to pour millions into the military. Great Britain also pursued an aggressive foreign policy and one which was expensive, indeed more expensive than its French counterpart. If we compare French and British expenditures on war, we find that up to 1763, the two countries spent approximately the same amount on the army and navy. However, in the years between 1776 and 1783, years which correspond with the American war of independence, the picture changes and dramatically. Not too surprisingly, the American war cost the British a great deal more than it cost the French. For France total expenditures on the American revolt came to 1.3 million *livres*, or about three times an ordinary budget in time of peace. England, by comparison, spent 80 million pounds sterling, or seven times the annual budget in a normal year. But the British exchequer was not brought to its knees as was the French treasury. How did the French go wrong?

Many historians would answer "by borrowing too much at too great a cost." Until recently, irresponsible borrowing was considered a peculiarity of Necker's first tenure as minister. But borrowing constituted one of the principal sources of revenue long before Necker became minister.[66] French ministers relied upon two basic kinds of loans, or *rentes*: the *rentes perpetuelles*, or perpetual annuity loan; and the *rentes viagères*, or life annuity loan. The *rentes perpetuelles*

was an annual income terminated by repayment of the capital, in
other words interest on a loan. The *rentes viagères* was an annual income terminated by the death of one or more persons named in the
contract. When an individual purchased a life annuity he abandoned
his capital and therefore received a higher income than under the
rentes perpetuelles.[67] Generally, the French, both as borrowers and
lenders, preferred the life annuity loans. Just why is not clear. Contemporaries castigated those who purchased *rentes viagères* for selfishly abandoning their descendants and saw the popularity of the life
annuities as proof of the decay of morals.[68] More likely, the preference
for life annuities reflected French men and women's need to provide
for their old age or even pure greed, for these annuities always carried
higher interest rates—especially after the creation of the tontine.
Under Louis XIV a certain Lorenzo Tonti, a Neapolitan banker, "invented" the tontine and it was used from 1689 to 1770.[69] The scheme
worked as follows: a certain number of individuals would "subscribe"
to a royal loan, abandoning their capital in return for an annual payment. As the individuals in the group died, their payments would
be distributed among the survivors, usually with a certain amount
deducted for the king. Tontine annuities were issued throughout
the eighteenth century and under slightly different circumstances.
Usually, the king established "classes" of individuals according to
age so that the youngest received the lowest annual payment and the
older a relatively high annual payment. By such a device, the king
saved himself money, but the tontines were still profitable to the subscribers. The *Encyclopédie méthodique* mentions a women who died
in 1726 at the age of 96. The last survivor of the second class of the
tontine of 1689, in the last year of her life she received 73,500 *livres*
on her initial 300 *livres* investment.[70]

Two further innovations made the life annuities even more profitable. In 1758, the king created a tontine which abandoned the distinction between ages and promised the same interest rate to all,
whatever their age. Tontines disappeared; but the life annuity without distinction of age survived, indeed became routine in the 1770s.
And in 1771 Genevan bankers found a way of packaging life annuities which reduced risk and rendered them attractive to the public.
Profiting from the uniform returns on life annuities, the Genevans
would purchase a host of annuities and settle them on the heads of

thirty young and healthy Swiss maidens. They then pooled the annuities, formed a syndicate, and sold shares in Paris and Amsterdam. The profits reaped could be enormous, so enormous that it is indeed "incredible," as George V. Taylor remarked, "that a government of a great power should have sold annuities on these terms . . ."[71] And the king could still exploit traditional forms of borrowing, like loans from the clergy, the provincial Estates, or one of the other corporate bodies. He could create new venal offices or, more likely, "refinance" old ones. He could always float loans through the intermediary of the Hôtel de Ville, loans with fixed interest rates or rates set by lottery. In any event, borrowing provided a substantial portion of the French revenue, indeed as we have seen a growing portion of that revenue.

But the mere fact of borrowing was not in itself a problem. Britain financed its maritime supremacy the same way France financed its foreign ambitions: by borrowing. According to Mathias and O'Brien, the British Crown used loans to fund 85 percent of the cost of the War of Austrian Succession, 81 percent of the cost of the Seven Years War, and 100 percent of the American war of independence.[72] By 1782, the British Crown like its French equivalent dragged after it a huge burden of debt inherited from the foreign adventures of the past. In fact, the similarities were greater than the differences. In 1782, the British debt amounted to 230 million pounds and servicing it absorbed 9 million pounds or 70 percent of the annual budget.[73]

Unlike its neighbor across the channel, however, France found it impossible to absorb its debt. The problem, virtually all historians agree, was that France had to pay more for money; simply put, it borrowed at a higher interest rate. Just what this interest rate was is hard to determine. The extreme variety of French financial instruments (venal offices, *rentes perpetuelles*, and a host of different life annuities) makes the interest rate hard to calculate. The "cheapest" portion of the royal debt was loans from the corporate bodies, that is the Assembly of the Clergy and the provincial Estates. Here the Crown acquired money on the most favorable terms. Even in the troubled 1780s, Necker and Joly de Fleury could borrow from the provincial Estates at between 4 and 5 percent interest.[74] Refinancing venal office—basically borrowing from the officers—also cost relatively little. In 1744, a 20.6 million augmentation of the *finance* on certain offices cost the Crown a moderate 5 percent in interest.[75] This latter type of loan tended to disappear over the course of the century at the cost of higher interest payments. In the 1750s, real yields on *rentes perpetuelles* amounted to 4.6 percent but this was the very cheapest portion of the voluntary debt.[76]

Once we enter the realm of loans accompanied by lotteries, tontines, and a host of other premiums, the cost of money to the French Crown became really astonishing. The highest rate conferred by the lottery wheel at the Hôtel de Ville between 1731 and 1751 was 8.33 percent.[77] The first lottery loan issued by Necker carried a "prize" of 11.1 percent. Admittedly, the government did not pay all subscribers this premium rate. But according to contemporary estimates and subsequent scholarship, these loans still cost on the average a high 6.66 percent.[78]

The *rentes viagères* cost a great deal more. David Weir calculates the internal rates of return on the tontine loans to have averaged about 9 percent.[79] Of course, the French abandoned such loans in 1770, but only a year later Terray issued a simple life annuity, known as the Loan of Holland because it was designed to attract Dutch investors, at a rate of 12 percent. It was common in the 1780s for life annuities to promise a 10 percent return. According to Lüthy, Necker made it possible for some of his Genevan friends to borrow at 13 percent; but Harris disputes the point and argues that the loans yielded less. Still, in the 1780s the French Crown offered life annuities at 10 percent or more, an extremely high rate of return.[80]

Calculating the overall interest rate on the French debt is hazardous. According to a contemporary, Joly de Fleury, the French debt was serviced in 1781 at an average rate of 6.5 percent. Average is the important qualifier here, for while certain old loans contracted under Louis XIV no longer required any more than 1 or 2.5 percent interest, more recent loans had been contracted—as we have seen—at much higher rates.[81] More recent estimates of the average French interest rate are higher. Weir advances a figure of 7.5 percent in the 1780s. Moreover, along with Mathias and O'Brien he figures the ratio between debt service and tax revenues to have been 61.9 percent in 1788.[82] Of course, for the interest payments made by the French Crown to look truly exaggerated one must prove that they were substantially higher than the rates paid by private individuals who borrowed money. Determining the private interest rate in France in this period is even more difficult than determining the public rate. But James Riley estimates that the real private interest rate in the period 1760–69 equalled 2.5 percent while the real public rate amounted to 3.2 percent, a significant difference.[83]

The British Crown apparently fared much better. According to Harris, the English acquired loans at an average nominal interest rate of 3.74 percent.[84] Weir advances a virtually identical estimate of 3.8 percent interest for the British debt in the year 1788 and further enlivens the story by pointing out that the fledgling United States paid only 4 percent on its huge debt. And when similar debt instruments are compared, it is clear that the French paid roughly 2 percent more than the British throughout much of the eighteenth century.[85]

Historians have offered a variety of explanations for why this was the case. Some cite the shape of the debt. Riley and Weir wonder why the French government continued to offer life annuity loans, even tontines, at high rates when the English and the Dutch had abandoned such offerings in favor of straight perpetual loans. Riley concludes that the French ministers of finance were "inept" and lacked the experience and the intellect to assess accurately the French financial situation.[86] Certainly, the French financial ministers lacked training in a modern sense, but I doubt that they failed to notice how much the loans, especially the ruinous tontines, cost. In fact, the French abandoned the tontine in favor of life annuities in 1770.[87] As for the life annuities, Morineau argues that they proved disastrous because of lengthening life expectancy in the eighteenth century. Based upon their knowledge of the past, French financial officers expected the life annuities to be "extinct" within a 20 year period and generally that was the case. But in the late eighteenth century, French men and women lived longer so it took longer to retire this particular kind of loan. New demographic circumstances wreaked havoc with the Crown's planning and the debt accumulated at an unexpected rate. In Loménie de Brienne's 1788 budget, only 23 million *livres* out of 101 million *livres* in *rentes viagères* had been "extinguished." Contemporaries would have estimated 30 million, leaving an error of 7 million—not huge but significant nonetheless. Was the French fisc "stabbed in the back by changing demography"?[88]

The work of P. G. M. Dickinson suggests another way in which the shape of the French debt led to high interest rates. Dickinson has emphasized that the English debt was usually "consolidated" and borrowing was tied to new levies designed to retire the debt.[89] Here the English were not that different from the French. Loans were often tied to specific revenues, the income from the tobacco monopoly for example, and the French were careful to promise that revenues would be assigned to loan redemption. Indeed, Marion criticizes French ministers for their "mania for redemption," which amounted to making "impolitic" promises to creditors.[90] In 1749 and 1764 the French authorities created *caisse d'amortissements*—a special treasury into which tax revenues flowed directly and whose sole purpose was redemption of the debt. In 1766, the Caisse d'Escompte took on much the same role.[91] But this did not prevent, as Marion has observed, "the chasm from growing." Still other scholars claim that France's problems stemmed from the lack of a national bank. No one can doubt that France would have benefited from an institution like the Bank of England; Calonne tried unsuccessfully to transform the Caisse d'Escompte into a genuine national bank.[92] Everyone deplores the lack of a French national bank, but no one explains it. Similarly, all scholars lament that the French Crown paid such high interest rates but none explains why it was obliged to. One is tempted like Michel Morineau to conclude that the difference between French and English public interest rates remains "enigmatic."[93]

Enigmatic too remain the fundamental causes of the French financial collapse of 1788. All of the explanations and interpretations offered by historians thus far deal with structural problems in the Old Regime fisc. Privilege, inadequate administrative machinery, peculiarly high interest rates—all of these problems existed long before 1788. Indeed, one could argue that the French Crown was in deeper trouble—certainly in deeper debt—at the death of Louis XIV than it was in 1788. But the existence of the monarchy was never seriously questioned. Throughout the eighteenth century, the Crown contended with high collection costs, fiscal immunities, and the lack of a national bank. But the revolution only occurred in 1788. Why?

In order to answer this question, I propose to examine in detail two earlier fiscal crises: that of 1720, which followed the collapse of John Law's system: and that of 1763, which occurred in the aftermath of the French defeat in the Seven Years War. In both instances, the treasury stood on the very brink of bankruptcy. In both

cases, political conflict complicated the financial situation and corporate bodies questioned the prerogatives of the Crown. But in both
cases the ultimate crisis was avoided. The monarchy managed to
survive and absolutism emerged damaged but fundamentally intact.
The strategies employed by royal officers during these crises to avert
bankruptcy and dispel resistance have a great deal to tell us about the
substance of absolutism. They also reveal just how important were
political ideas, especially those concerning taxes, for new thinking
could either enliven resistance or strengthen monarchical authority.
Finally, an analysis brings us closer to understanding what went
wrong in 1788 and how this bankruptcy became a revolution.

≺ II ≻

The Fiscal Crisis of 1720

At quarter past eight on the morning of 1 September 1715, Louis XIV
died. He left a minor on the throne; a nephew as regent; and a legend
as an absolute monarch, the most powerful sovereign in Europe. He
also left his treasury in a plight that one historian has observed "sur-
passed all ordinary considerations."[94] The royal debt stood at nearly
two billion *livres*, not including over six hundred million in short-
term unfunded government paper. Income for 1721 had been anticipated and spent and inroads had already been made into the revenue
for 1722. Revenues for 1721 were about 69 million *livres*, but expenditures were 146 million. Debt service alone, if met, would run over
86 million. The continuous wars of the end of the reign had sapped
the economy. Peasants passively resisted the tax collector, and the
costs of collecting some indirect impositions (the tax farm had just
been introduced in 1714) exceeded the revenue they brought to the
Crown. The regent's advisor, the duc de Saint Simon, advised bankruptcy and the convocation of the Estates General.[95]

If the state of the French monarchy ever seemed parlous, it did
in 1715. With a minor on the throne and bankruptcy imminent few
would have predicted that the Bourbon monarchy would survive. But
it did and it even emerged stronger than ever from the Law crisis.
Generally, historians describe the regency as a period of monarchical
weakness. But the duc d'Orléans's handling of financial affairs was

bold, autocratic, and thoroughly absolutist. Nevertheless, important sources of resistance formed at this time, especially within the Parlement and in the work of Montesquieu. The history of the treasury in this period has a great deal to tell us about absolutism, both its prerogatives and its limitations.

At the time the regent assumed leadership of the kingdom, the financial situation was desperate. In the next seven years he deployed the complete arsenal of absolutist tactics for reducing loans and extracting revenue. Typically absolutist means—a so-called *visa* followed by the last *chambre de justice*—were used to reduce the debt. In 1716, the government called in the outstanding obligations of the state, examined them, sorted them, and then reduced both capital and interest. The Crown ran roughshod over its creditors and casually reneged upon past agreements. By such high-handed means, the regent reduced the royal debt from 600 million to only 250 million and reissued the remaining paper at only 4 percent interest.[96] No one complained that such maneuvers came very close to theft and this particularly sweeping regalian right remained unquestioned, perhaps because *visa* operations were normally followed by a *chambre de justice*.[97] In the same year, the regent formed such a tribunal and began prosecuting financiers. The *chambre* constituted a particularly petty example of a fundamental pattern in absolutist behavior. The Crown here—as in its dealings with the provincial Estates and the venal office holders—operated what was essentially a protection racket.[98] It threatened to prosecute (or levy taxes) and in return for a certain sum of money agreed to desist. However, this time the *chambre de justice* proved less profitable than in the past. The minister Noailles had predicted that the operation would bring in 500 to 600 million *livres*; in 1722, the court was still trying to recover money that was pledged and had netted only 1 million in specie.[99] Such strong arm, absolutist tactics appear to have run their course.

Such was, in fact, the opinion of John Law at least before he offered his services to the regent. Law's system constituted a novelty, indeed a rather wild experiment. We need not review here the history of his scheme. Excellent accounts exist already.[100] Suffice it to say that Law convinced the regent to establish a bank in 1716 and in 1718 it became a royal bank. The regent bestowed upon Law the colonial concessions of the Company of the West and decreed that investors could purchase the Company's shares in Law's bank notes. Soon, company and bank became one; Law adopted a series of measures to see that the bank notes would replace specie. Speculation ran wild as vast fortunes were made in the rue Quincampoix, where the bank offices were located. On demand, Law faithfully redeemed his notes; but signs of trouble appeared in January of 1720 when the value of the notes began to decline on the Amsterdam stock market. By fall 1720, the system had collapsed. A new *visa* operation cleaned up the fiscal detritus left by the system. The debt was brought down to 1,512,899,633 *livres*. The Crown issued 400 million *livres* in *rentes viagères* payable in Law's paper money.[101]

The balance sheet of the system has been drawn up many times.[102] The monarchy should probably be placed among the winners, especially considering the risks that had been run. The forced write down of government loans, or *visa*, of 1721 largely negated the financial ill effects of the system. Some towns and corporate bodies did profit from the inflation to settle their back taxes; Toulouse for example purchased an immunity, thereby depriving the Crown of revenue in the long run.[103] Still, in 1722, the king's debts amounted to only 51.5 million, an amount similar to the debt in 1718 and substantially lower that the sum owed at Louis XIV's death.[104]

Law's system appears to have left barely a mark on the royal fisc. Monarchical pretensions, however, were badly scarred. Historians have generally overlooked the political implications of Law's experiment but recently Thomas Kaiser has revealed just how significant the financial debacle was.[105] Regalian rights emerged from the crisis more or less intact but the limits of the king's power were plain to see. Law's scheme demonstrated that the monarchy might do many things but it could not create public confidence and with it a national bank. Law believed (or at least maintained) that "an absolute prince who knows how to govern can extend his credit further and find the funds he needs at a lower interest rate than a prince who is limited in his authority."[106]

To do so, however, the prince needed to cultivate public "confidence," and Law himself did so by dutifully delivering specie in return for notes and by engaging in a small public relations campaign. He abolished some of the unpopular customs taxes around Paris, attached premiums to stock issues and notes, and eschewed—at least for a while—dictatorial methods of which he disapproved.[107] Still, the monarchy and Law its agent found it difficult to create confidence. Frenchmen persisted in behaving as if "the absolute authority chases away confidence . . ."[108]

Finally, Law had recourse to the very means he had decried. When Parisians proved reluctant to exchange their specie for bank notes, Law decided to force them to do so. Between September 1719 and December 1720, Law altered the price of gold twenty-eight times and that of silver thirty-five times while holding bank notes constant.[109] Such manipulations came close to an abuse of property and they were accompanied by the abuse of persons. In February of 1720, the monarchy decreed that individuals who made payments in specie were subject to criminal prosecution, house searches, and seizure of property. Public confidence, however, proved elusive and the system fell precisely because the absolute monarch could not dispel his subjects' fears.

Law's failure vindicated those who believed that absolute monarchy and a public bank were incompatible. Though Law took pains to reassure Frenchmen that "it is impossible that the king ever touch the system," most thinkers believed that sooner or later an absolute monarch would confiscate his own bank.[110] As Saint-Simon told the regent, "as good as this establishment (a bank) could be in itself, it could not exist except in a republic or in a monarchy like England, whose finances are governed absolutely by those alone who provide them and who provide them only as much as it pleases." In a state like France, Saint Simon believed, "solidity and consequently confidence . . . is necessarily lacking, because a king, or in his name, a mistress, a minister of favored interests, most especially in extreme necessity . . . could overturn the Bank whose resources are too great and at the same time too accessible."[111]

Law tried to dispel such fears by claiming that the monarch shared the interests of his subjects and would never do anything to endanger his own credit.[112] But Law's policies constantly undercut such pronouncements. Indeed, his pronouncements frequently contradicted themselves. For Law, the monarch could indeed create—or destroy— anything. All property "held in full ownership belongs to you only on the condition that you use it in a manner useful to society," a manner defined only by the prince.[113]

Small wonder then that Montesquieu considered Law "one of the greatest promoters of despotism yet seen in Europe."[114] Law's monarch exercised untrammeled power. Had the system survived, Law would have revolutionized French finance. The British ambassador claimed that Law wanted to drive the interest rate down to 2 percent or lower. Law also harbored a desire to redeem venal offices, which he considered a particularly onerous form of debt.[115] The Crown would just will a new kind of fiscal structure into existence regardless of the damage done to his subjects' private property.

Eventually, Law's absolutist policies brought him into conflict with the sovereign court, the Parlement of Paris. According to the royal declaration of Vincennes, the magistrates had the duty (or right) to register the king's edicts so that they would be enforced in the Parlement and subordinate courts. When an edict transgressed the law of the land, the magistrates could refuse to register it and could read a *remontrance* to the king. If the monarch chose he could then force registration in a special session known as a *lit de justice*. The sovereign courts therefore had extremely limited powers; they could protest or remonstrate but that was about all. During the last years of Louis XIV's reign, the magistrates had been most docile indeed. But with the regency, they became bolder. Jansenism was the issue that most engaged them at first, and the initial decrees concerning Law's bank slipped past because as Law maintained "they did not appreciate their importance."[116] But Law's rough handling of state creditors and his frequent monetary mutations finally drew the fire of the parlements. The magistrates declined to register the king's edicts and drew up remonstrances. The regent tried to engineer a compromise but finally on 21 July 1720 he exiled the Parlement to Pontoise. For the first time in years, the monarch's will met with resistance.

But such timid resistance! The days when the magistrates would proclaim themselves representatives of the people and defenders of the ancient constitution of France were far off. The Parlement of the early eighteenth century was a very meek institution indeed. The magistrates always proclaimed their loyalty and their deep attachment to the monarchy. One would expect such protestations of affection, but the mental world of the magistrates appears to have been bounded, indeed created, by the monarchy. When remonstrating against the king's manipulation of currency, the Parlement spoke timidly of the "inconveniences" which these changes caused.[117] When the Parlement condemned the king's arbitrary reduction of interest rates on government loans, it did so in the meekest of language. The magistrates did not rail against the monarch for this violation of the right of property. On the contrary, they admitted that the king had the right to set the interest rate on his loans and timidly observed that arbitrary variations in the rate "could create hardship among his subjects."[118] The *parlementaires* never invoked a constitution, never defended the ancient liberties of the French, and only once reached back into French history to establish the limits of the monarchy. "We have no powers save those bestowed upon us by your predecessors" the magistrates asserted, and their dependence upon the monarchy appeared complete.[119] The magistrates of 1720 simply lacked the intellectual tools to fashion a truly adversary stance for themselves. They *were* the king's creation and they could contrive no intellectual counterweight to absolutism. In 1720, the French constitution had only a shadowy existence in the minds of the magistrates and they showed little ability to defend constitutional liberties.

If a serious political crisis failed to materialize in 1720 as it did in 1788, it was not because the financial situation lacked gravity. Rather it was because the forces of opposition lacked an ideology. The mental world of the magistrates was the mental world of absolutism and the Parlement of Paris seemed to justify Montesquieu's contention that the sovereign courts were "in decline."[120] Even Montesquieu displayed little interest in challenging royal prerogative when it came to taxation. It was in his guise as sociologist, as dispassionate observer, that he approached government finance; and his goal was to establish the rules or laws that govern revenue collection.

In *The Spirit of the Laws*, Montesquieu analyzes the relationship between taxes, different forms of government, and liberty. In Book 13, Montesquieu states flatly that "the public revenues are a portion each citizen gives of his property in order to secure or enjoy the remainder." He explores the point no further but goes on to describe how heavy taxes are in different kinds of government. Moderate governments, Montesquieu believes, tax their citizens more heavily than do despotic governments. They do so because they can, "because the citizen who thinks he is paying himself cheerfully submits to them (taxes)." As for the kind of taxes, Montesquieu believes

that the "natural tax of moderate government is the duty laid on mer-
chandise."[121] Here Montesquieu is clearly thinking of England and he
observes the operation of English credit very carefully. He says that
England's credit is "without blemish" and that things are so arranged
that the "creditor of the state, by the sums he contributes pays himself."[122] England in conjunction with Holland and Switzerland also
provided the basis for Montesquieu's discussion of banks. Like most
of his contemporaries, Montesquieu believed that some relationship
existed between republican or "moderate" governments and national
banks. Only in such states could banks prosper; an absolute monarch
would not tolerate organized private interests, banking or otherwise,
to protrude into political affairs. Indeed, the absolute monarch would
seize the bank, for "in a government of this kind, none but the prince
had or can ever have a treasure; and wherever there is one, it no sooner
becomes great than it becomes the treasure of the prince."[123]

For Montesquieu, absolutism and a public bank were incompatible; history would prove him correct. Part of the legacy of the
Law crisis was that France did not in fact receive a public bank. The
idea continued to tantalize; ministers and pamphleteers continued
to suggest the establishment of such a beneficial institution. But the
shadow of Law made the establishing of a bank impossible and even
the revolutionaries had to contend with the banker's ghost when creating the *assignat*. Law's debacle also had another, less well known
legacy: the monetary mutations so common under Louis XIV and
employed by Law disappeared. From Fleury on, France's ministers
pursued a policy of monetary stability which would only be broken—
and then in good faith—at the time of Calonne.

The crisis of 1720 had yet another, more profound legacy. Law
with his high handed methods, his disregard for property, and his
belief in the limitless efficacy of the monarch, became the standard
of despotism, particularly of the fiscal sort. He helped define despotism and so helped create an anti-monarchical position which would
eventually undermine the Crown.[124] In 1720 though, the strong arm
policies of absolutism saved the monarchy. The *visa* in 1721 cleansed
the royal fisc of the nefarious affects of the Law system. To a certain degree, absolutist fiscal policy saved the monarchy and restored
its financial health. But the cure proved temporary, and within forty
years the treasury was ailing again.

≺ III ≻

The Crisis of 1763

In 1763, the Crown once again faced near bankruptcy, the treasury returning "to the desperate financial position it had occupied at the death of Louis XIV . . ."[125] Revenues had risen: in 1758 the king collected 365.3 million *livres* and in 1763 425.4 million *livres*. But expenditures had risen faster: in 1758 they equalled 366.4 million *livres* and in 1763 442.2 million *livres*.[126] The villain is not hard to ascertain: the Seven Years War. The growing cost of war made this the most expensive war France had fought in the eighteenth century and the treasury would never recover from the conflict. Indeed, the Seven Years War—not the American war of independence—"gave" France her revolution some twenty six years later. The treasury never paid off the war and dragged the debt it accrued up to and beyond 1789. The era of heavy government borrowing and exorbitant interest rates began in the late 1760s, not in the 1780s under Necker—as historians previously believed.[127] Signs that the French treasury had acquired a debt that it would never pay off and would service only with great difficulty first became apparent in 1763.

Moreover, the financial difficulties of the Crown were complicated by a political crisis of virtually unprecedented dimensions. Conflict between the king and his parlements sharpened and accelerated. "For the first time," according to one student of the parlements, "the ingredients of crisis were combined in a way that was dangerous for the survival not just of the ministry in power but of strong monarchial government."[128] The struggle between the king and the sovereign courts brought the question of royal finances into the public domain, and the financial crisis sparked a small public controversy. Encyclopedists and physiocrats debated how best to restore financial health and reorganize the fiscal system. Proponents of the *thèse royale* (reform through a strong monarchy) and the *thèse nobiliaire* (reform through aristocracy and representative institutions) confronted each other. Demands that the Estates General be called were heard. "In terms of ideas," James Riley claims, "France seemed to be ready for a revolution around 1760."[129]

And yet a revolution did not occur. Indeed, the Old Regime would limp along for another twenty years, albeit beset by huge deficits and harassed by all segments of the intelligentsia. Somehow, though the moment seemed ripe for it, revolution was averted in 1763. The *parlementaires* still lacked the ammunition to bring down the monarchy; the "economists" or physiocrats actually shored it up; and the treasury's officers bandaged its financial wounds.

The primary remedy applied by the treasury was borrowing. The Seven Years War appears to have cost some 1,325 million *livres*, or 189 million annually—a figure which does not include the ordinary costs of government. In the short run, the king made some small economies for the sake of the conflict, primarily in his own court, and resorted to short term credit. When this kind of borrowing is added to the cost of the war, the annual bill for the war was 225 million. The monarchy chose to meet the costs of the war by credit (59 percent), the refinancing of offices (5 percent), tax increases (29 percent), and miscellaneous revenues (7 percent).[130] When one bears in mind that "finance" on venal offices differed little—if at all—from loans, the role of borrowing is even greater, 64 percent to be exact.[131] Debt accumulated quickly and by the late 1760s, debt service (which was mainly interest payments) required some 196 million *livres* annually—more than 60 percent of expenditures and double the portion of 1753.[132]

Certainly, the French Crown was no stranger to debt. The royal debt at the death of Louis XIV was just as large, indeed larger in real terms. But the ministers after 1722 adopted two policies which would prove disastrous. First, they eschewed the *visas*, which had allowed the monarch to clean house and reduce the debt in the past. The ministers Fleury and Machault wooed the poor creditor instead of beating him. The Crown had always been obliged to issue loans at relatively high interest. But in the 1760s it tended to favor the life annuity, an onerous form of borrowing as we have seen, at 10 percent. Such a return constituted a genuine bargain, for Dutch government securities at the same time brought a return 3 percent smaller.[133] Clearly, the French government had to pay a premium for money.

Why? Investors were not lacking. Right up until the Revolution, French fiscal officers had little trouble marketing government securities. Some difficulties were experienced in 1788, but until then, French paper sold easily. And no wonder: it brought a high return, one which, once the secondary market developed, made fortunes.[134]

Of course, high returns in the eighteenth century, as today, only come in return for high risk.[135] And what else than risk could the premium paid by the government denote? As events both before and after the Law debacle show, the French government felt little compunction about reneging on its previous agreements and canceling or reducing government obligations. To be sure, the *visa* of 1722 was the last such operation, and the sort of terrorist tactics associated with the *chambre de justice* had ended in 1716. But absolutism was not dead and partial defaults still occurred in the 1750s and beyond. At the end of the War of Polish Succession the authorities had written off the claims of arms suppliers. During the Seven Years War, payments were suspended in 1759 and 1760 on two leading instruments of short-term credit—the *billets* issued by the farmers general and the *rescriptions* of the receivers general. Payments on these notes were resumed in 1761 but nine years later, the abbé Terray again suspended payment on the *rescriptions* in the most famous partial bankruptcy of the century.[136] As Montesquieu knew, an absolute monarch could not be trusted; he would seize any treasure in his domains. Worse yet, he would not live up to his own agreements.

Ironically, the ministers of mid century tried to quell investor fears and render investment in French government securities less risky. They tried to behave like their counterparts in Holland and England, where governments borrowed money at the market rate.[137] They introduced a "new standard of fiscal behavior," for the Law debacle had taught them not to toy with the money stock, and they resolved to preserve the "sanctity" of public credit, if possible. James Riley argues that this fiscal conservatism was "the innovation that undermined royal finances."[138] My own view is that it was this conservatism mixed with occasional recourse to absolutist methods (bankruptcies) that weakened the French fisc. Louis XV's ministers both courted and abused creditors, creating not confidence (and with it lower interest rates) but confusion. The king's servants refused to employ the most dramatic (and effective) weapons in the absolutist, fiscal arsenal and avoided the *visa* operations which had previously cleansed the treasury and allowed the Crown to put its financial house in order. Louis XV's ministers foreswore such drastic measures in the interest of courting the creditor. But they still had recourse to suspensions of payments and partial write downs which undermined confidence and failed to restore fiscal health. Too timid and yet too bold, Louis XV's ministers had the worst of both worlds. The monarchy neither repudiated its debts nor created creditor confidence.

Of course, the king's ministers could have taken another approach to the troubled royal finances: they could have imposed new taxes, raised old levies, or rendered existing charges more profitable. All these strategies were attempted. In 1756, the king imposed a second *vingtième* and ordered it continued until ten years after the conclusion of a peace treaty. In 1769, he suspended exemptions from the *taille* enjoyed by venal office holders (exception was made for the magistrates of the sovereign courts) and bourgeois until two years after the peace. In 1759, he raised postal fees and customs duties on leather goods entering Paris. In September of the same year, the finance minister Silhouette asked for a wholly new tax, a so-called "subvention territoriale," which would be levied on all income from land with no regard for privilege or traditional immunities. A third *vingtième* (added to the two others) and a host of new excise taxes soon followed.[139]

The result was a torrent of remonstrances from the sovereign courts and *lits de justice* (enforced registration). Conflict between the king and his magistrates was not new. But in the 1760s it became both more frequent and more dangerous. In 1720, the regent had only the Parlement of Paris to contend with. But in 1763, the most rebellious courts lay in the provinces. At Rouen, Pau, Besançon, Grenoble, and Toulouse, parlements opposed the royal will. There were too many courts, too scattered, to be easily coerced; coercion would require money. Henceforth, some of the most spectacular conflicts between king and parlement would occur outside Paris, in Brittany and Languedoc.[140]

The parlements' revival sprang from two sources: Jansenism and Adrien LePaige's two-volume work on the history of the sovereign courts. As Dale Van Kley has recently shown, Jansenism stoked the fires of resistance and led to a magisterial *prise de conscience*.[141] From opposition to royal ultramontanism to resistance to royal taxation were but short steps and the magistrates emerged from the struggle over Gallican liberties more assertive and more aware of their role in the polity. At the same time, the publication of Adrien LePaige's *Lettres historiques sur les fonctions essentielles du parlement* in 1753 and 1754 gave the magistrates the vocabulary with which to

articulate their position. Le Paige virtually reinvented French constitutionalism and made the sovereign courts the only defense against
despotism. According to Le Paige, as the descendants of the Merovingian councils the Parlement of Paris as well as its provincial "ema-
nations" "was just as old as the monarchy." The duties of the courts
consisted as they did in the time of Clovis of "never doing or regis-
tering anything contrary to the laws of the realm . . ." As reposito-
ries of the constitution and descendants of the ancient Merovingian
councils, the parlements owed the king counsel, by which LePaige
meant something more than just advice. Like the Merovingian councils which "murmured" dissent, the Parlement had the right or rather
duty to remonstrate or approve the king's actions. "No edict, ordonnance or other acts have the force of public law in the realm before
they have been deliberated in the parlement which represents today
those princes and those assemblies."[142] Indeed, the parlements represented the old medieval assemblies which had brought together all
the king's subjects. Though he never clearly enunciated it, LePaige
comes close to the principle of popular sovereignty and he implies
that a contract exists between monarch and people.

Emboldened by Le Paige's historical argument, the parlements
went out to do battle with the king. The fiscal edicts of 1756 through
1763 and beyond raised a storm of protest in the parlements. The
magistrates castigated the king for trying to prolong the wartime impositions into peacetime; for suspending interest payments on royal
securities; and for trying to impose an "arbitrary" assessment, the
third *vingtième*. The principle which linked these remonstrances was
the belief that the monarch should and must abide by his own agreements. When he promised that certain loans would be secured by
certain taxes, he must not assign these same tax revenues to another
loan. The remonstrances of 9 August 1763 go on for pages describing
the king's defaults and bankruptcies, his tendency to renege on his
agreements and repudiate loans. The king, the parlements appear to
be saying, must keep his word and honor his contracts.[143]

The implications of such talk were clear but the provincial parlements went beyond mere insinuation. Rouen for example railed
against the government in the following terms:

When the Estates General came to an end, fiscal measures broke down all
the dikes and inundated France and covered it with onerous debts. Eager per-

haps that nothing be legal and everything be arbitrary, (the crown) reversed
the order and levied taxes without consent; one eluded and disdained ancient
forms, which conserve the good of the state and the legitimate liberty of its
members; one tore down sacred barriers, the august monuments of our earliest existence . . . Give us back, Sire, our precious liberty; give us back our
Estates General . . . the essence of a law is that it is accepted . . . the right to
consent to a law is the right of a nation . . . This right exists and your Majesty
recognizes it in addressing his edicts to the magistrates who can substitute
for the nation in verifying them. Exercised during the absence of the Estates
by those whom the nation regards as the depositaries of legislation, the right
is sacred . . .[144]

Stronger language would not be heard in the 1780s and the Parlement clearly connected liberty, popular sovereignty, and right of the
nation to consent to taxes. But not all parlements were so advanced.
The Parlement of Paris balked at mentioning the Estates General,
and even in the 1780s, conservative magistrates (like LePaige himself) had grave doubts about the institution.[145]

The Revolution was years away and absolutism had far from run
its course. Indeed, in many quarters the *thèse royale* still enjoyed
considerable prestige. Among monarchy's most avid supporters were
the intellectuals who talked the most often and the most construc-
tively about taxes—the physiocrats. Outside of this group, few French
thinkers worried about state finance, so the "economists" monopo-
lized the fiscal question. One of their number, the chevalier de Jaucourt, wrote the entry entitled "taxes" for Diderot's *Encyclopédie*.[146]
For Mirabeau, Quesnay, Mercier de la Rivière, and to a lesser degree
Turgot, the king did and should exercise absolute power. Property
they believed to be a natural right but they maintained that the king
was a "co-proprietor" of all property, that is he had the right to seize
property if he wished and to tax at will.[147] Neither representation nor
consent was necessary; indeed, Mirabeau found both most undesir-
able. "The Monarch," Mirabeau explained, "gathers in himself two
sacred rights, that of authority and that of property; it follows therefore that he alone, the unique leader will establish and administer
regular taxation." The right to "contest or establish taxes," Mirabeau
maintained, was "incompatible with monarchy"; and he regarded
most representative institutions as little better than a nuisance.[148]
National assemblies "are little better than gatherings of blind people
. . . who create confusion of languages, the conflict of wills, disdain,

noise, plots, smoke, farce and contempt for authority." The English
Parliament, for example, "flatters itself," Dupont de Nemours believed, "that it opposes sovereign authority, an opposition that only
earns (the English) a stormy constitution."[149] Still, the physiocrats,
in particular Turgot, promoted the establishing of local assemblies—
but assemblies with very limited powers. These groups' only purpose
was to apportion taxes; they were to have no say in how much individuals were taxed or by what means. Of course, the physiocrats en-
dorsed a single tax on the income of landowners, the so-called *impôt
territorial*. The notion of a single, simple tax was extremely popular
in the eighteenth century and a host of individuals, including finance
ministers Silhouette and Calonne, called for such a measure. But the
physiocrats' tax differed in that it was designed not only to fill the
treasury, but also to benefit the economy. The physiocrats believed
that excise taxes were particularly harmful to landowners and to an
agrarian country like France. In this regard, they viewed taxes from
a new perspective; and their reliance upon natural law and utility
instead of history held out the promise of creating new sources of
political authority. But their notions had little to do with liberty or
freedom in a political sense. For Mirabeau, liberty consisted almost
solely of economic liberty: "Liberty consists," he explains, "in not
being prevented from acquiring property by work or enjoying property that one has acquired."[150]

In short, the physiocrats constituted no serious threat to royal
power and consequently thinking about fiscal policy, which they mo-
nopolized, had little to do with opposition to the monarch. They
therefore must be accounted among the forces which shored up
the Crown in the crisis of 1763. Similarly, parlementary resistance,
seemingly so profound, never really damaged the king's prerogatives.
Whatever the courts' constitutional pretensions, the king still had
the right to register any edict by *lit de justice* and he could exile his
magistrates at will. In 1770, the chancellor Maupeou took the next
step: he dissolved the sovereign courts altogether and set up his own
judicial bodies. France lived quite happily for four years without the
magistrates.[151] Because they were the creation of the monarchy, the
magistrates never constituted an independent source of resistance.
They could annoy the monarch and constitute a nuisance, but they
could not overturn the monarchy in 1763 or thereafter. As for the

fiscal situation, the ministers' mixed policy of restraint and force
kept the Crown together financially—but just barely—for another
twenty-five years.

< IV >

The Fiscal Crisis of 1788

The time has now come to consider not how a revolution was averted
but why one occurred in 1789. We need not review the events of
1787–88 here for there are many excellent accounts. What we must
do is isolate the forces that brought down the French treasury. Traditionally, the difficulties of the Crown have been ascribed to "bankruptcy"—that is, to the inability of the king to borrow. Standard
accounts of 1788 invoke the "death of credit" which preceded the
Revolution and point to the unwillingness of the state's creditors
to continue to provide funds.[152] Certainly, Loménie de Brienne and
Necker scrambled to find money; but they were able to float loans.
As David Weir and François Velde recently have demonstrated, the
Crown had no trouble attracting creditors.[153] To be sure, the king did
pay a risk premium on some (though not all) of his loans: the public
demanded higher yields or default premia on those loans which were
perceived as particularly vulnerable based on the experience of default in 1759 and 1770.[154] Most vulnerable were loans with "unreason-
able" or "exorbitant" rates of return which could be branded as "excessive" and earmarked for default. But the king employed an array
of financial instruments, some of which were unlikely to be targets
of default. These kinds of government securities easily found buyers
at the Bourse in 1788.[155] Therefore one cannot say that the inability
to borrow precipitated the convocation of the Estates General.

So why did the king have recourse to the Estates? There were a
number of other possible strategies. Terray, in the aftermath of the
Seven Years War in 1770, had enacted a selective write down. Such
a move was now impossible, however, because Louis XVI had promised upon ascending to the throne to renounce defaults. The Crown
could have also adopted another strategy, that of raising taxes, abol-
ishing some old imposts, and creating new ones. But this course
was as risky and perhaps more difficult. New taxes—and then loans

secured by new revenue—would have alleviated the Crown's financial miseries without alienating creditors through default or write
down. But Louis XVI could not, it appears, levy new taxes. His unwillingness or inability to create new impositions hamstrung the French
fisc and made the fiscal crisis of 1788 into the constitutional crisis of
1789. More than any other factor, the inability to tax brought down
the French treasury and with it the absolute monarchy. The political impasse which prevented the Crown from raising taxes lay at the
heart of the kingdom's fiscal problems and it is this impasse that now
bears closer scrutiny. The groups which created this political impasse
were the magistrates of the sovereign courts, the government itself,
the French taxpayers, and contemporary political thinkers. No one
group can be considered in isolation; their actions intersected and
supported one another. No one group alone could have successfully
brought down the throne; they lacked either the force, the imagination, or the desire to do so.

    Let us begin with the magistrates of the sovereign courts. Recent
scholars have expressed reservations about the old concept of an "aristocratic revolution," one arguing that the parlements came out of the
Maupeou experiment badly discredited and thoroughly cowed.[156] But
bloodied and bowed, the parlements nevertheless constituted an an-
noyance for the royal fisc. In the 1780s, the most radical elements in
the courts shed their conservative constitutionalism and LePaige's reliance on history and adopted instead the more radical rhetoric of the
philosophes. Nature and reason replaced the Merovingian monarchy
as the basis for the magistrates' pretensions, and this development
could only contribute to resistance.[157] To be sure, some of the magistrates remained attached to the old notion of liberty, in the sense
of provincial liberties or fiscal immunities. But most abandoned it,
especially after the convocation of the Estates General.[158]

    Thus fortified with a new vocabulary of resistance, the parlements
of the 1780s mounted concerted resistance to the government's fiscal
policies. Certainly, the monarchy could and sometimes did use the *lit
de justice* to sweep away parlementary resistance. But this does not
mean that the parlements were harmless. They thwarted the monarchy in two important ways. First, their resistance often accompanied
the issuing of government paper and embarrassed the government at
a crucial moment. It did the monarchy's credit rating little good to

have the magistrates air before the public examples of the king's bad faith to his creditors.

Second, and more important, the parlements made levying new taxes virtually impossible. If the ministers of the 1770s and 1780s relied heavily upon borrowing, it was because they had to, because they could not increase or alter levies. Their English equivalents were not so fettered. According to J. E. D. Binney, the English tax burden increased enormously in the 1780s: it was 66 percent greater in 1789 than it had been 20 years earlier.[159] Between 1783 and about 1789, Pitt and the British Parliament operated a financial redressment. They raised British taxes and increased the revenue from approximately 13 million pounds to 17.5 million pounds, which allowed them to retire some debts. By this bold but simple means, the amount of money needed to service the British debt was reduced to only 56 percent of the annual budget and investors could see the possibility of reducing it much further. The French ministers could not contemplate such a solution because the sovereign courts stood between them and the changes they sought.

This brings us to the monarchy itself. Historians have castigated and praised the ministers of the years between 1770 and 1788. They figure as either hapless fools or noble reformers, champions of centralization and forerunners of the modern, revolutionary state. The ministers between Terray and Brienne certainly don't deserve our scorn; they showed remarkable ingenuity in keeping the ship of state afloat. Their reputations as reformers and centralizers I also find questionable. By reformers, historians have generally meant ministers who sought to do away with fiscal immunities and thereby "reform" the fiscal structure. I have already dealt at length with historians' fixation on fiscal privilege; this notion of reform is yet another instance of the same policy. Calonne for example tried to abrogate privilege and tax the previously untaxed. But he also used every weapon in the arsenal of absolutism to extract revenue. He forced loans on the corporate bodies, refinanced offices, and generally worked every available avenue for revenue. He did not contemplate remaking or even reforming the institutional or fiscal structure of France.

With one exception. Calonne, along with Turgot and Necker, tried to establish provincial assemblies that would negotiate and apportion taxes. Historians since de Tocqueville have been so intent upon

finding signs of centralization that they have overlooked these attempts to create representative assemblies. The French ministers did
not seek just to centralize authority, but to fragment it. They desperately needed representative assemblies, and for several reasons. First,
each minister sought fair and rigorous tax assessment and we know
that only an assembly could succeed at this task. The intendants as
individuals easily bowed to power and influence and thereby deprived
the Crown of revenue. As the duc d'Orleans remarked in relation
to Calonne's project for assemblies, "this bad joke will cost 200,000
livres, for an assembly (unlike the Intendant) will surely make me
pay."[160] Second, only elected bodies could legitimate tax apportion-
ment and render levies less onerous to tax payers. The *cahiers de
doléances*, or lists of grievances, left no doubt: Frenchmen wanted
and would accept only levies apportioned equitably, which was to
say locally.[161] Finally, the monarchy desperately needed a representative body with which to negotiate taxes and thereby legitimize them.
The advantages of such a sovereign body were amply demonstrated
by the English Parliament. Pitt could raise taxes to per capita levels
not even dreamed of by the French ministers. He could also borrow
money at relatively low rates of interest. The fiscal exigencies of war
made a sovereign representative body, which could consent to taxation in the name of the nation, a virtual necessity. The level of revenue required by the rising cost of warfare—a cost which would soar
with the advent of citizen armies and military conscription—probably could not have been achieved without such institutions. The
French monarchy needed the Estates General and it was the king after
all who in August 1788 convoked them.

There was also the group which we have virtually ignored but
which deserves a leading role in this drama—the taxpayer. If anyone
brought the French fisc to its knees, it was the average Frenchman.
The parlements may have blocked new tax edicts, but the French taxpayer quietly thwarted all tax edicts, old or new. As James Riley has
observed, the real problem in late eighteenth century France was not
tax immunities or privilege but tax avoidance.[162]

Unfortunately we can neither measure exactly nor estimate approximately the degree of tax avoidance on the eve of the Revolution.
The best we can do is determine what the average French subject
thought about taxes; and here we have an excellent though certainly

flawed document, the *cahiers de doléances*. If we use the several hundred *cahiers* collected in the parlementary archives we can get a sense of the average city dweller's view of taxes on the very eve of the Revolution.[163] A number of themes appear in virtually all *cahiers*, be they from Normandy or Provence; be they of the church, the nobility, or the third estate. All *cahiers* declared their loyalty to the king; all expressed their hostility to his ministers and many blame their mismanagement for the fiscal crisis.

That the Crown was experiencing financial difficulties, the *cahiers* did not deny. But they tended to view these difficulties as passing or at least as relatively easy to remedy. The third estate of Agen believed that a careful examination of income and expenditures would produce a solution, that is a balanced budget.[164] The third of Albret insisted that after such an examination, suspect ministers be charged with peculation and brought before the courts.[165] Some *cahiers*, like that of the nobility of Alençon, maintained that the sale of the royal domains would suffice to retire the deficit and the debt.[166] Other *cahiers* provided more detailed and more realistic solutions for the fisc.

In regard to the debt, most *cahiers* accepted the accumulated debt, though a few specified that only the "legitimate" debts be honored by the new regime. Many, however, reaffirmed the duty of the Crown to meet its obligations and instructed the deputies to find a way to retire the debt after its "consolidation." French subjects apparently believed that little more than "economy" was needed to balance the French budget and retire the accumulated debt.[167] Lavish pensions would be reduced and the cost of tax collection lowered. Many *cahiers* suggested that the *receveurs-généraux* be abolished and a host of indirect taxes suppressed because their collection was annoying and wasteful. A single, land-based tax was preferred and the *cahiers* argued for the abolition of all existing imposts in favor of such a levy.

That such a tax would apply to all French subjects, regardless of their status or place of residence, was assumed by all the *cahiers*. The representatives of the nobility as well as the third estate called for the end of fiscal immunities, an act presented in at least one noble *cahier* as "a sign of disinterestedness."[168] Much has been made of the nobles' willingness to give up their fiscal privileges and if the *cahiers* are any indication the second estate was indeed prepared to relinquish its immunities.[169] But this measure—in contrast to what Calonne and subsequent historians would have us believe—was not presented as the panacea that would cure the French fisc. On the contrary, most *cahiers*, noble or commoner, requested that all fiscal immunities, privileges, and irregularities be abolished in the interest of equity, not higher tax returns. Geographical privileges were to disappear and the gap between *pays d'état* and *pays d'élection* was to vanish. Virtually all the *cahiers* that address the fiscal issue in detail call for the establishing of provincial Estates throughout France, which would assign taxes and oversee their collection. The power of the locality was to be enhanced at the expense of the central government and the *cahiers* ironically advocated the extension of Necker's reforms throughout the kingdom. Henceforth, French subjects, not envoys or venal officeholders, would apportion and collect taxes.

Virtually all *cahiers* called for an extension of the French subject's fiscal rights, or in a few cases, for a restoration of those rights. "Only taxes examined and approved by the Estates General are legitimate," proclaim most of the *cahiers*, and they located this right sometimes in history but more often in natural law. The first duty of the deputies to the Estates, many *cahiers* claim, was to "establish the French constitution and consecrate it in just laws."[170] The subject's right to examine and approve all royal levies was a part of this constitution, but it was a right which most French subjects, especially those of the third estate, felt little need to locate in the French past or justify by historical precedent. "All imposts established without the consent of the French subjects are illegitimate," proclaimed the third estate of Alençon, like so many others; and the notion of popular consent to taxation was so common in the *cahiers* that it constituted the principal point of unanimity in 1789. To assure that taxation with representation would be the rule in the future, most *cahiers* called for regular meetings at three, four, or five year intervals to vote new taxes and review the national budget.

Moreover, most *cahiers* clearly stated that all existing taxes were "illegitimate" because they had not been approved by the Estates General. "All current imposts are illegal," proclaimed the third estate of Amiens, thereby tacitly permitting French subjects to avoid paying them. More significantly on the political plane, the third of Amiens enjoined its deputies to defer voting new subsidies until the grave

constitutional issues facing the nation had been resolved.[171] This was
an extremely common theme in the *cahiers* and it revealed that the
deputies were expected to use the tax issue as a lever. No imposts
could be approved without the doubling of the third, the regular convocation of the Estates General, and the creation of provincial Estates
—in short, a massive empowering of French subjects at the expense of
the monarch. The *cahiers* were adamant: no financial measures until
the king had made concessions. One must remember that the issue
was a hot one in 1789, when the Estates were constantly threatened
with dissolution. The fiscal impasse was the lever, the instrument by
which the Revolution was born and the guarantee that the changes
undertaken in the spring of 1789 would come to completion.

The element which gave force to the Estates' "blackmail" was a
massive evasion of taxes from the spring of 1788. The already bleak
financial prospects of the Crown were made considerably worse by
what was in effect a tax strike. Taxes never brought in the revenues
they were supposed to, while even "reform" levies like the *vingtième*
produced only a fraction of their projected harvest. Marion is inclined
to blame the hapless Necker for this state of affairs and accuses him
of fostering the idea, very widespread by the fall of 1788, that the king
not only would permit tax evasion but wanted it.[172] While it does appear that there was a general belief that in calling the Estates the king
had called off all taxes, the events of 1788 alone are not to blame.
The problem was clearly structural and had plagued the French fisc
for years. Under any circumstances, the Crown simply lacked the
resources, technical or financial, to coerce every individual in the
country into paying his taxes.

Absolutist monarchies, indeed all governments, must to a certain
degree rely upon quasi-voluntary compliance. People may not like to
pay taxes but they must be persuaded to do so if the government is
to survive. Effective monitoring, the elimination of free riders, and
maximum equity—all contribute to legitimacy and with it compliance.[173] These were all qualities strikingly absent from the French
fiscal system so it comes as little surprise that French taxpayers did
not comply. Apparently (and we need a great deal more information
on this point) Frenchmen refused to pay or sought to avoid paying virtually all royal taxes, and with success. A representative, sovereign
body which permitted negotiation between taxpayer and government
would have created this sense of legitimacy which promoted compli-

ance. Though it too encountered resistance and evasion, the National Assembly created by the Revolution probably extracted huge sums from the reluctant French citizen—in a climate of disorder, economic depression, and numerous challenges to central authority.

Which brings us to the political thinkers of the late eighteenth century, who not only helped turn a fiscal crisis into a revolution but also shaped that revolution. Between 1763 and 1788 the intellectual climate changed. The old *thèse royale* had been thoroughly discredited during the Maupeou reform. Even the physiocrats, its most intelligent supporters, learned from their occupancy of the ministry that enlightened despotism would not lead to reform. The old *thèse nobiliaire* had not survived the 1770s either.[174] France had survived without the "stupid" judges, as Diderot called them, and it had become abundantly obvious that they had no program for reform of the royal fisc save weak admonitions to economy.

A fresh approach, a rethinking of royal finances, was desperately needed. Surprisingly, given the importance of the fiscal issue, relatively few pamphleteers in the years between 1770 and 1789 devoted themselves to the financial problem. Those authors who examined the Crown's financial difficulties usually did so from the perspective of the ever-changing ministries. Necker and Calonne both wrote treatises on finance which were scarcely veiled apologia for their own ministries.[175] Other pamphleteers rushed to defend or condemn various financial ministers, but the analysis went little further than personalities and accusations of corruption and stupidity. In 1787, Linguet did publish a treatise calling for a single, land tax and extolling the virtues of clarity and simplicity.[176] The visible success of the Bank of England also produced pamphlets calling for the consolidation and monetization of the debt along British lines.[177] Otherwise, creative thinking on the Crown's fiscal problems appears to have been scarce.

With the advent of the Revolution still fewer Frenchmen focused on the kingdom's financial difficulties. As a cursory glance at a catalog of French revolutionary pamphlets reveals, the fiscal issue was dwarfed in 1788 and 1789 by the grave constitutional problems facing the country. Thereafter, a host of other controversies came to preoccupy public opinion and only the *assignat* debacle brought financial problems to the fore again.[178] Consequently, discourse on taxation began—but also ended—with the notion of no taxation without rep-

resentation. This was no small achievement: without the fiscal crisis
and the political pressure which it allowed French subjects (be they
magistrates or commoners) to exert on the Crown there would have
been no Revolution. But it was still unclear how liberty, the sanctity
of private property, and compulsory taxation would be combined in
the "new order" ushered in by the Revolution.

The turmoil of the years between 1788 and 1799 meant that no
new theoretical approaches would emerge. As for the years after 1799,
the Napoleonic dictatorship brought all discussion of "liberty" to an
end. And to find a fresh approach to taxes we must look not forward
but backward to the eighteenth-century thinker who in so many
ways foreshadowed future developments, Rousseau. Rousseau did not
write a great deal about taxation. He addressed the subject only in the
Essay on Poland and, at greater length in the "Discourse on Political
Economy" that appeared in the *Encyclopédie*. He begins "The Discourse on Political Economy" with the following maxim: "It is true
that all imposts must be legitimately established by the consent of
the people or by its representatives . . ."[179] He then asserts that a just
government will "leave to each individual a part of the public administration so that the individual feels he is at home and believes that
the laws serve only to guarantee the community's liberty."[180] Thus far
Rousseau has not departed from the standard, Anglo-Saxon views on
taxation. But he is about to add a new element—equality. "One of the
most important tasks of government is to prevent extreme inequali-
ties of fortune . . . ," he asserts, and adds that the "most necessary
and perhaps difficult feat for a government is to act equitably and to
protect the poor from the rich."[181] Inequity diminishes freedom and
eventually destroys liberty. Taxation, Rousseau insists, could be used
"to prevent the accumulation of wealth, to prevent inequality."

This is a very modern notion of taxation; it argues that revenue
collection is not just a sophisticated form of tribute but a means of
social engineering. Taxation could discourage "luxury" and mitigate
the "inequity" that threatened social harmony and with it political freedom. Here we encounter a notion of freedom that pushes
the social contract described by the commoners of Bar-le-Duc, with
whom this chapter began, one step further. Fiscal demands here are
not just a part of the bargain between ruler and ruled; they are an instrument of social equity, an important part of modern liberty.

<>

Conclusion

PHILIP T. HOFFMAN AND KATHRYN NORBERG

THE CHAPTERS IN this volume suggest certain revisions in what one might call the Whig view of the relationship among liberty, representative institutions, and government finance. (By Whig view we mean a generalization of the English experience—and especially the experience of 1688–89.) Presuming that the English path was the only road to freedom, historians have assumed that representative institutions, such as the English Parliament, were the people's sole defense against a ravenous, absolutist fisc. They have portrayed the monarchs of continental Europe robbing their downtrodden subjects and riding roughshod over property and liberty. Such a view plunges its roots deep into English history: its origins reach back at least as far as John Fortescue in the fifteenth century and it resonates in the political rhetoric of the late seventeenth century, which depicts the subjects of absolute monarchies as slaves.[1] In condemning the continental monarchies, it implicitly supposes that the lighter the tax burden the greater the liberty, the weaker the state the more freedom the citizens enjoyed. So ingrained is this distinctly English view of early modern state building that much of it passes for common sense.

The story told in this volume suggests a different view of the political and fiscal history of early modern Europe. The notion that those who are freest are taxed least does not hold up in the light of comparative history. If we compare the rates of taxation in Spain, France, England, and the Netherlands, we find that in the absolutist states, Spain and France, taxation was relatively light. It is rather in the states with strong representative institutions, the Netherlands and eighteenth-century England, that taxation was extraordinarily heavy.

The comparison, of course, is fraught with difficulty, for reasons that the previous chapters describe in abundant detail: the available evidence is fragmentary and inaccurate, and for Spain and the Netherlands we have to make do with numbers from Castile and Holland alone. Furthermore, even when tax figures do exist they are likely to omit money that was collected and spent locally. And the difficulty of converting the available tax receipts into a common measure—days of labor or hectoliters of grain—makes it impossible to compare all four countries for the same single year or to find a period when they all face the same fiscal and economic conditions. Yet despite all the uncertainty the message the meager figures give seems clear (Table 1). The tax burden was light in early seventeenth-century England, particularly if we restrict ourselves to the customs and parliamentary taxation and note that the evidence derives from a period of warfare and thus of higher than usual taxation. But the burden was not really any heavier across the English Channel in absolutist France. In Castile, it is true, the fisc did bear down with somewhat greater weight, although I. A. A. Thompson would maintain that fiscal absolutism did not exist there. All these differences, though, pale to insignificance beside the enormous taxes levied in eighteenth-century England and even more so in Holland—precisely the examples of states with powerful representative institutions. And a more detailed comparison of eighteenth-century England and France suggests much the same.[2]

Of course, the Netherlands and England both enjoyed robust economies, which may account for much of their ability to bear heavy taxes. In a more general sense, all of the chapters in this volume point to economic strength as a necessary precondition for a strong fisc and therefore a strong state. When economies stagnated or fell behind, countries risked decline or retreat from the international arena, like Spain in the seventeenth century or the Netherlands in the eighteenth. Obviously, a state could not tax effectively when the economy produced little of value. Yet it would be wrong to reduce all the variation in tax burdens to economic strength alone: that at least is what a careful comparison of the tax rates in eighteenth-century France and Great Britain suggests. By the eve of the French Revolution, the British tax burden was not only higher in absolute terms; it also took up a far higher share of the per-capita incomes—nearly twice as much as in France. And it was this difference in the share

TABLE I

Comparative Per Capita Annual Tax Burdens, Selected Periods

Country	Period	Annual Tax Burden in Terms of		
		Wheat (Hectoliters per Person)	Unskilled Labor (Man Days per Person)	Skilled Labor (Man Days per Person)
England	1594–1603	0.1[a]	2.0[a]	1.3[a]
		0.2[b]	3.5–3.8[b]	2.3–2.5[b]
Great-Britain	1720	1.8	—	—
Holland	1650	1.8	16.9	12.6
	1721	4.5	27.8	20.1
Castile	1557	0.3	—	2.8
	1664	1.0	—	6.8
France	1560–69	0.2	2.1	1.1
	1590–99	0.1	2.5	1.3
	1600–09	0.2	3.0	1.5
	1650–59	0.6	8.8	4.4
	1720–29	0.7	9.5	4.8

SOURCE: Chapters 1, 3, 4, and 6, and Peter Mathias and Patrick O'Brien, "Taxation in Britain and France, 1715–1810: A Comparison of the Social and Economic Incidence of Taxes Collected for the Central Government," *JEEcH* 5 (1976): 601–50.

NOTE: The figures here will differ slightly from those given in the sources because they have all been rounded or (in the case of Holland) carried out to the same number of decimal places. David Sacks gives taxes in terms of skilled labor; to find the equivalent in terms of man days of unskilled labor, we followed E. A. Wrigley and R. S. Schofield, *The Population History of England 1541–1871*, 2d edition (Cambridge, 1989), 638, and assumed that a skilled craftsman's wage was 1.5 times an unskilled laborer's wage. Augustus Veenendaal's calculations concern unskilled labor but equivalents in terms of man days of skilled labor were derived from his wage source: Jan de Vries, "The Population and Economy of the Preindustrial Netherlands," *Journal of Interdisciplinary History* 15 (1985): 672. Finally, the French burdens in terms of man days of unskilled labor were converted from man days of skilled labor at the rate of 2.0 days of unskilled labor per day of skilled labor. This was the long term ratio of skilled to unskilled wages in the Paris building trades: Micheline Baulant, "Les salaires des ouvriers du bâtiment à Paris de 1400 à 1726," *Annales* 26 (1971): 463–83. Admittedly, the simplistic conversion of unskilled to skilled wages (or the reverse) introduces some uncertainty, as does the rounding. However, given the limited accuracy of all of these figures the resulting error is hardly a cause for worry.

[a] Customs and parliamentary subsidies only.

[b] Customs, subsidies, and other royal revenues.

of income going to the fisc, rather than any disparity in the income itself, that explains much of the heavier tax burden in Britain.[3]

To be sure, taxation itself acts on the economy and can stimulate or impede economic growth. In Castile, as Thompson points out, contemporaries bemoaned the burden placed on the economy by the confusing welter of local taxes; their effect, one could argue, was to throttle trade. In the Netherlands, as Augustus Veenendaal notes, the excise taxes were the targets of similar attacks, although it is far from clear that they actually damaged the economy. And all early modern monarchs risked having their fiscal policies unleash what contemporary economists refer to as "rent seeking"—that is, economic activity which produces nothing except, in this case, tax evasion. How interesting would it be to calculate the amount of time, effort, and money expended by the French peasantry on avoiding the *taille*? How much more effort and money was expended by the French fisc in attempting to subvert privileges and undermine discrepancies? Here undoubtedly was a great economic loss, one that might be masked, as in France, by a relatively light tax burden.

The effective early modern monarch tried to tax his subjects efficiently: in other words, he tried to raise revenue at the least possible cost. Here again, as the selections in this book demonstrate, the nature of the economy was crucial. When it was possible both politically and administratively, early modern monarchs preferred to tax trade. When it could be stopped at easily controlled bottlenecks, such as major ports or a small number of city gates, then taxing commerce was cheaper than taxing scattered wealth such as land. In the prosperous years of the sixteenth century, for example, the Spanish virtually wrote off taxing land and non-commercialized arable farming in Castile. They focused instead on trade and on the commercial part of agriculture, such as the raising of livestock. The English also relied heavily on indirect taxes such as customs and the famous excise. They were incredibly lucky: a vibrant commercial sector made it easy to levy indirect taxes and explains (if only in part) their ability to support both an army and a navy in the eighteenth century.

The French took in much less from indirect taxes.[4] Because their country was less urbanized and more agricultural than England, it was understandable that they relied more heavily on a land tax; in addition, trade in France was too scattered to tax easily. But what is surprising is that the French did not abandon levies on land, like the Spanish in sixteenth-century Castile. The reason, perhaps, was that arable farming was a bit more commercialized in France and relatively more important than stock raising in Castile. But in any event imposing taxes on land was still quite difficult in France, and many of the peculiarities of the French fiscal system discussed by Philip Hoffman and Kathryn Norberg stem from this fact. The Bourbon monarchs desperately sought ways of "unlocking" the money buried in land. Indeed, most of late eighteenth-century French fiscal history reflects this effort undertaken by a series of reforming ministers.

The early modern state made fiscal policy but fiscal policy also made the state. As James Jones points out in his chapter, some eighteenth-century Englishmen feared that the new financial interest would dominate Parliament. Their fears were hardly groundless. Indeed, most early modern states risked becoming hostages of the very groups they sought to tax or borrow from, and political life itself was shaped by seemingly inconsequential fiscal expedients. In Spain, for example, the king had to rely upon the cities for his income and quickly grew dependent upon them. In France, as Hoffman shows, the Crown came to rely upon the venal office holders for quick loans and subsidies. What was more typical of the Bourbon monarchy than the peculiar institution of venality and who was to prove more annoying that the venal office holders? The Bourbon kings could not live without them—nor with them as it turned out. In this case, the demands of the fisc came to shape the distribution of political power and with it the very texture of political life.

That the French and the Spanish kings were hamstrung by the very groups that provided funds points to another theme that runs through the chapters in this volume: the reevaluation of absolutism. For two decades now, historians (in particular those of seventeenth-century France) have deemphasized the absolute in absolutism. Where once they saw unlimited prerogatives, now they see a host of institutions and groups that opposed the king and curtailed his powers. Nowhere was this more evident than in the crucial realm of the fisc. Thompson, Hoffman, and Norberg all stress the enormous institutional barriers that frustrated the continental monarch's will. Both the French and the Spanish kings had to contend with a welter of local privileges and institutions that might obstruct their orders, from the Cortes and the city councils in Castile to the provincial estates and sovereign parlements in France. Often, these obstacles were the king's own creation. In Spain, as Thompson shows, the king's very council often acted as the most effective guarantor of constitutional privileges and liberties. In France, the venal office holders who staffed the sovereign courts and loaned the king money proved the most vigorous and effective champions of French constitutional liberties.

Why though did France hold off a real crisis much longer than Spain? Why did it prove the more robust of the two strong continental monarchies? Part of the answer lies with the lack of fiscal absolutism in Spain, the lack of a fiscal equivalent to the intendants, who could forcibly bring in taxation in a moment of military crisis, albeit at great long run cost both to the treasury and to the polity. The French had other advantages as well. Their economy was sounder, at least as the seventeenth century wore on, and the French Crown could borrow from a host of domestic lenders—municipalities, tax farmers, and office holders—and do so even during the crises years of the 1630s and 1640s. The Spanish Crown, by contrast, lost access to one of its main sources of credit, international capital, as bullion shipments from the Americas diminished. Forced by military necessity to abuse its other great creditors—the *juros* holders—it ultimately destroyed what had once been an extraordinary credit system.[5]

In a sense, the rulers of Spain and France faced greater obstacles than the kings of England. The will of the English Crown was not thwarted to the same degree by a host of local courts, representative institutions, and provincial bodies which deployed local privileges and local legal traditions to ward off the demands of the fisc. The English monarchs largely avoided such problems because they ruled over a smaller, more easily managed kingdom—one centralized, ironically, by conquest early in the Middle Ages. As David Sacks rightly observes, the Norman Conquest imposed on England a uniformity in law and custom that continental monarchs might well envy. While the king of England thus had only Parliament to deal with, the king of France found himself engaged in long and costly negotiations with local Estates and law courts; even Louis XIV in effect had to buy them all off. These local institutions guaranteed their constituency's "liberties" just as surely as did the Parliament of England.

The "liberties" guaranteed here were not rights but rather privileges, the privileges of a province or city, or the immunities of a powerful lord or corporation. Such privileges were not peculiar to France and Spain; they existed in all four of our countries, albeit with certain differences. Some dated back to the Middle Ages; many others—in France and Spain, in particular—were created by early modern monarchs in moments of fiscal desperation.[6] In the Netherlands, there were obstacles to creating privileges in this way: the

Union of Utrecht, which gave birth to the Dutch federation, made it difficult to create new privileges that might infringe upon the old or even to modify existing privileges. In France, privileges might be defended by local courts such as the provincial parlements. In Castile their defense might also come from the judicial system, but from its very summit, the royal councils, even when privileges had to be supported against the king himself.

Nearly all of these privileges were particularistic—peculiar to this or that province, city, or corporation. Only in England, so Sacks argues, does one begin to see broader liberties, liberties that belong to all free born Englishmen, not because of membership in a city or a corporation, but simply by virtue of their being English. According to Sacks, these general liberties first appeared at the beginning of the seventeenth century. Older and narrower privileges by no means vanished but one saw beside them broader liberties that distinguish England from France, Spain, and even the Netherlands.

In sum, all of the monarchs of early modern Europe had to confront powerful obstacles to their will; none raised revenue without negotiation, consultation, and sometimes bribery. Sometimes representative bodies played this role, as with the English Parliament. But sometimes other institutions championed liberties or privileges— the corporations of venal office holders in France or even the royal council in Castile. The chapters in this volume thus remind us that we cannot focus on representative institutions alone if we are to understand how liberty grew out of the contest between king and subject over revenue. They also suggest that the relationship between the fisc and representative bodies was not necessarily adversarial. A representative body could actually facilitate revenue extraction as the examples of the Netherlands and eighteenth-century England surely prove. The Dutch and the English paid more taxes than other nations and they did so because representative bodies helped sanction fiscal demands. The lesson of eighteenth-century England, where Parliament, albeit unwittingly, lent legitimacy to the fisc, was not lost on the kings of France. As Norberg argues, reforming ministers in France tried repeatedly to establish representative bodies on both the local and provincial level. They hoped that these bodies would legitimize royal demands and draw forth the new tax revenues which the French kings so desperately needed. The French Minister Calonne's Assembly of Notables was but the best known of these doomed efforts, and it underscored how hobbled the Bourbons were by the lack of something approaching the English Parliament.

In the end, representative institutions, not absolute monarchy, proved superior in revenue extraction. Where representative bodies held the ultimate authority, as in the Netherlands or eighteenth-century England, they facilitated taxing. Representation in the English Parliament created a willingness to pay; so did the older attitudes about contributing to the government which Sacks describes. Where forceful representative institutions were absent, though, fiscal paralysis was almost inevitably the result. In France, competing interests and the lack of a national representative body made it virtually impossible for the royal government to create desperately needed taxes. In Spain, the demise of the Cortes helped freeze taxation and usher in the end to Spain's status as a great power.

To tax, the monarch needed representative bodies; he also needed them in order to borrow. As this survey of the fiscal history of the early modern state reminds us, taxation was but one part of the financial baggage of the European monarchies. Borrowing was also essential to the fiscal and military health of early modern states. Taxes, after all, were never enough for war. No matter how great, they could not keep pace with the enormous sums needed when troops were suddenly mobilized and campaigns waged. States simply had to borrow to meet the expenses of war: only then could the expenses be spread into the future and paid off with taxes. Exceptions to this rule are rare: Prussia under Frederick William I might qualify as one, but otherwise one looks in vain for a country that did not mortgage the future to pay for its military ventures.[7]

Credit was necessary for fiscal health, and all the states described here borrowed, though with varying success—that is, at different rates of interest. Eventually all early modern monarchs had recourse to complicated fiscal devices, and most resorted to default as well, or to something approaching it. Even the English, thereafter so careful to meet their obligations, had their Stop of the Exchequer in 1672. The Bourbons were much more creative in this regard. As Hoffman shows, the French monarchs frequently repudiated debts, suspending payments and threatening financiers. Monetary manipulations were often added to the fiscal stew, but such maneuvers came to a halt after the financial debacle of the Law affair. Thereafter, the French king was much more circumspect about monetary manipulations, but the Crown could still not resist spectacular repudiations and write downs like Terray's famous "suspension" of debt payments in 1770.

After defaults of this sort, monarchs had to find ways to drum up new funds, and the French and Spanish kings were not without solutions. One device was to play lender off against lender. Early modern monarchies frequently resorted to such tactics in order to borrow anew after a default had frightened off creditors. In Spain, for example, at least until well into the seventeenth century, the Crown's numerous bankruptcies typically began with a suspension of interest due bankers on short term loans, pitting banker against banker in an effort to get additional funds. As Thompson points out, the most powerful bankers always emerged from these negotiations with a special deal in return for providing new credit. In France the monarchy also played lender against lender. There too politically powerful lenders were often repaid in moments of fiscal crises in order that future loans would be forthcoming and political disaster averted. As Hoffman shows, the kings of France also utilized a variety of expedients to reassure creditors and thereby borrow more—seeking loans from tax farmers, for example, or selling venal offices.

Such expedients worked but only temporarily and at considerable political cost. In France, they reinforced the privileges of the elite and made bitter negotiations with the privileged groups an unfortunate necessity. The negotiations could grow difficult and time consuming as the Crown scurried between one group and another hoping to find a solution. As the only unifying element in French political life, the king could be embroiled in quarrels among privileged groups and find himself wounded by the cross fire. Paralysis was the result—not a bad way to describe the French fiscal crisis of 1788.

The solution proposed by Calonne in the midst of this crisis—his Assembly of Notables—is revealing: it amounted to the creation of a national, somewhat representative institution. Calonne clearly thought that a representative body would allow him not only to raise new taxes but also to borrow money. Here, it seems, Calonne was correct, for representative institutions did facilitate borrowing, as the comparative rates of interest monarchs paid on their debt demonstrate. Again, any comparison is clouded by temporary fiscal crises;

it is further complicated by fragmentary records and by differences in loan terms and domestic inflation rates. But if one compares French and English rates on long term loans in the eighteenth century, it is clear that the king of France paid a risk premium of about 2 percent on his most creditworthy loans. This was a sizeable premium, and the French king paid even more for his riskier loans.[8]

Clearly the English enjoyed an advantage when it came to borrowing, an advantage due in large part to Parliament, which reassured creditors and thereby reduced the interest demanded for loans. Parliament did so in two important ways. First, it helped raise taxes, as we know, by conferring legitimacy on the fisc so that new impositions could be created with relative ease. New taxes could not be levied in late eighteenth century France, as Norberg shows, and the French fisc paid dearly, not just in terms of lost revenue but also in terms of high interest payments on its loans.

Parliament also facilitated borrowing directly. Because it could ultimately hold the Crown and the government accountable, it could guarantee that government loans would be repaid. Governments, after all, always need to convince potential lenders that they will pay their debts; like all borrowers, they have to make their commitments credible. For monarchies, this was no easy task in an era when kings did not hesitate to default. The king of France never entirely succeeded in reassuring his creditors—whence the risk premium on his loans. Ultimately, the king of Spain also failed his creditors, eventually defaulting even on the once secure *juros*. Only where strong representative bodies wielded fiscal power did monarchies manage in the long run to make credible promises to lenders. In England, the Parliament performed this task after the Glorious Revolution; the English therefore paid less for the money they borrowed. In the seventeenth century, the Dutch too, as Veenendaal shows, borrowed at phenomenally low rates, thanks in large part to their estates.

But simply having estates or a Parliament was not enough to reassure state creditors, for a representative body itself could abuse state creditors. In England, as Jones points out, there were no legal limits to what the English Parliament could have done to creditors in the aftermath of the Glorious Revolution. It could have acted against the Bank of England or suspended interest payments due on loans without violating the constitution, and its actions would have left creditors no possibility of redress in the courts. What kept it from exercising its growing powers and doing what certain modern assemblies have done—running up a deficit and then defaulting on its loans?

The answer, according to Jones, was in part ideological. Default was simply unthinkable, because it would have ruined the economy and destroyed a new but indispensable form of property—government loans and stock in the Bank of England. It would also have been difficult politically, for Parliament would have run afoul of the powerful financial interest, which had no trouble exercising its influence over MPs. And in the long run default would have violated the mutually beneficial trust and confidence that slowly grew up between investors and the state in the aftermath of the Glorious Revolution.

We can ask the same question of the Dutch Republic. Why did its estates avoid default? There too the answer is partly ideological: default would be an unthinkable violation of property in this republic of merchants. But there were political obstacles too. It would have been very hard for the estates not to back up government loans because their own members were prominent among the government's creditors.[9] They would be wounding themselves in case of default.

Although representative institutions were thus not enough to guarantee a good credit rating and high taxes, it was obvious that they helped immensely. Given their fiscal superiority, why then did they not triumph everywhere in early modern Europe? Why did they ultimately exercise such authority in only two of our four countries? How do we account for their demise in Old-Regime France and Spain? A partial answer here comes from political science. Certain political scientists maintain that representative institutions are more likely to develop where traders and merchants predominate. The argument has nothing to do with the bourgeoisie or Marxist classes; it is simply that merchants can influence a ruler because mercantile wealth is mobile. Even a grasping despot would be better off negotiating with merchants over taxes rather than imposing levies by force and then watching their assets slip away.[10] The same line of reasoning suggests that representative institutions will encounter difficulties in countries of peasants and landowners; their wealth is land, immobile and thus easy to seize. With them, a ruler obviously has less reason to strike a deal.

Although historians might shy away from such an abstract argument, it would seem to apply quite well to the four countries we have studied. Trade was important in the Netherlands, and in England as well, at least by the end of the seventeenth century. It was much less important in France and Spain, which remained predominately agricultural. The fate of representative institutions divides along the same lines: ultimately they exercised authority in the Netherlands and England but withered away in France and Spain.

Yet to reduce everything to economics would be a gross distortion, for too many other factors entered into play. To take but one example, let us consider France, whose size and diversity ruled out a representative assembly for the entire kingdom. Without a national assembly, it was easier for the king of France to pit privileged group against privileged group and thereby circumvent the local assemblies that the country did possess. In England, by contrast, such a strategy of divide and rule was bound to fail. Parliament became a national forum for political negotiation at an early date, as Sacks has shown, and it therefore helped keep the Crown from using divide and rule to establish an absolutist regime. Similarly, the common law and the early unification of the country also served as barriers to divide and rule.

The different political outcomes in our four countries reflected contrasts in political thought as well. One thinks, for instance, of the limits which English political traditions placed on the state's claims, or of the Castilian belief, stressed by Thompson, which subordinated individual liberty to the common good. Sheer accident also had a role to play: for example the Union of Utrecht unintentionally became the constitution of the Dutch Republic. There was just no simple path to representative government, no simple reason why representative institutions triumphed in one country and suffered defeat in another.

We end with a potent irony. Absolutist regimes despite their pretensions were not able to borrow or tax at will. Only government with strong representative institutions could extract huge revenues and borrow large sums. Taxation and despotism were in the end incompatible. Liberty and the institutions which protected it proved much more able to monopolize resources and extract revenue. The fiscal crises which allowed the representative institutions to negotiate a greater measure of liberty also allowed states to grow, to gain fiscal strength. In the end, liberty was a necessary precondition for the emergence of a strong state, a state of wealth and power.

REFERENCE MATTER

Abbreviations

ACC	*Actas de las Cortes de Castilla*
ACD	Archivo del Congreso de los Diputados (Madrid)
AGS	Archivo General de Simancas
	CJH Consejo y Juntas de Hacienda
	GA Guerra Antigua
	PR Patronato Real
AHE	*Archivo Histórico Español*
AHES	*Annales d'histoire économique et sociale*
AHN	Archivo Histórico Nacional (Madrid)
AHP	Archivo Histórico Provincial de
AHR	*American Historical Review*
AM	Archivo Municipal de
Annales	*Annales: économies, sociétés, civilisations*
AP	*Archives parlementaires*
AV	Archivo de la Villa de
BAE	*Biblioteca de Autores Españoles*
BIHR	*Bulletin of the Institute of Historical Research*
BL	British Library (London)
BMGN	*Bijdragen en Mededelingen betreffende de Geschiedenis der Nederlanden*
BNM	Biblioteca Nacional Madrid, Sección de manuscritos
Bod.L	Bodleian Library, Oxford
BRAH	*Boletín de la Real Academia de Historia*
CJH	*Canadian Journal of History*
CODOIN	*Colección de Documentos Inéditos para la Historia de España*, 113 vols (Madrid, 1842–95)
CSP	*Calendar of State Papers*
EcHR	*Economic History Review*
EHJ	*Economisch Historisch Jaarboek*
EHR	*English Historical Review*
FHS	*French Historical Studies*
HJ	*Historical Journal*
IVDJ	Instituto Valencia de Don Juan (Madrid)
JEEcH	*Journal of European Economic History*

JEH	Journal of Economic History
JMH	Journal of Modern History
leg.	legajo
MHE	Memorial Histórico Español
mrs.	maravedís
PRO	Public Record Office
RAH	Real Academia de Historia (Madrid)
RC	Real Cédula
RD	Real Decreto
RGP	Rijks Geschiedkundige Publicatien
RP	Real Provisión
SP	State Papers
TvG	Tijdschrift voor Geschiedenis

<>

Notes

INTRODUCTION

1. References for the fiscal history of England, France, the Netherlands, and Spain can be found in subsequent chapters. For an overview of government borrowing in the early modern period, see James Tracy, *A Financial Revolution in Habsburg Netherlands: Renten and Renteniers in the County of Holland, 1515–1565* (Berkeley, 1985) 7–27. The literature on fiscal crises spills over into the old debate on the crisis of the seventeenth century; for a brief summary, see Trevor Aston, *Crisis in Europe, 1560–1660* (New York, 1967).

2. Otto Hintze, *Staat und Verfassung*, ed. Gerhard Oestreich and Fritz Hartung, 3d ed. (Göttingen, 1970), especially his essay "Wesen und Wandlung des modernen Staats," 470–96; Roland Mousnier, *Les institutions de France sous la monarchie absolue, 1589–1789*, 2 vols. (Paris, 1974–1980); Hans Rosenberg, *Bureaucracy, Aristocracy, and Autocracy: The Prussian Experience 1660–1815* (Boston, 1958).

3. The recent exceptions include works by William Beik, David Bien, Richard Bonney, John Brewer, James Collins, Daniel Dessert, Françoise Bayard, and James Tracy, all of which are cited in subsequent chapters. The older works of F. L. Carsten, *Princes and Parliaments in Germany* (Oxford, 1959) and *The Origins of Prussia* (Oxford, 1954), also linked policies and fiscal detail. The subject has also attracted the interest of economic historians and social scientists; see, in particular, the essay by Douglass C. North and Barry Weingast, "Constitutions and Commitment: Evolution of the Institutions Governing Public Choice in Seventeenth-Century England," *JEH* 49 (1989): 803–32.

4. Tracy, *Financial Revolution*, 9–21; Carsten, *Princes and Parliaments*. Professor Anthony Molho of Brown University is preparing a book on state finance in Renaissance Italy. His research should answer many of our questions for Italy, much as Carsten's book does for parts of Germany.

5. In keeping with the generally accepted usage for France and other parts of Europe, we call the various Dutch representative bodies "estates" rather than the term sometimes reserved for them, "states."

CHAPTER I

1. Justice Oliver Wendell Holmes in *Compania de Tabacos v. Collector* (1904), 275 U. S. 87, 100.

2. Chief Justice John Marshall in *McCulloch v. Maryland* (1819), 4 Wheaton 431; cf. Justice Holmes's remark in *Panhandle Oil Co. v. Knox* (1928), 277 U. S. 223: "The power to tax is not the power to destroy while this Court sits."

3. See F. C. Lane, "Economic Consequences of Organized Violence," *JEH* 18 (1958): 401–17.

4. Jean Bodin, *Les Six Livres de la Republique*, 1576 ed., 6 vols. (Paris, 1986), 6:35; see also Jean Bodin, *The Six Bookes of a Commonweale: A Facsimile reprint of the English Translation of 1606 Corrected and supplemented in the light of a new comparison with the French and Latin texts*, ed. Kennneth Douglas McRae (Cambridge, MA, 1962), 649.

5. Joseph Schumpeter, "The Crisis of the Tax State," trans. W. F. Stolper and R. A. Musgrave, *International Economic Papers*, no. 4, ed. Alan T. Peacock et al. (London, 1954), 6–7.

6. Bodin, *Six Livres* 2:31; Bodin, *Six Bookes*, 197.

7. On the "theory of predatory rule," see Margaret Levi, *Of Rule and Revenue* (Berkeley, 1988), chap. 2.

8. Bodin, *Six Livres* 2:35, 43; Bodin, *Six Bookes*, 200, 204.

9. Michael Mann, "The Autonomous Power of the State: Its Origins, Mechanisms and Results," in Michael Mann, *States, War and Capitalism: Studies in Political Sociology* (Oxford, 1988), 5–9 and *passim*.

10. Sir John Fortescue, *The Governance of England: otherwise called The Difference between an Absolute and a Limited Monarchy*, ed. Charles Plummer (Oxford, 1885), 109–10. See also Sir John Fortescue, *De Laudibus Legum Anglie*, ed. and trans. S. B. Chrimes (Cambridge, 1942), chaps. 9, 13, 14, 18, 19, 35–36; *De Natura Legis Naturae*, in *Life and Works of Sir John Fortescue*, 2 vols., ed. and trans. Lord Clermont (London, 1869), 1: pt. 1, chaps. 16, 22–26.

11. Bodin, *Six Livres* 2:43, see also 35; Bodin, *Six Bookes*, 204, see also 200.

12. See Bodin, *Six Livres* 1:51, 113; Bodin, *Six Bookes*, 14, 47.

13. See John Brewer, *The Sinews of Power: War, Money and the English State, 1688–1783* (New York, 1989), 143, 247.

14. See e.g. Samuel E. Finer, "State and Nation-Building in Europe: The Role of the Military," in Charles Tilly, ed., *The Formation of National States in Western Europe* (Princeton, 1975), 85.

15. For a discussion of Fortescue that anticipates some of the following remarks, see Alan MacFarlane, *The Origins of English Individualism: Family Property and Social Transition* (New York, 1979), 179–83.

16. Fortescue, *De Laudibus Legum Anglie*, 68–71.

17. Ibid., 42–45.   18. Ibid., 68–69.

19. Ibid., 66–69.   20. Ibid., 80–83.

21. Ibid., 86–87.

22. G. R. Elton, "'The Body of the Whole Realm': Parliament and Representation in Medieval and Tudor England," in G. R. Elton, *Studies in Tudor and Stuart Politics and Government*, 3 vols. (Cambridge, 1974–83), 2:28–29; see G. R. Elton, *The Parliament of England, 1559–1581* (Cambridge, 1986), chap. 2.

23. Fortescue, *De Laudibus*, 82–85; Fortescue, *Governance*, 114–15.

24. Fortescue, *Governance*, 115.

25. Fortescue, *De Laudibus*, 86–89.

26. Fortescue, *Governance*, 115, 116. Fortescue recognized, however, that the French king manages to extract at least twice as much revenue as his English counterpart, but he does so by oppression and because these taxes "be not goodly taken . . . the might of the realm is . . . destroyed thereby," ibid., 116–17.

27. Fortescue, *De Laudibus*, 88–89.

28. Fortescue, *De Natura* 1:213–14; see also Fortescue, *De Laudibus*, 88–89; Fortescue, *Governance*, 116.

29. Fortescue, *De Natura* 1: pt. 1, chap. 26; Fortescue *Governance*, 117; Fortescue, *De Laudibus*, 27, 35.

30. Fortescue, *De Laudibus*, 88–89.

31. Ibid., 27.

32. Ibid., 86–87.

33. See e.g. G. M. Trevelyan, *History of England*, 3d ed. (New York, 1952).

34. E. P. Thompson, "The Peculiarities of the English," in E. P. Thompson, *The Poverty of Theory and Other Essays* (New York, 1978), 245–310, esp. 257; see also Philip Corrigan and Derek Sayer, *The Great Arch: English State Formation as Cultural Revolution* (Oxford, 1985).

35. MacFarlane, *Origins of English Individualism*, 163, 165.

36. See J. C. Holt, "Rights and Liberties in Magna Carta," in J. C. Holt, *Magna Carta and Medieval Government* (London, 1985), 210–15.

37. See William A. Morris, "Magnates and Community of the Realm, 1264–1327," *Medievalia et Humanistica*, fasc. 1 (Boulder, 1943), 58–94; F. M. Powicke, *The Thirteenth Century* (Oxford, 1953), 130–37, 141–42, 145–46; F. M. Powicke, *King Henry III and the Lord Edward: The Community of the Realm in the Thirteenth Century*, 2 vols. (Oxford, 1947), 1:28–38.

38. The main guide to this development is still Frederick Pollock and F. W. Maitland, *The History of English Law before the Time of Edward I*, 2d ed., 2 vols. (Cambridge, 1968); but see also S. F. C. Milson, *Historical Foundations of the Common Law* (London, 1969), 1–50; Doris Stenton, *English Justice Between the Norman Conquest and the Great Charter, 1066–1215* (Philadelphia, 1964); R. C. van Caenegem, *Royal Writs in England from the Conquest to Glanville: Studies in the Early History of Common Law* (Selden Soc. 77, 1959); R. C. van Caenegem, *The Birth of the English Common Law* (Cambridge, 1973).

39. See e.g., K. B. McFarlane, " 'Bastard Feudalism,' " in K. B. McFarlane, *England in the Fifteenth Century* (London, 1981), 23–43; K. B. McFarlane, "The Wars of the Roses," in ibid., 231–61; K. B. McFarlane, *The Nobility of Later Medieval England* (Oxford, 1973), 1–18, 102–21.

40. James H. Ramsay, *A History of the Revenues of the Kings of England, 1066–1399*, 2 vols. (Oxford, 1925), 1:60.

41. Charles M. Gray, "Plucknett's 'Lancastrian Constitution,' " in Morris S. Arnold et al., eds., *On the Laws and Customs of England: Essays in Honor of Samuel E. Thorne* (Chapel Hill, 1981), 195–230; the quoted passages are on 196, 222; see also T. F. T. Plucknett, "The Lancastrian Constitution," in R. W. Seton Watson, ed., *Tudor Studies Presented by the Board of Studies in the University of London to Albert Frederick Pollard* (London, 1974), 161–81.

42. J. G. Edwards, " 'Justice' in Early English Parliaments," reprinted in E. B. Fryde and Edward Miller, *Historical Studies of the English Parliament*, 2 vols. (Cambridge, 1970), 1:280–97; the quote is on 297. For an overview of medieval parliamentary history, see Ronald Butt, *A History of Parliament: The Middle Ages* (London, 1989).

43. Elton, " 'The Body of the Whole Realm,' " 22.

44. Ibid., 29–30.

45. F. W. Stenton, *Anglo-Saxon England* (Oxford, 1943), 406–7; G. L. Harriss, *King, Parliament and Public Finance in Medieval England to 1369* (Oxford, 1975), 5–6.

46. Harriss, *King, Parliament and Public Finance*, 9–10; see also Sidney Painter, *The Reign of King John* (Baltimore, 1949), 132.

47. Harriss, *King, Parliament and Public Finance*, 19–26, 509–17; the quoted passages appear on 21, 511; G. L. Harriss, "War and the Emergence of the English Parliament, 1297–1360," *Journal of Medieval Studies* 2 (1976): 43, 53; G. L. Harriss, "The Management of Parliament," in G. L. Harriss, ed., *Henry V: The Practice of Kingship* (Oxford, 1985), 141–44.

48. Harriss, *King, Parliament and Public Finance*, 29–33.

49. Ibid., 42.

50. Harriss, "War and the Emergence of the English Parliament," 45–47; Harriss, *King, Parliament and Public Finance*, chap. 18.

51. See B. P. Wolffe, *The Royal Demesne in English History: The Crown Estate in the Governance of the Realm from the Conquest to 1509* (London, 1971), chaps. 1–2; B. P. Wolffe, *The Crown Lands, 1461–1536: An Aspect of Yorkist and Early Tudor Government* (London, 1970), 15–23.

52. On the history of fiscal feudalism see Joel Hurstfield, *The Queen's Wards: Wardship and Marriage under Elizabeth I* (Cambridge, MA, 1958); Robert Constable, *Prerogativa Regis: Tertia Lectura Roberti Constable de Lyncolnis Inne Anno II Henry VII*, ed. S. E. Thorne (New Haven, 1949), intro. *passim*. On the exploitation of the feudal aid in the early days of the Hundred Years War see Harriss, *King, Parliament and Public Finance*, 410–19.

53. Harriss, *King, Parliament and Public Finance*, chaps. 15–16; for the later history of purveyance, see Allegra Woodworth, *Purveyance for the Royal Household in the Reign of Queen Elizabeth* (Transactions of the American

Philosophical Society 35 [1945]]; G. E. Aylmer, "The Last Years of Purveyance," *EcHR*, 2d ser., 10 (1957): 81–93.

54. Ramsay, *History of the Revenues of the Kings of England* 2:144–45; Joseph R. Strayer, "Introduction," in William A. Morris and Joseph R. Strayer, eds., *The English Government at Work. 1327–1336, 2: Fiscal Administration* (Cambridge, MA, 1947), 4–7; Harriss, *King, Parliament and Public Finance*, 253–69; 509–46; Harriss, "War and the Emergence of Parliament," 52; Wolffe, *The Royal Demesne*, chaps. 1–2; Wolffe, *The Crown Lands*, 15–23; G. L. Harriss, "Aids, Loans and Benevolences," *HJ* 6 (1963): 1–19.

55. Wolffe, *Royal Demesne*, chaps. 3–8; Wolffe, *Crown Lands*, 23ff; B. P. Wolffe, "Acts of Resumption in the Lancastrian Parliaments, 1399–1456," *EHR* 73 (1958): 583–613. For a recent discussion of these issues, see David Starkey, "Which Age of Reform?" in Christopher Coleman and David Starkey, eds., *Revolution Reassessed: Revisions in the History of Tudor Government and Administration* (Oxford, 1986), 13–27; G. R. Elton, "A New Age of Reform?" *HJ* 30 (1987): 709–16.

56. S. B. Chrimes, *English Constitutional Ideas in the Fifteenth Century* (Cambridge, 1936), 76; Elton, " 'The Body of the Whole Realm,' " 36.

57. On this point see ibid., 36; David Harris Sacks, "Parliament, Liberty, and the Commonweal," in J. H. Hexter, ed., *Parliament and Liberty from Elizabeth I to the English Civil Wars* (Stanford, 1992), 86–93.

58. Elton, " 'The Body of the Whole Realm,' " 26, 53–55.

59. J. S. Roskell, *The Commons in the Parliament of 1422* (Manchester, 1954), 131; May McKisack, *The Parliamentary Representation of the Boroughs during the Middle Ages* (Oxford, 1932), 109–10; J. E. Neale, *The Elizabethan House of Commons* (London, 1949), 146–48.

60. G. L. Harriss, "War and the Emergence of the English Parliament," 42; see also Harriss, *King, Parliament and Public Finance*, chaps. 10–11. On *plena potestas* see J. G. Edwards, "The *Plena Potestas* of English Parliamentary Representatives," in Fryde and Miller, *Historical Studies of the English Parliament* 1:136–49; Gaines Post, "*Plena Potestas* and Consent in Medieval Assemblies," in Gaines Post, *Studies in Medieval Legal Thought: Public Law and the State, 1100–1322* (Princeton, 1964), chap. 3; Helen Maud Cam, "The Theory and Practice of Representation in Medieval England," *History*, n.s. 38 (1953): 11–26.

61. Chrimes, *English Constitutional Ideas in the Fifteenth Century*, 121–25; Elton, " 'The Body of the Whole Realm,' " 33–35.

62. G. R. Elton, *The Tudor Constitution: Documents and Commentary*, 2d ed. (Cambridge, 1982), 277; see also the Dispensations Act of 1534, ibid., 361.

63. Elton, " 'The Body of the Whole Realm,' " 33.

64. Thomas Smith, *De Republica Anglorum: A Discourse on the Commonwealth of England*, ed. Mary Dewar (Cambridge, 1982), 78–79.

65. Karl Polanyi, *The Great Transformation: The Political and Economic Origins of Our Time* (Boston, 1944), chap. 4.

66. Diarmaid McCulloch, "Bondmen under the Tudors," in Claire Cross,

David Loades, and J. J. Scarisbrick, eds., *Law and Government under the Tudors: Essays Presented to Sir Geoffrey Elton Regius Professor of Modern History in the University of Cambridge on the Occasion of his Retirement* (Cambridge, 1988), 91–109. For some later cases, see Eric Kerridge, *Agrarian Problems in the Sixteenth Century and After* (London, 1969), 71–72, 87–93; Charles M. Gray, *Copyhold, Equity and Common Law* (Cambridge, MA, 1963).

67.   See Robert Brenner, "Agrarian Class Structure and Economic Development in Pre-Industrial Europe," in *The Brenner Debate: Agrarian Class Structure and Economic Development in Pre-Industrial Europe*, ed. T. H. Aston and C. H. E. Philpin (Cambridge, 1985), 10–63; Robert Brenner, "The Agrarian Roots of European Capitalism," in ibid., 213–327, esp. 246–64, 284–99, 307–19; M. M. Postan and John Hatcher, "Population and Class Relations in Feudal Society," in ibid., 64–78; M. M. Postan, *The Medieval Economy and Society: An Economic History of Britain in the Middle Ages* (Harmondsworth, 1975), esp. chaps. 8–9; Edward Miller, ed., *The Agrarian History of England and Wales*, vol. 3: 1348–1500 (Cambridge, 1991), chaps. 6–8.

68.   See e.g. Joan Thirsk, "Industries in the Countryside," in F. J. Fisher, ed., *Essays in the Economic and Social History of Tudor and Stuart England in Honour of R. H. Tawney* (Cambridge, 1961), 70–88.

69.   Joan Thirsk, *Economic Policy and Projects: The Development of a Consumer Society in Early Modern England* (Oxford, 1979), chaps. 1–2; G. D. Ramsay, *English Overseas Trade during the Centuries of Emergence: Studies in Some Modern Origins of the English Speaking World* (London, 1957); G. D. Ramsay, *The City of London in International Trade at the Accession of Elizabeth Tudor* (Manchester, 1975), chaps. 1–2, 4–5, 7–8; David Harris Sacks, *The Widening Gate: Bristol and the Atlantic Economy, 1450–1700* (Berkeley, 1991), chap. 1; David Harris Sacks, *Trade, Society and Politics in Bristol, 1500–1640*, 2 vols. (New York, 1985), 1: chaps. 7–9.

70.   E. A. Wrigley and R. S. Schofield, *The Population of England, 1541–1871: A Reconstruction* (Cambridge, MA, 1981), 208, 531–33.

71.   E. A. Wrigley, "Urban Growth and Economic Change: England and the Continent in the Early Modern Period," in E. A. Wrigley, *People, Cities and Wealth: The Transformation of Traditional Society* (Oxford, 1987), 158–63; see also Jan de Vries, *European Urbanization, 1500–1800* (Cambridge, MA, 1984), 28–77, 171–72.

72.   Wrigley, "Urban Growth and Economic Change," 158–63.

73.   See E. H. Phelps Brown and Sheila V. Hopkins, "Seven Centuries of the Prices of Consumables, Compared with Builders' Wage-Rates," in E. M. Carus-Wilson, ed., *Essays in Economic History*, 3 vols. (London, 1954–62), 2:194–95.

74.   C. G. A. Clay, *Economic Expansion and Social Change: England, 1500–1700*, 2 vols. (Cambridge, 1984), 2:100–101.

75.   See David Underdown, *Revel, Riot and Rebellion: Popular Politics and Culture in England, 1603–1660* (Oxford, 1985), esp. chaps. 1–4.

76. As regards the city of Bristol see Sacks, *Trade, Society and Politics* 1: chaps. 2–3; Sacks, *Widening Gate*, chaps. 1–7.

77. Linda Levy Peck, *Court Patronage and Corruption in Early Stuart England* (Boston, 1990), chap. 6; Robert Ashton, *The City and the Court, 1603–1643* (Cambridge, 1979), chaps. 3–4; Robert Ashton, "Conflicts of Concessionary Interest in Early Stuart England, in D. C. Coleman and A. H. John, eds., *Trade, Government and Economy in Pre-Industrial England* (London, 1976), 113–31; Thirsk, *Economic Policy*, chaps. 3–4; Robert Ashton, *The Crown and the Money Market, 1603–1640* (Oxford, 1960).

78. Brewer, *Sinews of Power*, 252 n. 1.

79. Mann, "Autonomous Power of the State," 4; emphasis in the original.

80. See Lawrence Stone, *Family and Fortune: Studies in Aristocratic Finance in the Sixteenth and Seventeenth Centuries* (Oxford, 1973), chap. 1; Hurstfield, *The Queen's Wards*, chaps. 11–15; Joel Hurstfield, *Freedom, Corruption and Government in Elizabethan England* (London, 1973), chaps. 5, 7. See in general John Neale, "The Elizabethan Political Scene," in John Neale, *Essays in Elizabethan History* (London, 1958), 59–84; Wallace T. MacCaffrey, "Partronage and Place in Elizabethan Politics," in S. T. Bindoff, Joel Hurstfield, and C. H. Williams, eds., *Elizabethan Government and Society* (London, 1961), 95–126; Lawrence Stone, *The Crisis of the Aristocracy, 1558–1641* (Oxford, 1965), chap. 8; Peck, *Court Patronage*, esp. chaps. 2, 3, 5, 6.

81. Sacks, *Trade, Society and Politics* 2:727–30; see also Peck, *Court Patronage*, chap. 6, esp. 143ff.

82. G. E. Aylmer, *The King's Servants: The Civil Service of Charles I* (London, 1961), 239–52; Clay, *Economic Expansion and Social Change* 2:253.

83. T. E. Hartley, ed., *Proceedings in the Parliaments of Elizabeth I. Volume 1: 1558–1581* (Leicester, 1981), 199; see also 244; J. E. Neale, *Elizabeth I and Her Parliaments, 1559–1581* (London, 1953), 188–90.

84. See Quentin Skinner, *The Foundations of Modern Political Thought*, 2 vols. (Cambridge, 1978) 1:ix–x; 2:352–58.

85. See John Guy, *Tudor England* (Oxford, 1988), 352; see also Victor Morgan, "Whose Prerogative in Late Sixteenth- and Early Seventeenth-Century England?" in A. Kiralfy, M. Slatter, and R. Virgoe, eds., *Custom, Courts and Counsel* (London, 1983), 39–64.

86. "The Maxims of State," in *The Works of Sir Walter Ralegh, Kt. now first Collected*, 8 vols. (Oxford, 1829), 8:1; on the provenance of this work see Pierre Lefranc, *Sir Walter Ralegh Ecrivain* (Paris, 1968), 67–70; J. G. A. Pocock, *The Machiavellian Moment: Florentine Political Thought and the Atlantic Republican Tradition* (Princeton, 1975), 355–56.

87. Mann, "Autonomous Power of the State," 4.

88. Thomas Starkey, *A Dialogue between Reginald Pole and Thomas Lupset*, ed. Kathleen M. Burton (London, 1948), 57. Quentin Skinner sees Starkey's formulation as an early example in English of the idea of the state as an impersonal constitutional order: see Skinner, *Foundations of Modern Political Thought* 2:356–57; but Thomas Mayer's analysis comes closer to

the correct interpretation; see Thomas F. Mayer, *Thomas Starkey and the Commonweal: Humanist Politics and Religion in the Reign of Henry VIII* (Cambridge, 1989), 125–26. It is clear that Starkey also often used "state" to mean "estate" or "condition," as both Skinner and Mayer note.

89. See *Oxford English Dictionary.*

90. Alan Everitt, "The County Community," in E. W. Ives, ed., *The English Revolution, 1600–1660* (New York, 1971), 48, 49.

91. Peter Laslett, *The World We Have Lost: England before the Industrial Age,* 1st ed. (New York, 1965), 22, 26, 27.

92. E. P. Thompson, "Patrician Society, Plebian Culture," *Journal of Social History* 7 (1973–74): 395–96.

93. Thomas Elyot, *The Boke Named The Governor,* ed. H. H. S. Croft, 2 vols. (London, 1883), 1:1–3.

94. Smith, *De Republica Anglorum,* ed. Dewar, 73–77.

95. Ibid., 64, 77.

96. Thomas Wilson, *The State of England, Anno Dom. 1600,* ed. F. J. Fisher, Camden Miscellany 16 (Camden Soc., 3d ser. 52, 1936): 19, 23; Mac-Caffrey, "Place and Patronage in Elizabethan Politics," 99; see also David Palliser, *The Age of Elizabeth: England Under the Later Tudors, 1547–1603* (London, 1983), 70, 72; Mildred Campbell, *The English Yeoman Under Elizabeth and the Early Stuarts* (London, 1942), 219.

97. Gregory King, "Natural and Political Observations upon the State and Condition of England," in Joan Thirsk and J. P. Cooper, eds., *Seventeenth-Century Economic Documents* (Oxford, 1972), 780–81; Palliser, *Age of Elizabeth,* 72; Campbell, *English Yeoman,* 219–20; Clay, *Economic Expansion and Social Change* 1:chap. 5; G. E. Mingay, *The Gentry* (London, 1976), 59; J. P. Cooper, "The Social Distribution of Land and Men in England, 1436–1700," *EcHR,* 2d ser., 20 (1967): 419–40.

98. King, "Observations," 772; King estimates that there were about 110,000 families of merchants, shopkeepers, and artisans in England in 1688, but not all of these would necessarily have lived in towns: see ibid., 780; in general see Peter Clark and Paul Slack, *English Towns in Transition, 1500–1700* (Oxford, 1976), chap. 8.

99. See Penry Williams, *Tudor Regime* (Oxford, 1979), chap. 3, 293–305; J. H. Hexter, "The Education of the Aristocracy in the Renaissance," in J. H. Hexter, *Reappraisals in History: New Views on History and Society in Early Modern Europe,* 2d. ed. (Chicago, 1979), 45–70.

100. See Guy, *Tudor England,* chap. 13.

101. See Aylmer, *King's Servants,* chap. 7.

102. Williams, *Tudor Regime,* 107; Aylmer, *King's Servants,* 470–87.

103. See K. R. Andrews, *Trade, Plunder and Settlement: Maritime Enterprise and the Genesis of the British Empire, 1480–1630* (Cambridge, 1984), 25–26, 104–5, 230–45, 362–63.

104. G. R. Elton, *The Tudor Revolution in Government: Administrative Changes in the Reign of Henry VIII* (Cambridge, 1960); Williams, *Tudor Regime,* chaps. 1–2; Guy, *Tudor England,* chap. 6.

105.   Neale, "The Elizabethan Political Scene," 54–89; Peck, *Court Patronage*, chaps. 2–3.

106.   See J. D. Alsop, "The Structure of Early Tudor Finance, c. 1509–1558," in Christopher Coleman and David Starkey, eds., *Revolution Reassessed: Revisions in the History of Tudor Government and Administration* (Oxford, 1986), 135–62; Christopher Coleman, "Artifice or Accident? The Reorganization of the Exchequer of Receipt, c. 1554–1572," in ibid., 163–98; J. D. Alsop, "The Exchequer in Late Medieval Government," in J. G. Rowe, ed., *Late Medieval Government and Society* (Toronto, 1987); see also G. R. Elton, "Mid-Tudor Finance," *HJ* 20 (1977): 737–40; J. D. Alsop, "The Revenue Commission of 1552," *HJ* 22 (1979): 511–33.

107.   F. C. Dietz, *English Public Finance, 1485–1641*, 2 vols., 2d ed. (London, 1964), 1:13.

108.   See Wolffe, *Crown Lands*, chaps. 2–3; B. P. Wolffe, "Acts of Resumption in the Lancastrian Parliaments, 1399–1456," *EHR* 73 (1958): 583–613; Wolffe, *Royal Demesne*, chaps. 4–7; see also David Starkey, "Which Age of Reform?" in Coleman and Starkey, eds., *Revolution Reassessed*, 13–28; G. R. Elton, "A New Age of Reform?" *HJ* 30 (1987): 709–16.

109.   J. L. Kirby, "The Issues of the Lancastrian Exchequer and Lord Cromwell's Estimates of 1433," *BIHR* 24 (1951): 121–51; Wolffe, *Crown Lands*, 37–38 and chap. 3; Williams, *Tudor Regime*, 57–58.

110.   Elton, *Tudor Revolution*, 190, 198; W. C. Richardson, *Tudor Chamber Administration, 1485–1547* (Baton Rouge, 1952), 322–26; Williams, *Tudor Regime*, 63; see also W. C. Richardson, *History of the Court of Augmentations, 1536–1554* (Baton Rouge, 1961), chap. 10.

111.   Dietz, *English Public Finance* 1:147–49, 183, 198; Williams, *Tudor Regime*, 64, 67, 68; see also H. J. Habakkuk, "The Market for Monastic Property, 1539–1603," *EcHR*, 2d ser., 10 (1957–58): 362–80.

112.   Dietz, *English Public Finance* 2:296, 302; R. B. Outhwaite, "The Price of Crown Land at the Turn of the Sixteenth Century," *EcHR*, 2d ser., 20 (1967): 231–40; G. R. Batho, "Landlords in England," in Joan Thirsk, ed., *The Agrarian History of England and Wales*, vol. 4: 1500–1640 (Cambridge, 1967), 265–73; Eric Kerridge, "The Movement of Rent, 1540–1640," in Carus-Wilson, ed., *Essays in Economic History* 2:208–29; Williams, *Tudor Regime*, 71.

113.   Dietz, *English Public Finance* 2:299; see also Aylmer, *King's Servants*, 64.

114.   Williams, *Tudor Regime*, 71; Batho, "Landlords in England," 265–73; Aylmer, *King's Servants*, 64; Clay, *Economic Expansion and Social Change* 2:252.

115.   Robert Constable, *Prerogativa Regis*, intro.; Hurstfield, *Queen's Wards*, chap. 1.

116.   Joel Hurstfield, "The Profits of Fiscal Feudalism. 1541–1602," *EcHR*, 2d ser., 8 (1955–56): 53–61; the unofficial profits of feudalism to officeholders probably amounted to three times the figure going directly into the monarch's account, ibid., 58.

117. Dietz, *English Public Finance* 2:303.
118. Ibid., 263 n. 24.
119. G. E. Aylmer, "The Last Years of Purveyance, 1610–1660," *EcHR*, 2d ser., 10 (1957–58): 81–86; see also Dietz, *English Public Finance* 2:423–24. For an account of the operations of the Purveyors under Elizabeth I, see Woodworth, *Purveyance for the Royal Household*; see also Eric Lindquist, "The King, the People and the House of Commons: The Problem of Early Stuart Purveyance," *HJ* 31 (1988): 549–70; Peck, *Court Patronage*, 147–48.
120. Thirsk, *Economic Policy*, 33–34, 51–60, 89, 97–101; Clay, *Economic Expansion and Social Change* 2:252–53, 255–57; W. R. Scott, *The Constitution and Finance of English, Scottish and Irish Joint-Stock Companies to 1720*, 3 vols. (Cambridge, 1910–12), 1:214.
121. See N. S. B. Gras, *The Early English Customs System: A Documentary Study of the Institutional and Economic History of the Customs from the Thirteenth to the Sixteenth Century* (Cambridge, MA, 1918), 59–85; Harriss, *King, Parliament and Public Finance*, 423–25, 457–59; T. S. Willan, ed., *A Tudor Book of Rates* (Manchester, 1962), xii–xxvi.
122. Dietz, *English Public Finance* 1:25; Williams, *Tudor Regime*, 58.
123. Williams, *Tudor Regime*, 69; see also Dietz, *English Public Finance* 1:103–4, 206–9.
124. F. C. Dietz, *The Exchequer in Elizabeth's Reign* (Smith College Studies in History 8, no. 2, 1923), 80–90; Williams, *Tudor Regime*, 71.
125. See Dietz, *English Public Finance* 2:314–61; Robert Ashton, "Revenue Farming under the Early Stuarts," *EcHR*, 2d ser., 8 (1955–56): 310–22; Robert Ashton, "Deficit Finance in the Reign of James I," *EcHR*, 2d ser., 10 (1957–58): 15–29; Robert Ashton, *The Crown and the Money Market*; Robert Ashton, "Charles I and the City," in Fisher, ed., *Essays in the Economic and Social History*, 138–63; Robert Ashton, "Conflicts of Concessionary Interests in Early Stuart England," 113–31; Robert Ashton, *The City and the Court, 1603–1643* (Cambridge, 1979); Valerie Pearl, *London and the Outbreak of the Puritan Revolution: City Government and National Politics, 1625–1643* (Oxford, 1961), chap. 3; Clay, *Economic Expansion and Social Change* 2:255–56, 270–72.
126. Dietz, *English Public Finance* 2:269, 335, 366–68; Willan, ed., *Tudor Book of Rates*, xliii–xlvii.
127. Dietz, *English Public Revenue* 2:362–79; see also F. C. Dietz, *The Receipts and Issues of the Exchequer during the Reigns of James I and Charles I* (Smith College Studies in History 13, no. 4, 1928), 150.
128. See Dietz, *Receipts and Issues of the Exchequer*, 152.
129. J. F. Willard, *Parliamentary Taxes on Personal Property, 1290–1334* (Cambridge, MA, 1934); Dietz, *English Public Finance* 1:13–16, 54–59; 2:382; R. S. Schofield, "Parliamentary Lay Taxation, 1485–1547" (Ph.D. diss., Cambridge, 1963), chap. 3.
130. Schofield, "Parliamentary Lay Taxation," 160–61.
131. See ibid., chaps. 4, 5, 7; R. S. Schofield, "Taxation and the Political

Limits of the Tudor State," in Cross, Loades, and Scarisbrick, eds., *Law and Government under the Tudors*, 227–55; Dietz, *English Public Finance* 2: 382–88, 391–93; Helen Miller, "Subsidy Assessments of the Peerage in the Sixteenth Century," *BIHR* 28 (1955): 15–34; Lawrence Stone, *The Crisis of the Aristocracy, 1558–1641* (Oxford, 1965), 496–97; Clay, *Economic Expansion and Social Change* 2:258.

132.   Williams, *Tudor Regime*, 64–67; Dietz, *English Public Finance* 2:389 n. 17.

133.   Historical Manuscripts Commission, *Calendar of the Manuscripts of the . . . Marquess of Salisbury . . . Preserved at Hatfield House* 15:1–2; Conrad Russell, *The Causes of the English Civil War* (Oxford, 1990), 168. Cecil estimated wartime expenditures in Ireland, France, and the Low Countries in these years as amounting to £2,750,950, excluding the costs of naval operations.

134.   Dietz, *English Public Finance* 2:392–93.

135.   *Statutes of the Realm*, 26 Hen. 8, c. 19.

136.   See e.g. Hartley, ed., *Proceedings in the Parliament of Elizabeth I* 1:183–87, esp. 184.

137.   See Schofield, "Parliamentary Lay Taxation," 23–30; G. R. Elton, "Taxation for War and Peace in Early-Tudor England," in Elton, *Studies in Tudor and Stuart Politics and Government* 3:216–33; J. D. Alsop, "The Theory and Practice of Tudor Taxation," *EHR* 97 (1982): 1–30; J. D. Alsop, "Innovation in Tudor Taxation," *EHR* 99 (1984): 83–93; Clive Holmes, "Parliament, Liberty, Taxation, and Property," in Hexter, ed., *Parliament and Liberty*, 144–53. G. L. Harriss has argued for the persistence of medieval doctrine in "Medieval Doctrines in the Debates on Supply, 1610–1629," in Kevin Sharpe, ed., *Faction and Parliament* (London, 1978), 93–103; "Thomas Cromwell's 'New Principle' of Taxation," *EHR* 93 (1978): 721–38; and "Theory and Practice in Royal Taxation: Some Observations," *EHR* 97 (1982): 811–19.

138.   For a rough estimate of the tax burden ca. 1600 see the appendix below and the conclusion to the volume.

139.   See Clay, *Economic Expansion and Social Change* 2:253, 256, 262; Brewer, *Sinews of Power*, 20–21; Margaret Levi, *Of Rule and Revenue*, chap. 5; see also Richard Bean, "War and the Birth of the Nation State," *JEH* 33 (1973): 212–17.

140.   See Dietz, *The Exchequer in Elizabeth's Reign*, 80–90; Dietz, *Receipts and Issues of the Exchequer in the Reigns of James I and Charles I*, 135–52.

141.   Edward Hall, *Hall's Chronicle containing the History of England during the Reign of Henry the Fourth and the Succeeding Monarchs to the End of the Reign of Henry the Eighth* (London, 1809), 656; see also Schofield, "Parliamentary Lay Taxation," 31ff.

142.   G. W. Bernard, *War, Taxation and Rebellion in Early Tudor England: Henry VIII, Wolsey and the Amicable Grant of 1525* (New York, 1986), 115–17.

143.   BL, Cotton MS Titus F. ii, fol. 51r.

144.   See Russell, *Causes of the English Civil War*, chap. 7; Conrad Russell, *The Fall of the British Monarchies, 1637–1642* (Oxford, 1991), 72–73, 130–36; Conrad Russell, *Parliaments and English Politics 1620–1629* (Oxford, 1979), 49–53, 64–84; Conrad Russell, "Parliament and the King's Finances," in Conrad Russell, ed., *The Origins of the English Civil War* (London, 1973), 91–116. For Russell's recent qualifying comments on the importance of consent in English politics, see Russell, *Fall of the British Monarchies*, 7–13, 97, 113.

145.   BL, Cotton MS Titus F. ii, fol. 51r.

146.   Simonds D'Ewes, *The Journals of all the Parliaments during the Reign of Queen Elizabeth* (London, 1682), 659.

147.   BL, Cotton MS Titus F. ii, fol. 30r.

148.   Michael Roberts, *The Military Revolution, 1560–1660* (Belfast, 1956); Finer, "State- and Nation-Building in Europe," 102 ff.; Geoffrey Parker, "The 'Military Revolution,' 1560–1660—a Myth?," *JMH* 48 (1976): 195–214; Geoffrey Parker, *The Military Revolution: Military Innovation and the Rise of the West, 1500–1800* (Cambridge, 1988); Michael Duffy, ed., *The Military Revolution and the State, 1500–1800* (Exeter Studies in History, no. 1, 1980), 1–9, 49–85; William McNeill, *The Pursuit of Power: Technology, Armed Force, and Society since A. D. 1000* (Chicago, 1982), 79 ff.; J. R. Hale, *War and Society in Renaissance Europe, 1450–1620* (New York, 1985).

149.   See Bean, "War and the Birth of the Nation State," 203–21; Michael Mann, "State and Society, 1130–1815: An Analysis of English State Finances," in Mann, *States, War and Capitalism*, 73–123.

150.   Clay, *Economic Expansion and Social Change* 2:261; Dietz, *English Public Finance* 2:216.

151.   Russell, *Parliaments and English Politics*, 73.

152.   Williams, *Tudor Regime*, 66–67, 70, 75–77.

153.   Clay, *Economic Expansion and Social Change* 2:259 and 259 n. 12; Dietz, *English Public Finance* 2:238 n. 66; Aylmer, *King's Servants*, 65.

154.   Harriss, "Aids, Loans and Benevolences," 1–19.

155.   Elizabeth Read Foster, ed., *Proceedings in Parliament, 1610*, 2 vols. (New Haven, 1966), 2:411; on this subject more generally, see Clive Holmes, "Parliament, Liberty, Taxation, and Property," 138–42 and *passim*; Johann P. Sommerville, *Politics and Ideology in England, 1603–1640* (London, 1986), 151ff.; John Spelman, *The Reports of Sir John Spelman*, ed. J. H. Baker, 2 vols. (Selden Soc., 44, 1978), intro. 2:178ff.

156.   Quoted in Richard Cust, *The Forced Loan and English Politics, 1626–1628* (Oxford, 1987), 175.

157.   John Rushworth, ed., *Historical Collections of Private Passages of State*, 8 vols. (London, 1659–1701), 2:486, 505.

158.   Margeret A. Judson, *The Crisis of the Constitution: An Essay in Constitutional and Political Thought in England, 1603–1645* (New Brunswick, 1949), esp. chap. 1; Thomas Cogswell, "A Low Road to Extinction? Supply and Redress of Grievances in the Parliaments of the 1620s," *HJ* 33 (1990): 283–303.

159.   On these points, see Mann, "The Autonomous Power of the State," 1–

32 and Mann, "States, Ancient and Modern," in Mann, *States, War and Capitalism*, 33–72; see also Michael Mann, *The Sources of Social Power. Volume I: A History of Power from the Beginning to A. D. 1760* (Cambridge, 1986).

160. See e.g. Smith, *De Republica Anglorum*, 48–58; Richard Hooker, *The Laws of Ecclesiastical Polity* 8: pt. vi. 11; H. C. Porter, "Hooker, the Tudor Constitution and the Via Media," in W. Speed Hill, ed., *Studies in Richard Hooker: Essays Preliminary to an Edition of His Works* (Cleveland, 1972), 77–116; Guy, *Tudor England*, 375ff.

161. For this view see J. S. Roskell, "Perspectives in English Parliamentary History," in Fryde and Miller, eds., *Historical Studies of the English Parliament* 2:296–323; Conrad Russell, "Introduction," in Conrad Russell, *Unrevolutionary England, 1603–1642* (London, 1990), ix–xxx; Conrad Russell, "The Nature of a Parliament in Early Stuart England," in ibid., 1–29; Conrad Russell, "Parliamentary History in Perspective, 1604–1629," in ibid., 31–57; Russell, *Parliaments and English Politics*, chap. 1; Russell, *Causes of the English Civil War*, 178–84; see also Kevin Sharpe, "Introduction: Parliamentary History 1603–1629: In or Out of Perspective?" in Sharpe, ed., *Faction and Parliament*, 1–42.

162. G. L. Harriss, "Medieval Doctrines in the Debates on Supply, 1610–1629," in Sharpe, *Faction and Parliament*, 73–103; J. D. Alsop, "Parliament and Taxation," in D. M. Dean and N. L. Jones, eds., *The Parliaments of Elizabethan England* (Oxford, 1990), 91–116; David Harris Sacks, "The Countervailing of Benefits: Monopoly, Liberty and Benevolence in Elizabethan England," in Dale Hoak, ed., *Tudor Political Culture* (Cambridge, forthcoming); see also J. H. Hexter, "Power, Parliament and Liberty in Early Stuart England," in Hexter, *Reappraisals*, 163–218; Thomas Cogswell, "A Low Road to Extinction?" 283–303.

163. Sacks, "The Countervailing of Benefits."

164. See Sacks, "Parliament, Liberty, and the Commonweal," 93–101; David Harris Sacks, "Private Profit and Public Good: The Problem of the State in Elizabethan England," in Gordon Schochet, ed., *Law, Literature and the Settlement of Regimes* (Washington, D.C., 1990), 121–42; Frank Smith Fussner, "William Camden's 'Discourse Concerning the Prerogative of the Crown,'" *Proc. Amer. Phil. Soc.* 101 (1957): 207. Fussner's identification of the author of the "Discourse" as Camden is "doubtful": see G. R. Elton, *Parliament of England*, 24 n. 25.

165. This paragraph and the next are adapted from David Harris Sacks, "Parliament, Liberty, and the Commonweal," 93–94, 110.

166. See below chaps. 3 through 7 and the conclusion.

167. Foster, ed., *Proceedings in Parliament, 1610* 2:194.

168. Ibid., 195.

169. Ibid., 196.

170. Ibid., 191.

171. See Harriss, "Medieval Doctrines in the Debates on Supply, 1610–1629," 73–103; see also David Harris Sacks, "The Countervailing of Benefits."

172. T. B. Howell, ed., *Cobbett's Complete Collection of State Trials* (London, 1816), 2:387–94.

173. See *Darcy v. Allen*, Noy, 173–85 in *English Reports* 72:1131–41.

174. PRO, SP 12/286/47.

175. Sacks, "Parliament, Liberty, and the Commonweal," 85–121.

176. See Sacks, "Parliament, Liberty, and the Commonweal," 85–121, esp. 93–101; David Harris Sacks, "The Corporate Town and the English State: Bristol's 'Little Businesses,' 1625–41," *Past and Present* 110 (1986): 102–3.

177. Ronald Syme, *The Roman Revolution* (Oxford, 1960), 59.

178. See e.g. John Lilburne, *ENGLAND'S BIRTH-RIGHT Justified Against all Arbitrary Usurpation, whether REGALL or PARLIAMENTARY, or under what Vizor soever* (London, 1645); A. S. P. Woodhouse, ed., *Puritanism and Liberty; Being the Army Debates (1647–1649) from the Clarke Manuscripts with Supplementary Documents*, 2d ed. (Chicago, 1951), 1–124.

179. David Iagomarsino and Charles T. Wood, eds., *The Trial of Charles I: A Documentary History* (Hanover, 1989), 64–66, 74–82, 86–87, 111–18.

180. George Bishop et al., *The Cry of Blood* (London, 1656), 10; see Sacks, *Widening Gate*, 311–12.

181. Historical Manuscripts Commission, *Manuscripts of the . . . Marquess of Salisbury* 15:1–2; Foster, ed., *Proceedings in Parliament* 2:19–20; Russell, *Causes of the English Civil War*, 168.

182. Figure calculated from Dietz, *English Public Finance, 1558–1641* 2:328n.

183. Skilled builders' wages in this period were approximately 12d per ten-hour work day; see Phelps Brown and Hopkins, "Seven Centuries of Building Wages," in *Essays in Economic History*, ed. Carus-Wilson, 2:177.

184. Wrigley and Schofield, *Population History of England*, 208.

185. Wheat prices estimated from W. G. Hoskins, "Harvest Fluctuations and English Economic History, 1480–1619," in *Essays in Agrarian History*, ed. W. E. Minchinton, 2 vols. (New York, 1968), 1:115. According to Hoskins, these years were marked by bad harvests in 1594 and 1595 and dearth in 1596 and 1597. Using Hoskins's 31-year moving averages for wheat prices, the sum of £274,000 translates into about 1,525,400 bushels or about 555,000 hectoliters of wheat.

CHAPTER 2

1. See John Brewer, *The Sinews of Power* (London, 1989); Brewer coins the term.

2. C. D. Chandaman, *The English Public Revenue 1660–1688* (Oxford, 1975), 200–205.

3. Anchitell Grey, *Debates of the House of Commons* (London, 1769), 2:129–31, 184, 205, 220–21.

4. Ibid., 398.

5. Ibid., 218.

6. Ibid., 404–7; 3:2, 320; 4:134.

7. The Heads of Grievances, Declaration, and Bill of Rights all declared this method illegal in 1689. Lois G. Schwoerer, *The Declaration of Rights* (Baltimore, 1981), 295, 299; E. N. Williams, *The Eighteenth-Century Constitution* (Cambridge, 1960), 28.

8. Grey, *Debates* 2:393.

9. J. A. Downie, "The Commission of Public Accounts and the Formation of the Country Party," *EHR* 91 (1976): 33–51; J. R. Jones, *Country and Court* (London, 1978), 159.

10. Grey, *Debates* 1:267, 272–73, 352.

11. Ibid., 188, 315.

12. Ibid., 187, 266–67, 273.

13. Ibid., 188, 274, 315, 316, 319, 350–53.

14. J. Keith Horsefield, "The 'Stop of the Exchequer' Revisited," *EcHR* 2d ser. 35 (1982): 511–28.

15. Grey, *Debates* 3:321; 9:127.

16. Ibid. 3:322; Basil D. Henning, ed., *The House of Commons 1660–1690* (London, 1983) 2:445–48.

17. Horsefield, " 'Stop of the Exchequer' Revisited," 519.

18. MPs' suspicions received retrospective confirmation from seeing that Sir Thomas Clifford, the chief Court and Treasury spokesman in the Commons, became the chief minister in the implementation of royal policies in 1672–73. See C. H. Hartmann, *Clifford of the Cabal* (London, 1937), although this now needs revision.

19. Grey, *Debates* 2:393.

20. Ibid., 394.

21. Ibid. 3:322.

22. Howard Nenner, "Liberty, Law, and Property: The Constitution in Retrospect from 1689," in J. R. Jones, ed., *Liberty Secured? Britain Before and After 1688* (Stanford, 1992), 88–121.

23. Grey, *Debates* 3:304.

24. Ibid., 322.

25. Ibid. 2:233.

26. Ibid. 6:30, 98, 100–101; J. R. Jones, *The First Whigs* (London, 1970), 27–30.

27. Grey, *Debates* 8:359.

28. Chandaman, *English Public Revenue*, 256–61.

29. See Sir Roger L'Estrange, *An Answer to a Letter to a Dissenter* (London, 1687); *Animadversions on a late paper, entituled a Letter to a Dissenter* (London, 1687); *A Third Letter from a Gentleman in the Country* (London, 1687).

30. These words are from James's 1687 Declaration of Indulgence: J. P. Kenyon, *The Stuart Constitution* (Cambridge, 1966), 410.

31. *Animadversions on a late paper*, 14–15.

32. Charles D'Avenant wrote that he was not wedded to conclusions

which he would not change "upon better conviction. To write of the income and expense of a whole people and the public revenues is travelling in an undiscovered country," and that Petty's findings must all be revised because he had had to work with incomplete materials: Sir Charles Whitworth, ed., *The Political and Commercial Works of Charles D'Avenant* (London, 1771), 1:287.

33. The Marquis of Lansdowne, *The Petty Papers* (London, 1927), 1:26–72, 171–250; 2:49–58, 98–131, 185–93.

34. Ibid. 1:xiv–xvii, xxxviii, 36–37, 173, 256–57, 265; 2:185–86.

35. J. R. Jones, "James II's Revolution: Royal Policies, 1686–92," in Jonathan I. Israel, ed., *The Anglo-Dutch Moment* (Cambridge, 1991), 69–70.

36. Kenyon, *Stuart Constitution*, 439–41.

37. Lansdowne, *Petty Papers* 1:7–8.

38. Grey, *Debates* 1:240–42, 276–77, 401.

39. Joyce Appleby, *Economic Thought and Ideology in Seventeenth-Century England* (Princeton, 1978), 41–49.

40. Ibid., 82.

41. The standard work on Colbert is still C. W. Cole, *Colbert and a Century of French Mercantilism* (New York, 1939, and London, 1964), especially 1:278–532 and 2:1–560.

42. Lionel Rothkrug, *Opposition to Louis XIV* (Princeton, 1965), 234–43, 342–49.

43. J. G. A. Pocock, *Virtue, Commerce and History* (Cambridge, 1985), 32, 48–49, 108–110; *The Machiavellian Moment* (Princeton, 1975), 446–61; Albert O. Hirschman, *The Passions and the Interests* (Princeton, 1977), 32, 40n, 43, 48, 49.

44. The best guide to post-1688 governmental finance is P. G. M. Dickson, *The Financial Revolution in England* (London, 1967).

45. Geoffrey Holmes, *British Politics in the Age of Anne* (London, 1967), 148–82.

46. John Giuseppi, *The Bank of England* (London, 1966), 31–32, 37. The original statute was 5 Wm. and Mary, c. 20.

47. Nenner, "Liberty, Law, and Property," in Jones, ed., *Liberty Secured?* 98–100.

48. Williams, *Eighteenth-Century Constitution*, 32.

49. T. B. Howell, ed., *A Complete Collection of State Trials* 13 (London, 1812): 537–758.

50. Williams, *Eighteenth-Century Constitution*, 28.

51. *Lords Journals* 12:328–29; twenty-nine peers protested the bill's passage, of whom twelve were bishops; 28 March 1670; Grey, *Debates* 1:251.

52. *The Examiner* 37 (19 April 1711), reprinted in H. Davies, ed., *Prose Works of Jonathan Swift* (Oxford, 1940), 3:134.

53. John Carswell, *The South Sea Bubble* (London, 1961), 18. The statute was 3 and 4 Anne, c. 9.

54. John Childs, *The Nine Years' War and the British Army 1688–1697* (Manchester, 1991), supersedes earlier studies.

55. Henry Horwitz, *Revolution Politicks* (Cambridge, 1968), 167–69, 181–90, 197–99.

56. *The Examiner* 13 (2 November 1710); Davies, ed., *Prose Works of Swift* 3:7.

57. Lois G. Schwoerer, *No Standing Armies! The Anti-Army Ideology in Seventeenth-Century England* (Baltimore, 1974), 155–87.

58. Pocock, *Machiavellian Moment*, 430–32.

59. Schwoerer, *No Standing Armies!* 184–87.

60. This thesis was applied to current politics by Clarendon's son Rochester in the preface and dedication he wrote to the first volumes of the *History of the Rebellion* when first published in 1702–3. See the edition by W. D. Macray (Oxford, 1888), 1:xvii–lvi.

61. Pocock, *Machiavellian Moment*, 383–400; *The Ancient Constitution and the Feudal Law* (Cambridge, 1957), 124–47.

62. W. C. Costin and J. S. Watson, *The Law and Working of the Constitution* (London, 1952), 1:117.

63. Whitworth, ed., *Works of Charles D'Avenant* 1:153–56, 158–60.

64. Ibid., 128.

65. Ibid., 276; 4:299.

66. Geoffrey Holmes, "The Attack on 'The Influence of the Crown' 1702–16," *BIHR* 39 (1966): 48–50.

67. Whitworth, ed., *Works of Charles D'Avenant*, 2:301.

68. Clayton Roberts, "The Constitutional Significance of the Financial Settlement of 1690," *HJ* 20 (1977): 59–76.

69. Downie, "Commission of Public Accounts," *EHR* 91:33–51.

70. Holmes, *British Politics in the Age of Anne*, 79, 172–74.

71. B. W. Hill, *Robert Harley Speaker, Secretary of State and Premier Minister* (New Haven, 1988), 134–45.

72. Colin Brooks, "Public Finance and Political Stability: The Administration of the Land Tax, 1688–1720," *HJ* 17 (1974): 282–84, 287–96, 297–300.

73. See Paul Langford, *The Excise Crisis: Society and Politics in the Age of Walpole* (Oxford, 1975).

74. Williams, *Eighteenth-Century Constitution*, 42–46.

75. Ibid., 59. The importance of this change has been emphasized by Douglass C. North and Barry R. Weingast, "Constitutions and Commitment," *JEH* 49 (December 1989): 804, 806, 829.

76. W. Cobbett, ed., *Parliamentary History of England* 21 (London, 1814): 340–68, 374–86.

77. Appleby, *Economic Thought and Ideology*, 237, 239–40: J. K. Horsefield, *British Monetary Experiments 1650–1710* (London, 1960); Samuel Grasscomb, *An Account of the Proceedings of the House of Commons* (London, 1696), which the Commons ordered to be burned: reprinted in *A Collection of Scarce and Valuable Papers* (London, 1712).

78. Sir George Clark, ed., Sir William Temple, *Observations upon the United Provinces of the Netherlands* (Oxford, 1972), 110.

79. Whitworth, *Works of Charles D'Avenant* 1:77.

CHAPTER 3

1. For the Burgundian dukes, predecessors of the Habsburgs, see R. Vaughan, *Philip the Good; The Apogee of the Burgundian State* (London, 1970); J. Calmette, *Les grands ducs de Bourgogne* (2d ed. Paris, 1979); H. P. H. Jansen, "Modernization of the Government: The Advent of Philip the Good," in *BMGN* 95 (1980): 254–64.

2. In December 1427 the towns of Holland were convened in Haarlem and agreed to pay 75,000 schilden, in exchange for a promise of the duke not to transfer the government into other hands without their permission: W. Prevenier and J. G. Smit, eds., *Bronnen voor de geschiedenis der dagvaarten van de Staten en steden van Holland voor 1544*, vol. 1 (1276–1433) pt. 2:teksten. RGP, Grote serie 202 ('s-Gravenhage, 1987), nr. 1193.

3. See for the development of the "bede," J. A. M. Y. Bos-Rops, "Van incidentele gunst tot jaarlijkse belasting: de bede in het vijftiende-eeuwse Holland," in *Fiscaliteit in Nederland. 50 jaar Belastingmuseum "Prof. Dr. Van der Poel"* (Zutphen-Deventer, 1987), 21–32.

4. See also Jansen, "Modernization of the Government."

5. About the financial "revolution," see J. D. Tracy, "The Taxation System of the Country of Holland during the reigns of Charles V and Philip II, 1519–1566," *EHJ* 48 ('s-Gravenhage, 1985): 71–117, and his later *A Financial Revolution in the Habsburg Netherlands. Renten and Renteniers in the County of Holland, 1515–1565* (Berkeley, 1985).

6. Tracy, "The Taxation System," 86.

7. For the finances of the Netherlands under the Habsburgs, see M. Baelde, "Financiële politiek en domaniale evolutie in de Nederlanden onder Karel V en Filips II (1530–1560)," *TvG* 76 (1963): 14–33.

8. Ibid., 91–92.

9. It is impossible to give a complete survey of all works on the Dutch revolt, and a short list must suffice: P. Geyl, *The Revolt of the Netherlands 1555–1609*, 2d ed. (London, 1958); G. Parker, *The Dutch Revolt* (London, 1977); H. A. Enno van Gelder, *The Two Reformations in the Sixteenth Century. A Study of the Religious Aspects and Consequences of Renaissance and Humanism*, 2d ed. (The Hague, 1961); for a strictly economic explanation E. Kuttner, *Het hongerjaar 1566* (Amsterdam, 1949).

10. F. H. M. Grapperhaus, *Alva en de Tiende Penning* (Zutphen, 1982); G. Parker, *The Army of Flanders and the Spanish Road, 1567–1659* (London, 1972), 141, 287.

11. Grapperhaus, *Alva*, 309–314.

12. Ibid., 295. For the opposition against Alba's tax reform see also O. van Rees, *Geschiedenis der staathuishoudkunde in Nederland tot het einde der achttiende eeuw*, 2 vols. (Utrecht, 1865–1868), 2:145–50.

13. For the complete Dutch text of the Union of Utrecht see S. Groenveld and H. L. Ph. Leeuwenberg, "Die originale unie metten acten daernaer gevolcht," in S. Groenveld and H. L. Ph. Leeuwenberg, eds., *De Unie van*

Utrecht. Wording en werking van een verbond en een verbondsacte (Den Haag, 1979), 5–55. A translation into English is in E. H. Kossmann and A. F. Mellink, eds., *Texts Concerning the Revolt of the Netherlands* (London, 1974) 165–73; an abbreviated text in H. H. Rowen, ed., *The Low Countries in Early Modern Times: A Documentary History* (New York, 1972), 69–74.

14. Kossmann and Mellink, eds., *Texts*, 267–68.

15. Still invaluable for a complete description of the constitution of the Dutch Republic is R. Fruin, *Geschiedenis der staatsinstellingen in Nederland tot den val der Republiek*, uitgegeven door H. T. Colenbrander, 2d ed. ('s-Gravenhage, 1980). Less complete is S. J. Fockema Andreae, *De Nederlandse staat onder de Republiek*. Verhandelingen der Koninklijke Nederlandse Akademie van Wetenschappen, Afd. Letterkunde Nieuwe Reeks 68, 3 (Amsterdam, 1978). For a succinct survey see A. Th. van Deursen, "Staatsinstellingen in de Noordelijke Nederlanden 1579–1780, in *Algemene Geschiedenis der Nederlanden* 5 (Haarlem, 1980): 350–87.

16. For a recent survey of the position of the stadholders in the Dutch Republic, see H. H. Rowen, *The Princes of Orange: The Stadholders in the Dutch Republic* (Cambridge, 1988).

17. C. Wilson, *The Dutch Republic and the Civilisation of the Seventeenth Century* (New York, 1977), 55.

18. See Van Deursen, "Staatsinstellingen," 361–66.

19. For the legal system in the Dutch Republic, see Fruin-Colenbrander, *Staatsinstellingen*, 115–49 and 254–63; and R. H. Hartog, *Onrechtmatige overheidsdaden in de Republiek der Verenigde Nederlanden* (Deventer, 1971).

20. W. van Iterson, *Geschiedenis der confiscatie in Nederland. Een rechtshistorische studie aan de hand van Noord-Nederlandse, een aantal Zuid-Nederlandse en andere bronnen* (Utrecht, 1957).

21. F. N. Sickenga, *Bijdrage tot de geschiedenis van de belastingen in Nederland* (Leiden, 1864), 123, 269, 288, 426–28.

22. Douglass C. North and Robert Paul Thomas, *The Rise of the Western World: A New Economic History* (Cambridge, 1973), 134–38.

23. This section is based on J. H. Huizinga, *Dutch Civilisation in the Seventeenth Century* (New York, 1968); P. Geyl, *The Revolt of the Netherlands*; and H. A. Enno van Gelder, *Getemperde Vrijheid* (Groningen, 1972). For a recent study of the liberties in the Dutch Republic see E. H. Kossmann, "Freedom in Seventeenth-century Dutch Thought and Practice" in Jonathan I. Israel, ed., *The Anglo-Dutch Moment. Essays on the Glorious Revolution and its World Impact* (Cambridge, 1991), 281–98.

24. Kossmann, "Freedom in Seventeenth-century Dutch Thought and Practice."

25. L. J. Rogier, "De Vestiging van de Ware Vrijheid (1648–1672)," in *Algemene Geschiedenis der Nederlanden* 7 (Utrecht-Antwerpen, 1953): 1–26; here 25.

26. J. J. Woltjer, "Dutch Privileges, Real and Imaginary," in J. S. Bromley

and E. H. Kossmann, eds., *Britain and the Netherlands* 5 (The Hague, 1975): 19–35.

27. D. J. Roorda, *Partij en Factie. De oproeren van 1672 in de steden van Holland en Zeeland; Een krachtmeting tussen partijen en facties* (Groningen, 1961), 46; K. H. D. Haley, *The Dutch in the Seventeenth Century* (London, 1972), 52.

28. For the difference between "general petition" and "state of war," see A. Th. van Deursen, "Staat van oorlog en generale petitie in de jonge Republiek," *BMGN* 91 (1976): 44–55; for the system of quota, H. L. Zwitzer, "Het quotenstelsel onder de Republiek der Verenigde Nederlanden alsmede enkele beschouwingen over de generale petitie, de staat van oorlog en de repartitie," in *Mededelingen van de Sectie Militaire Geschiedenis Landmachtstaf* 5 (1982): 5–57.

29. A complete but not altogether dependable list of the convoy duties in the seventeenth century appears in H. E. Becht, *Statistische gegevens betreffende de handelsomzet van de Republiek der Vereenigde Nederlanden gedurende de 17e eeuw (1579–1715)* ('s-Gravenhage, 1908). For critical comments on this work see J. C. Westermann, "Statistische gegevens over den handel van Amsterdam in de zeventiende eeuw," *TvG* 61 (1948): 3–15. There is a complete and generally dependable list for the eighteenth century in Joh. de Vries, *De economische achteruitgang der Republiek in de achttiende eeuw* (Amsterdam, 1959), 185–93; for Zeeland only, in F. Snapper, "Statistische gegevens betreffende de Zeeuwse convooien en licenten uit de 17e en 18e eeuw," *EHJ* 29 (1963): 260–301. The duties became so complex that a new tariff was drawn up in 1725; for the new tariff, see J. L. F. Engelhard, *Het generaal-plakkaat van 31 juli 1725 op de convoyen en licenten en het lastgeld op de schepen* (Assen, 1970).

30. For the evasion of convoy duties see Westermann, "Statistische gegevens," 4–5; and the postscript to Westermann's article by J. G. van Dillen, in *TvG* 61: 16–30, here 23.

31. Sir William Temple, *Observations upon the United Provinces of the Netherlands* (Oxford, 1972), 129.

32. For these discussions see J. W. Veenendaal-Barth, ed., *Particuliere notulen van de vergaderingen der Staten van Holland 1620–1640 door N. Stellingwerff en S. Schot* 2 (Sept. 1623-May 1625), RGP, grote serie 200 ('s-Gravenhage, 1987).

33. On taxation in Holland in general P. H. Engels, *De geschiedenis der belastingen in Nederland van de vroegste tijden tot op heden* (Rotterdam, 1848); F. N. Sickenga, *Bijdrage tot de geschiedenis van de belastingen in Nederland* (Leiden, 1864); and A. C. J. de Vrankrijker, *Geschiedenis van de belastingen* (Bussum, 1969).

34. For a complete listing see Engels, *Geschiedenis der Belastingen*.

35. A. Th. van Deursen, *Het Kopergeld van de Gouden Eeuw*, 4 vols. (Assen, 1979), 3:27–31.

36. Ibid., 35.

37. De Vrankrijker, *Belastingen*, 47.

38. Although all the literature on taxation already mentioned gives the stamp duty as a Dutch invention, there is some indication that a taxation along these lines was already practiced in Tuscany and France and copied in Holland in 1623. Veenendaal-Barth, *Particuliere Notulen*, 28.

39. R. Dekker, *Holland in Beroering. Oproeren in de 17de en 18de eeuw* (Baarn, 1982), 33.

40. The result of this registration, the first official census in Holland, gave the total population of this province as 671,675. This figure is probably somewhat too low, as certain categories were excluded. Also, some fraud must have been practiced, as the census was carried out for tax purposes. J. H. van Dillen, "Summiere staat van de in 1622 in de provincie Holland gehouden volkstelling," *EHJ* 21 (1940): 167–89.

41. For the hundredth and thousandth penny see R. C. J. van Maanen, "Hollandse vermogensheffingen in de zeventiende en achttiende eeuw," in *Nederlands Archievenblad. Tijdschrift van de Vereniging van Archivarissen in Nederland* 88 (1984): 61–72; and P. W. Klein, "De heffing van de 100e en 200e penning van het vermogen te Gouda, 1599–1722," *EHJ* 31 (1967): 41–62.

42. Van Maanen, "Hollandse vermogensheffigen," 71.

43. Sickenga, *Bijdrage*, 442.

44. P. H. Engels, *De belastingen en de geldmiddelen van den aanvang der Republiek tot op heden* (Utrecht, 1862), 133–34.

45. De Vrankrijker, *Belastingen*, 43–45.

46. For the personal *quotisation* see W. F. H. Oldewelt, ed., *Kohier van de Personeele Quotisatie te Amsterdam over het jaar 1742*, 2 vols. (Amsterdam, 1945); for the element of progression J. G. van Dillen, *Van Rijkdom en Regenten. Handboek tot de economische en sociale geschiedenis van Nederland tijdens de Republiek* ('s-Gravenhage, 1970), 277.

47. D. Houtzager, *Hollands lijf- en losrenteleningen vóór 1672* (Schiedam, 1950), 44–46.

48. Ibid., 52.

49. Ibid., 54–62.

50. Ibid., 78–79; also N. Japikse, *Johan de Witt*; 2d ed. (Amsterdam, 1928), 233–37.

51. Houtzager, *Hollands lijf- en losrenten*, 85–86.

52. About the reduction of the rate of interest and its temporary salutary effect on the finances of Holland and its admiralties, see J. R. Bruijn, *De admiraliteit van Amsterdam in rustige jaren, 1713–1751. Regenten en financiën, schepen en zeevarenden* (Amsterdam-Haarlem, 1970), 87–91; R. Liesker, "Tot zinkens toe bezwaard. De schuldenlast van het Zuiderkwartier van Holland 1672–1794," in *Bestuurders en Geleerden. Opstellen aangeboden aan Prof. dr. J. J. Woltjer* (Amsterdam-Dieren, 1985), 151–60, here 155.

53. Sickenga, *Belastingen*, 439–40.

54. J. A. van Houtte, *An Economic History of the Low Countries, 800–1800* (London, 1977), 304.

55. Bruijn, *Admiraliteit*, 72.

56. J. Aalbers, *De Republiek en de vrede van Europa. De buitenlandse politiek van de Republiek der Verenigde Nederlanden na de vrede van Utrecht (1713), voornamelijk gedurende de jaren 1720–1733* (Groningen, 1980), 3–7.

57. Charles Wilson stresses this point in his "Taxation and the Decline of Empires: An Unfashionable Theme," *Bijdragen en Mededelingen van het Historisch Genootschap* 77 (1963): 10–23.

58. John Brewer, "The English State and Fiscal Appropriation, 1688–1789," *Politics and Society* 16 (1988): 336.

59. J. Aalbers, "Holland's Financial Problems (1713–1733) and the Wars against Louis XIV," in A. C. Duke and C. A. Tamse, eds., *Britain and the Netherlands* 6 (The Hague, 1977): 79–93.

60. This point is stressed by Joh. de Vries in his *De economische achteruitgang*.

61. For the Amsterdam money market, see J. C. Riley, *International Government Finance and the Amsterdam Capital Market 1740–1815* (Cambridge, 1980).

62. Aalbers, *De Republiek*, 117.

63. Liesker, "Tot zinkens toe bezwaard," 156.

64. Temple, *Observations*, 69.

65. P. C. A. Geyl, *Revolutiedagen te Amsterdam, augustus-september 1748. Prins Willem IV en de Doelistenbeweging* ('s-Gravenhage, 1936).

66. For Haarlem in 1747–48, see Y. A. F. de Jongste, *Onrust aan het Spaarne. Haarlem in de jaren 1747–1751* ('s-Gravenhage, 1984).

67. De Jongste, *Onrust aan het Spaarne*, 288–91.

68. It was estimated that before 1747 only one quarter of the revenues collected by the tax farmers actually reached the treasury of the states. After 1750 this figure rose to about half, while the rest was used for the cost of collection. Engels, *Belastingen en geldmiddelen*, 43.

69. J. Hovy, *Het voorstel van 1751 tot instelling van een beperkt vrijhavenstelsel in de Republiek* (Groningen, 1966). See also Sickenga, *Belastingen*, 271–72.

70. See J. Hovy, "Institutioneel onvermogen in de 18de eeuw," in *Algemene Geschiedenis der Nederlanden* 9 (Haarlem, 1980), 126–38, where the several proposed measures of reform are discussed. See also J. M. F. Fritschy, *De patriotten en de financiën van de Bataafse Republiek. Hollands krediet en de smalle marges voor een nieuw beleid (1795–1801)* ('s-Gravenhage, 1988), 27–73.

71. My estimate for the tax burden in Holland in 1721—an estimate subject to considerable uncertainty—is 4.5 hectoliters of wheat per person; see the appendix for the details and a discussion of the problems with the meager data available for the Netherlands. Similar calculations for Britain and France—calculations that are themselves highly uncertain—yield

much lower figures: 1.78 hectoliters per person in Britain in 1720, and 0.72 hectoliters in France in 1720–29. But the same was true in the seventeenth century. I estimate that the tax burden in Holland in 1650 was 1.8 hectoliters per person, versus 0.60 hectoliters in France in 1650–59 and roughly 0.2 hectoliters in England circa 1600. The figures for Britain and France here are taken from Peter Mathias and Patrick O'Brien, "Taxation in Britain and France, 1715–1810. A Comparison of the Social and Economic Incidence of Taxes Collected for the Central Governments," *JEEcH* 5 (1976): 620, and chaps. 1 and 6 of this volume. See the conclusion, below, for a more detailed comparison of tax burdens.

72. Van Deursen, "Staat van Oorlog," 54.

73. Engels, *Belastingen*, 137–47 and 172–74.

74. The convoy duties, from De Vries, *De economische achteruitgang*, 186–92.

75. See J. M. F. Fritschy, "Overheidsfinanciën," *EHJ* 48 (1985): 28, 35.

CHAPTER 4

1. G. Parker, *The Army of Flanders and the Spanish Road, 1567–1659* (Cambridge, 1972), 231–63; F. Braudel, "Les emprunts de Charles-Quint sur la place d'Anvers," in *Charles-Quint et son temps* (Paris, 1959), 191–201.

2. C. Sánchez Albornoz, "The Frontier and Castilian Liberties," in A. R. Lewis and T. F. McGann, *The New World Looks at its History* (Austin, TX, 1963), 27–46: "the great frontier duel of Medieval Spain . . . made the Castilians the most free of European peoples of that day," 30.

3. E. Lourie, "A Society Organized for War: Medieval Spain," *Past and Present* 35 (1966): 54–76.

4. C. Sánchez Albornoz, "Conséquences de la Reconquête et du repeuplement sur les institutions féudo-vassaliques de Léon et de Castille," in *Les Structures Sociales de L'Aquitaine* (1969), 17–40, and "The Frontier and Castilian Liberties," 27–46; D. W. Lomax, *The Reconquista of Spain* (London, 1978); J-M. Font y Rius, "Les villes dans l'Espagne du moyen age. Histoire de leurs institutions administratives et judiciaires," in *Recueils de la Société Jean Bodin*, VI, *La Ville* (Brussels, 1954) 1ère partie, 263–95; A. MacKay, *Spain in the Middle Ages, From Frontier to Empire, 1000–1500* (London, 1977); J. F. O'Callaghan, *A History of Medieval Spain* (Ithaca, 1975).

5. MacKay, *Spain in the Middle Ages*, 121, sees in Spain "the most advanced version of absolutism to be found in the whole of later-medieval Europe," and see also 133; O'Callaghan, *Medieval Spain*, 563, 564, 580.

6. J. M. Nieto Soria, *Fundamentos ideológicos del poder real en Castilla (siglos XIII–XVI)* (Madrid, 1988), 238.

7. For a recent survey of the vexed question of feudalism in Spain, L. García de Valdeavellano, *El feudalismo hispánico y otros estudios de historia medieval* (Barcelona, 1981); and from a different perspective, R. Pastor,

"Reflexiones sobre los comienzos de la formación política feudo-vasallática en Castilla y León," in A. Rucquoi, *Realidad e imágenes del poder, España a fines de la Edad Media* (Valladolid, 1988), 11-22.

8.   J. A. Maravall, *Estado moderno y mentalidad social (siglos XV a XVII)* (Madrid, 1972), 1:352-56.

9.   A. García Gallo, *Manual de Historia del Derecho Español* 1 (Madrid, 1959): 1295-1301; J. Beneyto Pérez, *Los orígenes de la ciencia política en España* (Madrid, 1949), 286; M. A. Ladero Quesada, "Aristocratie et régime seigneurial dans l'Andalousie du XVe siècle," *Annales* 38 (1983): 1346-68, at 1346-47; F. Javier de Ayala, *Ideas políticas de Juan de Solórzano* (Seville, 1946), 285; D. E. Vassberg, *Land and Society in Golden Age Castile* (Cambridge, 1984), chap. 1; Beneyto Pérez, *Los orígenes*, 296, on the concreteness of liberties.

10.   "Est enim libertas res inestimabilis," Javier de Ayala, *Juan de Solórzano*, 283; Beneyto Pérez, *Los orígenes*, chap. 8; J. A. Maravall, "Saavedra Fajardo: moral acomodaticia y carácter conflictivo de la libertad," in *Estudios de Historia del Pensamiento Español* 3, *Siglo XVII* (Madrid, 1975), 161-96, esp. 187-92; L. Pereña and V. Abril, *Bartolomé de las Casas, Derechos civiles y políticos* (Madrid, 1974), 61ff., 155.

11.   A. González Palencia, *La Junta de Reformación, 1618-1625, AHE* 5 (Valladolid, 1932): 86 (23 May 1621); B. Hamilton, *Political Thought in Sixteenth-Century Spain* (Oxford, 1963), 57, quotes Suárez, "The common good must take precedence over the private good, and a man is bound to lose his life for the sake of the common good."

12.   *ACC* 18:460 (4 Dec. 1599).

13.   W. Piskorski, *Las Cortes de Castilla en el período de tránsito de la Edad Media a la Moderna (1188-1520)*, new ed. by J. Valdeón (Barcelona, 1977); J. F. O'Callaghan, *The Cortes of Castile-León 1188-1350* (Philadelphia, 1989); J. M. Pérez-Prendes, *Cortes de Castilla* (Barcelona, 1974); *Las Cortes de Castilla y León en la Edad Media*, 2 vols. (Valladolid, 1988); S. de Dios, "La evolución de las Cortes de Castilla durante el siglo XV," in Rucquoi, *Realidad e imágenes del poder*, 137-69.

14.   *Reino*, literally realm, or kingdom, was also applied synecdochically to the institutions which represented the kingdom. How *Reino* is to be understood in any particular instance, as the Cortes, the cities of the Cortes, the Cortes or the cities, the Cortes and the cities, the Cortes of the cities, involves constitutional as well as situational judgments. For that reason I use *Reino* when what is meant is neither the Cortes alone, nor the cities alone, but one or the other, or both together in their institutional relationship. The untranslated *Reino* both retains that crucial ambiguity and serves as a continual reminder that the meaning of *Reino* is the central problem of the early-modern Castilian "constitution."

15.   For example, *ACC* 31:35 (10 Nov. 1617). This point has been the subject of some contention; my position accords entirely with that of Pérez-

Prendes, *Cortes de Castilla*, 136–51; the most recent survey is O'Callaghan, *Cortes of Castile-León*, chap. 7.

16. *Recopilación de las Leyes destos Reynos* (Madrid, 1640) [*Nueva Recopilación*], ley ii, tit. 7, lib. VI, "Que sobre hechos grandes y arduos se fagan Cortes," fasc. ed., 3 vols. (Valladolid, 1982), 2:124v.

17. *Nueva Recopilación*, ley i, tit. 7, lib. VI.

18. A. Rodríguez Villa, *La Corte y Moñarquía de España en los años 1636 y 1637* (Madrid, 1886), 13; "Cartas de Jesuitas," in P. de Gayangos, ed., *Cartas de algunos Padres de la Compañía de Jesús sobre los Sucesos de la Monarquía entre los años 1634 y 1648*, MHE, vols. 13–19, (Madrid, 1861–65), 13:437–38.

19. O'Callaghan, *Medieval Spain*, 583; S. de Dios, *El Consejo Real de Castilla (1385–1522)* (Madrid, 1982).

20. J. M. Pérez-Prendes, *Curso de historia del derecho español*, 2 vols. (Madrid, 1978), 1:503ff.; F. Tomás y Valiente, *Manual de historia del derecho español* (Madrid, 1981), 243, 270; E. N. Van Kleffens, *Hispanic Law until the End of the Middle Ages* (Edinburgh, 1968), esp. 220ff. On the importance of the *Partidas* and *Recopilaciones*, Van Kleffens, *Hispanic Law*, 155–215; Pérez-Prendes, *Curso* 1:534, 575ff., 600ff., 741ff.; Tomás y Valiente, *Manual*, 265–70.

21. García-Gallo, *Manual*, 1302; Tomás y Valiente, *Manual*, 291; F. Elias de Tejada Spínola, *Gerónimo Castillo de Bovadilla* (Madrid, 1939), 119–20; B. González Alonso, "La fórmula 'Obedézcase, pero no se cumpla' en el derecho castellano de la Baja Edad Media," *Anuario de Historia del Derecho Español* 50 (1980): 469–87.

22. "It is always understood that the laws of princes are to be observed to the letter whenever, wherever, and however is good for the honor and advantage of the prince and his state, and as the virtues of prudence, justice and discretion etc. dictate," Fr. Juan de Victoria, OP, "Noticias de la Invencible," *CODOIN* 81:231, condemning Medina Sidonia and Diego Flores for their handling of the Armada and countering the defense that they were simply adhering to the king's instructions.

23. J. A. Maravall, *La philosophie politique espagnole au XVIIe siècle* (Paris, 1955), 221, 225, 227. F. Vermúdez de Pedraza, *El Secretario del Rey* (1620), (Madrid, 1973), 25, argued the importance of the councils in giving the populace confidence in the resolutions of government. In the view of the Council of State in 1705, "the tribunals are the depositories of wise counsel, of the oath taken by the king of Spain, and of that which he has received from his subjects," H. Kamen, *Spain in the Later Seventeenth Century, 1665–1700* (London, 1980), 26. For the constitutional role of the councils, P. Fernández Albaladejo, "Monarquía, Cortes y 'cuestión constitucional' en Castilla durante la edad moderna," *Revista de las Cortes Generales* 1 (1984): 11–34; and B. Cárceles, "The Constitutional Conflict in Castile between the Council and the Count-Duke of Olivares," *Parliaments, Estates and Representation* 7 (1987): 51–59. In "La Junta de Competencias durante el reinado

de Felipe IV. Un proyecto institucional en la monarquía hispana," *Critica storica/bolletino A.S.E.* (1980), 15, Cárceles cites the Council of Castile's insistence that government should follow "what is established by law, statute, custom and form, from which it is impossible to diverge without threatening the principles and foundations upon which good government rests."

24. See, for example, the part played by the Council of Castile and the *Chancillería* of Granada in bringing an end to the sale of common wastes in Andalusia in the 1640s: A. Domínguez Ortiz, "La comisión de D. Luis Gudiel para la venta de baldíos de Andalucía," in his *Estudios de historia económica y social de España* (Granada, 1987), 89–103; for other examples, I. A. A. Thompson, *War and Government in Habsburg Spain, 1560–1620* (London, 1976), 42–47.

25. C. Rahn Phillips, "Time and Duration: A Model for the Economy of Early-Modern Spain," *AHR* 92 (1987): 531–62, the most recent short, general survey of the early-modern Spanish economy, presents a full bibliography and useful material, directed to a dubious thesis. On population, A. Molinié Bertrand, *Au siècle d'or. L'Espagne et ses hommes: la population du royaume de Castille au XVIe siècle* (Paris, 1985); V. Pérez Moreda, *Las crisis de mortalidad en la España interior: siglos XVI–XIX* (Madrid, 1980).

26. M. R. Weisser, "The Agrarian Depression in Seventeenth-Century Spain," *JEH* 42 (1982): 149–54; A. García Sanz, *Desarrollo y crisis del Antiguo Régimen en Castilla la Vieja. Economía y sociedad en tierras de Segovia de 1500 a 1814* (Madrid, 1986), 95; in Murcia diocese total agricultural production doubled 1530s to 1560s, stabilized 1560s to 1590s, and was down by half by the 1640s: G. Lemeunier, "La coyuntura murciana: población y producción en el Siglo de Oro (1500–1650)," *Estudios de Historia de la Región Murciana, Cuadernos de Historia de España* 10 (1983): 165–233, at 178.

27. In 1610 the *tercias* were put at about one-quarter of the value of the *encabezamiento general*, some 700,000 ducats: *ACC* 25:632.

28. Rahn Phillips, "Time and Duration," 543; F. Ruiz Martín, "Un testimonio sobre las manufacturas de paños en Segovia por 1625," in *Homenaje al Profesor Alarcos García* (Valladolid, 1967), 2:787–807; J. I. Fortea Pérez, *Córdoba en el siglo XVI: las bases demográficas y económicas de una expansión urbana* (Cordoba, 1981), 440; in Toledo textile production plunged 1606–7 and 1619–20: M. R. Weisser, "The Decline of Castile Revisited: The Case of Toledo," *JEEcH* 2 (1973): 614–40.

29. J. C. Salyer, "La política económica de España en la época del mercantilismo," *Anales de Economía* 8 (1948): 303–27, at 312–15; C. Rahn Phillips, "The Spanish Wool Trade, 1500–1780," *JEH* 42 (1982): 775–95; L. M. Bilbao and E. Fernández de Pinedo, "Exportations des laines, transhumance et occupation de l'espace en Castille aux XVI, XVII et XVIIIème siècles," in *Migrations, Population and Occupation of Land (Before 1800)*, Eighth International Economic History Congress (Budapest, 1982), 36–48.

30. V. Vázquez de Prada, *Historia económica y social de España* 3, *Los siglos XVI y XVII* (Madrid, 1978), sees a clear reversal of the trend after

1592. On the problems of early-seventeenth century Seville, M. Moret, "Aspects de la société marchande de Séville au début du XVIIe siècle," *Revue d'Histoire Economique et Sociale* 42 (1964): 170–219; and 546–90, at 580–85. On the American trade, P. and H. Chaunu, "The Atlantic Economy and the World Economy," in P. Earle, ed., *Essays in European Economic History 1500–1800* (Oxford, 1974), 113–26; P. Chaunu, *Séville et l'Amérique, XVIe–XVIIe Siècle* (Paris, 1977), handier than his megalithic *Séville et l'Atlantique (1504–1650)*, 12 vols. (Paris, 1955–60); A. García-Baquero González, *Andalucía y la Carrera de Indias (1492–1824)* (Seville, 1986). On bullion imports, E. J. Hamilton's figures, in his *American Treasure and the Price Revolution in Spain 1501–1650* (Cambridge, MA, 1934), have been modified by E. Lorenzo Sanz, *Comercio de España con América en la época de Felipe II*, 2 vols. (Valladolid, 1979); D. O. Flynn, "Fiscal Crisis and the Decline of Spain (Castile)," *JEH* 42 (1982): 139–47; A. Domínguez Ortiz, "Las remesas de metales preciosos de Indias en 1621–1665," *Anuario de Historia Económica y Social* 2 (1969): 561–85; M. Morineau, *Incroyables Gazettes et Fabuleux Métaux. Les retours des trésors américains d'après les gazettes hollandaises (XVIe–XVIIIe siècles)* (Cambridge, 1985), 262, 321; Kamen, *Spain in the Later Seventeenth Century*, 134–40.

31.   Hamilton, *American Treasure and the Price Revolution in Spain*, 241.

32.   E. J. Hamilton, *War and Prices in Spain 1651–1800* (Cambridge, MA, 1947), 28, for silver premiums (Hamilton estimates that *vellón* made up over 92 percent of monetary transactions in Castile by the 1650s); Kamen, *Spain in the Later Seventeenth Century*, 361, for Crown spending.

33.   Reflected in differential tax rates and *arbitrio* values; in the 1650s the *millones* on wine were charged at 60 and 34 mrs. per *arroba* in New Castile, 34 and 24 mrs. in Old Castile: J. de la Ripia, *Práctica de la Administración y Cobranza de las Rentas Reales*, 3d ed. (Madrid, 1769), 112–13.

34.   See the complaint of Don Juan de Cañas for Burgos 1629, BL, Add. MSS 9938, fols. 86–87. A short-lived attempt at redress, collecting the *millones* at the point of production, was repealed 5 Oct. 1659; Ripia, *Práctica*, 112–13.

35.   Lomax, *Reconquista*, 157; M. A. Ladero Quesada, "Estado y hacienda en Castilla durante la baja edad media," in B. Bennassar et al., *Estado, Hacienda y Sociedad en la Historia de España* (Valladolid, 1989), 13–43, at 23, 32. Castilian royal finances in the fifteenth and sixteenth centuries have been covered comprehensively by M. A. Ladero Quesada, *La hacienda real de Castilla en el siglo XV* (La Laguna, Tenerife, 1973); J. A. Llorens, "Spanish Royal Finances in the Sixteenth Century," (Ph.D. diss., Harvard, 1951); R. Carande, *Carlos V y sus banqueros 2, La Hacienda Real de Castilla* (Madrid, 1949); M. Ulloa, *La hacienda real de Castilla en el reinado de Felipe II*, 2d ed. (Madrid, 1977); F. Ruiz Martín, "Las finanzas españolas durante el reinado de Felipe II (alternativas de participación que se ofrecieron para Francia)," *Cuadernos de Historia. Anexos de la Revista Hispania* 2 (1968): 109–73;

and most recently, M. J. Rodríguez Salgado, *The Changing Face of Empire. Charles V, Philip II and Habsburg Authority, 1551–1559* (Cambridge, 1988). The seventeenth century, with a less coherent financial history and less accessible records, has received less thorough treatment: A. Domínguez Ortiz, *Política y Hacienda de Felipe IV* (Madrid, 1960); F. Ruiz Martín, *Las finanzas de la monarquía hispánica en tiempos de Felipe IV (1621–1665)* (Madrid, 1990); M. Garzón Pareja, *La hacienda de Carlos II* (Madrid, 1980); Kamen, *Spain in the Later Seventeenth Century*; and, the more ambitious, M. Artola, *La hacienda del Antiguo Régimen* (Madrid, 1982), for the period 1591–1808.

36.   Ladero, *Hacienda real en el siglo XV*, 239.

37.   J. M. Carretero Zamora, *Cortes, monarquía, ciudades. Las Cortes de Castilla a comienzos de la época moderna (1476–1515)* (Madrid, 1988), 75.

38.   Carretero, *Cortes, monarquía, ciudades*, 64.

39.   Gerónimo Castillo de Bovadilla, *Política para Corregidores y Señores de Vasallos* [1597], facs. of Antwerp, 1704, ed. (Madrid, 1978), V. v. 4, vol. 2: 595; D. Garcí Pérez de Araciel, "Discurso en que se trata si los Reyes de Castilla pueden imponer nuevos tributos sin concession de las Ciudades que tienen voto en las Cortes," BL, Egerton MSS 347², fol. 620.

40.   Ladero, *Hacienda real en el siglo XV*, 226; S. Haliczer, *The Comuneros of Castile. The Forging of a Revolution 1475–1521* (Madison, WI, 1981), 91, on sale of *juros* by the Catholic Kings; A. Castillo Pintado, "Los juros de Castilla. Apogeo y fin de un instrumento de crédito," *Hispania* 23 (1961): 43–70, at 51–52 (36.6 percent in 1522, 103.9 percent in 1560).

41.   In 1667 only 7 percent of the revenues of the Council of Finance were "in administration": Kamen, *Spain in the Later Seventeenth Century*, 357.

42.   Haliczer, *Comuneros*, 119, 147, 221; F. Tomás y Valiente, "La Diputación de las Cortes de Castilla (1525–1601)," in his *Gobierno e instituciones en la España del Antiguo Régimen* (Madrid, 1982), 89–92. For the "denaturization" of the *alcabalas* and *servicios*, Carretero, *Cortes, monarquía, ciudades*, 90–92.

43.   Domínguez Ortiz, *Política y hacienda de Felipe IV*, app. 1, 333–42.

44.   A. Domínguez Ortiz, "La desigualdad contributiva en Castilla durante el siglo XVII," *Anuario de Historia del Derecho Español* 21–22 (1951–52): 1222–72, at 1228.

45.   M. Steele, "La hacienda española en el siglo XVI, 1516–1598," in *Historia General de España y América* 6, ed. V. Vázquez de Prada (Rialp, Madrid, 1985): 3; Sancho de Moncada, *Restauración Política de España*, ed. J. Vilar (Madrid, 1974), 158, "the greatest danger for kingdoms is if the king's credit is lost."

46.   On the "asiento" system, R. Carande, *Carlos V y sus banqueros*, 3 vols. (Madrid, 1943–67); H. Lapeyre, *Simón Ruiz et les asientos de Philippe II* (Paris, 1953); F. Ruiz Martín, introd. to *Lettres marchandes échangées entre Florence et Medina del Campo* (Paris, 1965); J. C. Boyajian, *Portuguese Bankers at the Court of Spain 1626–1650* (New Brunswick, NJ, 1983); C. Sanz Ayán, *Los banqueros de Carlos II* (Valladolid, 1988).

47. Significantly, 1647 was the first "bankruptcy" not to have major international repercussions: Boyajian, *Portuguese Bankers*, 178.

48. In addition to Boyajian, *Portuguese Bankers*, see N. Broens, *Monarquía y capital mercantil: Felipe IV y las redes comerciales portuguesas (1627–35)* (Madrid, 1989).

49. Kamen, *Spain in the Later Seventeenth Century*, 361–62.

50. Between 1627 and 1641 *vellón* was inflated three times and deflated four, to be followed by further alterations in 1642, 1651, 1652, 1658, 1660, 1664, 1680, and 1684: Hamilton, *War and Prices*, 13–21. For criticism of royal monetary policy, Juan de Mariana, "Tratado y Discurso sobre la Moneda de Vellón," *BAE* 31 (Madrid, 1872): 577–93. On the *erarios*, F. Ruiz Martín, "La banca en España hasta 1782," in *El Banco de España. Una historia económica* (Madrid, 1970), 1–196, at 59ff. B. Bennassar, "Impôts et crédit public en Espagne du XVIe siècle à nos jours (traits dominants d'une mutation)," *Finances Publiques d'Ancien Régime*, Spa Colloquium 1971 (Brussels, 1972), 180, "Thanks to an extremely astute inflationary policy, the country's specie stocks made it possible to get over the trough of the seventeenth century."

51. F. Ruiz Martín, "Procedimientos crediticios para la recaudación de los tributos fiscales en las ciudades castellanas durante los siglos XVI y XVII: el caso de Valladolid," in A. Otazu, *Dinero y Crédito (siglos XVI al XIX)* (Madrid, 1978), 37–47; J. Fayard, "Crédit public en Espagne au XVIIe siècle: les emprunts sur la ville de Madrid," in *La documentación notarial y la historia. Actas del II Coloquio de Metodología Histórica Aplicada* 2 (Santiago de Compostela, 1984): 253–65; J. I. Martínez Ruiz; "Donativos y empréstitos sevillanos a la Hacienda Real (siglos XVI–XVII)," *Revista de Historia Económica* 2 (1984): 233–44; A. Gutiérrez Alonso, "Un aspecto poco conocido de la Crisis del siglo XVII: el endeudamiento municipal. El ejemplo de la ciudad de Valladolid," *Investigaciones Históricas* 6 (1986): 9–37. That this was also a shift in creditworthiness is suggested by the president of Castile's recommending in 1646 the allocation of *juros* to private individuals through the intermediacy of the provincial capitals, "because they will prefer to have the cities specifically obligated for their payment rather than Your Majesty alone," *CODOIN* 95:248. Unfortunately, the credit and finances of the later half of Philip IV's reign are matters of which we still remain in the deepest ignorance.

52. For a subtle analysis of the earlier "bankruptcies," F. Braudel, *The Mediterranean and the Mediterranean World in the Age of Philip II*, 2 vols. (London, 1972), 1:500–517.

53. M. Steele, "International Financial Crises during the Reign of Philip II, 1556–1598" (Ph.D. diss., Univ. of London, 1986), 417.

54. A. Castillo, " 'Decretos' et 'Medios Generales' dans le système financier de la Castille. La crise de 1596," in *Mélanges en l'honneur de Fernand Braudel* (Toulouse, 1973), 1:137–44; Rodríguez Salgado, *Changing Face of Empire*, 232–43, for 1557. Also A. W. Lovett, "The Castilian Bankruptcy of 1575," *HJ* 23 (1980): 899–911, and "The General Settlement of 1577: an aspect

of Spanish finance in the early modern period," *HJ* 25 (1982): 1–22, though his general thesis is untenable, see Steele, "International Financial Crises," 240–41.

55. *Juros* came in many different types with different rates of return. A. Castillo Pintado has dealt with the *juro* in a series of articles, "Los juros de Castilla. Apogeo y fin de un instrumento de crédito," *Hispania* 23 (1963): 43–70; "Dette flottante et dette consolidée en Espagne de 1557 à 1600," *Annales* 18 (1963): 745–59; "El mercado del dinero en Castilla a finales del siglo XVI. Valor nominal y curso de los juros castellanos en 1594," *Anuario de Historia Económica y Social* 3 (1970): 91–104. See also P. Toboso Sánchez, *La deuda pública castellana durante el Antiguo Régimen (Juros) y su liquidación en el siglo XIX* (Madrid, 1987), 167, 156.

56. Junta del Decreto, 16 Dec. 1597, AGS, CJH 254 (359).

57. BL, Egerton MSS, 356², fol. 413. The total number of *juro* bonds extant by the eighteenth century exceeded 64,000: Toboso, *Deuda pública castellana*, 190.

58. An attempt to fund *juros* on "extraordinary" income from the Indies at the start of Philip II's reign proved not to be a success: F. Ruiz Martín, "Un expediente financiero entre 1560 y 1575. La hacienda de Felipe II y la Casa de Contratación de Sevilla," *Moneda y Crédito* 92 (1965): 3–59.

59. *CODOIN* 81:534–35; *ACC* 30:366–69.

60. The *millones* contract of 1601 applied 500,000 ducats of the grant every year to the liquidation of the consolidated debt. A condition of that agreement was that the king would make no further *asientos*, or if they were unavoidable only after giving notice to the *Reino*, in a form acceptable to the *Reino*, and signed "in the name of the king and kingdom" ("a voz de Rey y reino"). Those conditions would have made it almost impossible for the king to conduct an independent foreign policy. The attempts of the Cortes to intervene in relations with the bankers were seen by the Council as an outrage: "In asking of the king a detailed account of the proceeds of the Settlement, which is an *arbitrio*, and insisting that it be terminated, they are saying two things to him: the first is that he give account of the effects on which they have been spent, itemizing everything, thus providing the opportunity for censure by those who have not, and should not attribute to themselves such authority, neither is it right or proper that they should do so; the second is to prevent Your Majesty either redeeming the *juros* which are encumbering the royal revenue, or reducing their rate of interest. The best thing of all is that Your Majesty order the speedy conclusion of these Cortes," AGS, PR 89, fol. 223.

61. The reduction from 14 to 20 "al millar" on 26 Oct. 1621 produced about 3 million ducats, Toboso, *Deuda pública castellana*, 158. Its significance lies not only in its timing (six months after the ending of the truce with the Dutch), but in that this was the first time such a reduction had been applied to "juros al quitar," which were not royal *mercedes* but contractual obligations.

62. *Juros* were being discounted in the 1590s, but moderately—by 7 per-

cent on the *encabezamiento*, 14 percent on the *rentas arrendadas*: Castillo, "El mercado del dinero," 103. By 1623 the Council of Finance was claiming that most *juros* were being traded at half or one-third their face value: Toboso, *Deuda pública castellana*, 183. D. Francisco de Guadalfajara in Sala de Millones, 10 Mar. 1684, AGS, CJH 1079 (1476).

63. Toboso, *Deuda pública castellana*, 167, 156.

64. Ladero, *Hacienda real en el siglo XV*, 242–45; M. L. Lunenfeld, *The Council of the Santa Hermandad. A Study of the Pacification Forces of Ferdinand and Isabella* (Coral Gables, FL, 1970); Carretero, *Cortes, monarquía, ciudades*, 66, 68–85, 86–91.

65. E. Hernández Esteve, *Creación del Consejo de Hacienda de Castilla (1523–1525)* (Madrid, 1983); R. Rodríguez Raso, ed., *Maximiliano de Austria, gobernador de Carlos V en España. Cartas al emperador* (Madrid, 1963), 210.

66. Haliczer, *The Comuneros of Castile*, chap. 6; Tomás y Valiente, "Diputación de las Cortes," 95; Carande, *Carlos V y sus banqueros* 2:249.

67. For the part played by the aristocracy in the rejection of the *sisa* in the 1538 Cortes: A. Cánovas del Castillo, "Carlos V y las Cortes de Castilla," *La España Moderna* 1 (1889): 73–115; J. Sánchez Montes, *1539. Agobios carolinos y ciudades castellanas* (Granada, 1974), chap. 6; Carande, *Carlos V y sus banqueros* 2:536–37.

68. Ulloa, *Hacienda de Felipe II*, 175; J. I. Fortea Pérez, *Fiscalidad en Córdoba. Fisco, economía y sociedad: alcabalas y encabezamientos en tierras de Córdoba (1513–1619)* (Cordoba, 1986), 66–67, 59; in the Cordoba district the *encabezamiento* of 1557–61 was in real terms little more than half that of 1513–17, and the real cost per household only 38.6 percent of 1528–29 (p. 63).

69. Carande, *Carlos V y sus banqueros* 3:27–34 and tables. Between 1536 and 1556 *asientos* were taken for 22 ½ million ducats, half of them after 1551, at an average rate of 46 percent.

70. Hamilton, *American Treasure*, 34; Lorenzo Sanz, *Comercio de España con América* 2:163ff.; Carande, *Carlos V y sus banqueros* 3:420–26; S. de Moxó, "Las desamortizaciones eclesiásticas del siglo XVI," *Anuario de Historia del Derecho Español* 31 (1961): 327–61; J. Cepeda Adán, "Desamortización de tierras de las Ordenes Militares en el reinado de Carlos I," *Hispania* 146 (1980): 487–527; H. Nader, *Liberty in Absolutist Spain. The Habsburg Sale of Towns, 1516–1700* (Baltimore, 1990), 99–129; D. E. Vassberg, "The Sale of *Tierras Baldías* in Sixteenth-Century Castile," *JMH* 47 (1975): 629–54; M. Cuartas Rivero, "La venta de oficios públicos en Castilla-León en el siglo XVI," *Hispania* 158 (1984): 495–516; I. A. A. Thompson, "The Purchase of Nobility in Castile, 1552–1700," *JEEcH* 8 (1979): 313–60. The *alcabalas* of about 1,000 places were sold under Charles V and Philip II: S. de Moxó, *La alcabala. Sus orígenes, concepto y naturaleza* (Madrid, 1963), 88–92.

71. *Juro* payments on the "ordinary rents," made largely in compensation for the seizure of private bullion from the Indies no less than ten times between 1535 and 1558, tripled during the reign: Castillo, "Dette flottante et dette consolidée," 757; "Relacion de todos los juros" (end 1552), 300 *cuentos*

(capital 2,333 *cuentos*), AGS, CJH 13 (23), fol. 378; "Valor de todas las rentas del reino," 8 June 1556, 364 *cuentos* for *juros*, AGS, CJH 19 (29), fol. 263; bullion seizures, 1554, AGS, CJH 15 (25), fol. 248; Rodríguez Salgado, *Changing Face of Empire*, 68–71, 208–12.

72. AGS, Estado 139, fol. 293, *juros* 1,262,000 ducats (473 *cuentos*), general needs 1,684,000, debts 7,000,000 plus; Rodríguez Salgado, *Changing Face of Empire*, 231–52.

73. *CSP, Venetian* 7:204 n. 158; Ulloa, *Hacienda de Felipe II*, chaps. 4, 24, 19–21; Thompson, *War and Government*, 68, 288; I. Cloulas, "Le 'subsidio de las galeras,' contribution du clergé espagnol à la guerre navale contre les Infidèles de 1563 à 1574," *Mélanges de la Casa de Velázquez* 3 (1967): 289–326.

74. Ulloa, *Hacienda de Felipe II*, 780–94; and further details in A. W. Lovett, "Juan de Ovando and the Council of Finance, 1573–1575," *HJ* 15 (1972): 1–21.

75. The high point of the 1520s has been established in regions as different and as geographically removed as Cordoba and Alava: Fortea, *Fiscalidad en Córdoba*, 64 and n. 7.

76. Ulloa, *Hacienda de Felipe II*, 174–80; C. Jago, "Philip II and the Cortes of Castile: The Case of the Cortes of 1576," *Past and Present* 109 (1985): 24–43; J. I. Fortea Pérez, *Monarquía y Cortes en la Corona de Castilla. Las ciudades ante la política fiscal de Felipe II* (Salamanca, 1990), 508ff.

77. Castillo, "Dette flottante et dette consolidée," figure at 752 for *asientos*; S. de Moxó, "La venta de alcabalas en los reinados de Carlos I y Felipe II," *Anuario de Historia del Derecho Español* 41 (1971): 487–554; Vassberg, "Sale of *Tierras Baldías*," 650; J. Hellwege, *Zur Geschichte der spanischen Reitermilizen. Die Caballería de Cuantía unter Philipp II, und Philipp III. (1562–1619)* (Wiesbaden, 1972), 131.

78. President of Castile, 23 Mar. 1593, "it can indeed be said that all the measures and expedients which His Majesty could employ are exhausted," *ACC* 12:373. Commutation of *caballeros de cuantía* was suspended in 1593 after opposition in the Cortes, *ACC* 12:285, 13:87; Vassberg, "Sale of *Tierras Baldías*," 648–50; Moxó, "Venta de alcabalas," 526 (at 42½ times rent 1550s, 30 times 1580s and 90s).

79. Hamilton, *American Treasure*, 34; Lorenzo Sanz, *Comercio de España con América* 2:395, 409–10; Moret, "Société marchande de Séville," 582, 585 for drop in *alcabalas* and *almojarifazgos* in the 1600s. The Council of Finance (2 Oct. 1607) directly linked the fall in revenues with the decline of population, trade, and commerce, AGS, GA 670.

80. AHN, Consejos, leg. 4438, 1662, n. 34, "Apuntamientos que se hace del valor que en cada un año tendran los servicios de Millones concedidos por el Reyno," 31 May 1662, gives 9.4 million plus "8000 soldados," and the *encabezamiento*, *cientos* and *servicios* are to be added.

81. *ACC* 26:381–96, "Escritura del repartimiento," 1 Feb. 1611.

82. I. Pulido Bueno, *Consumo y fiscalidad en el reino de Sevilla: el ser-*

vicio de millones en el siglo XVII (Seville, 1984), 72, thinks the differential as far as the *millones* are concerned was not very great. The *millones* were set officially at 440 mrs. per *vecino* in the cities, 327 in the *tierras*, *ACC* 13:149. With the *alcabalas*, however, the per capita burden was proportionately greater the larger the town: in the Montes de Toledo, for example, M. R. Weisser, *The Peasants of the Montes* (Chicago, 1976), 63; or in Cordoba where, at the end of the sixteenth century, each *vecino* paid 3,500 mrs. in the city, 1,200–1,300 in the *pueblos*: Fortea, *Fiscalidad en Córdoba*, 133. In Galicia a more or less direct comparison can be made: in Viana del Bollo, the town paid 1,200 mrs. per *vecino* in *alcabalas*, the *tierra* 152: Council of Finance, 21 Dec. 1606, AGS, CJH 341 (467). The distribution of the *millones* was very different: in Viveiro, the town paid 215 mrs. per *vecino*, the rural parishes 243: P. Saavedra, *Economía, Política y Sociedad de Galicia. La provincia de Mondoñedo. 1480–1830* (Madrid, 1985), 505.

83. BL, Add. MSS 9936, fols. 214–15, 1649; the contrast with the situation 30 years earlier is striking—by 1619 Castile had overpaid the "18 *Millones*" of 1601 by 2.1 million ducats, *ACC* 33:135. During Philip IV's reign the *encabezamiento general* fell from 2,917,000 ducats to 2,584,000, the *almojarifazgo de Indias* from 295,000 to 43,000, the Maestrazgos from 295,000 to 217,000, the *Lanzas* from 400,000 to 150,000, the paper duty from 500,000 to 300,000; see Domínguez Ortiz, *Política y Hacienda de Felipe IV*.

84. For the Union of Arms, J. H. Elliott, *The Count-Duke of Olivares. The Statesman in an Age of Decline* (Yale, 1986), chap. 7. For Portugal, P. T. Rooney, "The Habsburg Government of Portugal in the Reign of Philip IV (1621–40)" (Ph.D. diss. Univ. of Keele, 1988), chaps. 4 and 5; for Naples, G. Muto, "La economía del *mezzogiorno* continental de la segunda mitad del *cinquecento* a las crisis de los años cuarenta del siglo XVII (Interpretaciones más recientes)," *Cuadernos de Investigación Histórica* 1 (1977): 191–213, esp. 211–13, and the bibliography there.

85. For Olivares's failure, Elliott, *Count-Duke of Olivares*, pt. 3.

86. Trujillo, for example, was paying 1,475 ducats a month to the army in Extremadura for "utinselios," AHN Consejos, leg. 7176, 1666, n. 95; Avila was paying over 7,000 ducats a year for billeting and also maintaining 364 soldiers in the field, AHP Avila, Libro de Acuerdos 1667, fol. 91, *ayuntamiento* of 29 Nov. 1667; Cáceres, with a population of 500 *vecinos*, supported cavalry in billet from 8 July 1664 to 4 Apr. 1665 with 85,073 *reales* and was being asked for another 32,540 *reales*, discountable from royal taxes, as in Trujillo, Council of War, 24 Apr. 1665, AGS, CJH 872. The Galician cities were having to supply straw, firewood, hay, lodging, and pay for the troops, AM Santiago, Libro de Consistorios 1667, fols. 463, 469, 499. As A. J. Sánchez Pérez writes, "the war ended up being a national struggle financed for the most part by the region directly involved," *Poder municipal y oligarquía. El concejo cacereño en el siglo XVII* (Cáceres, 1987), 155.

87. AGS, CJH 842 (1152), Sala de Millones, 10 July 1662: Zamora offers to

farm "los servicios, ympuestos y quiebras de Millones" for 1662–64; Council of Finance, 18 Dec. 1662: Palencia took the farm of the "24 *Millones*," "8000 soldados" and "nuevas sisas" from 1 Oct. 1658. Cáceres agreed to take the "cabezón de alcabalas y cientos" of the town and its jurisdiction for 1670–72 under threat that otherwise the Council of Finance would send in *jueces administradores* to collect at the full 14 percent: AM Cáceres, Libro de Actas 1669–73, fols. 67v, 74, 31 Jan. and 16 Mar. 1670.

88.   Domínguez Ortiz, "Desigualdad contributiva," 1233–37, and app. 1, 1269; Garzón Pareja, *Hacienda de Carlos II*, 342–62. Pardons and remissions of criminal sentences, even for homicide, were negotiated by the 1638 "donative" commissioners. P. Hernando de Salazar in 1643 wanted each contributor to be given a written assurance that no other taxes would be imposed upon him, "as if the contract and transaction had been made with him alone, so that the individual obligation is added to the corporate one," cited in A. Cratchley, "The Arbitristas of the Mid-Century: Programmes of Reform and Their Reception 1643–1667" (D.Phil thesis, Oxford, 1981), 125.

89.   RD, 3 Sept. 1669, ending the "quiebras de millones" from 1 Jan. 1669 and remitting all sums outstanding, reducing the "servicio de milicias" from 30 to 20 ducats, remitting debts on all "donatives" from 1625 to 1658, and making various administrative changes: AHN, Consejos, libro 1474, fols. 176–77; "Memorial que el año de 1686 se dió al Rey sobre el estado de la Monarquía de España," 4 Dec. 1686, RAH Jesuitas 5, fols. 83–93v. "It is certain that for many years Castile has never been so relieved of taxes than since Your Majesty's happy reign" (fol. 84), referring to further concessions: the general pardon for monies owed on all taxes and "services" prior to 1674, calculated to be in excess of 12 million ducats (10 Feb. 1680); the reduction of nearly one-third of the price of the new *encabezamiento* (1683); the abolition of the new taxes called the "carnes nuevas" and the "service of 3 million" ducats (3 Feb. 1685); and the halving of the four *cientos* on the *alcabalas*; F. Gil Ayuso, *Noticia bibliográfica de textos y disposiciones legales de los Reinos de Castilla impresos en los siglos XVI y XVII* (Madrid, 1935), 346, no. 1492. Kamen, *Spain in the Later Seventeenth Century*, 366.

90.   Kamen, *Spain in the Later Seventeenth Century*, 367–69; Garzón Pareja, *Hacienda de Carlos II*, 18–22; Artola, *Hacienda del Antiguo Régimen*, 216–21; RAH, Pellicer 20, fols. 262–67.

91.   J. I. Fortea Pérez, "Trayectoria de la Diputación de las Cortes," in *Las Cortes de Castilla y León en la Edad Moderna*, (Valladolid, 1989), 33–87, at 59, 75, 77.

92.   A point made by D. Luis Moreno Ponce de León in joint meeting of Council of Finance and Sala de Millones, 10 Mar. 1684, AGS, CJH 1079 (1476).

93.   Kamen writes that Charles II's was "fiscally the most progressive reign of the Habsburg epoch": *Spain in the Later Seventeenth Century*, 360.

94.   For the fiscal history of the eighteenth century, H. Kamen, *The War of Succession in Spain 1700–15* (London, 1969), chap. 9; Artola, *Hacienda del Antiguo Régimen*, 249ff.; M. Garzón Pareja, *Historia de la Hacienda*

Española, 2 vols. (Madrid, 1984), 1:593ff; J. Lynch, *Bourbon Spain 1700–1808* (Oxford, 1989), 61–62, 110–15.

95.   For the overall fall in the real per capita burden of taxation between the 1520s and the 1570s, C. Rahn Phillips, *Ciudad Real, 1500–1750: Growth, Crisis and Readjustment in the Spanish Economy* (Cambridge, MA, 1979), 78; Fortea, *Fiscalidad en Córdoba*, 63. The low point should be located at the end of the 1550s.

96.   J. Gentil da Silva, *En Espagne. Développement économique, subsistance, déclin* (Paris, 1965), 92, estimates Castile's national income in 1570 at c. 73 million ducats; the 105 million proposed by A. Domínguez Ortiz, *The Golden Age of Spain* (London, 1971), 198, seems rather high. Domínguez Ortiz thinks that under Philip IV the Crown took c. 11 percent of Castile's 180 million ducats of national income (*Política y Hacienda de Felipe IV*, 183), but the latter figure is surely excessive. On the other hand, an official calculation of the 1750s that total taxes then were the equivalent of 4 percent of income from all sources suggests that my own estimate may well be at the upper end of the range: R. Herr, *Rural Change and Royal Finances in Spain at the End of the Old Regime* (Berkeley, 1989), 9. J. U. Nef, *Industry and Government in France and England 1540–1640* (Ithaca, NY, 1957), 129, puts Louis XIII's revenues at over 10 percent of national income, Charles I's at 2–3 percent.

97.   García Sanz, *Desarrollo y crisis*, 333, 336.

98.   Contemporary estimates ranged wildly, from 10 percent, see M. Grice-Hutchinson, *Early Economic Thought in Spain 1177–1740* (London, 1978), 157, to the more usual one-third. For two official calculations: BL, Add. MSS 9936, fols. 214–15, 1649, 3.1 of 9.6 million; and AHN, Consejos, leg. 4438, 1662, n. 34, 5.6 of 9.8 million.

99.   Council of Finance, 31 Aug. 1660 and 17 Oct. 1661, AGS, CJH 807 (1111).

100.   Saavedra, *Mondoñedo*, 506; in the Montes de Toledo there could be a nearly eight-fold variation (Weisser, *Peasants of the Montes*, 63), in the region of Cordoba a six- or seven-fold variation (Fortea, *Fiscalidad en Córdoba*, 157). D. Juan de Lacalle, councillor of the Indies and *procurador de Cortes* for Toro, claimed there were places with 1,000 *vecinos* paying twice as much as others with 6,000: 26 Apr. 1655, *ACC* 59[1]:118.

101.   Saavedra, *Mondoñedo*, 499; E. Diez Sanz, *Soria y su tierra ante el sistema fiscal de Felipe II* (Soria, 1987), 45; Fortea, *Fiscalidad en Córdoba*, 143.

102.   B. Bennassar, *Valladolid au siècle d'or: une ville de Castille et sa campagne au XVIe siècle* (Paris, 1967), 254–57. In seventeenth century Ciudad Real, however, less than half the *juro* payments stayed within the city: Rahn Phillips, *Ciudad Real*, 109. For Burgos, BL, Egerton MSS 356[2], fol. 413.

103.   Between 36 and 40 percent of the price of meat and 33 to 60 percent of the price of wine was tax, depending on local excises: AHN, Consejos, leg. 7175, 1664, n. 27; ACD, Libro 2[0] Cortes de 1655, fol. 206; AV Madrid, Libro de Acuerdos 80, fol. 291 (29 Aug. 1667). The Junta de Fraudes was formed in June 1682 to check contraband in Seville; its authority was extended throughout

the kingdom in January 1683: Junta de Fraudes, 8 July 1683: AGS, CJH 1069 (1462); D. Carlos de Herrera, 8 Jan. 1683, AGS, CJH 1069 (1462), reports from Cordoba and Seville.

104.   Cortes, 22 Mar. 1596, *ACC* 16:400, for one complaint of hundreds; and sixty years later, the same complaint, A. Paz y Melia, ed., *Los Avisos de Jerónimo de Barrionuevo*, BAE 220–21 (Madrid 1968–69), 1:134.

105.   16,000 according to Gerónimo Hurtado, *procurador de Cortes* for Toledo, 1649–51, costing 5,840,000 ducats a year in salaries and the same again in trouble and inconvenience: BL, Add. MSS 9938, fol. 50; 65,000 according to Diego de Villoslada, 1644: RAH, Salazar y Castro K 112, fols. 2–11v; 100,000 according to Osorio y Redín: Grice-Hutchinson, *Early Economic Thought in Spain*, 157; 150,000 according to the *Contador* Antolín de la Serna, c. 1616: AGS, PR 89, fol. 289; 232,000 according to a memorialist of 1667, Domínguez Ortiz, *Política y Hacienda de Felipe IV*, 182.

106.   For an authoritative view, President of Castile, 20 July 1643, *CODOIN* 95:95.

107.   *ACC* 32:58, *procurador de Cortes* for Murcia, 13 July 1618; Domínguez Ortiz, *Política y Hacienda de Felipe IV*, 191 n. 52 (Arjona); Garzón Pareja, *Hacienda Española* 1:570; P. Fernández Martín, "Las ventas de las villas y lugares de behetría y su repercusión en la vida económico-social de los pueblos de Castilla," *Anuario de Historia Económica y Social* 1 (1968): 261–80, at 273 on the behavior of the bailiffs, etc.

108.   D. Juan de Cañas, Oct. 1644, BL, Add. MSS 9938, fol. 94; Junta in Granada, c. 1657, "There would be no end to describing the extortions, tyrannies, and humiliations that in these present circumstances men of good will are suffering. They are the ones whose gain it is to free themselves from them and live in liberty, rid of their present slavery": BL, Add. MSS 9936, fols. 8–11.

109.   For the profound reservations to be applied in the reading of this appendix, see pp. 156–57 above. Not the least problem is the definition of "taxation." For present purposes, I have not included *arbitrios*, transactions, and (with much uncertainty) the *media anata* and other retentions of *juros* (worth c. 3,500,000 ducats a year in 1664) for which "satisfaction" was given. For 1557, see my "Taxation, Military Spending and the Domestic Economy in Castile in the Later Sixteenth Century," in I. A. A. Thompson, *War and Society in Habsburg Spain: Selected Essays* (Aldershot, 1992), chap. 8; and (with slightly lower figures) L. M. Bilbao, "Ensayo de reconstrucción histórica de la presión fiscal en Castilla durante el siglo XVI," in E. Fernández de Pinedo, ed., *Haciendas Forales y Hacienda Real* (Bilbao, 1990), 37–62. For Philip IV's reign, Domínguez Ortiz, *Política y hacienda de Felipe IV*, pt. 3 and app. 1. New Castilian wheat prices and Valladolid wage rates were selected to permit strict comparability between the two periods. For wheat prices, Hamilton, *American Treasure and the Price Revolution in Spain 1501–1650*, app. 4; and *War and Prices in Spain 1651–1800*, app. 1. For wages, B. Bennassar, *Valladolid au siècle d'or*, 297; A. Gutiérrez Alonso, *Estudio sobre la*

decadencia de Castilla. La ciudad de Valladolid en el siglo XVII (Valladolid, 1989), 181. For population (another uncertain variable), Molinié-Bertrand, *Au Siècle d'Or. L'Espagne et ses hommes;* A. Domínguez Ortiz, *La sociedad española en el siglo XVII* 1 (Madrid, 1964), 113.

CHAPTER 5

1. C. D. Hendricks, "Charles V and the Cortes of Castile" (PhD diss., Cornell, 1976); C. Jago, "Habsburg Absolutism and the Cortes of Castile" *AHR* 86 (1981): 307–26; P. Fernández Albaladejo, "Monarquía y Reino en Castilla, 1538–1623," Istituto Internazionale di Storia Economica "Francesco Datini" (Prato, 1982); I. A. A. Thompson, "Crown and Cortes in Castile, 1590–1665," *Parliaments, Estates and Representation* 2 (1982): 29–45; *Las Cortes de Castilla y León en la Edad Moderna* (Valladolid, 1989). See the survey of recent developments in S. de Dios, "Evolución de las Cortes de Castilla durante los siglos XVI y XVII," in *Hispania. Entre derechos propios y derechos nacionales, Per la storia del pensiero giuridico moderno* 34/35 (Milan, 1990): 593–755.

2. S. Haliczer, *The Comuneros of Castile. The Forging of a Revolution 1475–1521* (Madison, WI, 1981), chap. 6.

3. J. A. Maravall, *Las Comunidades de Castilla: Una primera revolución moderna* (Madrid, 1963). See also J. Pérez, *La révolution des "Comunidades" de Castille (1520–1521)* (Bordeaux, 1970).

4. This largely follows B. González Alonso, "Las Comunidades de Castilla y la formación del estado absoluto," in his *Sobre el Estado y la Administración de la Corona de Castilla en el Antiguo Régimen* (Madrid, 1981), 7–56. De Dios, "Evolución de las Cortes de Castilla," 150–57, gives the fullest account of the Cortes program of the Comuneros.

5. Hendricks, "Charles V and the Cortes of Castile"; Haliczer, *The Comuneros of Castile,* chap. 9; De Dios, "Evolución de las Cortes de Castilla," 157–64.

6. For these developments, C. Jago, "Philip II and the Cortes of Castile: The Case of the Cortes of 1576," *Past and Present* 109 (1985): 24–43; I. A. A. Thompson, "Cortes y Ciudades: tipología de los procuradores (extracción social, representatividad)," in *Las Cortes de Castilla y León en la Edad Moderna,* 193–248, at 208–13; and for an exhaustive and persuasive account of the 1570s-1590s, J. I. Fortea Pérez, *Monarquía y Cortes en la Corona de Castilla. Las ciudades ante la política fiscal de Felipe II* (Salamanca, 1990), esp. 399–403.

7. An ironic consequence of the refusal of so many districts to accept the new *encabezamiento general* in 1575, leaving the *Diputación*, the permanent committee responsible for its management, unable to cope with the multitude of individual accounts without the help of royal experts; as a result the royal accounts office came to be permanently associated with the

Diputación in the management of a previously exclusive prerogative of the *Reino*; see J. I. Fortea Pérez, "Trayectoria de la Diputación de las Cortes," in *Las Cortes de Castilla y León en la Edad Moderna*, 58–60.

8. M. Danvila, "Nuevos datos para escribir la historia de las Cortes de Castilla en el reinado de Felipe III," *BRAH* 8 (1886): 259–61; AHN, Consejos, lib. 1532, fol. 111, President of Castile, 19 Jan. 1639.

9. For the following paragraphs, Thompson, "Crown and Cortes in Castile," 33–37.

10. *ACC* 16:476–80.

11. *ACC* 18:565 (29 Dec. 1599). A not dissimilar declaration had been made in 1574 with reference to the *encabezamiento*. The latter, however, was always understood to be an agreement with the cities, rather than with the Cortes, in that it did not bind any of the cities which did not agree to it and preferred to have their *alcabalas* collected at the full rate. Moreover, the 1574 declaration, though perhaps of significance as a precedent, seems to have been an isolated statement which did not become regularized and formalized until 1599: *ACC* 4:302 (15 Nov. 1574).

12. F. Gil Ayuso, *Noticia bibliográfica de textos y disposiciones legales de los Reinos de Castilla impresos en los siglos XVI y XVII* (Madrid, 1935), nos. 864, 885, 928.

13. See the account by the President of Castile, D. Fernando de Acevedo, of the agreement renewing the *millones* in 1618, in M. Escagedo Salmón, "Los Acebedos," *Boletín de la Biblioteca Menéndez Pelayo* 7 (1925): 182.

14. Thompson, "Cortes y Ciudades," 238–39. Secretary Angulo to duke of Lerma, 20 July 1618, "todos quieren mostrarse gente de República," AGS, PR 89, fol. 305; Junta de Asistentes, 8 Mar. 1647, complaining of 15 or 16 *procuradores* "concerned only to oppose and delay Your Majesty's service"; M. Danvila, "Nuevos datos para escribir la historia de las Cortes de Castilla en el reinado de Felipe IV," *BRAH* 16 (1890): 279–80. Junta de Cortes, 17 July 1610, *ACC* 26:46; Olivares in Cortes, 16 Sept. 1623, speaking to "the arguments put forward by some that the 'Reino' should not accept any measure that is fixed, certain, and permanent so that the king always be dependent and obliged to summon the Cortes," J. H. Elliott and F. de la Peña, *Memoriales y Cartas del Conde Duque de Olivares*, 2 vols. (Madrid, 1978–81), 1:21. L. Cabrera de Córdoba, *Relaciones de las cosas sucedidas en la Corte de España desde 1599 hasta 1614* (Madrid, 1857), 311; the Cortes accepted the king's promise "that he would give his pledge and royal word as firmly as necessary for its compliance" (1 Sept. 1607). The condition that the Cortes be convoked every three years was revoked in 1608, AGS, PR 87², fol. 555.

15. Undated paper of responses to conditions of new *millones* agreed by Cortes on 23 Sept. 1617, AGS, PR 91, fol. 6. Council of Finance, 25 Sept. 1618, AGS, CJH 402 (555); Junta de Presidentes, 15 Nov. 1618, Danvila, "Nuevos datos," *BRAH* 8:275–79. President of Finance to Cortes, 7 July 1609, *millones* producing 1,303,593 ducats less than what is assigned on them as result of

failures and delays in process of collection and delivery in private interests of receivers and *regidores, ACC* 25:302–3; almost identical complaint from Junta de Asistentes, 27 Oct. 1621, M. Danvila, "Nuevos datos para escribir la historia de las Cortes de Castilla en el reinado de Felipe IV," *BRAH* 15 (1889): 403–5. For the full details of the "repartimiento de los dos millones" of 1611, *ACC* 26:381–96.

16.   On the *De mutatione monetae*, BNM MS. 12179, fol. 138, "Memoria para leerse luego" (1609). See also J. Vilar, *Literatura y economía. La figura satírica del arbitrista en el siglo de oro* (Madrid, 1973).

17.   RAH, Pellicer 14, fols. 68–73v, "Tocante a los Servicios de Cortes contra los dos escribanos mayores de los Reinos," c. 1620, at fol. 71v.

18.   Initially an equal number of royal ministers were associated with the *procuradores* who made up the *Comisión* (1632). By 1643 it consisted of five royal ministers and only two *procuradores*. An abortive attempt had been made to incorporate the *Comisión* into the royal Council of Finance in 1647; see Fortea, "Trayectoria de la Diputación de las Cortes," 41–44, 77–80; and Jago, "Habsburg Absolutism," 322–24.

19.   Jago, "Habsburg Absolutism," 322–23; complaint of Granada, 9 Mar. 1632, *ACC* 49:214, 256; *ACC* 50:219; *consulta* of Cortes 20 Dec. 1634, AHN, Consejos, leg. 51445; *Avisos de Barrionuevo* 1:215, 225; complaint of Cordoba in the Cámara, 26 Feb. 1642, AHN, Consejos, leg. 4428, 1642, n. 11; complaint and new condition 12 in "escritura" of Nueve Millones de Plata 3 Jan. 1647, AHN Consejos, libro 1532, fols. 150bis-156v; complaints in Valladolid, 19 Oct. 1647, AM Valladolid, Libro de Actas 42, 4 Jan. 1649, Libro de Actas 43; *procurador* for León, 29 Apr. 1655, *ACC* 59¹:149; *procurador* for Jaén, 9 Jul. 1655, *ACC* 59¹:380; *ayuntamiento* of Madrid, 3 Aug. 1667, AV Madrid, Acuerdos 80, fols. 258–61. The "Quiebras" were administered by the *Comisión del Reino* and *corregidores*, RC, 6 Jan. 1647, AHN, Consejos, libro 1532, fols. 172–73.

20.   For the great reform decree, sent to the cities in October 1622, and the salt tax of 1631, which established compulsory quotas for every region, see F. Ruiz Martín, "La banca en España hasta 1782," in *El Banco de España. Una historia económica* (Madrid, 1970), 93, and J. H. Elliott, *The Count-Duke of Olivares. The Statesman in an Age of Decline* (Yale, 1986), 115–27.

21.   I treat this episode at length in my "Cortes y Ciudades," 215–21.

22.   Junta de Asistentes, 17 Mar. 1645, M. Danvila, "Nuevos documentos para escribir la historia de las Cortes de Castilla en el reinado de Felipe IV," *BRAH* 16 (1890): 154–57.

23.   The new levies were a third extra "ciento," doubling of paper duty, and a "nueva sisa de la carne," all in 1656 and estimated at 3 million ducats *vellón* a year; and 3 million over three years on wine, vinegar, and oil in 1657: RAH, Pellicer 14, fols. 34–38, 44; M. Danvila, "Nuevos documentos para escribir la historia de las Cortes de Castilla en el reinado de Felipe IV," *BRAH* 17 (1890): 274–77.

24. "Proposición Real," 7 Apr. 1655, *ACC* 59[1]:33.

25. ACD, Libro de las Cortes de 1660–64, 5 Oct. 1663. *Avisos de Barrionuevo* 2:295 (24 Nov. 1663).

26. I. A. A. Thompson, "The End of the Cortes of Castile," *Parliaments, Estates and Representation* 4 (1984): 125–33.

27. AV Madrid, Libro de Acuerdos 80, fols. 257–61 (3 Aug. 1667).

28. Thompson, "Cortes y Ciudades," 195.

29. Cited in A. Domínguez Ortiz, "Concesiones de votos en Cortes a ciudades castellanas en el siglo XVII," in his *Crisis y decadencia de la España de los Austrias* (Barcelona, 1969), 97–111, at 101 n. 3; and Acevedo, 21 Sept. 1618: "they are hated in their cities," AGS, PR 91, fol. 1. For other condemnations, President Contreras, 25 Feb. 1622, BL, Add. MSS 14017, fol. 139; Juan de Mariana, "Tratado y Discurso sobre la Moneda de Vellón," *BAE* 31 (Madrid, 1872): 578; Lisón y Viedma, J. Vilar, "Formes et tendances de l'opposition sous Olivares: Lisón y Viedma 'Defensor de la Patria,'" *Mélanges de la Casa de Velázquez* 7 (1971): 263–94, at 285 n. 1; Sancho de Moncada, *Restauración Política de España*, 190; Quevedo, J. A. Maravall, "El tema de las Cortes en Quevedo," in his *Estudios de historia del pensamiento español* (Madrid, 1975), 3:345.

30. D. Miguel de Salamanca, *procurador* for Burgos, 30 June 1632: *ACC* 50:201–6; *Actas de las Juntas y Diputaciones del Principado de Asturias (1652–1672)*, ed. M. D. Andujar Polo (Oviedo, 1964), 7:58–59.

31. Vilar, "Formes et tendances de l'opposition sous Olivares," 263–94; Elliott, *Count-Duke of Olivares*, 109–10. D. Gerónimo de Carvajal, *regidor* of Salamanca, proposed in *ayuntamiento* 13 Nov. 1648, "que si fuera posible, no solo las ciudades por votos de sus caballeros Regidores, pero tambien los braços eclesiastico y militar, y el comun avian de votar en sus decisiones," AM Salamanca, Libro de Acuerdos 32, fols. 378v-39.

32. This was the case with the new 2 percent tax on rents in 1642, which the Cortes defended against the opposition of some cities as in line with its desire for "general measures, which it would not be at the option of any place to vary": AHN, Consejos, leg. 51446, fol. 511; in 1663 the Cortes condemned a proposal by Madrid to take over the excises collected in its province as a means of servicing an advance of 500,000 ducats to the king, as "greatly prejudicial to the public service and the authority of the Cortes" and as a device by which Madrid was aiming to escape its common burdens ("pretende quedar exsimida y desagregada del cuerpo unibersal del Reyno y esenta de las contribuciones comunes"), ACD, Libro de las Cortes de 1660–64, *consulta* of 18 July 1663.

33. A decree of 1669 restored the administration of the revenues to the justices and commissioners of the cities and ordered all *administradores*, executors, and special and private judges of the tax-farmers to cease their operation: RD to President of Council, 3 Sept. 1669, AHN, Consejos, libro 1474, fols. 176–77. In 1673, in return for the regrant of the *millones*, their

administration was again conceded to the justices and commissioners of the provincial capitals whenever they were "en administración": AHP Avila, *ayuntamiento* of 3 June 1673; the qualification was, of course, important.

34. At the time, as well as since; see Mariana in G. Lewy, *Constitutionalism and Statecraft during the Golden Age of Spain* (Geneva, 1960), 55; R. Giesey, *If Not, Not. The Oath of the Aragonese and the Legendary Laws of Sobrarbe* (Princeton, 1968), 3–15.

35. "Should [the conditions] not be complied with, or if any of them be contravened, the said services shall be of themselves as naught and shall be suspended and cease *ipso facto*, just as if they had never been granted" (condition 20 of 15 July 1628, BL, Add. MSS 9936, fol. 59); ministerial objections to "nullity clause" in *ACC* 60¹:342, 344–46. L. González Antón, *Las Cortes de Aragón* (Zaragoza, 1978), for the revisionist view.

36. A. García Gallo, "El pactismo en el Reino de Castilla y su proyección en América," in L. Legaz y Lacambra et al., *El pactismo en la historia de España* (Madrid, 1980), 143–68.

37. *Comisión de Millones* 20 Mar. 1647, disincorporated 9 Mar. 1649; Fortea, "Trayectoria de la Diputación de las Cortes," 78; on overselling of offices, RP 2 Aug. 1647, AHN, Consejos, libro 1532, fols. 198–99; *ACC* 59²: 910.

38. Good statements in *capítulo* 3 of 1588 Cortes, 9 June 1590: *ACC* 9: 384–86; in "Cortes del año de 1596," BNM, MS. 1750, fols. 293–95v; and in Sancho de Moncada, *Restauración política de España*, 189. See also J. Laures, *The Political Economy of Juan de Mariana* (New York, 1928); M. Grice-Hutchinson, *Early Economic Thought in Spain 1177–1740* (London, 1978), 134–36.

39. See, for example, the "proposición" of the President of Castile to the Cortes, 13 Nov. 1599: *ACC* 18:426–28.

40. IVDJ, envío 43, fol. 180, Junta in Aranjuez, 4 June 1591: a proposal to tax the movement of grain was referred by the Crown to four judges of the Sala del Consejo; three of them declared against and it was dropped; BL, Add. MSS 9936, fol. 273, probably 1642–43, the *fiscal* appealed to the Royal Council against "the unjust refusal of the Cortes in not giving their consent"; A. Rodríguez Villa, *Corte y Monarquía de España en los años 1636 y 1637* (Madrid, 1886), 13 (20 Jan. 1636); "Cartas de Jesuitas," 24 June 1636, *MHE* 13:437; D. Garcí Pérez de Araciel, BL, Egerton MSS 347², fols. 620–23.

41. Gerónimo Castillo de Bovadilla, *Política para Corregidores y Señores de Vasallos* [1597], facs. of Antwerp, 1704, ed. (Madrid, 1978), V. v. 1–4; F. Elias de Tejada Spínola, *Gerónimo Castillo de Bovadilla* (Madrid, 1939), 133.

42. There was no new *general* taxation, but frequent "donatives" and other local impositions, which were taxes in all but name; see the majority vote of Dr. D. Joseph de la Serna in *ayuntamiento* of Salamanca, 14 Feb. 1691, that the levy of paid and uniformed troops which had cost Salamanca nearly 200,000 *reales* in the previous few years "is in substance a new tax"

and so should have consent of "el Reyno combocado," AM Salamanca, Libro de Actas 75, fol. 35v. The levy on salt was also increased in 1694, apparently with the consent of the cities: M. Garzón Pareja, *La hacienda de Carlos II* (Madrid, 1980), 334.

43. A. Domínguez Ortiz, *Política fiscal y cambio social en la España del siglo XVII* (Madrid, 1984), 88, 97, quotation on 86.

44. J. de la Ripia, *Práctica de la Administración y Cobranza de las Rentas Reales*, 3d ed. (Madrid, 1769), 2. Localization of administration enabled municipal governments to "denaturize" impositions like the "donative"; in Soria in 1667, as in 1659 and 1664, the "donative" was raised by "medios generales" rather than by a levy on "individuals": AM Soria, *ayuntamiento* 8 Aug. 1667.

45. Calculated from A. Domínguez Ortiz, *Política y Hacienda de Felipe IV* (Madrid, 1960), app. 1, pp. 333–42. The count of Chinchón paid over 70,000 ducats in forced loans between 1633 and 1645; the duke of Osuna spent over 100,000 in sixteen years on the raising of regiments and other services; the marquis of Poza was owed 277,000 for *medias anatas*, retained and unassigned *juros*, costs of military levies, and losses on alterations of the coinage, all incurred between 1647 and 1664: Domínguez Ortiz, *Política fiscal y cambio social*, 111; AHN, Consejos, leg. 4440, 1667, n. 23, and leg. 4438–39, 1664, n. 10.

46. Domínguez Ortiz, "La desigualdad contributiva en Castilla durante el siglo XVII," *Anuario de Historia del Derecho Español* 21–22 (1951–52): 1261–63, and 1262 (quoting Novoa).

47. Domínguez Ortiz, *Política fiscal y cambio social*, 86.

48. Petition of Cordoba, 1646, "businessmen of great wealth trading here and in the Indies pay nothing, not even in sales taxes, because they charge their costs, taxes, and profit to the purchaser," AHN Consejos, leg. 51448.

49. *Regidores* of Burgos vote for *media anata de juros*, 12 Oct. 1645. Opposition of Cortes to "repartimientos personales," *ACC* 26:381–96.

50. On the clergy, A. Domínguez Ortiz, *La sociedad española en el siglo XVII*, vol. 2, *El estamento eclesiástico* (Madrid, 1970), chap. 8; Q. Aldea Vaquero, "La resistencia eclesiástica," in J. H. Elliott and A. García Sanz, *La España del Conde Duque de Olivares* (Valladolid, 1990), 399–414. For clerical agitation against the *millones* for example, AGS, PR 86, fols. 68, 190.

51. Domínguez Ortiz, *Estamento eclesiástico*, 200–204; the Court news reported on 18 Apr. 1637 a sermon by Fr. Ocaña, SJ, against the stamped paper duty and "so much taxation," "arguing that still it should all be borne if employed in the defence of the kingdom, but that it was not to be suffered to be spent on irrelevances and useless buildings" (sc. Buen Retiro Palace), Rodríguez Villa, *Corte y Monarquía de España*, 127.

52. See, for example, the "Parecer . . . sobre el servicio de los 500 Quentos" of three royal confessors, 30 July 1598, *ACC* 16:568–70.

53. For the new *corregimientos*, AHN, Consejos, leg. 4428, 1643, n. 70; *ACC* 60²:628–30. The quotations are from A. Sacristán y Martínez, *Munici-*

palidades de Castilla y León, 1877 (new ed. Madrid, 1981), 443, 544; H. Nader, *Liberty in Absolutist Spain. The Habsburg Sale of Towns, 1516–1700* (Baltimore, 1990), 128.

54. *ACC* 25:789–91; *ACC* 13:271, 370; *ACC* 16:274–79 (Cordoba) and 105 (Cuenca); AHN, Consejos, leg. 4428, 1642, n. 7.

55. Bujalance spent 80,000 ducats; Logroño voted in *concejo abierto* by 881 votes to 19 to restore its elective offices at a cost of 52,267 ducats, AM Logroño, Libro de Actas 8, 7 Aug. 1596; it had fewer than 1,000 *vecinos*. Valverde (Madrid) took *censo* in 1576 to buy its own jurisdiction; in 1607 its 45 *vecinos* were paying interest of 139,586 mrs. (some 30 days of labor per household, or as much as all royal taxes), and owed over 1,000,000 and its creditors had sequestrated *propios* and foreclosed on property of some householders; Valverde now wanted to resell its jurisdiction to redeem its debt: Consejo de Hacienda, 12 Jan. 1607, AGS, CJH 345 (473). For the celebrations, Nader, *Liberty in Absolutist Spain*, 159, 168.

56. BL, Add. MSS 9936, fols. 120–31.

57. There were 137 grandees and titled nobles created by Philip III and Philip IV, 354 by Charles II: A. Domínguez Ortiz, *La sociedad española en el siglo XVII* I (Madrid, 1963): 209–10; some 7,000 grants of knighthoods of the military orders were made in Philip IV's reign: E. Postigo Castellanos, *Honor y privilegio en la Corona de Castilla. El Consejo de las Ordenes y los Caballeros de Hábito en el siglo XVII* (Soria, 1988), 119; for the sale of *señoríos*, A. Domínguez Ortiz, "El fin del régimen señorial en España," in J. Godechot, *La abolición del feudalismo en el mundo occidental* (Madrid, 1979), 73; for the *cuantiosos*, J. Hellwege, *Zur Geschichte der spanischen Reitermilizen. Die Caballeria de Cuantia unter Philipp II, und Philipp III (1562–1619)* (Wiesbaden, 1972), 131; for the sale of offices, Domínguez Ortiz, *Política fiscal y cambio social*, chap. 5; for communal lands, B. Yun Casalilla, *Sobre la transición al capitalismo en Castilla. Economía y sociedad en Tierra de Campos (1500–1830)* (Salamanca, 1987), 304–6; D. E. Vassberg, *Land and Society in Golden Age Castile* (Cambridge, 1984), 175; A. García Sanz, *Desarrollo y crisis del Antiguo Régimen en Castilla la Vieja. Economía y sociedad en tierras de Sogovia de 1500 a 1814* (Madrid, 1986), 272–74.

58. By agreements of 12 Mar. 1573 and 25 Apr. 1574, Seville paid 800,000 ducats "por el qual se le dieron en empeño ciertas villas del maestrazgo de Santiago": AGS, PR 87², fol. 541; Madrid paid 150,000 ducats to stop exemptions from her jurisdiction, 9 Mar. 1630: AV Madrid, Libro de Acuerdos 46.

59. F. Tomás y Valiente, "La venta de oficios de regidores y la formación de oligarquías urbanas en Castilla (siglos XVII y XVIII)," *Historia, Instituciones, Documentos* 2 (1975): 523–47, and "Ventas de oficios públicos en Castilla durante los siglos XVII y XVIII," in his *Gobierno e instituciones en la España del Antiguo Régimen* (Madrid, 1982), 151–77. *ACC* 25:789–91, petition against exemptions, 25 Jun. 1610.

60. Olivares, in Elliott and Peña, *Memoriales y Cartas* 2:171–72. For the

1680s, opinion of Los Vélez, *Superintendente General de la Hacienda*, 1687, in M. Garzón Pareja, *Historia de la Hacienda Española*, 2 vols. (Madrid, 1984), 1:116; Sala de Millones, 10 Mar. 1684, AGS, CJH 1079 (1476); D. Rafael Sanguineto, AV Madrid, Libro de Acuerdos 104, 14 Feb. 1691. Domínguez Ortiz, "Desigualdad contributiva," 1260, 1264; J. M. de Bernardo Ares, "Gobierno municipal y violencia social en Córdoba durante el siglo XVII," *Axerquia* 1 (1980): 15–52; M. R. Weisser, *The Peasants of the Montes* (Chicago, 1976), 102; Fortea, *Monarquía y Cortes*, 341–42.

    61.   Dr Alexandro Parenti, AHN, Consejos, leg. 7179, 1669, n. 98.

    62.   P. Saavedra, *Economía, Política y Sociedad de Galicia. La provincia de Mondoñedo. 1480–1830*, (Madrid 1985), 500–504, suggests the responsiveness of the fiscal system to local needs and its reasonably equitable nature was one reason why there was so little resistance to taxation, compared with other parts of Europe. For what little is known about popular disturbances in early-modern Spain, see A. Domínguez Ortiz, *Alteraciones andaluzas* (Madrid, 1973); H. Kamen, *Spain in the Later Seventeenth Century, 1665–1700* (London, 1980), 175–82.

    63.   J. Sánchez Montes, "Sobre las Cortes de Toledo de 1538–39. Un procurador del Imperio en un momento difícil," in *Carlos V (1500–1558)*, *Homenaje de la Universidad de Granada* (Granada, 1958), 595–663, at 662; *corregidor* of Murcia, 1 Oct. 1576, *ACC* 5 adicional:357; Granada, BL, Add. MSS 9936, fol. 8; AHP Orense, Actas, vol. 34, fols. 43–46, 10 July 1673.

    64.   Saavedra, *Mondoñedo*, 501. A similar case could be made elsewhere. In Palencia, where part of the *encabezamiento* was raised by *repartimiento*, of 1478 *vecinos* in 1601, 36.7 percent paid nothing, the top 8.9 percent paid 54.5 percent; the top 1 percent paid more than the bottom 71.7 percent: AM Palencia, Libro Antiguo de Contabilidad, no. 14 and Inventario de 1758, leg. 22. Weisser, *Peasants of the Montes*, 46–47, also has such figures.

    65.   *ACC* 25:789–91. For one such case, I. A. A. Thompson, "El Concejo Abierto de Alfaro en 1602: la lucha por la democracia municipal en la Castilla seiscientista," *Berceo* 100 (1981): 307–31.

    66.   Domínguez Ortiz, "Desigualdad contributiva," 1234: in 1625 the *corregidor* of Madrid, with a *regidor*, parish priest, and notary visited each householder personally, going to smaller towns and villages on feast days to catch the residents on leaving mass; other examples, *MHE* 13:60 (10 June 1634), *CODOIN* 67:123 (6 Aug. 1677).

    67.   M. J. Rodríguez Salgado, *The Changing Face of Empire. Charles V, Philip II and Habsburg Authority, 1551–1559* (Cambridge, 1988), 68–71, 208–12, 226–27.

    68.   "Tratado que se dio al Rey el año 1643 sobre materias del Govierno y de hacienda," BNM, MS 2375, fols. 204–73, at fol. 211.

    69.   BL, Egerton MSS 347, fols. 117–18v, "Informe y relacion que don Matheo de Lison y Biedma, 24° de la Ciudad de Granada hiço a Su Magd . . . sobre la contradicion de la Benta de los bassallos" (11 June 1626).

    70.   *MHE* 13:60 (10 June 1634); *CODOIN* 67:123 (6 Aug. 1677). Pellicer's

Avisos of 29 Jan. 1641 tell of "un papel muy atrevido y desvergonzado" protesting on behalf of *juro*-holders against the retention of one-third; Domínguez Ortiz, "Desigualdad contributiva," 1233–41, and on hostility to "donatives," 1238, 1240.

71. On the reversibility of alienated offices, F. Tomás y Valiente, "Legislación liberal y legislación absolutista sobre funcionarios y sobre oficios públicos enajenados: 1810–1822," *Actas del IV Symposium de Historia de la Administración* (Madrid, 1983), 703–22, at 715; *Nueva Recopilación*, lib. 5, tit. 10, ley 3, prohibits royal donations of towns and villages of the Corona Real, and ley 15, "that grants made by the will of kings alone can be revoked in their totality."

72. Juan de Hevia Bolaños, *Curia Philipica* (1603), 1783 ed., fol. 307, nos. 7, 31–35; *Nueva Recopilación*, lib. 5, tit. 11, ley 1, "Que pone el remedio del engaño en más del justo precio" *(laesio ultra dimidium)*.

73. Council of Castile, Nov. 1654, BL, Egerton MSS 332, fols. 291v-292; other justifications for the revocation of *mercedes* in *AHE* 5:38–44.

74. BNM, MS 1750, fols. 293–95v, "Cortes del año de 1596": "the king may withhold from what he owes his creditors everything he needs for the inexcusable obligations which as king he has." For the abrogation of *asientos* with bankers, *AHE* 5:219; Barrionuevo, *Avisos*, 19 Aug. 1662, on the *Decreto* of that year, says the justification is exorbitant interest.

75. For the retention of *medias anatas* and "valimiento de juros," Cámara, 3 June 1643, AHN, Consejos, leg. 4429–30, 1646, n. 27. The dubiety of the measure (see BL, Egerton MSS 332, fol. 288) was possibly one reason why the king continued to ask the cities for their consent for these retentions. The compensations available tended to transform the *media anata* into a forced sale of *arbitrios*, though not necessarily on bad terms: D. Alonso de Ribadeneyra was allowed to buy the territory and revenues of the villages of Boecillo and Laguna (Valladolid) for 60,000 ducats owed him for *juros*: Council of Finance, 5 June and 24 Oct. 1662, AGS, CJH 842 (1152); marquis of Camarasa compounds for *alcabalas* of Castroxeriz and Astudillo for 21,065,452, of which 12,207,738 from *medias anatas de juros* and 1,358,414 salary debts: Council of Finance, 10 Sept. 1660, AGS, CJH 807 (1111). Royal ministers were getting jurisdictions as compensation for unpaid salaries: an *asesor* of the Council of War, D. Francisco de Solis Ovando, had 26,500 *reales* he owed for such a purchase offset against either his salary or the *medias anatas* of his *juros*: D. Juan de Góngora, 9 Dec. 1662, AGS, CJH 842 (1152).

76. Dr. Don Alonso de Agreda of Consejo y Cámara to Soria, 11 Apr. 1607, "esta es cedula de gracia de Su Magestad y como tal y cossa de Corte no tiene otro tribunal," AGS, PR 87², fol. 168. J. Lalinde Abadía, *Derecho Histórico Español* (Barcelona, 1974), 286–87. Don Juan de Góngora to king, 17 Apr. 1662: recently the duke of Pastrana, "in a contract, made a considerable service in money so that Your Majesty would not retain the *media anata* of his *juros*," and therefore he should not be included in the current suspension of exemptions from *medias anatas* of *juros* as his exemption was not "reserva

de gracia . . . sino de justicia por el contrato nuevo y servicio que pagó," AGS, CJH 841 (1152–53).

77. Sir Walter Aston to Secretary Conway, Madrid, 8 Aug. 1624, BL, Add. MSS 36449, fol. 135v.

78. "la Hazienda (que es el nervio de la autoridad)," F. Tomás y Valiente, Los Validos en la monarquía española (Madrid, 1963), 173.

79. A. Pellegrini, Relazioni inedite di ambasciatori lucchesi alla corte di Madrid (sec. XVI–XVII) (Lucca, 1903), 90.

80. Response of Queen Regent to protest of Council against indemnity to Francisco Centani for engrossing and tax evasion granted as condition of asiento for 240,000 escudos vellón, AHN, Consejos, leg. 7176, 1666, n. 66. On export licenses for silver as bonuses for asientos, ACC 32:84. On the increasing demands of the asentistas in the mid-seventeenth century, C. Sanz Ayán, Los Banqueros de Carlos II (Valladolid, 1988), 107–12.

81. AHN, Consejos, leg. 4436, 1658, n. 18.

82. Domínguez Ortiz, Política fiscal y cambio social, chap. 5.

83. AHN, Consejos, leg. 4427, 1639, n. 35; AHN, Consejos, leg. 7162, Council of Castile, 3 Feb. 1652.

84. I. Pulido Bueno, Consumo y fiscalidad en el reino de Sevilla: el servicio de millones en el siglo XVII (Seville, 1984), 26; Nader, Liberty in Absolutist Spain, passim. In the "alcaldía mayor y partido" of Almodovar every village had bought its exemption and jurisdiction bar one hamlet of 30 households, Junta, 15 May 1593, IVDJ, envío 43, fol. 410; 24 of 28 villages in jurisdiction of Guadalajara had gained exemption by 1636: A. Domínguez Ortiz, "Ventas y exenciones de lugares durante el reinado de Felipe IV," Anuario de Historia del Derecho Español 34 (1964): 172; complaint of Valladolid in Council of Finance, 24 Oct. 1662, AGS, CJH 842 (1152). But even places subject to the jurisdiction of others could buy augmentations of the value of cases they could try in the first instance from 600 to 4,000 mrs.: Cámara 3 Mar. 1636, AHN, Consejos, leg. 4426, 1636, n. 64.

85. Consulta of Council of Castile, Nov. 1654: "with so many exemptions from the ordinary jurisdiction of the Crown the voice of justice has been reduced to a confusion of tongues and to continuous conflicts of jurisdiction," BL, Egerton MSS 332, fol. 288v.

86. I. Atienza Hernández, "'Refeudalización' en Castilla durante el Siglo XVII: ¿Un tópico?," Anuario de Historia del Derecho Español 56 (1986): 889–919; B. Yun Casalilla, "La aristocracia castellana en el seiscientos. ¿Crisis, refeudalización u ofensiva política," Revista Internacional de Sociología 2a época, 45 (1987): 77–104; R. Giuffrida, "La politica finanziaria spagnola in Sicilia da Filippo II a Filippo IV (1556–1665)," Rivista Storica Italiana 88 (1976): 310–41, at 329.

87. The Contador de la Razón certified that 76,818½ vasallos (perhaps 350,000 individuals) had been sold, in addition to free grants, Council of Castile, 26 Mar. 1669, BL, Egerton MSS 332, fol. 299; Domínguez Ortiz, "Ventas

y exenciones de lugares," 171, gives 53,089 *vasallos* sold in 1626–70, including self purchases but not free grants.

88. In 1634 the Crown sold lords the right to appoint the justices and other judicial officials of their villages, M. Garzón Pareja, *Historia de la Hacienda Española*, 2 vols. (Madrid, 1984), 1:200; in 1639 lords were being sold the right to suppress the primary jurisdiction of their village justices (*alcaldes ordinarios*) and to administer justice directly through their own judges (*alcaldes mayores*), AHN Consejos, leg. 4427, 1639, n. 70. Council of Finance, 24 Nov. 1637, notes 3,621 places in Castile whose *alcabalas* went to private persons, particularly in Galicia, León, and Burgos: A. Domínguez Ortiz, *Política y Hacienda de Felipe IV* (Madrid, 1960), 223 n. 11. As early as 1598 a document put the numbers paying their *alcabalas* to a private lord at 31 percent of the population, Bod.L, Tanner MS. 99, fol. 175.

89. R. Benítez Sánchez Blanco, "Expulsión de los mudéjares y reacción señorial en la Serranía de Villaluenga," *Andalucía Moderna (Siglos XVI–XVII)* (Cordoba, 1978), 1:109–17, at 116–17. For other examples of concessions to the grandees for the same consideration, Domínguez Ortiz, *Política y Hacienda de Felipe IV*, 201.

90. Nader, *Liberty in Absolutist Spain*, 3–4, 208.

91. R. L. Kagan, *Lawsuits and Litigants in Castile, 1500–1700* (Chapel Hill, NC, 1981), 225.

92. A. Domínguez Ortiz, "La conspiración del duque de Medina Sidonia y el marqués de Ayamonte," *Archivo Hispalense* 106 (1961): 22.

93. Lord Mahon, *Spain under Charles the Second* (London, 1844): 18.

94. Tomás y Valiente, "Ventas de oficios públicos," 176; sales of *regimientos* were effectively stopped by a royal decree of 9 May 1669: *Autos Acordados* 3:373; A. Domínguez Ortiz, "La comisión de D. Luis Gudiel para la venta de baldíos de Andalucía," in his *Estudios de historia económica y social de España* (Granada, 1987), 101; Nader, *Liberty in Absolutist Spain*, 127; Domínguez Ortiz, "Ventas y exenciones de lugares," 171; of 78 places in the province of Segovia whose taxes were alienated from the Crown in the seventeenth century, only two were sold after 1677: García Sanz, *Desarrollo y crisis*, 340; there were no new sales of revenues in Tierra de Campos after 1685: B. Yun Casalilla, *Sobre la transición al capitalismo en Castilla*, 325–29.

95. The list is celebrated: "Don Felipe, por la gracia de Dios, Rey de Castilla, de León, de Aragón, de las dos Sicilias, de Jerusalem, de Portugal, de Navarra, de Granada, de Toledo, de Valencia, de Galicia, de Mallorca, de Sevilla, de Cerdeña, de Córdova, de Corcega, de Murcia, de Jaén . . . de las Indias Orientales y Occidentales . . . Conde de Barcelona, Señor de Vizcaya y de Molina . . . Archiduque de Austria, Duque de Borgoña, y de Brabante y Milán, Conde de Apsburg, de Flandés y de Tirol etc."

96. For the very different and largely ceremonial "Spanish" Cortes of the eighteenth century, P. Molas Ribalta, "Las Cortes de Castilla y León en el siglo XVIII," in *Las Cortes de Castilla y León en la Edad Moderna*, 143–69.

CHAPTER 6

1. For a discussion of Richelieu's statement, see James Collins, *Fiscal Limits of Absolutism: Direct Taxation in Early Seventeenth-Century France* (Berkeley, 1988), 1. Except in the opening sections of this chapter, which describe the French economy, the structure of governance, and system of taxation, I shall restrict myself to the period before 1700. For tax revenues, representative institutions, and fiscal crises in the eighteenth century, see chap. 7.

2. Denis Richet, *La France moderne: L'esprit des institutions* (Paris, 1973), 77; see also William Beik, *Absolutism and Society in Seventeenth-century France: State Power and Provincial Aristocracy in Languedoc* (Cambridge, 1985); Collins, *Fiscal Limits of Absolutism*; Daniel Dessert, *Argent, pouvoir et société au grand siècle* (Paris, 1984). Even social historians have become interested in taxes in recent years: Philip T. Hoffman, "Taxes and Agrarian Life in Early Modern France: Land Sales, 1550–1730," *JEH* 46 (1986): 37–55.

3. I derived population figures from Jacques Dupâquier, ed., *Histoire de la population française*, 4 vols. (Paris, 1988), 1:513–24, 2:64–68. See also Roland Mousnier, *The Institutions of France Under the Absolute Monarchy, 1589–1789*, trans. Arthur Goldhammer and Brian Pearce, 2 vols. (Chicago, 1979–84), 1:682–86; and Table 1, sources. The estimates of the agricultural population come from E. A. Wrigley, "Urban Growth and Agricultural Change: England and the Continent in the Early Modern Period," *Journal of Interdisciplinary History* 15 (1985): 683–728; because of the difficulty of counting workers who divided their time between agriculture and cottage industry, these estimates are subject to great uncertainty.

4. Richard J. Bonney, "The Failure of the French Revenue Farms, 1600–60," *EcHR*, 2d ser., 32 (1979): 11–32. The taxes on trade here include all of what Bonney defines as indirect taxes: the *aides*, the *gabelle*, the *fermes*, etc. The *gabelle* was more of a royal monopoly on the sale of salt, though, than an excise tax.

5. Jean Meuvret, *Le problème des subsistances à l'époque de Louis XIV*, 3 vols. (Paris, 1977–88), vol. 3, pt. 1 (*Texte*):47–187, and pt. 2 (*Notes*):115–47; Jan de Vries, *European Urbanization 1500–1800* (Cambridge, MA, 1984), 167; Fernand Braudel, *L'identité de la France*, 3 vols. (Paris, 1986), 1:55–60; Henri Cavaillès, *La route française: Son histoire, sa fonction* (Paris, 1946).

6. Bordeaux: David Parker, *The Making of French Absolutism* (New York, 1983), 17; guilds, local monopolies, and tax collection: Gail Bossenga, "La Révolution française et les corporations: trois exemples lillois," *Annales* 43 (1988): 405–26.

7. Albert N. Hamscher, *The Parlement of Paris after the Fronde, 1653–1673* (Pittsburgh, 1976), 153–54, 196–202. For a different opinion, see Mousnier, *Institutions of France* 2:632.

8. Such a view of the monarchy is one that emerges from a number of recent works, including Beik, *Absolutism and Society* and "Etat et société

en France au XVIIe siècle: La taille en Languedoc et la question de la re-distribution sociale," *Annales* 39 (1984): 1270–98; David Parker, *Making of French Absolutism*; Dessert, *Argent*; Robert Harding, *Anatomy of a Power Elite: The Provincial Governors of Early Modern France* (New Haven, 1978); Joseph Bergin, *Cardinal Richelieu: Power and the Pursuit of Wealth* (New Haven, 1985); Françoise Bayard, *Le monde des financiers au XVIIe siècle* (Paris, 1988); and Collins, *Fiscal Limits of Absolutism*. A more traditional view would pit the monarchy against the aristocracy and argue that it acted in the interests of the *bourgeois* or of the *commissaires*.

9. John Bell Henneman, "Nobility, Privilege, and Fiscal Politics in Late Medieval France," *FHS* 13 (1983): 1–17.

10. A summary of the evolution of the tax system can be found in Collins, *Fiscal Limits of Absolutism*, 18–64. See also the somewhat rapid account in Pierre Chaunu, "L'état," in Fernand Braudel and Ernest Labrousse, eds., *Histoire économique et sociale de la France*, 4 vols. (1970–82), 1, pt. 1:9–228. For the earlier period, see J. B. Henneman, *Royal Taxation in Fourteenth-Century France: The Captivity and Ransom of John II, 1356–1370* (Philadelphia, 1976) and *Royal Taxation in Fourteenth-Century France: The Development of War Financing, 1322–1356* (Princeton, 1971). There are also a number of older works, now somewhat superseded, including J. J. Clamageran, *Histoire de l'impôt en France*, 3 vols. (Paris, 1867–76; reprint, Geneva, 1980). For the financiers, see Bayard, *Le monde des financiers*; and Dessert, *Argent*. They collected taxes, made payments, worked as tax-farmers, and even devised new levies for the Crown. Their main function, though, was to raise funds among the wealthy for government loans.

11. J. Russell Major, *Representative Government in Early Modern France* (New Haven, 1980), 58–69 and *passim*. The distinction between royal officials who collected the direct taxes and private farmers who administered the indirect taxes is in many ways artificial. By the late seventeenth century, at least, the financial officials and tax-farmers participated in one another's ventures, and to a great extent the two groups overlapped. See Dessert, *Argent*, 42–109.

12. See, for example, the otherwise excellent book by J. Bosher, *French Finances, 1770–95* (Cambridge, 1970). Bosher attributes the failings and rigidity of the French fisc to the intermingling of public and private funds and the corruption it bred. The sort of intermingling he has in mind includes tax farming. Bosher and like-minded historians see this and other practices as inexplicable and archaic. Archaic they may have been, but they have a ready explanation, as we shall see below.

13. Beik, "Etat et société en France."

14. For Vauban, see Alain Lefebvre and Françoise Tribouillard, "Fiscalité et population dans l'élection de Valognes de 1540 à 1660," *Annales de Normandie* 21 (1971): 207–33, n. 13. For earlier problems assessing a land tax, see Bernard Guenée, *L'occident aux XIVe et XVe siècles: Les états* (Paris, 1971),

173. Parts of southern France did of course have marvelous land tax registers at a very early date.

15. Richard Bonney, *The King's Debts* (Oxford, 1981), 15. One solution to the problem of salt smuggling would be to require taxpayers to purchase quantities of high priced salt, precisely what was done in areas of the so-called *grande gabelle.*

16. Beik, *Absolutism and Society,* 247.

17. Collins, *Fiscal Limits of Absolutism,* 126–31. For more on the difficulties of shipping bullion, see Dessert, *Argent,* 27–41. For further examples of how little money reached Paris, see Daniel Hickey, *The Coming of French Absolutism: The Struggle for Tax Reform in the Province of Dauphiné, 1540–1640* (Toronto, 1986).

18. Beik, *Absolutism and Society,* 250–51.

19. Collins, *Fiscal Limits of Absolutism,* 131–35.

20. Beik, *Absolutism and Society,* 247–69, and "Etat et société." Ensuring that tax revenues were spent locally had a long political history. The taxes levied in the fourteenth century to support the first standing army, for example, were used to pay for local soldiers.

21. Dessert, *Argent,* 27–41, 155–209.

22. For tax farming, see Bayard, *Le monde des financiers,* 104–62; and Richard Bonney, "The Failure of the French Revenue Farms, 1600–1660." There were other reasons for the reliance on tax farming as well. The most notable was the relationship between tax farming and lending, to be discussed below.

23. Bonney, *King's Debts,* 274. In 1647, when France was embroiled in war with Spain, the government seriously discussed the possibility of royal bankruptcy but ruled it out because of the effect it would have on future borrowing: see ibid., 201. Numerous examples of broken promises can be found in Bayard, *Le monde des financiers,* 163–227, 318–39.

24. Bernard Schnapper, *Les rentes au XVIe siècle: Histoire d'un instrument de crédit* (Paris, 1957), 151–64; Roger Doucet, *Finances municipales et crédit public à Lyon au XVIe siècle* (Paris, 1937) and "Le grand parti de Lyon au XVIe siècle," *Revue historique* 171 (1933): 473–513, and 172 (1933): 1–41; Richard Gascon, *Grand commerce et vie urbaine au XVIe siècle: Lyon et ses marchands,* 2 vols. (Paris, 1971), 1:255–58. In the seventeenth century, many of the *rentes* issued by the monarchy continued to be little more than forced loans: see Dessert, *Argent,* 21–26. One of the first steps toward undermining the *rentes sur l'hôtel de ville* in the sixteenth century was the king's reassertion of control over the taxes that funded the *rentes.* Later in the Old Regime, it is worth noting, the *rentes sur l'hotel de ville* no longer involved such elaborate city backing.

25. Bayard, *Le monde des financiers,* 228–66, 285–89, 318–39; Bosher, *French Finances,* 17–19, and "*Chambres de justice* in the French Monarchy," in *French Government and Society, 1500–1850: Essays in Memory of Alfred Cobban,* ed. J. Bosher (London, 1973), 19–40; Bonney, *King's Debts,* 19–20;

Dessert, *Argent*, 128–29, 238–310. Bayard found evidence of bankruptcy for at least 14 percent of the financiers she studied, and she argues that the real rate of bankruptcy was much higher, on the order of 20 to 25 percent. Dessert found an 18 percent bankruptcy rate among his financiers, and he too thinks that the real rate was 20 to 25 percent. In both cases the financiers included tax farmers, *traitants*, and other individuals involved in tax collection, who combined their various activities with lending to the Crown. It should be stressed that by the second half of the seventeenth century the *chambres de justice* ceased doing real damage to the financiers; they had become little more than a threat used to prod renegotiation. It was also worth noting that the behavior of the Crown was not the only uncertainty lenders faced. The *traitants*, for example, who made short term loans to the Crown, usually had to get their *traités* registered by a sovereign court. If the court balked or refused, the *traitant* would have to renegotiate.

26. See appendix.

27. Bayard, *Le monde des financiers*, 228–66; Bonney, "The Failure of the French Revenue Farms, 1600–1660," *EcHR* 32 (1979): 11–32; Dessert, *Argent*, 21–26, 42–65.

28. David Bien, "Les offices, les corps et le crédit d'état: L'utilisation des privilèges sous l'ancien régime," *Annales* 43 (1988): 379–404; see also Dessert, *Argent*, 21–26, 42–65; Collins, *Fiscal Limits of Absolutism*, 78.

29. Bien, "Les offices"; Bonney, *King's Debts*, 176–77. Forced loans were only one of the fiscal abuses that corporate office holders had to endure during the first half of the seventeenth century, before the system described here was in place; see Bonney, *King's Debts*, 201–5, and the account of the Fronde below. But even in the late seventeenth century the loans supposedly extorted from the office holders were often not forced at all; see Dessert, *Argent*, 21–26.

30. For a seventeenth-century example, see Beik, *Absolutism and Society*, 267–69. For more on borrowing and financial expedients, see Bayard, *Le monde des financiers*, 228–66; and Richard Bonney, *Political Change in France under Richelieu and Mazarin* (Oxford, 1978), 171–72. Some borrowing via corporate bodies—municipalities, for example—was destructive of local privileges, for it justified royal interference in municipal affairs as early as the sixteenth century; see Doucet, *Finances municipales*, 87, 94–95, 125. One might wonder whether these expedients were ultimately more costly to the monarchy in purely monetary terms than a policy of keeping its promises would have been. This amounts to asking whether the money it saved by default was enough to compensate for the high interest rates it paid, or, in other words, whether the high interest rates amounted to something more than merely the monetary losses of default. Unfortunately, this is a question we shall never be able to answer. Even indirect sources of evidence (the profits from involvement in government finance and the value of financial office) cannot unlock the secret. It might well be the case though that as certain expedients grew more costly the monarchy switched to new

forms of finance: one thinks, for example, of how raising money from existing officers replaced the sale of new venal offices.

31. Cf. David Bien, "Manufacturing Nobles: The Chancelleries in France to 1789," *JMH* 61 (1989): 445–86; he argues that Louis XIV's effort to restrict access to the nobility was undertaken for fiscal reasons. The government raised money when *traitants* undertook investigations of the nobility (*recherches de noblesse*); and once the state controlled access to the nobility, it could profit by selling expensive ennobling offices.

32. The necessary calculation has been performed only for the case of Languedoc, and then only in the seventeenth century. See Beik, *Absolutism and Society*, 245–69, and "Etat et société en France." As mentioned above, 33 percent of the taxes collected in Languedoc went directly to local notables; roughly another 19 percent was spent under their direction.

33. J. R. Mallet, *Comptes rendus de l'administration financière de la France* (London-Paris, 1789); F. Forbonnais, *Recherches et considérations sur les finances de la France* (Liège, 1758). Works relying upon Mallet include Clamageran, *Histoire de l'impôt en France*; Pierre Chaunu, "L'état"; and Alain Guéry, "Les finances de la monarchie française sous l'ancien régime," *Annales* 33 (1978): 216–39. Françoise Bayard, in her *Le monde des financiers*, 22–44, and Richard Bonney, in *The King's Debts*, 304–5, have collected new figures from manuscript sources, but they do not differ greatly from Mallet's.

34. Beik, "Etat et société en France"; James Collins, "Sur l'histoire fiscale du XVIIe siècle: Les impôts directs en Champagne entre 1595 et 1635," *Annales* 34 (1979): 325–47, and *Fiscal Limits of Absolutism*, 108–65.

35. Table 1 converts the revenue into both grain and man-days of labor. One might argue that conversion to grain was irrelevant or misleading, because it and other agricultural commodities presumably did not enter into government expenditure and because the price of agricultural goods rose more rapidly than other prices in the sixteenth century. Such an argument overlooks the fact that the government did purchase grain and agricultural goods to feed soldiers and horses; furthermore, even if the government never spent a penny on agricultural goods, conversion of tax revenues into grain equivalent would help us understand the burden of taxation since grain was the major product of the French agricultural economy. As for the steeper increase in the price of grain, that is to be expected when population rises and is hardly a reason to dismiss the use of the price of grain.

36. On the expedients, see Bayard, *Le monde des financiers*; Bonney, *The King's Debts*; and Collins, *Fiscal Limits of Absolutism*. Barring a revolution in state borrowing—a revolution that did not take place in France—the regular tax revenues ultimately limited the funds that the monarch could mobilize. In France, a difficulty with many of the fiscal expedients was that they were undependable, and therefore it was the regular taxes that ultimately constrained the size of the royal budget. Furthermore, tax revenues never grew fast enough (even during the periods of vertiginous tax increases)

to base a permanent state debt on the expectation of greater government revenues in the future. The problem was that the economy was sluggish, and with interest rates on government loans exceeding by a wide margin the rates at which taxes revenues grew, the payments due on a permanent government debt would quickly outstrip the Crown's income.

37. For local tax series, see Beik, "Etat et société en France"; Collins, *Fiscal Limits of Absolutism* and "Sur l'histoire fiscale du XVIIe siècle"; Alain Lefebvre and Françoise Tribouillard, "Fiscalité et population dans l'élection de Valognes de 1540 à 1660," *Annales de Normandie* 21 (1971): 207–33; Emmanuel Le Roy Ladurie, *Les paysans de Languedoc*, 2 vols. (Paris, 1966), 2:1026; Llewain Scott van Doren, "War Taxation, Institutional Change, and Social Conflict in Provincial France—the Royal *Taille* in Dauphiné, 1494–1559," *Proceedings of the American Philosophical Society* 121 (1977): 70–96, and "Civil War Taxation and the Foundations of Fiscal Absolutism: The Royal Taille in Dauphiné, 1560–1610," *Proceedings of the Third Annual Meeting of the Western Society for French History* (1976), 35–53. For permanent taxation and the Hundred Years War, see Major, *Representative Government*, 10–30; Henneman, *Royal Taxation in Fourteenth-Century France, 1322–1356* and *Royal Taxation in Fourteenth-Century France, 1356–70*. The imposition of the taxation during the early stages of the war was revolutionary. In Montpellier, as Major points out, taxes in 1370 were twenty times what they had been in 1328, despite both depopulation and declining prices.

38. J. S. Roskell, "Perspectives in English Parliamentary History," in *Historical Studies of the English Parliament*, ed. E. B. Fryde and Edward Miller, 2 vols. (Cambridge, 1970), 2:304–5; Gerald Harriss, "War and the Emergence of the English Parliament, 1297–1360," *Journal of Medieval History* 2(1976): 35–56; Major, *Representative Government*, 10–30, 33–45; Georges Picot, *Histoire des Etats généraux*, 2d ed., 5 vols. (Paris, 1888), 1:xvii, 390–92. What I have said about the subsequent role of the Estates General applies as well to the sporadic assemblies of notables.

39. Major, *Representative Institutions*, 45. For the influence of the Estates General on legislation, see Picot, *Histoire des Etats généraux*. The Ordonnance of Orléans (1561) was probably the piece of legislation that bore the clearest imprint of an Estates General, yet even though parts of it copied directly the language of the cahiers of the Estates General of Orléans, it was still drawn up by the king's chancellor and councilors. See Picot, *Histoire des Etats généraux* 2:214, and François Olivier-Martin, *Histoire du droit français des origines à la Révolution*, 2d ed. (Paris, 1951), 374–77.

40. Major, *Representative Institutions*, 45; Picot, *Histoire des Etats généraux* 1:390–92, 2:10–13; Neithard Bulst, "Vers les états modernes: le tiers état aux Etats généraux de Tours en 1484," in *Représentation et vouloir politiques: Autour des Etats généraux de 1614*, ed. Roger Chartier and Denis Richet (Paris, 1982), 11–24. At the Estates General of Tours, concern with monetary grievances also played into the hands of the Crown and helped di-

vert the Estates General from demanding a greater role vis à vis the Crown;
see Harry Miskimin, *Money and Power in Fifteenth-Century France* (New
Haven, 1984), 106–21.

41. Major, *Representative Government*, 10–30, 38–39. One might wonder whether royal taxes, which fell disproportionately on the peasantry,
would cut into land rents and so provoke the ire of organized elites who
owned rural property. That taxes did not have this effect was the result of
the exemptions, which spared rural property held by the elites from taxation. In practice, if not always in theory, the tenants who worked such rural
property escaped their share of taxation, and the land rents they paid therefore remained insulated from most of the effects of higher taxation. On this
point, see Hoffman, "Taxes and Agrarian Life," 37–55.

42. Major, *Representative Government*, 31–200; Beik, *Absolutism and
Society*; Bonney, *Political Change*, 350–83. Provincial estates were not the
only bodies that had some voice in taxation. Governments of large cities
negotiated with the king, particularly before the seventeenth century, and
the assembly of the clergy negotiated the terms of their *don gratuit* from the
mid-sixteenth century to 1789. For the significance of these assemblies, see
Richet, *L'esprit des institutions*, 95–104.

43. For the increasing manpower the Crown employed, see Chaunu,
"L'état."

44. Major, *Representative Institutions*, 663–64.

45. Ibid., 450–672; Bonney, *Political Change*, 350–83, 419–52; Beik,
Absolutism and Society and "Etat et société en France," where the author
shows that the fiscal protection afforded by the provincial estates disappeared by the time of Colbert.

46. David Parker, *Making of French Absolutism*, 6–8, 61–64; Major,
Representative Institutions, 670; Collins, *Fiscal Limits of Absolutism*, 216;
Dessert, *Argent*, 155–71; Geoffrey Parker, *The Military Revolution: Military
Innovation and the Rise of the West, 1500–1800* (Cambridge, 1988), 39–46,
62–81, 146–51. Although the central government figures omit numerous
military expenses, they do demonstrate that the cost of the court was not
what provoked the tax increases and fiscal problems of the early seventeenth
century; see Bayard, *Le monde des financiers*, 22–44.

47. Bonney, "French Revenue Farms."

48. Collins, *Fiscal Limits of Absolutism*, 73–77, 216.

49. The interpretation here is taken from ibid., 77–87. For other opinions,
see Roland Mousnier, *La vénalité des offices sous Henri IV et Louis XIII*, 2d
ed. (Paris, 1971), 594–605, and Bonney, *King's Debts*, 61–62, who stress the
revenues to be gained from the sale of offices. See also Major, *Representative
Institutions*, 389–91, and "Bellièvre, Sully, and the Assembly of Notables of
1596," *Transactions of the American Philosophical Society* 44 (1974): 3–34;
he emphasizes the desire to decrease noble patronage.

50. Collins, *Fiscal Limits of Absolutism*, 65–66, 97–107, 135–46, 193–96,
203–13.

NOTES TO PAGES 245-48

51.   Ibid., 146, 163–66, 203–213; Bonney, *Political Change*, 163, 176–84, 219. For the reconstruction of the financial system after the Fronde, most of which is associated with Colbert, see Bayard, *Le monde des financiers*, 339; Bonney, "French Revenue Farms"; and Dessert, *Argent*.

52.   It is James Collins, in *Fiscal Limits of Absolutism*, who invokes the partial bankruptcy of 1634 to explain why the monarchy decided to post the intendants in the provinces; Richard Bonney's *Political Change* gives a broader view of the reasons behind the decision. For the repeated fiscal crises of the 1630s and 1640s, see Bonney, *King's Debts*, 159–241, especially 189.

53.   Bonney, *King's Debts*, 195–209; Bayard, *Le monde des financiers*, 339.

54.   Bonney, *King's Debts*, 195–209; Omer Talon, *Mémoires de Omer Talon, avocat général en la cour de Parlement de Paris, continués par Denis Talon, son fils*, ed. Joseph-François Michaud and Jean-Joseph François Poujoulat, Nouvelle collection des mémoires pour servir à l'histoire de France, ser. 3, vol. 6 (Paris, 1851): 195–296; Hamscher, *Parlement of Paris*, 71–81; Lloyd Moote, *The Revolt of the Judges: The Parlement of Paris and the Fronde, 1643–1652* (Princeton, 1971).

55.   Hamscher, *Parlement of Paris*, 71–81.

56.   Ibid., 63–65, 71–81; Pierre Clément, ed., *Lettres, instructions et mémoires de Colbert*, 8 vols. (Paris, 1861–82), vol. 2, pt. 1:42. As Hamscher points out, the Crown continued to appease influential magistrates. When in 1665 the Crown infuriated the sovereign courts by reducing the financial return on magistrates' offices (the *gages*), Colbert bargained with the leading judges and appeased them by paying their *gages* in full.

57.   Cf. Bonney, *Political Change*, 440–521. Like the Estates General, the provincial estates did influence legislation; the legislative power, though, was still the king's. In looking over the fate of the estates in France, it is tempting to interpret their weakness in the light of a theoretical argument elaborated by Robert Bates and Donald Lien. Using a game-theoretic model of a monarch and taxpayers, Bates and Lien demonstrate that taxpayers with mobile assets are more likely to exert control over the monarch. Their interpretation is that countries with mobile assets are more likely to witness the development of representative institutions, while countries overendowed with immobile assets such as land are less likely to do so. France, with its wealth in land and not in trade, would seem to fall decisively in the group of countries overendowed with immobile assets. See Robert Bates and Da-Hsiang Donald Lien, "A Note on Taxation, Development, and Representative Government," *Politics and Society* 14 (1985): 53–70.

58.   William Farr Church, *Constitutional Thought in Sixteenth-Century France: A Study in the Evolution of Ideas* (Cambridge, MA, 1941); Roland Mousnier, "Comment les français du XVIIe siècle voyaient la constitution," *XVIIe siècle* 25–26 (1955): 9–36; Denis Richet, "La polémique en France de 1612 à 1615," in *Représentation et vouloir politiques*, 151–94, and *L'esprit des institutions*, 135–48; Christian Jouhoud, *Mazarinades: La Fronde des mots* (Paris, 1985), 37–39, 93–94, 155–83, 237–39. Even a cursory comparison

of political pamphlets written during the Fronde and the English Civil War will bear out the contrast in political language.

59.   Church, *Constitutional Thought*, 19, 231–42, 315–35; Mousnier, "Comment les Français du XVIIe siècle voyaient la constitution," 14–17; Talon, *Mémoires*, 208–12. Bodin speaks of "le franc suget"; see Church, 241. The distinction between monarchy and despotism was standard and occurred even in the works of radical authors at the time of the Fronde. See Richet, *L'esprit des institutions*, 136; Jouhoud, *Mazarinades*, 156–57.

60.   Talon, *Mémoires*, 293–96; Bonney, *King's Debts*, 208–9; Beik, *Absolutism and Society*, 250–51; Jean Meuvret, "Comment les français du XVIIe siècle voyaient l'impôt," *XVIIe siècle* 25–26(1955): 59–82.

61.   Meuvret, "Comment les français du XVIIe siècle voyaient l'impôt," 64–67. Liberty boiled down to privilege elsewhere in Western Europe as well. For a discussion and a comparison of liberties and privileges in various countries, see the conclusion.

62.   For the Cour des Aides and the case of "la liberté publique des Français," see Meuvret, *Le problème des subsistances*, vol. 2, pt. 1 (*Texte*): 59; pt. 2 (*Notes*): 106. The *chambre de justice* of 1716 and the treatment of financiers in the late seventeenth century demonstrate the Crown's growing respect for elite property: the Crown did not tamper with the legal subterfuges by which the financiers sheltered their wealth. See Dessert, *Argent*, 110–52, 210–76. The investigations into the nobility (*recherches de noblesse*), which by tightening the definition of nobility reinforced the value of property embodied in ennobling offices, are further signs of the same regard for elite property. In a sense, the *recherches de noblesse* also strengthened the privileges of those already securely noble. For additional examples of the strengthening of privileges in the late seventeenth century, see Dessert, *Argent*, 82–109, 341–78; and Beik, *Absolutism and Society*. One could contrast these late seventeenth-century examples with evidence from the sixteenth century or from the early seventeenth century, which would show a monarchy that was on occasion more ruthless in its treatment of elite privileges and property. For one example, which concerns the Crown's seeking precisely the sort of information about private wealth that would have been considered shocking in the late seventeenth century, see Doucet, *Finances municipales*, 87.

63.   For agriculture and transportation: Philip T. Hoffman, "Institutions and Agriculture in Old-Regime France," *Politics and Society* 16 (1988): 241–64, and "Taxes and Agrarian Life in Early Modern France: Land Sales, 1550–1730"; Jean-Laurent Rosenthal, *The Fruits of Revolution: Property Rights, Litigation and French Agriculture 1700–1860* (Cambridge, 1992); Steven Laurence Kaplan, *Provisioning Paris: Merchants and Millers in the Grain and Flour Trade during the Eighteenth Century* (Ithaca, 1984), 83–87; Cavaillès, *La route française*, 118–22. In "Taxation in Britain and France, 1715–1810: A Comparison of the Social and Economic Incidence of Taxes Collected for the Central Government," *JEEcH* 5 (1976): 601–50, Peter Mathias and Patrick O'Brien argue that taxes did not sink the French economy, but their argu-

ment overlooks effects at the margin. In this regard, it would be a worthwhile enterprise to compare marginal rates of land taxes in early modern Europe in order to assess the effects of taxes on agriculture. For France, several examples suggest that the *taille* and other direct taxes amounted to between 15 and 40 percent of rent in the seventeenth century, a figure certainly high enough to have discouraged investment—particularly in livestock, the prize of the tax collector. For the nascent financial network and the talent mobilized by the fisc: Doucet, *Finances municipales*, 92–93, 103–19; Dessert, *Argent*, 42–65, 82–109, 379–411. In the eighteenth century, at least, the level of government debt in Britain was higher than in France, as is shown by David Weir, "Tontines, Public Finance, and Revolution in France and England, 1688–1789," *JEH* 49 (1989): 95–124. One might therefore argue that the French fisc could not have siphoned off an excessive amount of capital and talent. One way to rebut such an argument would be to stress less the actual financial capital than the extraordinary human talent wrapped up in getting a post within the French fiscal system.

64.   Sources: [Henri] Germain-Martin and Marcel Bezançon, *L'histoire du crédit en France sous le règne de Louis XIV* (Paris, 1913), 26–27, 31, 51, 55–59, 62, 90–91; Daniel Dessert, *Argent, pouvoir et société au grand siècle* (Paris, 1984), 21–26, 42–65; Roger Doucet, "Le grand parti de Lyon au XVIe siècle," *Revue historique* 171(1933): 483–88, and 172(1933): 3–10; Richard Gascon, *Grand commerce et vie urbaine au XVIe siècle: Lyon et ses marchands*, 2 vols. (Paris, 1971), 1:255–58.

CHAPTER 7

1.   "Cahier général des plaintes et doléances du tiers-état du bailliage de Bar-le-Duc," in *Archives parlementaires*, ed. M. J. Mavidal and M. E. Laurent (Paris, 1879), 2:192.

2.   See Simon Schama, *Citizens: A Chronicle of the French Revolution* (New York, 1989), 33.

3.   Charles Alexandre de Calonne, *Réponse de Monsieur Calonne à l'écrit que Monsieur Necker à publié en avril 1787* (London, 1788); Loménie de Brienne, *Mémoires*, in Jean-Louis Soulavie, *Mémoires historiques et politiques du règne de Louis XVI* (Paris, 1806), 6: 237–54; Jacques Necker, *De l'administration des finances de la France* (Paris, 1784), 3 vols; and *Sur le compte rendu . . . nouveaux éclaircissements* (Paris, 1787). On the difficulties presented by Necker's work see R. D. Harris, "Necker's *Compte rendu* of 1781: A Reconsideration," *JMH* 42 (1970): 170–76. Not just disgraced ministers published analyses of the Crown's financial distress; so too did a host of minor officials and fiscal agents. For a good discussion of this literature see J. F. Bosher, *French Finances, 1770–1795: From Business to Bureaucracy* (Cambridge, 1970), 125–41.

4.   Though apparently unaware of the degree to which the revolutionaries' views colored his own thinking, Bosher provides an excellent summary

of the principal arguments made both in the National Assembly and in the press after 1789 (see Bosher, *French Finances*, 215–52).

5. Frédéric Braesch, *Finances et monnaies révolutionnaires. Recherches, études et documents* (Nancy, 1934); René Stourm, *Les finances de l'Ancien Régime et de la Révolution: Les origines du système actuel*, 2 vols. (Paris, 1885); Robert Schnerb, "Technique fiscale et partis pris sociaux: l'impôt foncier en France depuis la Révolution," *AHES* 50 (1938): 116–38; Marcel Marion, *Histoire financière de la France*, 6 vols. (Paris, 1914) and *Les impôts directs sous l'ancien régime* (Paris, 1910).

6. Bosher, *French Finances*; J. D. Harris, "French Finances and the American War, 1777–83," *JMH* 48 (1976): 233–58 and *Necker, Reform Statesman of the Ancien Régime* (Berkeley, 1979) and *Necker and the Revolution of 1789* (Boston, 1986); James C. Riley, *The Seven Years War and the Old Régime in France: The Economic and Financial Toll* (Princeton, 1986).

7. Lucien Febvre in the introduction to Schnerb, "Technique fiscale et partis pris sociaux," *AHES* 50 (1938): 115.

8. See Eugene White, "Was there a Solution to the Ancien Regime's Financial Dilemna?" *JEH* 49 (1989): 545–68; David Weir, "Tontines, Public Finance, and Revolution in France and England, 1688–1789," *JEH* 49 (1989): 95–124. Also François R. Velde and David R. Weir, "The Financial Market and Government Debt Policy in France, 1746–1793," *JEH* 52 (1992): 1–39.

9. Dale Van Kley, *The Damiens Affair and the Unraveling of the Ancien Régime* (Princeton, 1984); Keith Baker, "The Ideological Origins of the French Revolution," in *Intellectual History*, Dominic LaCapra and Steven Kaplan, eds., (Ithaca, 1980), 197–220; Bailey Stone, *The French Parliaments and the Crisis of the Old Regime* (Chapel Hill, 1986) and *The Parlement of Paris, 1774–1789* (Chapel Hill, 1981).

10. Marion, *Histoire financière* 1:271.

11. Riley, *The Seven Years War*, 50–52.

12. Ever since Dale Van Kley's path-breaking book on Jansenism and the parlements, *The Damiens Affair*, no scholar can doubt that the magistrates' religious resistance quickly translated into resistance to fiscal decrees.

13. On Calonne's interpretation see Bosher, *French Finances*, 167.

14. For the Parlement of Paris's remonstrances see Jules Flammermont, *Remontrances du Parlement de Paris au XVIIIe siècle*, 3 vols. (Paris, 1883).

15. For the nobility's *cahiers de doléances* or lists of grievances see Francois Hincker, *Les français devant l'impôt sous l'ancien régime* (Paris, 1971), 99–105.

16. See Emmanuel Sieyès, *Qu'est-ce que le tiers état?* (Geneva, 1970), 158–66.

17. This is the interpretation given to this concession by Guy Chaussinand-Nogaret in "Le fisc et les privilégiés sous l'Ancien Régime," in *La fiscalité et ses implications sociales en Italie et en France aux XVIIe et XVIIIe siècles*, Colloque organisé par l'école française de Rome en collaboration avec l'archivia di stato di firenze et l'institut français de Florence (Rome, 1980), 191–206.

18. C. R. Behrens, "Nobles, Privileges and Taxes in France at the end of the Ancien Régime," *EHR* 15 (1962): 451–75. In "Nobles, Privileges and Taxes in France. A Revision Reviewed," *FHS* 8 (1974): 681–92, G. J. Cavanaugh provides a convincing critique of Behrens's interpretation.

19. Duc d'Orléans cited in Guy Chaussinand-Nogaret, "Le fisc et les privilégiés," 204.

20. Necker himself believed that the *pays d'état* got off fairly easily and their favored status was one of the issues at the Assembly of Notables (Robert Schnerb, "La répartition des impôts," 135).

21. The towns' exemptions from the *taille* could have serious consequences for fellow tax payers. In the élection of Paris alone, there were thirty tax-exempt municipalities, which thrust a disproportionate *taille* burden on the rural dwellers. See Georges Lizerand, "Observations sur l'impôt foncier sous l'Ancien Régime," *Revue d'histoire économique et sociale* 36 (1958): 20. Still, the towns did not get off scot free. According to Necker's figures, the urban population paid a disproportionate share of the excise taxes and therefore of taxes overall. The average Parisian for example paid 140 *livres* while the rural populations of the *élections* of nearby Soissons and Orléans paid only 25 and 30 *livres* respectively. See Michel Morineau, "Budgets de l'état et gestion des finances royales," *Revue historique* 264 (1980): 322 n. 93.

22. Schnerb, "La répartition des impôts," 138.

23. Lavoisier cited in ibid., 135.

24. Schnerb, "La répartition des impots," 143.

25. James Collins, *Fiscal Limits of Absolutism: Direct Taxation in Seventeenth Century France* (Berkeley, 1988), 33.

26. Georges Lizerand, "Observations sur l'impôt foncier," 24.

27. Schnerb, "La répartition des impôts," 22.

28. See Marion, *Histoire financière* 1:171–231.

29. Riley, *The Seven Years War*, 40.

30. A clear and concise discussion of the *vingtième* and other taxes appears in ibid., 46–55. No better introduction to the subject exists.

31. Ibid., 54–55.

32. Marion, *Histoire financière* 1:123–24.

33. David Bien, "The secrétaires du roy: Absolutism, Corps and Privilege under the Ancien Régime," in *Vom ancien Regime zur französischen Revolution*, Ernst Hinrichs, ed., (Göttingen, 1978), 153–68.

34. Riley, *The Seven Years War*, 185.

35. Marcel Marion, *Histoire financière* 1:380.

36. Arthur Young, *Travels in France During the years 1787, 1788 and 1789*, Jeffrey Kaplow, ed. (Gloucester, MA 1969).

37. Georges Lizerand, "Observations sur l'impôt foncier," 40–41.

38. Ernest Labrousse, *La crise de l'économie française à la fin de l'ancien régime et au début de la Révolution* (Paris, 1944), 473.

39. Michel Morineau, "Budgets de l'état et gestion des finances royales," 314. The per capita figures given here are Morineau's. Because they are based on different sources and concern individual years rather than decades, they

differ slightly, though not substantially, from the decennial figures in table 1 of chapter 6.

40. Peter Mathias and Patrick O'Brien, "Taxation in Britain and France, 1715–1810: A Comparison of the Social and Economic Incidence of Taxes Collected for the Central Government," *JEEcH* 5 (1976): 601–5. Because they used a different price series and different sources, Mathias and O'Brien's figures differ slightly from those in chapter 6, table 1.

41. Morineau, "Budgets de l'état et gestion des finances royales," 319. Because disparities in wealth were so great in Paris, Morineau's calculations may be a bit misleading. His numbers, it should be noted, differ slightly from those in chapter 6, table 1, because he used different sources.

42. Labrousse, *La crise de l'économie française,* xliv.

43. L. de Cardenal, "Le citoyen de 1791, payait-il plus ou moins d'impôt que le sujet de 1790?" *Notices, inventaires et documents: comité des travaux historiques et scientifiques* 22 (1936): 61–110.

44. Readers should note that the depreciation of the *assignats* has not been taken into account in these figures. All statistics here come from René Stourm, *Les finances de l'ancien régime et de la révolution* (New York, 1968), 2:413, 417, 429.

45. Mathias and O'Brien, "Taxation in Britain and France," 601–5.

46. Riley, *The Seven Years War,* 52.

47. Calonne cited in William Doyle, *The Origins of the French Revolution* (Oxford, 1978), 43.

48. Bosher, *French Finances,* 6, 306.

49. Ibid., 6.

50. Yves Durand, *Les fermiers généraux au XVIIIe siècle* (Paris, 1966).

51. George T. Matthews, *The Royal General Farms in Eighteenth-Century France* (New York, 1958).

52. Jean Villain, *Le recouvrement des impôts directs sous l'ancien régime* (Paris, 1952), 37–40.

53. Bosher, *French Finances,* 251.

54. Vuhrer cited in Morineau, "Budgets de l'état et gestion des finances royales," 318 n. 83.

55. Riley, *The Seven Years War,* 60–61.

56. Mathias and O'Brien, "Taxation in Britain and France," 642.

57. Morineau, "Budgets de l'état et gestion des finances royales," 303–4.

58. Ibid., 306–8.

59. A much more extensive discussion of the ill effects of the Seven Years War than is possible to include here can be found in Riley, *The Seven Years War.*

60. Morineau, "Budgets de l'état et gestion des finances royales," 308–9.

61. Ibid., 311.

62. Ibid., 318.

63. Marcel Marion, *Machault d'Arnouville, étude sur l'histoire du controle général des finances 1749 à 1754* (Paris, 1892).

64. See Marion, *Histoire financière* 1: 213–349.

65. Thomas Paine, *The Rights of Man* (New York, 1969), 99.

66. J. D. Harris, *Necker, Reform Statesman of the Ancien Régime*, (Berkeley, 1979).

67. This description of the rentes comes from George V. Taylor, "The Paris Bourse on the Eve of the Revolution," *AHR* 67 (July, 1962): 960.

68. Marion, *Histoire financière* 1:187–88.

69. On the tontines see Weir, "Tontines, Public Finance, and Revolution"; Taylor, "The Paris Bourse," 961; Marion, *Histoire financière* 1:295.

70. *Encyclopédie méthodique* cited in Marion, *Histoire financière* 1:157.

71. Taylor, "The Paris Bourse," 963.

72. Mathias and O'Brien, "Taxation in Britain and France."

73. R. D. Harris, "French Finances and the American War, 1777–1783," *JMH* 48 (1976): 235–58.

74. Marion, *Histoire financière* 1:343–44; Harris, *Necker, Reform Statesman*, 125.

75. Riley, *The Seven Years War*, 168 n. 12.

76. Ibid., 172.

77. Marion, *Histoire financière* 1:472; Riley, *The Seven Years War*, 173.

78. J. D. Harris, *Necker, Reform Statesman*, 126; A. Vuhrer, *Histoire de la dette publique en France*, 2 vols. (Paris, 1886), 1:270.

79. Weir, "Tontines, Public Finance and Revolution," table 4.

80. Harris, *Necker, Reform Statesman*, 126–28; Hubert Lüthy, *La banque protestante*, 2 vols. (Paris, 1961), 2:496ff. The interest rates here are nominal rates, the effective yield of course depending on the life span of the person named in the life annuity. For the numerous annuities bought on the lives of children—the life annuities could depend on the lives of third parties—the yield was extremely high. See Velde and Weir, "The Financial Market," 28–36.

81. Joly de Fleury cited in R. D. Harris, "French Finances and the American War," 250.

82. Weir, "Tontines, Public Finance and Revolution," table 1.

83. Riley, *The Seven Years War*, 171.

84. Harris, "French Finances and the American War," 250.

85. Weir, "Tontines, Public Finance, and Revolution," table 1; Velde and Weir, "The Financial Market," 15–19.

86. Riley, *The Seven Years War*, 190.

87. Weir, "Tontines, Public Finance, and Revolution," 95–124.

88. Morineau, "Budgets de l'état et gestion des finances," 328.

89. P. G. M. Dickinson, *The Financial Revolution in England, 1688–1740* (London, 1967).

90. Marion, *Machault d'Arouville*, 368.

91. Marion, *Histoire financière* 1:234–37.

92. Ibid., 386–402.

93. Morineau, "Budgets de l'état et gestion des finances," 327.

94. James D. Hardy, Jr., *Judicial Politics in the Old Regime* (Baton Rouge, 1967), 71.

95. Ibid., 72–73.

96. Edgar Faure, *La banqueroute de Law, 17 juillet 1720,* (Paris, 1977), 116.

97. On the *chambre de justice* see chap. 6.

98. I owe this term to Margaret Levy, *Of Rule and Revenue* (Berkeley, 1988), 12.

99. Faure, *La banqueroute de Law,* 125.

100. The best to my mind remains Faure, *La banqueroute de Law;* also of enormous value is Paul Harsin's analysis in John Law, *Les oeuvres complètes de John Law* (Liège, 1934).

101. Marion, *Histoire financière* 1:109–11.

102. For a good discussion of the aftermath of Law's system see Faure, *La banqueroute de Law,* 536–623.

103. Marion, *Histoire financière* 1:111.

104. Ibid., 112.

105. See Thomas Kaiser, "Money, Despotism, and Public Opinion in Early Eighteenth-Century France: John Law and the Debate on Royal Credit," *JMH* 63 (1991): 1–28.

106. John Law cited in Kaiser, "Money, Despotism, and Public Opinion," 6.

107. Faure, *La banqueroute de Law,* 298.

108. John Law, "Lettres sur le nouveau system des finances, extrait du mercure de France, février 1720," in *Collection des principaux économistes,* vol. 1: *Economistes financiers du 18ième siècle,* Eugene Daire, ed. (Osnabruck, 1966), 655.

109. See Kaiser, "Money, Despotism, and Public Opinion," 16.

110. Law, "Lettres sur le nouveau système," 655.

111. Saint Simon cited in Kaiser, "Money, Despotism, and Public Opinion," 5.

112. See ibid., 6.

113. John Law cited in ibid., 19.

114. Montesquieu, *Oeuvres complètes,* (Paris, 1964), 535.

115. Faure, *La banqueroute de Law,* 402–3.

116. Law cited in ibid., 117.

117. Flammermont, ed., *Remontrances du Parlement* 1:81.

118. Ibid., 127.

119. Ibid., 77.

120. Montesquieu cited in Mark Hulling, *Montesquieu and the Old Regime* (Berkeley, 1976), 53.

121. Montesquieu, *Spirit of the Laws,* Thomas Nugent, trans. (New York, 1959), 214–15.

122. Ibid., 395.

123. Ibid., 322.

124. Kaiser, "Money, Despotism, and Public Opinion," 1–9.

125. Riley, *The Seven Years War*, xix.
126. Ibid., 137–38.
127. Indeed, J. D. Harris has exonerated Necker and forced us to abandon the comfortable old cliché which held that the American war of independence and the debts France incurred at that time led to the revolution of 1789. See J. D. Harris, "French Finances and the American War, 1777–1783," *JMH* 48 (1976): 233–58.
128. David Hudson, "The Parliamentary Crisis of 1763 in France and Its Consequences," *CJH* 7 (1972): 116.
129. Riley, *The Seven Years War*, xix.
130. Ibid., 142.   131. Ibid., 138–39.
132. Ibid., 184.   133. Ibid., 187.
134. See Taylor, "The Paris Bourse on the Eve of the Revolution."
135. Riley, *The Seven Years War*, 187.
136. Ibid., 188–89; Marion, *Histoire financière* 1:254–55.
137. Riley, *The Seven Years War*, 185–87.
138. Ibid., 162.
139. Marion, *Histoire financière* 1:192–97.
140. Bailey Stone, *The French Parliaments and the Crisis of the Old Regime* (Chapel Hill, 1986).
141. Van Kley, *The Damiens Affair*.
142. LePaige cited in ibid., 186–87.
143. Flammermont, ed., *Remontrances du Parlement de Paris* 2:110–20, 322, 348, 390.
144. Requisitory of the Parlement of Rouen, 10 May 1760, cited in Marion, *Histoire financière* 1:207.
145 Stone, *The French Parlements and the Crisis of the Old Regime*, 100–101.
146. Chevalier de Jaucourt cited in Francois Hincker, *Les français devant l'impôt* (Paris, 1971), 136–37.
147. Georges Weulersse, *La physiocratie à la fin du règne de Louis XV* (Paris, 1959), 80, 90.
148. Mirabeau cited in ibid., 90.
149. Dupont de Nemours cited in ibid., 132.
150. Mirabeau cited in ibid., 81.
151. On the Maupeou reform see Durand Echeverria, *The Maupoeu Revolution: A Study in the History of Libertarianism, France 1770–1774* (Baton Rouge, 1985).
152. A standard account of the "death of credit" appears in Simon Schama, *Citizens* (New York, 1989).
153. Velde and Weir, "The Financial Market," 34, 36.
154. Ibid., 36–37.
155. See ibid., 28.
156. William Doyle, "The Parlements of France and the Breakdown of the Old Regime, 1771–1788," *FHS* 6 (1970): 415–58.

157. See Stone, *The French Parlements and the Crisis of the Old Regime;* also Flammermont, *Les remontrances,* 3.

158. See Jean Egret, *Le Parlement de Dauphiné,* 2 vols. (Paris, 1933).

159. J. E. D. Binney, *British Public Revenue and Administration, 1774–1792* (Oxford, 1958).

160. Duc d'Orleans cited in Marion, *Histoire financière* 1:389.

161. Hincker, *Les français devant l'impôt,* 136–40.

162. Riley, *The Seven Years War,* 40–46.

163. We need not recapitulate here all the problems posed by the *cahiers.* I would caution the reader that I am concerned here only with the *cahiers* drawn up at the *bailiwick* or secondary level. I will have nothing to say about the parish *cahiers.* Certainly, taxes play a prominent role in these brief documents, but the villagers' complaints are so local that only a profound understanding of village history makes these documents meaningful. Moreover, my main concern here is the broader political issue of the king's ability to tax his subject with or without consent.

164. *AP* (1862), 1:709.

165. Ibid., 703.   166. Ibid., 715.

167. Ibid. 2:79.   168. Ibid. 1:681.

169. Recent arguments concerning the "enlightened aristocracy" make a great deal of the generosity displayed by the nobility in the *cahiers.* See Guy Chaussinand-Nogaret, *La noblesse au XVIIIe siècle. De la féodalité aux lumières* (Paris, 1976). This generosity was real; there are in the *Archives parlementaires* remarkably few noble *cahiers* which do not make this concession. But the nobles' generosity was contingent: they always specified that *all* fiscal immunities, both personal and geographic, had to be abolished, and they complained that a class of individuals, the "capitalists," bore a lighter fiscal burden then they. The abolition of fiscal immunities here is not as grand a gesture as some would have us believe because these immunities were probably not very substantial at the end of the Old Regime and the fiscal concessions were usually accompanied by a staunch adherence to the political prerogatives of the nobility, in particular vote by order in the Estates.

170. *AP* 2:8. This is not the place to discuss the differing views on the French constitution and its components which emerged in the latter half of the eighteenth century. Suffice it to say, that one tradition, largely noble, believed that a constitution had always existed throughout French history and it only needed to be revived in 1789. Another school of thought, that of the "patriot party" whose most articulate spokesman on this issue was Sieyès, argued that there was no French constitution and it needed to be created. See the brief but excellent account of constitutional thinking in Marina Valensise, "La constitution française," in *The Political Culture of the Old Regime,* ed. Keith Michael Baker (Chicago, 1987), 441–69.

171. *AP* 2:745.

172. Marion, *Histoire financière* 1:429.

173. This whole line of thought was suggested to me by Margaret Levi's *Of Rule and Revenue.*

174. Echeverria, *The Maupoeu Reform*, 227.

175. Necker, *De l'administration des finances de la France*.

176. Linguet, *L'impôt territorial et ses avantages* (Paris, 1787).

177. See for example the work of the future Girondin Clavière, *Lettre d'un citoyen* (Paris, 1788) and that of François Forbonnais, *Prospectus sur les finances dedié aux bons citoyens* (Paris, 1789).

178. I have read through the inventory of French revolutionary writings prepared by André Martin and Gérard Walter, *Catalogue de l'histoire de la Révolution française* (Paris, 1954), which lists all the holdings of the Bibliothèque nationale in this area. Because Martin and Walter provide only the titles of pamphlets I may have missed some works on finance. Still my impression is that no more than 10 percent (if that) of the pamphlets produced during the Revolution dealt with taxes or state finance.

179. J.-J. Rousseau, "Discours sur l'économie politique," *Oeuvres* (Paris, 1967), 3:270.

180. Ibid., 258.

181. Ibid., 264.

CONCLUSION

1. See chaps. 1 and 2.

2. Peter Mathias and Patrick O'Brien, "Taxation in Britain and France, 1715–1810: A Comparison of the Social and Economic Incidence of Taxes Collected for the Central Government," *JEEcH* 5 (1976): 601–50. The year 1557 may underestimate the Castilian tax burden somewhat because, as I. A. A. Thompson shows in chapter 4, tax revenues had been declining since the 1520s. Nonetheless, the point about higher taxes in Holland and eighteenth-century Britain still holds, even if we compare with the heavy Castilian tax levies of 1664.

3. Mathias and O'Brien, "Taxation in Britain and France." Mathias and O'Brien estimate that in 1780, for example, the per capita tax burden in Britain (measured in terms of wheat) was 1.8 times what it was in France. They also estimate that it was 21 percent of per capita income in Britain versus only 12 percent of per capita income in France—a far lower share. If these estimates can be trusted, then the difference in the share of income going to taxes explains in and of itself nearly all the difference in tax burdens. Mathias and O'Brien's estimates for 1775 and 1785 lead to very similar conclusions. To be sure, one should be aware of the margin of error in the income estimates and not place too much weight on a comparison of tax burdens in terms of the price of wheat alone. Nonetheless, the conclusion seems clear.

4. Mathias and O'Brien, "Taxation in Britain and France," 622.

5. In addition to chaps. 4 and 6, see Richard Bonney, *The King's Debts* (Oxford, 1981), 166–67, 188–89, 275, and *Political Change in France under Richelieu and Mazarin* (Oxford, 1978), 443.

6. For the medieval background here, see Alan Harding, "Political Liberty in the Middle Ages," *Speculum* 55 (1980): 423–43.

7. Otto Hintze, *Die Hohenzollern und ihr Werk* (Berlin, 1915), 298.

8. In addition to chap. 7, see François R. Velde and David R. Weir, "The Financial Market and Government Debt Policy in France, 1746–1793," *JEH* 52 (1992): 1–40. In the sixteenth century, it is true, Spain paid relatively low rates of interest on its long term loans, the *juros*. Despite its representative institutions, the Dutch Republic could not do as well on its own long-term loans until the beginning of the seventeenth century, undoubtedly because of the uncertainties surrounding the outcome of its war against Spain. See chaps. 3 and 4, and James D. Tracy, *A Financial Revolution in the Habsburg Netherlands* (Berkeley, 1985), 108–9, 206–11; and Hermann van der Wee, "Monetary, Credit and Banking Systems," in *The Cambridge Economic History of Europe*, vol. 5: *The Economic Organization of Early Modern Europe*, ed. E. E. Rich and C. H. Wilson (Cambridge, 1977), 374.

9. In addition to Veenendaal's chapter here, see Tracy, *Financial Revolution*, 216–17.

10. Robert Bates and Da-Hsiang Donald Lien, "A Note on Taxation, Development, and Representative Government," *Politics and Society* 14 (1985): 53–70. There is of course an enormous sociological literature relevant to this problem, from Barrington Moore, *Social Origins of Dictatorship and Democracy: Lord and Peasant in the Making of the Modern World* (Boston, 1967), to Jack A. Goldstone, *Revolution and Rebellion in the Early Modern World* (Berkeley, 1991).

Index

In this index an "f" after a number indicates a separate reference on the next page, and an "ff" indicates separate references on the next two pages. A continuous discussion over two or more pages is indicated by a span of page numbers, e.g., "57–59." *Passim* is used for a cluster of references in close but not consecutive sequence.

Library of Congress Cataloging-in-Publication Data

Fiscal crises, liberty, and representative government, 1450–
1789 / edited by Philip T. Hoffman and Kathryn Norberg.
    p.   cm. — (The Making of modern freedom)
Includes bibliographical references and index.
ISBN 0-8047-2292-7 (alk. paper)
    1. Finance, Public—Europe—History.   2. Representative
government and representation—Europe—History.   3. Liberty.   I. Hoffman, Philip T., 1947–   II. Norberg, Kathryn,
1948–   . III. Series.
HJ1000.F55 1994
336.4—dc20   93-29864
                                                    CIP